Birding
Illinois

Sheryl DeVore

FALCON®

HELENA, MONTANA

A FALCON GUIDE ®

Falcon® Publishing is continually expanding its list of recreational guidebooks. All books include detailed descriptions, accurate maps, and all the information necessary for enjoyable trips. You can order extra copies of this book and get information and prices for other Falcon® guidebooks by writing Falcon, P.O. Box 1718, Helena, MT 59624 or calling toll-free 1-800-582-2665. Also, please ask for a free copy of our current catalog. Visit our website at www.FalconOutdoors.com or contact us by e-mail at falcon@falcon.com.

1 2 3 4 5 6 7 8 9 0 MG 04 03 02 01 00

Falcon and FalconGuide are registered trademarks of Falcon® Publishing, Inc.

Project Editor: Gayle Shirley
Production Editor: Brynlyn Lehmann
Maps by Tony Moore
Page compositor: Darlene Jatkowski
Book design by Falcon® Publishing, Inc.

Library of Congress Cataloging-in-Publication Data

DeVore, Sheryl.
  Birding Illinois / Sheryl DeVore.
      p.   cm.
  Includes bibliographical references (p.   ).
  ISBN 1-56044-689-7 (pbk.)
  1. Bird watching—Illinois Guidebooks. 2. Birding sites—Illinois Guidebooks.
  3. Birds—Illinois.   4. Illinois Guidebooks.
  I. Title.
  QL684.I3D48 1999
  598' .07'234773—dc21   99-35148
                                                           CIP

CAUTION

Outdoor recreational activities are by their very nature potentially hazardous. All participants in such activities must assume the responsibility for their own actions and safety. The information contained in this guidebook cannot replace sound judgment and good decision-making skills, which help reduce risk exposure, nor does the scope of this book allow for disclosure of all the potential hazards and risks involved in such activities.

Learn as much as possible about the outdoor recreational activities in which you participate, prepare for the unexpected, and be cautious. The reward will be a safer and more enjoyable experience.

 Text pages printed on recycled paper.

Look at six eggs
in a mockingbird's nest.
Listen to six mockingbirds
Flinging follies of O-be-joyful
Over the marshes and uplands.

Look at songs
hidden in eggs.

—*Carl Sandburg*
Galesburg, Illinois

Contents

Foreword

Before I moved to Illinois, my only experience birding the Prairie State was when my family drove through on our way to the Rockies during summer vacation. Admittedly, some great birds—the Red-headed Woodpecker and Dickcissel—seemed to be everywhere. But my overwhelming impression was that Illinois consisted of vast areas that were virtually uninhabitable for birds.

That opinion, however, changed in 1984 when I came to work for the Illinois Natural History Survey in Champaign. Now I have come to love both watching and studying birds in Illinois.

The waterfowl migrations along Illinois' rivers are among the largest in the world. Most of the continent's American Golden-Plovers pass through Illinois during the spring migration. In my first week in Illinois, I saw more golden-plovers than I had in my previous 16 years of birding in North America.

I am also amazed at the numbers of Smith's Longspur that pass through the state. Birders who live in east-central Illinois seem to spend large parts of their spring season showing Smith's Longspur to birders from other states.

The Bald Eagle roosts in Illinois are legendary, and the sight of hundreds of thousands of Canada Geese passing over the cornfields heading south after the first severe cold front of the winter still provides a thrill in spite of the problems created by geese in urban areas.

My own favorite birding spots in Illinois include the Mississippi River bluffs in southern Illinois and the Chicago lakefront. During the first ten days of May, a good birder can reliably see 30 to 33 species of warblers in one day in the western Shawnee National Forest. The Chicago lakefront and Springfield, Illinois, regions routinely harbor extreme rarities.

That is not to say that birds in Illinois aren't in jeopardy. Indeed, my initial research on breeding birds in Illinois did little to help the reputation of the state as a place for birds. For almost a decade, I found catastrophically low nesting success of the birds that were attempting to breed in the state's woodlands. When speaking to audiences outside Illinois, I used Illinois as an example of the most extreme consequences of habitat loss and fragmentation, arguing that the continued presence of many species breeding in the state depended on immigration from surrounding states.

More recently, however, my graduate students at the University of Illinois, other Illinois Natural History Survey employees, and I have been finding some areas and habitats in which nesting success is fairly high. Over the years, Illinois birders have helped enormously with this research. With the acquisition of such large habitats as the Midewin National Tallgrass Prairie and the Cache River Wetlands, Illinois' breeding bird populations may become less tenuous.

Because there is so little non-corn/soybean habitat in Illinois, the huge number of birds that migrate through the state must concentrate in small patches of habitat.

And because bird populations are so concentrated here, a birder armed with a guide to the good remaining habitat patches can see remarkable numbers of birds.

This book is exactly such a guide.

It is written by Sheryl DeVore, an enthusiastic and knowledgeable birder who enlisted the help of many of the state's best birders to ensure its completeness. Sheryl's work for eight years as chief editor of the Illinois Ornithological Society's quarterly publication, *Meadowlark,* has given her invaluable insights in preparing this guide.

A birder who uses this guide can be almost certain of finding large numbers and varieties of birds and will greatly increase the odds of seeing the rare species that makes birdwatching so exciting.

I will be using the book to find potential study sites as well.

Managers responsible for sites on public land can use the information herein for conservation planing at their sites. And, of course, we listers can use the guide to track down new species.

This guide appears at an opportune time. Birding is gaining rapidly in popularity as more and more people realize just how great a hobby it is. We now know far more about finding birds in the state than we did when the last guides were published, and that knowledge is here for you to use and enjoy.

Dr. Scott Robinson

DR. SCOTT ROBINSON

Dr. Scott Robinson is an avian ecologist at the Illinois Natural History Survey and a professor in the Department of Ecology, Ethology, and Evolution at the University of Illinois in Champaign. He is recognized worldwide for his research on neotropical migrants that breed in Illinois and spend winters in the tropics.

Acknowledgments

Many excellent Illinois birders and scientists contributed to this book, offering their time, talents, and knowledge to guide you to the best birding spots in the Prairie State. They read and reread various chapters and site guides to make sure directions were clear and accurate, and that the most reliable birding spots were highlighted. They shared their knowledge so that you could have the best chance at seeing some of the specialty birds of each site.

Four people deserve special mention. They are (in alphabetical order) Alan Anderson, Steven D. Bailey, Keith McMullen, and Michael P. Ward.

Keith McMullen, a biologist with the U.S. Army Corps of Engineers and Steve Bailey, an Illinois Natural History Survey ornithologist, have provided much of the information for some of the best places to bird in southern and central Illinois.

Steve and Keith, both Illinois Ornithological Society board members and longtime birders, lead many all-day field trips to the places they helped describe in this book.

Keith provided copious information and directions on the following sites: Crab Orchard National Wildlife Refuge, Union County Conservation Area, Cypress Creek National Wildlife Refuge, Atwood Ridge, Oakwood Bottoms, Pomona–Cave Creek, LaRue–Pine Hills Ecological Area, Lake Mermet, Giant City State Park, Horseshoe Lake State Park, Carlyle Lake, and Sauget Marsh.

Steve is well known for his ability to find bird nests, a skill that has aided the Illinois Natural History Survey in its task to understand breeding bird ecology in Illinois. Steve provided details on birding the Middle Fork River Valley, Castle Rock State Park, the Cache River State Natural Area, Forest Glen, Harry "Babe" Woodyard State Natural Area, Kennekuk County Park, Kickapoo State Park, Trail of Tears State Forest, and Horseshoe Lake Conservation Area. He also contributed to the Union County Conservation Area, LaRue–Pine Hills, and Atwood Ridge sites. In addition, Steve, one of the state's experts on bird distribution, spent many hours helping compile the first state distribution chart of its kind.

Mike Ward, a graduate student who researches birds for the Illinois Natural History Survey, provided most of the information for Beardstown Marsh, Banner Marsh, Green River Conservation Area, Siloam Springs State Park, and the Meredosia National Wildlife Refuge.

Because of Mike, Steve, and Keith, birders have some new areas to explore. Some of the birding spots they helped describe in this book have been relatively unknown to birders.

Alan Anderson, research chair and past president of the Chicago Audubon Society, deserves special credit for mapping the Chicagoland birding tour, walking the route several times to make sure the directions were accurate, and consulting with local birding experts to make corrections and additions to all the Cook County sites. Alan spent hours working on maps and directions for these sites and compiling breeding bird information for the Cook County sites.

I am also grateful to the following people for taking the time to show me the best places to bird in areas they know very well, and for reading and rereading the entries for accuracy. Some of them also compiled most of the birding information for particular sites.

*Robert Chapel, "Fall Field Notes" report editor for the Illinois Ornithological Society, for his help with Clinton Lake and Lake Shelbyville.

* Richard Bjorklund, professor emeritus, Eastern Illinois University, and his son, Sigurd, for their help with Lake Chautauqua and Sand Ridge State Forest.

* Dan Williams, past president of the American Birding Association, for help with Rock Cut State Park and the Sugar and Pecatonica River Forest Preserves.

* Kelly McKay, "Winter Field Notes" editor for the Illinois Ornithological Society, who wrote the accounts for Mississippi Palisades, Savanna Army Depot, the Keithsburg Division of the Mark Twain National Wildlife Refuge, and the Bald Eagle watching guide to northwestern Illinois.

* Ralph Herbst, past president of the Evanston North Shore Bird Club, and Etta Aubertin, president of the Kankakee Audubon Society for help with the Kankakee River State Park and Momence Wetlands entries.

*Al Stokie for his help with Illinois Beach State Park and the Iroquois Conservation Area.

* Sue Friscia and Wes Serafin for their help with the Palos Preserves.

* Ron Flemal, former Northern Illinois University geology professor, for his help with the Shabbona Lake State Park and Forest Preserve entry, as well as for his expert reviews of the Illinois landscape chapter.

* Justin Rink, who prepared the Woodford County Conservation Area entry, and Michael Retter, who prepared the Moraine View State Park entry.

* Jeff Walk, an Illinois Natural History Survey researcher, for his work on the Prairie Ridge State Natural Area.

*Irene Mondhink, Helen Weustenfeld, and Audrey Wiseman for their help with Pere Marquette State Park and the Mark Twain National Wildlife Refuge sites.

* Joe Milosevich, photographer for the Illinois Ornithological Society, for help with the Goose Lake Prairie State Natural Area and the Lake Renwick Heronry.

* Renee Baade, Gayle Wagner, and McHenry County Conservation District naturalist Brad Woodson, for their help with Moraine Hills State Park and Glacial Park.

* Denis Bohm, recording secretary for the Illinois Ornithological Society, for his help with Crabtree Nature Center, Blackwell Forest Preserve, and Chain O' Lakes State Park.

The following people also reviewed entries for specific sites:

* Cindy and John McKee: Starved Rock and Matthiessen State Parks.

* Peter Kasper and Illinois Ornithological Society art editor Denis Kania: Fermilab National Accelerator Laboratory.

* H. David Bohlen, Illinois State Museum curator: Lake Springfield.

* Ann Haverstock, steward for The Nature Conservancy: Nachusa Grasslands, Lowden-Miller State Forest and Franklin Creek.

* Danny Diaz: Waukegan Beach and Bowen Park.

* Douglas Stotz: Field Museum of Natural History biologist: Grant Park and Midewin National Tallgrass Prairie.

* Robert Montgomery: Max McGraw National Wildlife Foundation biologist and president of the Illinois Ornithological Society: early Illinois ornithologists.

If any names have been inadvertently omitted, I sincerely apologize. Any errors in this book are mine. I gladly will accept any notes delineating errors, so they can be corrected for future editions.

Many, many thanks are also due to the photographers who kindly allowed usage of their work in this book. They include Joe Milosevich, Dennis Oehmke, Eric Walters, and Kanae Hirabayashi, among others. Their work is also acknowledged elsewhere in this book.

Most important thanks go to Karl DeVore and Laurel Ann Kaiser for their support and encouragement.

A final thanks to all the Illinois birders who offered advice on which sites to list and for posting bird-finding information on the statewide birding website, Illinois Birders Exchanging Thoughts (IBET).

1. Introduction

Mention the state of Illinois and two images quickly come to mind: skyscrapers and farm fields. But some of the Midwest's best birding occurs here in the Prairie State—among the skyscrapers and farm fields, yes, but also in the woods, wetlands, hills, sandstone canyons, savannas, prairies, cypress swamps, and dunes, as well as along the expansive Lake Michigan shoreline and the miles of riverine habitat abutting the Mississippi, Illinois, and other rivers.

What can you experience while birding Illinois? The rushing sound of thousands of American Golden-Plover wings coursing through the sky across a cornfield in early spring, or the yellow-eyed stare of an adult Bald Eagle, perched quietly on a cottonwood overlooking the Illinois River, with snowflakes drifting through the air. Perhaps you'll startle at the sudden swoosh of thousands of famished, neotropical migrants, dropping in droves onto a peninsula of greenery along Lake Michigan, with the state's tallest buildings as a backdrop. In southern Illinois, you might hear the *"cuk-cuk-cuk-cuk"* of a Pileated Woodpecker, calling in a bald cypress–tupelo swamp, or in central Illinois, dozens of Bobolinks singing on the wing as they fly over the dewy, medium-tall grasses on a remnant prairie. In central Illinois, too, you might observe 20,000 Snow Geese crowded onto a large lake, resting before completing the journey northward to breeding grounds, or you might catch an Acadian Flycatcher building its nest in a tree along a river at the bottom of a canyon, or even glance up at a Northern Saw-whet Owl sitting on the branches of an arborvitae, its yellow eyes peering at yours, its demeanor seemingly tame.

Illinois hosts 9 national wildlife refuges, 262 state parks, and 236 state-designated natural areas. The state also has countless forest preserve and conservation districts that offer breeding and migrating habitat for 420 documented species of birds in Illinois; of these, 174 regularly breed here.

Early bird records

Illinois birders are fortunate because work by early naturalists, professional ornithologists, and interested observers has provided a detailed picture of the state's avifauna for nearly 100 years. Observers date to the early 1800s when John James Audubon reportedly stopped in Illinois on his journey along the Ohio River. Audubon and others who followed wrote of the fauna and flora that existed before settlement changed the state's natural habitats. Some of these observers rank as the most important ornithologists of their time. Included among them are E. W. Nelson, who published one of the state's earliest regional reports of bird life, and Robert Ridgeway, an Illinois native, who collected and assembled information for the first book on Illinois birds, *The Ornithology of Illinois*. Ridgeway later became a nationally recognized ornithologist and worked as the head of the ornithology department for the Smithsonian Institution.

Steven A. Forbes, a well-known scientist who directed some classical and important ecological studies, also contributed to Illinois' knowledge of birds. Director of the Illinois Natural History Survey in the early 1900s, Forbes led Alfred O. Gross and Howard Ray as they conducted the first systematic population study of the state's birds. Gross and Ray sampled different habitats across the state, recording not only the species present, but also the numbers they encountered. This information allowed them to calculate the population size of many of the state's most common species, and permitted identification of the most important habitats and a comparison among differing regions in the state.

Some 50 years later, husband and wife team, Drs. Richard and Jean Graber duplicated this census using the same techniques and where possible, the same routes. They published their study as an Illinois Natural History Survey Bulletin, titled, *A Comparative Study of Bird Population in Illinois in 1906–1909 and 1956–1958*. The Grabers also published a series of notes on Illinois birds.

Other early 20th century observers of the state's birds include H. K. Coale, C. W. G. Elfrig, T. E. Musselman, and B. T. Gault. Since this time, many important contributors have added to our knowledge of the distribution of the state's birds. Among these is H. David Bohlen, who wrote *An Annotated Checklist of the Birds of Illinois* in 1978, and *The Birds of Illinois* in 1989, a century after Ridgeway's first book of ornithology in Illinois.

Conservation

As birders improve their identification skills in Illinois, they also realize that knowing which bird is which could become a moot point if habitat is not preserved. Illinois bears the moniker Prairie State, but less than 1 percent of its original prairies remain. Only 5 percent of the state's natural wetlands and 10 percent of its woodlands still exist. Agriculture has replaced the prairie potholes and grasslands. Skyscrapers and development have replaced Chicago area wetlands. Logging and habitat fragmentation threaten the Shawnee National Forest in southern Illinois as well as woodlands statewide.

For the past several decades, volunteers and scientists have been expressing their passion for protecting the state's natural resources by restoring prairies, savannas, woodlands, and wetlands. They also are monitoring bird populations and educating themselves about the need for biodiversity, that is, protecting habitat that sustains many species of birds, plants, insects, mammals, reptiles, frogs, and salamanders in large enough areas to sustain gene pools, and hence, good populations of these species.

These people hail from countless agencies, including the Illinois Department of Natural Resources; the Illinois Endangered Species Protection Board; the Illinois Nature Preserves Commission; the Illinois Chapter of The Nature Conservancy; the U.S. Fish & Wildlife Service; the Illinois Audubon Society and its area chapters; the National Audubon Society's chapters, including the Chicago Audubon Society; the Illinois Natural History Survey; the forest preserve districts of Lake,

DuPage, and Cook Counties; conservation districts in McHenry and Vermilion Counties; and many, many more.

Scientists are passing their knowledge and data on to those who want to protect Illinois' habitats for birds. Focusing on their areas of expertise—savanna, woodland, grassland, and wetland—several state scientists conveyed a united message about birds and conversation at the state's first Birds and Habitat Conference held at Northeastern Illinois University in December 1997. Restoration can't be all things to all birds—and working together is the only way to save habitat for birds and other flora and fauna that live in the state's unique and rare ecosystems. Scientists agree that a species-by-species approach is expensive and frustrating and does not necessarily guarantee success.

Eighty percent of the nation's grassland species are declining. Recent research has shown that grassland species have specific requirements, for example, tall grasses, recently burned lands, or wetter prairies. The existence of some grassland sites in Illinois such as Goose Lake Prairie and the Midewin National Tallgrass Prairie in northern Illinois and the Greater Prairie-Chicken sanctuaries in southern Illinois, offer hope that some of the nation's most rapidly declining birds have a chance to survive.

Birds that prefer savannas for breeding are also in trouble. From 1966 to 1993, some 69 percent of bird species that breed in Illinois savannas have been decreasing, some of them significantly. Research is showing that breeding success is enhanced in restored savannas for several species, including Eastern Wood-Pewees, Red-headed Woodpeckers, and Baltimore Orioles.

The Chicago region is a major refueling site for migratory birds. Every little shrub becomes an important refuge during migration. Restoring the oak woodlands then becomes even more important because migratory birds tend to feed in oaks and not in maples, which are rapidly overtaking some oak woodlands in the Chicago region.

Research by Illinois scientists is also showing that Illinois forests are actually population sinks for birds. That means, these birds aren't reproducing enough to maintain a population here. That is happening because forest fragmentation increases the chance of cowbird parasitism and nest predation, among other things.

Many of the state's marshland breeding birds are listed with the state as threatened or endangered. Research is showing that a woven network of marshes and vegetation with fluctuating water levels is necessary for good reproductive success of many of these birds.

Birders are volunteering to help these scientists gather useful data on breeding, migrating, and wintering birds in northern Illinois. Opportunities for good birding as well as learning more about how to conserve their habitats continue to grow in Illinois. It is my hope that *Birding Illinois,* can serve as a catalyst for more people to join the movement to preserve the state's natural areas.

HOW TO USE THIS GUIDE

Rather than mirroring the multitude of books already available that help you identify birds, this book serves as an Illinois hotspot guide, and also reflects upon the conservation of the habitats in which you can find these birds. Indeed, if we do not work to preserve the places where birds breed and migrate, then we will eventually lose our ability to see them. The geological, ecological, and cultural information included should help you enjoy your birding adventure more fully.

The format presents opportunities for the new and casual as well as serious birders to visit some of the unique natural areas in Illinois. Whether you're a beginning or advanced birder, this book should provide you with a new perspective on how and where to bird in Illinois.

Chapter 2 describes Illinois' diverse landscape, from how our geological past paved the way for the habitats that attract our unique bird life to how human intervention has altered some of the habitats.

Chapter 3 is a month-by-month birding calendar.

Chapter 4 contains numerous trip-planning tips.

Chapter 5 covers an important part of birding—ethics.

Chapter 6 presents 80 of Illinois' best birding sites. Each site's commentary includes discussion of the following:

Habitats: Describes ecosystems found within the site.

Key birds: Identifies species you are likely to find in this area, focusing on those that birders often covet.

Best times to bird: Helps you plan when to visit the site. Some sites warrant a special visit in winter, others during migration, others during breeding season, still others year-round.

Directions: Tells you how to get to the site's main entrance or starting point on your journey from a major highway and town.

Birding: Takes you on a tour of the area, mentioning the best places to stop, what you'll likely see there and at what time of year. In some instances you'll find some specific directions to get you from one place to the next.

General information: Includes information about the site and what is being done to improve habitat for birds, as well as hazards you may encounter while birding there. Some of the sites listed establish hunting season goals beginning in September through early winter and sometimes in spring for turkey season. Each year the dates change at various sites. Call first, and be prepared for limited access. Whatever your feelings about hunting, know that people who fish and hunt in Illinois pay fees for licenses, and the money is used to manage lands to protect habitat for wildlife. Plenty of opportunities exist to bird at these sites.

ADDITIONAL HELP

DeLorme Illinois Atlas & Gazetteer (DeLorme IA&G) grid number: Indicates the page on which you will find this site in the *DeLorme Illinois Atlas & Gazetteer* (1996 edition). Available from DeLorme.

Contact: Refers to the organization to contact for more information, including hours, hunting season, and other pertinent information. An appendix provides addresses and phone numbers for your convenience.

Nearest gas, food, and lodging: Indicates the closest towns where you can find a place to stay overnight, plus nearby camping sites.

Accompanying maps: These pinpoint the site's location in Illinois and the areas mentioned in the text you will want to visit. This map is meant as an additional aid to be used with other maps already available including the *Illinois Atlas & Gazetteer,* the Official Illinois State Highway Map (free at some gas stations and tourist centers statewide), plus free maps and brochures of specific sites and trails that you can obtain at the sites or by calling site headquarters.

Chapter 7 is an Illinois Specialty Bird list.

Chapter 8 includes the state checklist, plus seasonal distributional charts divided roughly into north and south portions of the state.

Appendix A lists all the contact addresses and phone numbers for each of the 80 sites.

Appendix B includes the Illinois Ornithological Records Committee Rare Bird Documentation Form. If you find a rare bird in Illinois, please contact the committee so we may maintain an accurate checklist as well as continue to understand the distribution of birds in Illinois.

Appendix C is a Sensitive Bird Species list.

The bibliography lists published material that has contributed to our knowledge of Illinois bird life.

AUTHOR'S FAVORITE SITES

Following are some of my favorite places to see different groups of birds in Illinois at different times of year as well as the favorite places of some of the birders who helped me with this book.

Breeding herons, egrets, and cormorants

11 Baker's Lake and Ron Beese Park

29 Lake Renwick Heron Rookery Nature Preserve and Copley Nature Park

63 Pere Marquette State Park and Mark Twain National Wildlife Refuge—Brussels District

71 Union County Conservation Area and Associated Levees

74 Horseshoe Lake Conservation Area

79 Oakwood Bottoms and the Big Muddy River Levee

Migrating and wintering waterfowl

8 Glacial Park and Vicinity

10 Crabtree Nature Center, Palatine Marsh, and Vicinity

15 Gillson Park and Evanston Landfill

25 Saganashkee Slough

26 McGinnis Slough

39 Mississippi River Corridor

53 Clinton Lake

58 Lake Chautaqua National Wildlife Refuge

63 Pere Marquette State Park and Mark Twain National Wildlife Refuge—Brussels District

65 Horseshoe Lake State Park

71 Union County Conservation Area and Associated Levees

Migrating and wintering gulls

1 Montrose Harbor, the Magic Hedge, the Lincoln Park Bird Sanctuary, and Belmont Harbor

5 Waukegan Beach

15 Gillson Park and Evanston Landfill

28 Lake Calumet and Vicinity

39 Mississippi River Corridor

53 Clinton Lake

54 Lake Springfield and Washington Park

Winter finches

17 Morton Arboretum

37 Mississippi Palisades State Park

53 Clinton Lake

57 Sand Ridge State Forest

Migrating raptors

4 Illinois Beach State Park

5 Waukegan Beach and Bowen Park

18 Blackwell Forest Preserve

76 Atwood Ridge and Hamburg Hill

Wintering bald eagles

37 Mississippi Palisades State Park

39 Mississippi River Corridor

40 Starved Rock State Park and Matthiessen State Parks

58 Lake Chautauqua National Wildlife Refuge

63 Pere Marquette State Park and Mark Twain National Wildlife Refuge—Brussels District

71 Union County Conservation Area and Associated Levees

74 Horseshoe Lake Conservation Area

Wintering owls

3 Downtown Chicago Birding/Walking Tour

5 Waukegan Beach and Bowen Park

17 Morton Arboretum

19 Fermilab National Accelerator Laboratory

48 Middle Fork State Fish and Wildlife Area

51 Forest Glen Preserve and the Harry "Babe" Woodyard State Natural Area

66 Prairie Ridge State Natural Area and Newton Lake State Fish and Wildlife Area

72 Cypress Creek National Wildlife Refuge

Migrating shorebirds

5 Waukegan Beach and Bowen Park

6 Wadsworth Savanna and Wetlands Demonstration Project

8 Glacial Park and Vicinity

16 O'Hare Post Office Ponds

58 Lake Chautaqua National Wildlife Refuge

63 Pere Marquette State Park and Mark Twain National Wildlife Refuge—Brussels District

65 Horseshoe Lake State Park

67 Rend Lake

71 Union County Conservation Area and Associated Levees

Breeding and migrating wetland birds

6 Wadsworth Savanna and Wetlands Demonstration Project

7 Chain O' Lakes State Park

18 Blackwell Forest Preserve

30 Goose Lake Prairie and Heidecke Lake

47 Iroquois County Conservation Area

50 Kennekuk County Park

68 Sauget Marsh

79 Oakwood Bottoms and the Big Muddy River Levee

Migrating warblers and other songbirds

1 Montrose Harbor, the Magic Hedge, the Lincoln Park Bird Sanctuary, and Belmont Harbor

2 Jackson Park and the Paul O. Douglas Nature Sanctuary (Wooded Island)

12 Ryerson Conservation Area and the Des Plaines River Corridor

13 Chicago Botanic Garden

14 Skokie Lagoons

21 McClaughry Springs Woods

42 Lowden-Miller State Forest

50 Kennekuk County Park

51 Forest Glen Preserve and the Harry "Babe" Woodyard State Natural Area

55 Carpenter and Riverside Parks

61 Siloam Springs State Park

70 Giant City State Park

73 Cache River and Heron Pond State Natural Areas

75 Pomona–Cave Creek

77 Trail of Tears State Forest

Breeding warblers and other songbirds

34 Sugar River Forest Preserve

37 Mississippi Palisades State Park

40 Starved Rock and Matthiessen State Parks

42 Lowden-Miller State Forest

51 Forest Glen Preserve and the Harry "Babe" Woodyard State Natural Area

70 Giant City State Park

71 Union County Conservation Area and Associated Levees

73 Cache River and Heron Pond State Natural Areas

78 Pine Hills–LaRue Ecological Area

Breeding grassland birds

27 The Bartel and Orland Grasslands

30 Goose Lake Prairie and Heidecke Lake

31 Midewin National Tallgrass Prairie

43 Nachusa Grasslands and Franklin Creek State Natural Area

44 Green River Conservation Area

48 Middle Fork State Fish and Wildlife Area

66 Prairie Ridge State Natural Area and Newton Lake State Fish and Wildlife Area

2. *Illinois' Diverse Landscape*

Illinois' unique geographic location combined with its geologic past create conditions ripe for a rich and diverse landscape, and thus, a rich and diverse bird life. Because the state is so long, its climate varies considerably from the north to the south. The state's northern reaches have cool summers and cold winters, while southern areas experience mild winters and hot summers. Illinois generally receives abundant precipitation, although the state has experienced long, dry periods.

In northern Illinois January temperatures average 23 degrees F, while in extreme southern Illinois, the January average is 12 degrees warmer. Central Illinois average temperatures in January are 26.7 degrees. In July northern Illinoisans experience an average of 73.5 degrees, while central Illinoisans endure 3 more degrees on average. Southern Illinoisans suffer in the heat of an average of nearly 80 degrees in July. Rainfall averages 34 inches in northern Illinois, nearly 37 inches in the central part of the state, and approximately 45 inches down south.

Spring comes to southern Illinois several weeks before it comes to northern Illinois. Winter hits northern Illinois a bit more vengefully than it hits southern Illinois, and earlier, too. Southern Illinois birders can spot ten species of warblers plucking insects from flowering dogwood blossoms and other shrubs and trees, while trees are still bare in the north. Meanwhile, northern Illinois birders are still tallying late winter stragglers such as Red-breasted Nuthatches, Winter Wrens, and Yellow-bellied Sapsuckers, which have long left southern Illinois.

A natural boundary between the moist forests in the eastern United States and the drier prairies of the West passes through Illinois. The Prairie State spans 378 miles with latitudes from 37 to 42.5 degrees north. Situated along one of the nation's major flyways, the Mississippi, Illinois encompasses a surface area of 56,345 square miles. The state is bounded on the west by the Mississippi River, the east by Lake Michigan and the Wabash River, and the south by the Ohio River, each perfect entry and exit points for migratory and breeding birds.

Because of its location on a major flyway as well as its diversity of habitat, Illinois attracts massive numbers of migrating waterfowl, shorebirds, loons, raptors, and passerines, including an astounding passage of warblers in spring and fall. The state also hosts one of the largest wintering populations of Bald Eagles in the nation. These American icons winter along the Mississippi, Illinois, and other rivers, and their breeding numbers in the state have risen in the past decade.

Illinois' geological roots: What is now Illinois began as the rest of the world began, with the formation of the earth's crust some 4.6 billion years ago. The bare, hilly landscape punctuated with rivers and streams supported no life. The right mix of oxygen and other gases to support that life did not exist. Life did not even inhabit the region until 1 billion years later, when simple, unicellular creatures evolved.

At various times beginning some 500 million years ago, shallow seas covered large portions of Illinois. Creatures such as snails, clams, and other marine animals lived in the sea, and Illinois teemed with coral reefs, palm trees, and giant dragonflies in a tropical climate. As sea creatures lived, then died, and fell to the bottom of the earth, their calcium-rich shells formed the basis for limestone, and the muds and sands carried by rivers into the seas formed the shale and sandstone outcroppings, seen throughout Illinois today. These outcroppings rise to great heights in areas where the massive glaciers that came years later did not flatten the landscape. During the Ice Age, up to ten or more advances of heavy ice, sometimes one-quarter-mile thick, expanded, retreated, expanded, and retreated, laying down the diverse landscape we see in the northern half to two-thirds of Illinois.

Northeast and East-Central Region—Land of Prairies and Woods
Some 600 types of soils developed from the windblown silt overlying glacial debris in Illinois. One of the richest of these is the black soil beneath our prairies, for example, Goose Lake Prairie State Natural Area. Periods of drought and the flat topography allowed the quick spread of fires, which kept the prairies intact. The prairie grass and wildflowers developed deep root systems, sometimes 20 feet below the ground, adding the biomass and organic material needed for rich farmland.

Certain birds are attracted to breed in prairies—birds that sing on the wing and nest among the grasses. These include Bobolinks, Grasshopper and Henslow's Sparrows, Dickcissels, Upland Sandpipers, and Eastern and Western Meadowlarks, among others. These birds share common characteristics such as mottled brown-and-yellow plumages, offering camouflage against the grasses and forbs in which they build their nests.

As huge expanses of grassland were destroyed to create farmland, some of these birds' populations declined. Indeed, the Bobolink is one of the fastest declining songbirds in the nation, and Henslow's Sparrows, Short-eared Owls, and Northern Harriers are listed as endangered breeders in Illinois. The Greater Prairie-Chicken, which needs massive patches of grasslands in which to breed, is gone except from two state natural areas in Illinois just south of the east-central region.

Scattered among the prairies were wetlands in the north region and prairie potholes in the east-central region. The city of Chicago was, in fact, once a wetland complex consisting of wet prairie, sedge meadows, and marshes. South of the city, Lake Calumet offers clues to Chicago's geological past. Here the state-listed endangered Black-crowned Night-Heron, Pied-billed Grebe, and other birds confined to marshes nest. Their habitat is tenuous at best. Father south, in the east-central region are more wetland species, including bitterns and rails, as well as teals and other waterfowl breeding in the last remaining prairie potholes.

Growing among the prairies, too, are woodlands, which are generally found near waterways created by glacial meltwater or atop glacial ridges called moraines, where fire could not spread as quickly. In northern Illinois places such as

Ryerson Woods exist because it is situated next to the Des Plaines River. In central Illinois, the Vermilion River kept fire at bay, and amid the cornfields, which were once prairies, the river flows through bottomland woods where a wondrous group of birds such as Prothonotary Warblers and American Redstarts breed. These woodlands also host breeding forest birds such as Veeries, Wood Thrushes, and Scarlet Tanagers. However, the patchwork nature of Illinois' woods today, due to development, has created a major problem for breeding forest birds. The scenario has increased predation as well as brood parasitism by Brown-headed Cowbirds, which lay their eggs in other birds' nests.

Lake Michigan and its shoreline, formed in the northeastern region during the Ice Age, brings many birds to Illinois. The lake acts as a migratory funnel, and Illinois Beach State Park in the northeasternmost portion of Illinois is one of the best hawk-watching spots in the state, if not the Midwest. The Lake Michigan corridor and inland riverine corridors attract migrating songbirds traveling along these waterways looking for a patch of greenery for resting and feeding. Forty-one species of warblers have migrated through Illinois; most of them are seen each year, and May days can produce 20, 25, maybe even 30 species of warblers at one outing.

Today, the east-central region (as well as the northern part of the south region and parts of the west-central region) contains several large manmade lakes created by damming the miles of rivers that once flowed freely among the prairies. These lakes attract thousands of migratory ducks and other waterfowl. Protected riverine woodlands also offer respite for birds from the massive corn belt stretching through this part of the state.

Northwest and West-Central Region—Land of Hills, Rivers, and Valleys

The northwest region is known as the driftless area where rivers, especially the mighty Mississippi, have sculpted the landscape without interruption from glacial action for tens of thousands of years. The rivers continue to wind and bend through steep wooded valleys and hollows where Bald Eagles and Turkey Vultures soar and where Wild Turkeys once roamed, and are returning after being recently reintroduced.

Bordering the western part of the northwest and west-central regions in Illinois flows the mighty Mississippi River, which slowly erodes the region to create a rugged terrain of hills and limestone cliffs. As you drive from the palisades near the town of Savanna south, you can see the signs of river action. Away from the Mississippi toward the center of the northwest region is Starved Rock State Park, where 125-foot-tall sandstone bluffs, waterfalls, and canyons represent the constant erosive action of the Illinois River.

In the west-central region lies an area once covered with sloughs, wetlands, and woods where millions of migratory waterfowl and other birds fed. In the 1920s, agriculture development including diking and draining greatly disturbed the ecosystem. Restoration that began in the late 1930s has returned some of the natural floodplains within the Mississippi Flyway along the Illinois River, and soon 32,000 acres along the Illinois River will include bottomland forest, backwater lake, floodplain wetlands, and shorebird habitat. In fact, Lake Chautauqua National Wildlife Refuge within the west-central region is designated as an internationally important shorebird migratory stopover. This region attracts thousands of shorebirds annually, including dowitchers, phalaropes, yellowlegs, sandpipers, and plovers, as well as most, if not all of the ducks that have ever passed through Illinois.

A recent addition to the bird life here is the American White Pelican, a species that had been found occasionally years ago in this area, but now seems to have altered its migration course so that flocks of hundreds and sometimes even thousands come through these regions as well as the south region.

South Region—Land of the Shawnee Highlands and Cypress Swamps

The southernmost part of the state remained ice-free during Illinois' last ice age. Instead, geological action beneath the earth uplifted the ancient seabed to create the Shawnee highlands, what is now the national forest, which makes up most of the south region. Water running off these forested slopes cut deep canyons in the sandstone. Climatic and geologic activity together created a patchwork of habitats with different moisture, temperature, and soil conditions that meet the needs of various species. Here, bald cypress swamps remind you of a Louisiana bayou. Herons and egrets fish in the winding sloughs and backwaters, and Prothontoary Warblers nest in cavity holes overlooking the rivers. Sloping ravines attract Worm-eating Warblers to nest. High in the trees, are breeding Northern Parula, Yellow-throated, and Cerulean Warblers. River bottomlands provide habitat for breeding Louisiana Waterthrushes and Acadian Flycatchers. Some places in the South Region have hosted 36 species of migrating warblers and 19 species of breeding warblers.

A specialty of southern Illinois is the breeding Mississippi Kite, which finds trees along a backwater river a perfect place to build a nest. Yellow-crowned Night-Herons, listed as endangered in Illinois, breed here, too, feasting on the crayfish living in the backwaters. With all this variety in climate, ecosystem, and geological landscape, it is no wonder that Illinois is growing as an important birding state, one where some of the nation's rarest birds can be protected if only humans will work toward that end.

3. Birding Calendar

In Illinois, spring migration attracts as many birders as it does birds. With the chance to see up to 36 species of breeding plumaged warblers in one day, not to mention the flycatchers, thrushes, tanagers, and vireos, it's no wonder that many birders find May in Illinois to be one of the most productive months for birding. However, Illinois is a place to bird in all seasons. Choose any month and you'll find birders enjoying the season's avifauna statewide. Here's a look at the Illinois birding calendar, followed by information on how to best enjoy birding the 80 hotspots that follow.

January and February: Northern owls, finches, eagles, and gulls come to Illinois. Ducks begin courting.

In winter you can fairly easily find a Snowy Owl along the Lake Michigan shoreline and other places that simulate its tundra habitat. This is an irruptive species, meaning that when food sources get scarce in its northern home, it moves south into the northern states. Snowy Owls irrupt every five or more years, at which time they are rather common in northern Illinois during winter.

Red-breasted Nuthatches, Pine Siskins, and Common Redpolls are regular Illinois winter visitors, and are also somewhat tied to food production in their northern homes. You also have the chance to see Evening Grosbeaks in winter, as well as Red and White-winged Crossbills, and possibly, a really rare Illinois winter visitor, the Pine Grosbeak.

Many birders go owl prowling in January and February to listen for Eastern Screech-Owls, Barred Owls, and Great Horned Owls, year-round residents that begin breeding in winter. Birders also know the reliable places to find wintering Long-eareds, Short-eareds, and Northern Saw-whet Owls, three species that also migrate from Canada and other northern locations into Illinois for the winter.

Lake Michigan harbors hardy sea ducks, including, Oldsquaws, mergansers, goldeneyes, and scoters in winter. These birds begin pair-bonding and courting in January and February, so if you are willing to brave the cold, windy lakefront, you can have some fascinating birding experiences. Central and southern Illinois have large lakes, manmade and natural, that harbor wintering ducks. Birders are also lured to these same places in winter to find gulls. They know the reliable spots to find Thayer's, Iceland, and Glaucous Gulls during the cold months—several gull trips are planned annually statewide in the winter.

For a spectacular birding adventure, visit central and southern Illinois where wintering Snow Geese number in the thousands along the rivers and lakes. Or head to the Mississippi or Illinois Rivers to search for wintering Bald Eagles. The colder the winter, the farther south you can go to see large numbers of this majestic bird.

Still haven't found enough to whet your appetite for winter birding? Try scouting for Snow Buntings and Lapland Longspurs in fields or wintering American Tree Sparrows in shrubby areas. These hardy passerines brighten any winter day.

March: Migrating waterfowl return, and the American Woodcock goes courting.

As February eases into March, the numbers of waterfowl rise, so that 10,000 or more can be found in one large area in southern Illinois. March is the month for birders to go duck watching. Rewards include views of migrating Canvasbacks, Redheads, Ruddy Ducks, Northern Shovelers, and many others. In March you can see at least 19 species of waterfowl in southern and central Illinois.

American Woodcocks return in March, beginning their fascinating courtship ritual. Birders plan woodcock evenings as early as late February in the south and into April in the north. At dusk the male American Woodcock chooses a clearing near woods and utters the sound, *"peent"* several times, then flies into the air until he is out of human sight, as the female watches below. He returns to the same spot, his wings twittering on the way down.

Horned Larks, Eastern Meadowlarks, and Song Sparrows are also beginning courtship in March, singing from the fields and shrubs throughout the state. These species overwinter in southern Illinois.

April: Rails, snipes, herons, egrets, early songbirds, and shorebirds, including the American Golden-Plover return. Greater Prairie-Chickens return to leks to court. Hawks and owls are well into breeding.

Visit the Illinois wetlands at the end of March and April, depending on the weather and the location, to search for snipes, herons, egrets, rails, and early shorebirds. In April, herons and egrets return to their rookeries or establish new ones. The state-listed endangered Black-crowned Night-Heron returns to Lake Calumet and the Lake Renwick Herony Rookery, south of Chicago in April. Great Blue Herons and Great Egrets are also back, choosing their space in the colonial breeding grounds.

Lesser and Greater Yellowlegs and Solitary Sandpipers are already back in southern Illinois and winging their way north. In central Illinois you can tally 90 species on one day in April, including the coveted Smith's Longspur, and its more common cousin, the Lapland Longspur, ten species of sparrows, Yellow-bellied Sapsuckers, Winter Wrens, American Bitterns, and one of the most beloved Illinois shorebirds, the American Golden-Plover.

Loons return to northern Illinois glacial lakes, and birders usually plan a "looney" trip in Illinois during this month.

April brings migrant passerines to southern Illinois. Birders at Pere Marquette State Park sometimes find their first Eastern Phoebe and Louisiana Waterthrush in March. By the end of April, the Worm-eating and Prothonotary Warblers are singing full-force in southern Illinois while the Yellow-headed Blackbirds have selected the northern Illinois wetlands where they will breed.

Eastern Bluebirds are back, too, choosing the many boxes provided by humans to begin another breeding season, while migratory sparrows, kinglets, and other early passerines are arriving. Soras and Virginia Rails are stopping at various wetlands while migrating, and at dusk and dawn you should hear them call. The state-listed Least and American Bitterns return, and though their numbers are dwindling, they return to certain breeding areas with some consistency. Meanwhile, Bald Eagles have migrated to breeding grounds, while some remain to build their nests along Illinois waterways.

The rarest bird in the state, the federally listed endangered Greater Prairie-Chicken, begins its fascinating courtship ritual on leks set aside for its survival in southern Illinois. Schedule a trip in April to view the chickens in blinds.

Birders also find active Red-tailed and Cooper's Hawks as well as Barred and Great Horned Owl nests. By April, hawks and owls are feeding nestlings. The patient observer can enjoy this birding experience, as long as care is taken not to disturb the young. Horned Larks are also breeding in April; young are often hatched before the spring bird count in May.

May: Migrating passerines and grassland and savanna breeders arrive. Spring bird count occurs.

By the end of April as the last large numbers of ducks leave, the neotropical migrants begin to pour into southern Illinois. And by middle May, they are throughout the state—the warblers, tanagers, shorebirds, flycatchers, vireos. Migratory sparrows continue to fly through the state.

Spring Bird Count Day is on the first Saturday in May, and birders are scouting their territories.

In May you may see 30 species of warblers or more nearly anywhere in Illinois during the month. A 25-warbler day is not uncommon anywhere! You might count 15 species of shorebirds in a northern Illinois wetland in one hour. Birders plan Big Days in May—the record for the most number of species seen in Illinois within 24 hours, at this writing, is 184 species.

Many of these birds are flying farther north to breed, but some of them will remain in Illinois to breed.

Some of the Midwest's rarest birds arrive to claim territories on the grasslands. The Bobolink and Upland Sandpiper have returned from South America. Henslow's and Grasshopper Sparrows are just arriving, looking for the grassland with just the right height and moisture content in which to breed.

June: Grassland and woodland breeders song fills the Illinois air.

June is a spectacular month for hearing birds in Illinois. All the grassland and woodland breeders are singing. Pick a day almost anywhere at sunrise in June and choose almost any spot mentioned in this book and you will hear a chorus of breeders.

Visit Nachusa Grasslands at dawn to hear Henslow's, Grasshopper, and Savanna Sparrows, Eastern Meadowlarks, and Bobolinks. Visit a river bottomland woods and listen to the Prothonotary Warbler, American Redstart, and Acadian Flycatcher sing. Wood Thrushes and Veeries, with their flute-like trills, add a wonderful dimension to birding in June.

In the savannas, Great Crested Flycatchers shout, *"wheep"* while Eastern Wood-Pewees sing their name. Woodpeckers are feeding young, and you can observe the mottled plumage of the young Red-headed Woodpeckers as they beg for food from their more brilliantly plumaged parents.

The state-listed threatened Sandhill Cranes have hatched young in northern Illinois in June. Young Killdeer are scurrying about throughout the state.

In northern Illinois marshes, the state-listed endangered Yellow-headed Blackbird sings his lusty song, while the state-listed threatened Pied-billed Grebe shrieks a maniacal laughter from the background.

Throughout the woodlands and edges of the state, you may find 19 regularly breeding warblers, and three more that are rare. That's a lot of breeding warblers for a midwestern state!

July: Shorebirds return and songbirds fledge.

July is no time to put away your binoculars in Illinois. The shorebirds are returning from their northern breeding grounds. You can find them almost any time of day and the weather is balmy for birding. In early to middle July, the Greater and Lesser Yellowlegs are already back in southern Illinois, heading south for the winter.

You'll start seeing Semipalmated Plovers and Semipalmated, Least, and Pectoral Sandpipers statewide in July.

A stroll through the prairies can be uncomfortable in July, weather-wise, but you may see young Bobolinks, meadowlarks, and other grassland species feeding young. Fledgling Eastern Bluebirds remain close to their nest box sites, and you can observe parents and young dealing with the bird's equivalent of the human's "terrible twos" syndrome, i.e., the young want food and attention and the parents are getting tired of the whole routine.

August and September: Migrant shorebirds and land birds are numerous. Young herons and egrets wander.

It's time to learn your fall warblers and shorebirds! In mid-August, the warblers trickle into northern Illinois from their Wisconsin, Michigan, and Canadian breeding grounds, plus young warblers, vireos, and other songbirds that hatched in Illinois are dispersing and trying out their wings. As a result, you'll see warblers in many plumages, adults in worn breeding plumage, young in first-year plumage, and some gaining their winter plumages, all for the fascination of birders. Turnabout is fair play, so the warblers come through northern Illinois first—many of them along the Lake Michigan shores, and the birders down in southern Illinois have to wait for the birds to continue south.

The same holds true for shorebirds. Sanderlings return, wearing winter white and looking nothing like they did on their breeding grounds. More Pectoral and

Least Sandpipers arrive. Some are adults and some are young. Telling them apart can be an interesting challenge. Scopes are essential. A visit to Lake Chautauqua, listed as an internationally significant shorebird spot, should be on your agenda for late summer.

In August some herons and egrets are fishing in wetlands, river backwaters, and shallow lakes statewide. In some areas large groups of these birds find one great fishing spot where they feast in the early morning before the human fishermen arrive. Young Snowy Egrets and Little Blue Herons tend to wander in August; some of them appear north of where you'd expect them.

In late August, the American White Pelicans return to central and southern Illinois, migrating in numbers up to hundreds or even thousands. They will remain through November, sometimes later.

October and November: Ducks and hawks migrate in huge numbers.

When the ice descends on the lakes up north, the ducks fly south, many of them along the Mississippi Flyway, which runs through the state of Illinois. Buffleheads, mergansers, Ruddy Ducks, teals, and more fly into northern Illinois, resting on Lake Michigan as well as inland lakes and river backwaters.

Oldsquaws—some of the hardiest sea ducks—will remain throughout the winter. Flyby scoters, especially along Lake Michigan, are seen in October and November.

October is also the month for looking for the rare Purple Sandpiper in northern Illinois.

Probably the *piece de resistance* in October for Illinois birders is the chance to see up to 14 species of hawks in one day. Several hawk-watching spots rival the more well-known Hawk Mountain in Pennsylvania.

The flight actually begins in middle to late September, when thousands of Broad-winged Hawks ride the thermals. Following them are migrating Sharp-shinned and Cooper's Hawks, Northern Harriers, Merlins, Peregrine Falcons, American Kestrels, Red-tailed Hawks, and Red-shouldered Hawks, among others.

December: Christmas Bird Counts are held statewide.

Yes, you can see warblers in December in Illinois, you can hear Carolina Wrens singing, you can find a Snowy Owl, and you can find a Great Horned Owl nest—all in the same state. The proof is in the nearly 100 years of data gathered on Christmas Bird Counts done statewide in Illinois. The data show how bird life has changed in the state. For example, 50 years ago not a single goose was counted in Decatur in central Illinois. Now, the Canada Goose is one of the most common species seen on Christmas Bird Counts there as well as statewide.

The data also show how varied bird life is in Illinois from the southern to the northern end. Down south, birders are counting wintering White-crowned Sparrows, Loggerhead Shrikes, Carolina Wrens, and Yellow-rumped Warblers. Along the lakefront in northern Illinois, birders are counting the few Surf Scoters to be seen statewide, a Northern Shrike, plus Thayer's, Glaucous, Great Black-backed, and Lesser Black-backed Gulls among other birds. The number of species seen statewide during the Illinois Christmas Bird Count period is typically about 150.

The counts begin in middle December and don't end until right after New Year's Day. Whether a beginning or advanced birder, you should enjoy participating in the Christmas Bird Counts. You can contact any of the birding groups or websites listed in the next section to learn how you can join a count.

4. Planning Your Trip

Illinois is a land of extreme temperatures. Southern Illinois can be uncomfortably warm and humid in July and August, with temperatures rising near 100 degrees F. Northern Illinois can be downright frigid in winter, with temperatures dipping well below zero. Yet, walk a prairie in northern Illinois on a July day, and the hot sun can make you feel as if you were in a desert. Anywhere along lakeshores it can be cold and windy and wet in March and April when birders are scoping the fields and lakes for ducks.

Apparel for all weather conditions is readily available at outfitters and through catalogs, and if you are wearing the right clothes, you can have a comfortable birding experience. Plus some days in May and June as well as middle September through the end of October can be heaven, weather-wise and bird-wise for birders.

Wear layers of breathable, waterproof clothing when birding in winter in Illinois. You can always peel some of the layers if you get warm. Sturdy walking shoes and boots are essential, especially if you are going to explore the river backwaters and marshes, or climb the rugged cliffs and rolling terrain in various parts of the state. You'll need gloves and hats even in March and sometimes into April to keep warm.

In summer, light-colored clothing covering your body is necessary to protect you from mosquitos and ticks. Wear a wide-brimmed hat to keep the sun at bay, and bring plenty of drinking water. Even in April and May you should wear long pants to protect against ticks and from scratches when walking through brambles and areas where you may find snakes and poison ivy.

WHAT TO BRING

Water and food. When you embark on your trip, make sure you have a cooler stocked with water in any season. I can't stress how important this is—when I forget my water, I am very uncomfortable. And, have a stash of instant energy foods, whether it's sunflower seeds, chocolate bars, or fruit.

Extra clothes. Bring extra pairs of gloves, clothes, and shoes. My birding motto: more is better than not enough.

Binoculars and scopes. Don't forget your binoculars and spotting scope, which greatly enhance birding many of the spots described. Even if you're just going for a woodland migrant tour, stash your scope in the car—you never know when you'll come across a wetland or field with a flock of birds that you can't identify with only your binoculars. Don't forget to check your trunk every time you return to your vehicle to make sure you haven't left the scope somewhere in the field.

Field guides and checklists. You'll find field guides useful when identifying birds. Choose several that you like and get to know how to use them.

Many of the sites publish checklists. You'll find these helpful when out in the field looking for birds in specific habitats and at specific times of year. Call the contacts listed in Appendix A to obtain the checklists as well as brochures and other information to help you bird an area.

Maps and compass. Especially in central and southern Illinois, you'll want to bring maps with you, including the *DeLorme Illinois Atlas & Gazetteer,* the state's official highway map, this book, plus other maps that you have obtained by contacting the nature centers and preserves before going. If you plan to explore many of the southern Illinois sites off the main roads, you'll need a compass. I used several maps to help me in preparing the maps for this book, and I suggest you do the same to find your way around some of the backroads.

Field journal and pen. Taking notes in the field can be rewarding. When you have lunch with your birding friends you can relive the experiences. Take plenty of notes, and if you find a rare bird, contact the Illinois Ornithological Records Committee to obtain documentation forms. See Appendix B for more information.

Insect repellent, poison ivy ointment, and sunscreen. From April through September you may need repellent for mosquitos, ticks, chiggers, and other bothersome insects as well as poison ivy. Sunscreen can be useful year-round.

Tissue paper. In those backroad places where you find one little outhouse that is out of toilet paper, you may find tissue paper useful.

FIELD HAZARDS

Be aware and plan for the following hazards while birding.

Poison ivy: Poison ivy can be prolific, especially in southern Illinois. If you're susceptible, take precautions. Some new products can be taken before you embark on your birding trip. Even if you don't think you're susceptible, be cautious. For years, I thought I was immune to poison ivy, until I took a birding trip to southern Illinois in late June and spent the next four months battling the nasty, itchy condition. Staying on trails and learning to identify poison ivy can help.

Insects: Though few cases of Lyme disease have been reported in Illinois, you should be aware that deer and lonestar ticks can be found in the summer, especially when walking wet fields and prairies. Check for ticks carefully when you're done birding. Wear long pants tucked into your shoes. Light clothing is always the best choice when trying to avoid ticks or mosquitos, which can be plentiful from April through September in Illinois depending on where you are and the amount of rainfall and temperatures. Also avoid wearing perfume, which attracts insects, including bees in late summer.

Roads: Some roads can be hazardous, especially during rainy and snowy conditions. Some roads in southern Illinois should not be traveled after heavy rains except with an appropriate vehicle. Some in northern Illinois can contain high traffic volume. Use your judgment and read the "Birding" and "General information" in each of the sites carefully, to learn which roads may be hazardous.

Snakes: Don't let the word "snakes" scare you, but be cautious in southern Illinois when walking the trails and gravel roads. Good solid hiking shoes will help. Pay attention to where you walk.

Hunting season: Some of the birding sites listed are open for hunting season, which generally begins in September, October, or November (depending on the site) and lasts through part of winter. Some places also have turkey or squirrel hunting in spring. You can still bird most of these areas during these times, but should plan accordingly. Call the department of natural resources and other contacts given for each site before going during hunting season. Ask which sites are closed to public access and where you can and can't go. If you go, wear appropriate clothing, for example, blaze-orange vests. You can obtain an annual digest of hunting and trapping regulations from the Illinois Department of Natural Resources. Hunters and trappers purchase licenses; the funds are used to protect and restore wildlife habitat.

Crime: It is too bad that this topic comes up at all, but something must be said here. Personal safety is a concern—for some of these sites; birding is best done in groups. These potential problem areas are indicated in the text.

A more likely type of crime that birders may encounter is to find their cars broken into if they are left in remote parking lots. You should always be careful not to leave anything interesting or valuable in your car that can be seen from the outside.

WHERE TO STAY

Illinois has fine campgrounds, hotels, motels, and bed-and-breakfast inns where you can stay while on a birding trip. For an Illinois camping guide, call the Illinois Department of Natural Resources. You can also obtain a free *Illinois State Parks Magazine* from the department, which includes information on state park lodges and camping.

For a guide to Illinois bed and breakfasts, call the Illinois Bed & Breakfast Association, or the Illinois Department of Commerce and Community Affairs. Ask for the free Illinois Visitors Guide, which includes lodging information (also available on the internet).

Local chambers of commerce also provide helpful lodging information. See Appendix A for contact information.

BIRDING FIELD TRIPS AND HOTLINES

Illinois is lucky to have many birding groups that offer free walks as well as several rare bird alert hotlines and many websites describing field trips. In addition, people interested in birds participate in the statewide ListServ called Illinois Birders Exchanging Thoughts (IBET). If you have access to the Internet, you should find the following sites helpful when planning a birding trip. If you just have a phone, you can get great information as well, including up-to-date messages on birds seen in the area.

The amount of Illinois-based birding organizations and website available is huge. I'm sorry we can't fit them all here, but you can link to many more by checking the sites. See Appendix A for the list.

5. Birding Ethics

For the most part, birding is a low-impact activity; however, that does not mean we cannot damage habitats and ecosystems crucial to a bird's survival. You may think that traipsing into a wetland to see a bird's nest might have little impact since you are the only one there; but consider what would happen if everyone thought that way. The bird may abandon the nest.

Respect the landscape upon which you walk and the birds whose territories you may be entering. Respect private landowners' rights and those of your fellow birders.

The American Birding Association publishes and distributes a code of ethics to guide its members. Please give careful thought to these ethics before embarking on your birding trip.

AMERICAN BIRDING ASSOCIATION PRINCIPLES AND CODE OF ETHICS

Everyone who enjoys birds and birding must always respect wildlife, its environment, and the rights of others. In any conflict of interest between birds and birders, the welfare of the birds and their environment comes first.

1   Promote the welfare of birds and their environment.

1(a) Support the protection of important bird habitat.

1(b) To avoid stressing birds or exposing them to danger, exercise restraint and caution during observation, photography, sound recording, or filming. Limit the use of recordings and other methods of attracting birds, and never use such methods in heavily birded areas, or for attracting any species that is Threatened, Endangered, or of Special Concern, or is rare in your local area. Keep well back from nests and nesting colonies, roosts, display areas, and important feeding sites. In such sensitive areas, if there is a need for extended observation, photography, filming, or recording, try to use a blind or hide, and take advantage of natural cover. Use artificial light sparingly for filming or photography, especially for close-ups.

1(c) Before advertising the presence of a rare bird, evaluate the potential for disturbance to the bird, its surroundings, and other people in the area, and proceed only if access can be controlled, disturbance minimized, and permission has been obtained from private landowners. The sites of rare nesting birds should be divulged only to the proper conservation authorities.

1(d) Stay on roads, trails, and paths where they exist; otherwise, keep habitat disturbance to a minimum.

2 Respect the law and rights of others.

2(a) Do not enter private property without the owner's explicit permission.

2(b) Follow all laws, rules, and regulations governing use of roads and public areas, both at home and abroad.

2(c) Practice common courtesy in contacts with other people. Your exemplary behavior will generate goodwill with birders and nonbirders alike.

3 Ensure that feeders, nest structures, and other artificial bird environments are safe.

3(a) Keep dispensers, water, and food clean and free of decay or disease. It is important to feed birds continually during harsh weather.

3(b) Maintain and clean nest structures regularly.

3(c) If you are attracting birds to an area, ensure the birds are not exposed to predation from cats and other domestic animals, or dangers posed by artificial hazards.

4 Group birding, whether organized or impromptu, requires special care.

Each individual in the group, in addition to the obligations spelled out in Items #1 and #2, has responsibilities as a Group Member.

4(a) Respect the interests, rights, and skills of fellow birders, as well as people participating in other legitimate outdoor activities. Freely share your knowledge and experience, except where code 1(c) applies. Be especially helpful to beginning birders.

4(b) If you witness unethical birding behavior, assess the situation, and intervene if you think it prudent. When interceding, inform the person(s) of the inappropriate action, and attempt, within reason, to have it stopped. If the behavior continues, document it, and notify appropriate individuals or organizations.

Group Leader Responsibilities (amateur and professional trips and tours).

4(c) Be an exemplary ethical role model for the group. Teach through word and example.

4(d) Keep groups to a size that limits impact on the environment and does not interfere with others using the same area.

4(e) Ensure everyone in the group knows of and practices this code.

4(f) Learn and inform the group of any special circumstances applicable to the areas being visited (e.g., no tape recorders allowed).

4(g) Acknowledge that professional tour companies bear a special responsibility to place the welfare of birds and the benefits of public knowledge ahead of the company's commercial interest. Ideally, leaders should keep track of tour sightings, document unusual occurrences, and submit records to appropriate organizations.

Reprinted by permission of American Birding Association

Map Legend

Interstate	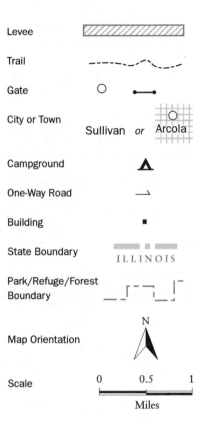	Levee	
US Highway		Trail	
State or County Road		Gate	
Forest Service Road	FR 224	City or Town	Sullivan *or* Arcola
Interstate Highway		Campground	
Paved Road		One-Way Road	
Secondary Paved Road		Building	
Gravel or Unimproved Road		State Boundary	ILLINOIS
Birding Site	17	Park/Refuge/Forest Boundary	
Parking Area	P		N
Lake, Dam,River/Creek,		Map Orientation	
Bridge		Scale	0 0.5 1
Marsh			Miles
Wetland			

24

6. *Illinois' Best Birding Sites*

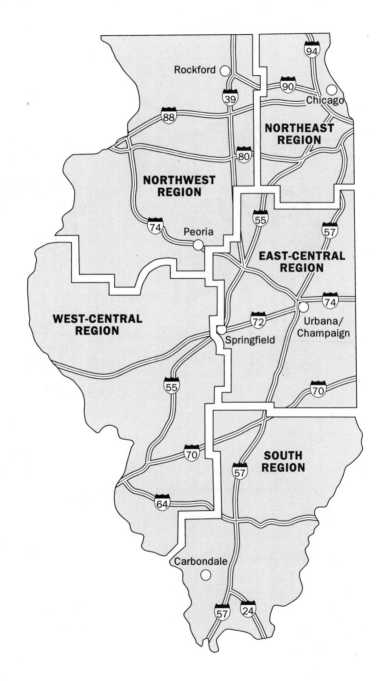

Sandhill Cranes drawing by Denis Kanis.

Northeastern Region

The Lake Michigan shoreline hugging the northeasternmost portion of the Prairie State attracts huge flocks of migratory birds, as well some of the state's rarest breeding birds. Just northwest of downtown Chicago, the Des Plaines River Valley serves as an important migratory passageway for the flycatchers, tanagers, orioles, warblers, and other songbirds. In fall and spring, the inland glacial lakes and sloughs pulse with migrating waterfowl, including loons and grebes, while Lake Michigan offers food for migrating ducks, terns, and other water-loving species.

Once a flat wetland, Chicago is now a conglomeration of skyscrapers and automobiles. Not much is left of the marshes, but the lake and the shrubs and trees hugging the shoreline serve as major funnels for birds that pass through two of the best birding spots in the state, Montrose Harbor and Jackson Park. Birders come to these places year-round, looking for rarities and watching the hordes of sparrows feeding in grassy patches next to tall buildings, or warblers flitting in trees planted by landscapers. In winter, Snowy Owls and other northern visitors fly south to Chicagoland.

Illinois Beach State Park at the northern tip of the state is arguably one of the Midwest's best hawk-watching spots. Hawk watchers report impressive raptor numbers here each season.

Chicago's northern and southern suburbs still hold vestiges of the past, marshes that provide habitat for the state-listed endangered Yellow-headed Blackbird, Black Tern, Forster's Tern, and Common Tern, found in Illinois only in the northeastern section. In 1979, the Sandhill Crane returned to breed in Illinois after more than a century, and birders find it only in the northern section of the state. Scattered among the wetlands, too, are small heron rookeries, where birders can observe the ritual of raising young from courtship through fledging.

Some of the state's most impressive prairies grow in northeastern Illinois. Henslow's Sparrows sing their *"tslicks,"* while Upland Sandpipers give their wolf whistles at the Midewin National Tallgrass Prairie. Bobolinks, one of the nation's fastest declining songbirds, breed here, too, as well as at the Bartel and Orland Grasslands.

CHICAGO

1 Montrose Harbor, the Magic Hedge, the Lincoln Park Bird Sanctuary, and Belmont Harbor

2 Jackson Park and the Paul O. Douglas Nature Sanctuary (Wooded Island)

3 Downtown Chicago Birding/Walking Tour

3a North River Walk

3b Southeast Walk

3c Grant Park/Museum Campuses Walk

CHICAGO SUBURBS NORTH

4 Illinois Beach State Park

5 Waukegan Beach and Bowen Park

6 Wadsworth Savanna and Wetlands Demonstration Project

7 Chain O' Lakes State Park

8 Glacial Park and Vicinity

9 Moraine Hills State Park

10 Crabtree Nature Center, Palatine Marsh, and Vicinity

11 Baker's Lake and Ron Beese Park

12 Ryerson Conservation Area and the Des Plaines River Corridor

13 Chicago Botanic Garden

14 Skokie Lagoons

15 Gillson Park and Evanston Landfill

16 O'Hare Post Office Ponds

CHICAGO SUBURBS WEST

17 Morton Arboretum

18 Blackwell Forest Preserve

19 Fermilab National Accelerator Laboratory

CHICAGO SUBURBS SOUTH—THE PALOS PRESERVES

20 Conkey Woods

21 McClaughry Springs Woods

22 Little Red Schoolhouse Nature Center and Nearby Sloughs

23 Swallow Cliff Woods

24 Camp Sagawau

25 Saganashkee Slough

26 McGinnis Slough

CHICAGO'S FAR SOUTH SUBURBS

27 The Bartel and Orland Grasslands

28 Lake Calumet and Vicinity

29 Lake Renwick Heron Rookery Nature Preserve and Copley Nature Park

30 Goose Lake Prairie and Heidecke Lake

31 Midewin National Tallgrass Prairie

32 Kankakee River State Park, Momence Wetlands, and Sod Farms

28

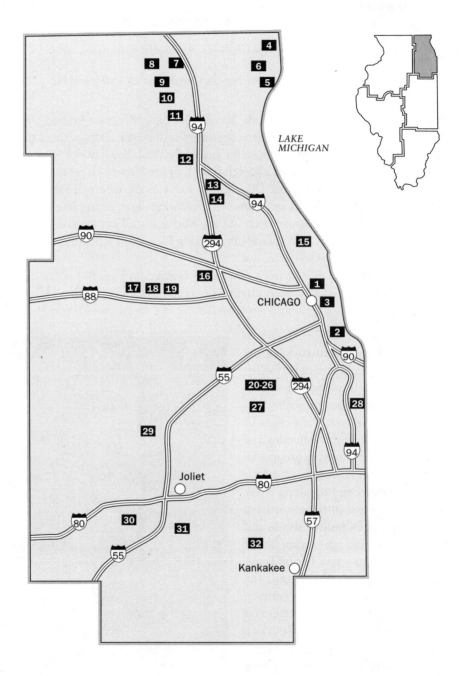

LAKE
MICHIGAN

94

94

294

90

15

16

1

CHICAGO 3

17 18 19

88

2

90

55

20-26 294

27

28

29

94

Joliet

80

80 30

31

57

55

32

Kankakee

1 Montrose Harbor, the Magic Hedge, the Lincoln Park Bird Sanctuary, and Belmont Harbor

Habitats: Lake Michigan shoreline, patches of trees and shrubs locally known as the Magic Hedge, meadow, and fenced-in woods at the sanctuary.

Key birds: Migratory waterfowl, hawks, shorebirds, gulls, terns, and songbirds.

Best times to bird: Year-round, but particularly during spring and fall migration.

Directions: In Chicago, exit from Lake Shore Drive onto Montrose Avenue. Drive east a few blocks, then turn right or southeast at the Bait Shop, a small gray building. Drive one block and park on the side of the road. You'll notice more cars parked here, too, bearing license plates that say they are birders. To get to the bird sanctuary, return to Lake Shore Drive going south to the next exit (about 0.5 mile), which is Irving Park Road. Turn east, following the signs to Lincoln Park. Look for the fenced-in sanctuary west of Lake Michigan and just south of the golf course and tennis courts. One mile south of Irving Park Road is Belmont Avenue, which you can take east to the harbor.

You can also take the bus from downtown Chicago to Lincoln Park and the hedge. Call the Regional Transportation Association (RTA) for details and times. (See Appendix A).

Birding: Go to the Magic Hedge north of downtown Chicago early in the morning at the right time of year when the winds are right and you should experience one of the best migratory fall-outs in the Midwest. Thousands of songbirds that have flown hundreds of miles from their wintering grounds in South and Central America across the Gulf of Mexico and up along rivers and lakes to get to their northern breeding grounds, find the shrubs and trees along the Chicago skyline one of the few places to refuel. For birds migrating along Lake Michigan, the Magic Hedge is an oasis in between all the city buildings. Those trees and hedges on a spit of land jutting out into the lake mean food to be gorged upon by birds tired and hungry from the long springtime commute.

Dunlin migrant at Montrose Beach.
ERIC WALTERS PHOTO

1 Montrose Harbor, the Magic Hedge, the Lincoln Park Bird Sanctuary, and Belmont Harbor

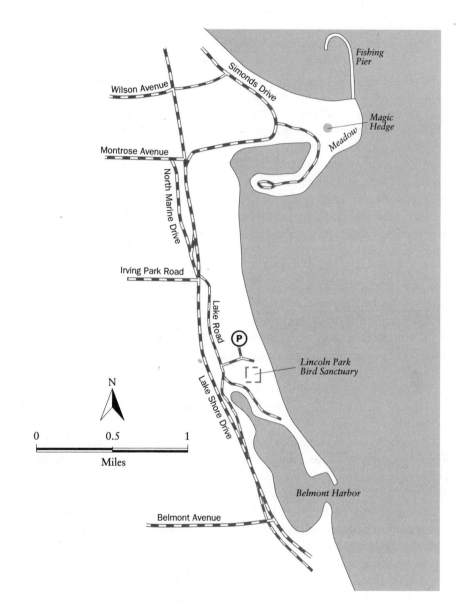

Wilson Avenue

Simonds Drive

Fishing Pier

Magic Hedge

Meadow

Montrose Avenue

North Marine Drive

Irving Park Road

Lake Road

P

Lincoln Park Bird Sanctuary

Lake Shore Drive

N

0   0.5   1

Miles

Belmont Harbor

Belmont Avenue

Observers have recorded at least 300 species of birds at the hedge, meadow, and nearby Lake Michigan shoreline. That number represents three-fourths of all bird species known to have occurred in Illinois.

The hedge is actually one small group of shrubs west of the lake, but now as more trees and shrubs are planted, you could say the whole area of greenery here is a Magic Hedge.

Many birders have added lifers to their lists by visiting the Magic Hedge, when for example, a Black Rail remained for several days, or a Red-necked Grebe stayed in the harbor for a few days. To experience the most exciting migration requires some weather watching. An overnight south to southwesterly wind with clear skies in late April or early May attracts the migrants to the hedge. Conversely, in fall, north to northeasterly winds often bring in the songbirds, as well as hawks, shorebirds, and other migrants.

Arrive at dawn or soon thereafter. By 9 or 10 A.M., bicyclists, joggers, picnickers, dog walkers, and ballplayers arrive to enjoy the lakeshore, and unfortunately, their activities sometimes disturb the birds.

After parking, cross the road and walk northeast toward the small bushes of honeysuckle, virburnum, elderberry, and spirea, where hosts of birds feed and rest during migration.

You'll also see a grassy meadow here, where you can walk to another set of trees and shrubs, which may be holding more birds. Don't be surprised if a Monk Parakeet flies by (see Jackson Park Site 2 for details on this species).

The songbird flight begins sometime in April, with many species of warblers arriving in the latter part of the month and well into May, sometimes even early June. If you're searching for the rare Connecticut Warbler, late May is a good time to come.

Check every green nook and cranny here, but please be careful not to disturb the birds or walk into shrubs or trees. Remember, these birds are famished and vulnerable.

Toward the end of August, you may find 21 species or more of warblers on a single day, along with Tree, Swamp, White-throated, White-crowned, Field, Song, Lincoln's, and House Sparrows, plus Brown Thrashers, both kinglets, redpolls, American Pipits, Winter Wrens, and more.

Before or after birding the Magic Hedge, walk east to the lake to search for gulls and shorebirds, as well as flyby ducks and hawks. Bring your scope. You can walk the sandy beach to search for shorebirds, or walk south to the fishing pier, where you might spot a Peregrine Falcon snatching a shorebird for breakfast. In late August, birders found Sanderlings, Semipalmated Plovers, and Semipalmated Sandpipers, Greater Yellowlegs, and Spotted Sandpipers along the beach. In September, the Black-bellied Plovers and American Golden-Plovers come.

Also in September, look for terns, including Caspian, Forster's, and Common, flying along the lakeshore. Later in fall, Sanderlings, Dunlins, and an occasional Red Knot feed on the beach. When October comes, look for loons and grebes as well as ducks, including scaups, mergansers, and scoters, many of which remain through March. Within two days in early November, a birder recorded 6 Common Loons, 2 Pied-billed Grebes, 1 Red-necked Grebe, a Least Bittern being chased by an adult Peregrine Falcon, 1 American Black Duck, hundreds of scaups and Red-breasted Mergansers flying over the lake, a male Hooded Merganser, a Northern Harrier, kestrels and merlins, several Black-bellied Plovers, Sanderlings, and Dunlin, plus Bonaparte's, Ring-billed, and Herring Gulls, and one Lapland Longspur among 80 Snow Buntings.

Birders usually record Snowy Owls here in winter, too—and some years when the species irrupts from the north, you can get excellent views.

A newcomer to the Hedge is the Eurasian Collared-Dove, just recently added to the Illinois State Checklist for Birds. This bird successfully bred in 1998 in a small group of maples at the base of a fishhook pier. Birders are debating whether this particular dove is a hybrid species.

After birding the hedge and shoreline, go to the Lincoln Park Bird Sanctuary, about 1 mile south. You can drive, or, if you have time, walk or bicycle from the Magic Hedge south along the trail all the way to the sanctuary.

Even if you've had a fruitful day at the hedge, you'll likely add more species to your list when you visit the sanctuary.

Birding is not so easy on the eyes here, though, because you'll have to peer through a tall fence that protects the woods from encroachment from humans and dogs. In spring, look to the tree branches for Black-crowned Night-Herons, which often roost there. Wet areas, best viewed from the east side, attract rails, including Virginia and Sora. The sanctuary has also produced its share of rarities, including a Brewer's Sparrow that spent the winter in 1997. Also check Belmont Harbor for migrating or wintering gulls and ducks.

General information: The Magic Hedge exists because of the U.S. Army missile base built in the 1950s along Lake Michigan. The government allowed shrubs and trees to grow around the base. When the army dismantled the base in 1970, it left the greenery. Since then, the Magic Hedge has attracted birders as well as controversy, especially lately as conservationists and park district officials discuss how to meet the needs of birders, dog walkers, fishermen, joggers, and other users of these parks. The Chicago Park District has developed an ecological restoration program, which officials say will include planting native species to provide cover and food for birds and other wildlife. Restrooms are available only at Lincoln Park.

ADDITIONAL HELP

DeLorme IA&G grid: 29.
Contact: Chicago Audubon Society and Chicago Park District.
Nearest gas, food, and lodging: Downtown Chicago.

2 Jackson Park and The Paul O. Douglas Nature Sanctuary (Wooded Island)

Habitats: 16-acre island of woods and shrubs surrounding open water.
Key birds: Migratory songbirds, and breeding Monk Parakeets.
Best times to bird: Early morning in late April through first three weeks in May and late August through September.

Directions: Take Interstate 55 to Lake Shore Drive (Illinois Highway 41), and drive south for about 3 miles to the museum entrance. Park on the south side of the museum and walk across the bridge to get to the island.

By CTA, from downtown Chicago, take the #6 (Jeffery) Express bus or the #10 (Museum of Science and Industry) bus, which runs all day during summer and weekends only the rest of the year. Or take the red or green line train to Garfield Station and transfer to an eastbound #55 (Garfield bus). The museum's north entrance is closest to public transportation. The Chicago Transportation Association (CTA) or Metra will take you right to the park.

Birding: Just like Montrose Harbor and the Magic Hedge north of downtown Chicago, a 16-acre island south of downtown Chicago has harbored more than 75 percent of all birds seen in Illinois. Some birders, including out-of-towners, have called Wooded Island in Jackson Park one of the best places in the Midwest during migration.

The chance for rarities is sweet here. For example, Illinois' rarest warbler, the Swainson's Warbler, spent some time in Jackson Park several years ago in May.

However, there's one caveat to this area where more than 268 species have been recorded, sometimes more than 100 in a day: It's not the safest place to be, especially in the afternoons and night, though the Chicago Park District is working on that.

Bird the park in groups in the morning, and consider taking one of the many free bird walks led by the Chicago Audubon Society's Doug Anderson on Wednesday and Saturday in spring, summer, and fall. The Chicago Audubon Society lists the bird walks on its website, as well as in its monthly newsletter, "The Compass."

Jackson Park is adjacent to the world-renowned Museum of Science and Industry. Wooded Island is on the south side of the museum.

You can walk a path in the island where you'll encounter mature trees, dense shrubs, and openings with periodic views of the lagoon.

From the parking lot, walk west to the lagoon, then south to a bridge that leads you onto the island. Begin walking clockwise, or southeast along the path. You'll walk past the Osaka Japanese Gardens, a little cove on your left. Check the gardens for migrants, then return to the main path, checking more little coves along the way for migrating birds, including Northern Waterthrush and Prothonotary Warbler.

As you walk south, you'll see the old rose gardens to the west. Check this area for migrants, too. When you reach the southern part of the island, walk west (or

2 Jackson Park and The Paul O. Douglas Nature Sanctuary (Wooded Island)

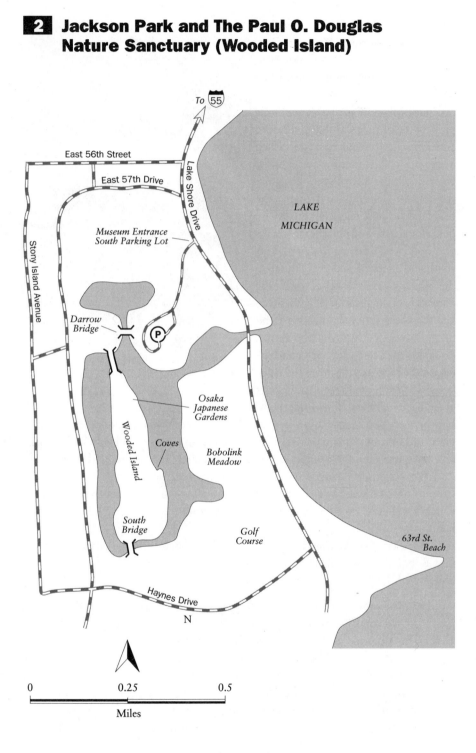

To 55

East 56th Street

East 57th Drive

Lake Shore Drive

LAKE MICHIGAN

Museum Entrance South Parking Lot

Stony Island Avenue

Darrow Bridge

P

Osaka Japanese Gardens

Wooded Island

Coves

Bobolink Meadow

South Bridge

Golf Course

63rd St. Beach

Haynes Drive

N

0   0.25   0.5

Miles

counterclockwise) to check a series of tangles for Mourning Warbler, Connecticut Warbler, and Yellow-billed Cuckoo, especially in middle to late May.

One bird you'll probably see at the park is the Monk Parakeet, a South American native that has established a breeding colony nearby. To get to the colony, exit the island via a bridge at the southern end. After crossing the bridge, walk east, checking the grassy fields for sparrows and other birds. As you walk, you'll see ballfields to your south and a fenced-in driving range to the east. Look for tall lights, where the parakeets build nests. The lights simulate the species' natural nesting habitat, tall trees in Argentina and Brazil. Look for the huge twig nests and listen for the raucous calls from the parakeets. The Monk Parakeet has a bright green back and head, gray underbelly,

Monk Parakeet nest near Jackson Park.
JASON SOUTH PHOTO

blue primary feathers, hooked beak, and pointed tail. This species probably colonized the Chicago area when several escaped from a home. The species may survive the harsh Chicago winters by visiting backyard bird feeders and gardens.

After hopefully having seen the parakeets, you can walk back west to the lagoon to observe swallows snatching insects or Blue-winged Teals dabbling in the water. You'll likely see Barn, Northern Rough-winged, Bank, and Cliff Swallows here.

Northeast of the lagoons is Bobolink Meadow, where, unfortunately, you rarely find Bobolinks. But you can find Yellow Warbler, thrashers, and other shrub-loving birds here.

General information: Frederick Law Olmsted, who designed Central Park in New York, also designed Wooded Island for the World's Columbian Exposition held in 1893. The Japanese government gave $500,000 to the world's fair and built a replica of the famous Phoenix Hall in Uji, Japan, here. A Japanese garden was later added, and in 1981, the Chicago Park District renovated the garden and added a waterfall. In 1992, Chicago officials renamed the area Osaka Garden to honor their sister city. Osaka donated $250,000 for a new entrance gate. Streams meander throughout the garden, a miniature island within Wooded Island.

Local birders, concerned about landscape plans and changes, belong to a lakefront birding task force, which should improve birding here.

You'll find outdoor restrooms near the driving range and inside the Museum of Science and Industry, which you might also enjoy visiting while birding the area.

ADDITIONAL HELP

DeLorme IA&G grid: A6.
Contact: Chicago Park District, Chicago Audubon Society, Museum of Science and Industry.
Nearest gas, food, and lodging: Downtown Chicago.

▮ 3 ▮ DOWNTOWN CHICAGO BIRDING/WALKING TOUR
North River Walk, Southeast Walk, and Grant Park/Museum Campuses Walk

Habitats: Lake Michigan lakefront, harbors, Chicago River, city parks, and plazas.
Key birds: Migratory ducks, gulls, warblers, sparrows, and other passerines; wintering Snowy Owl and breeding Peregrine Falcon.
Best times to bird: September through May.

Directions: The tour described should give you ample directions to find any of the places you wish by walking (or driving to see Snowy Owls in winter.) You can also take public transportation to many of these places. Here are some helpful hints: An underground walkway exists at the Washington Street stop for the Dearborn and State Street "El" lines. Follow the walkway east until it ends at Grant Park, which can be helpful to avoid stoplights, crowds, and unseasonable weather.

The #146 CTA bus runs from downtown to the Museum Campus from 6:30 A.M. to 7:30 P.M. (be sure to check this out before going; times change.) Downtown, the bus runs along State Street to Congress Parkway, to Michigan Avenue to the Museum Campus via Balbo Street and Columbus Drive. It stops at all three museums. The #12 (Roosevelt) bus also stops at the museum campus. To get to the southwest downtown birding locations, exit at the LaSalle Street stop on the Dearborn subway trains. Walk south 1 block to Harrison Street, and then west 2 blocks to the south branch of the Chicago River.

Birding: If you're vacationing or if you work in downtown Chicago, you can enjoy an hour or two of birding in the morning before you visit the museums for sightseeing or start your day's job. Or if you've planned a day of shopping downtown, you can start the morning birding first. Even lunch hour can be productive here during migration. While you may see fewer species than at the Magic Hedge at Montrose Harbor or Jackson Park (see Sites 1 and 2), you'll find some good birding

3 DOWNTOWN CHICAGO BIRDING/WALKING TOUR
North River Walk

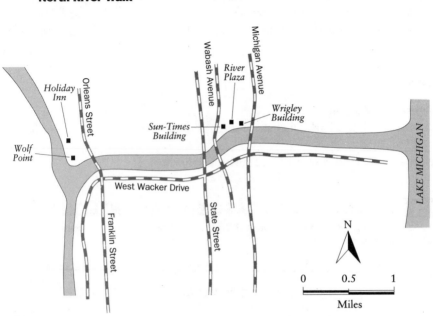

spots within walking distance of downtown hotels and offices. In addition, certain areas can attract large numbers of migrants at the right time.

In late fall, winter, and early spring, ducks and gulls congregate in lakefront harbors, open water, and in the Chicago River. During migration, you can see a number of migrant passerines feeding in downtown parks and plazas or flying on the lakefront and along the river. Snowy Owls often spend much of the winter near Meigs Field, and Peregrine Falcons nest on downtown building ledges.

What follows are three downtown birding tours you can take in a morning or during a lunch hour.

3a. North River Walk: River Plaza, along the Chicago River to Wolf Point (estimated one to two hours walking/birding time round trip). Start at River Plaza. Enter the plaza either through the Wrigley Building glass door entrance (just south of 400 North Michigan Avenue) or north of the Chicago Sun-Times Building, about 405 North Wabash Avenue. Two levels in the plaza have shrubs and trees that sometimes harbor migrants (mainly sparrows, thrushes, and warblers) in spring and fall. White-throated Sparrows and other birds sometimes winter here, too. Exit onto Wabash Avenue and walk south 1 block to West Wacker Drive on the south side of the Chicago River. Walk west (right) on the north side of West Wacker Drive. Check the trees and shrubs along the river for migrants (April through May, September through October), and the river for ducks and gulls (October through April). Here you often will get a straight-on look at the tops of the trees, and you won't have to worry about developing birder's neck.

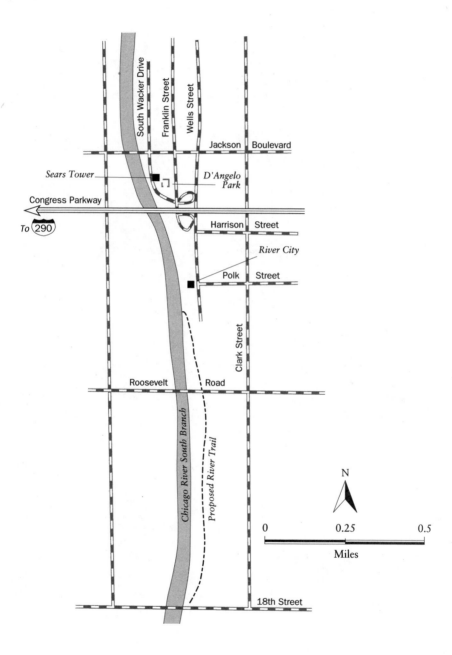

3 **DOWNTOWN CHICAGO BIRDING/WALKING TOUR**
Grant Park/Museum Campuses Walk

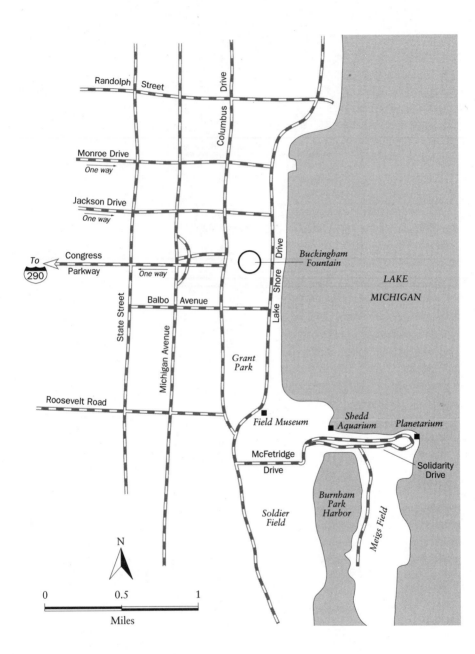

Continue along the north side of West Wacker Drive about a half mile until you reach the area where the river splits into the North and South Branches, just beyond Franklin and Orleans Streets (300 W.). After crossing Orleans, walk north on the bridge and go down the steps into the grassy area south of the Holiday Inn. This area is known at Wolf Point. Check the shrubs and trees along the river for migrant passerines in spring and fall, and for ducks in the river.

3b. Southeast Walk: Includes D'Angelo Park, Chicago River, and River City: (30 minutes to 1 hour birding/walking time round trip). Walk south from the Dearborn Street or State Street El stops at Jackson Street to Harrison Street, and then west 2 or 3 blocks (depending on how you define block) to South Franklin Street. D'Angelo Park, a small grassy city park bordered by shrubs and trees, is one-half block north of the intersection of Harrison and Franklin Streets. Passerines (especially warblers, sparrows, thrushes, flycatchers, and blackbirds) stop here during migration, especially in May through the first week of June, and again in September. Late migrants such as Mourning Warblers often linger into the first week of June. Next, walk back one block south on Franklin Street to check the Chicago River's South Branch for ducks and herons along the edge, and migrants in the shrubs and trees along the east bank. For another look at the river, walk to River City. Walk east on Harrison Street 1 block and south on Wells Street 1 block to Polk Street. Go into the cement parking and plaza area on the north side to view a small marina and the river for ducks, gulls, and herons. A riverwalk is planned from south of River City to Chinatown.

3c. Grant Park, Lake Michigan, and the Museum Campuses Walk: You can spend from one to four hours or more walking and birding these areas. Grant Park is an expansive parkland extending almost 2 miles on the city's lakefront. Hence, migrants are not concentrated as they are at the Lincoln Park Bird Sanctuary, Magic Hedge, or Jackson Park. However, if you don't mind walking the length of the park, from east of the Art Institute to the Field Museum (about 1.5 miles), you should be able to see quite a few migrant passerines during spring and fall migration. Sometimes Grant Park yields outstanding numbers of sparrows and warblers during migration.

Grant Park offers fruitful birding, especially for sparrows, in the spring when the winds are out of the southwest and in fall, when the winds are from the northwest. If you're birding here in March and April, you'll find sparrows, including different species; in May, you should find warblers and other sparrows. Between the north end of Grant Park and the Shedd Aquarium, birders found 14 species of sparrows in early October a few years ago.

Good areas in Grant Park for sparrows (and most other land birds) are around Soldier Field, especially the north end, the east side of the Field Museum, the north side (especially the northwest corner) of Burnham Harbor, the area around Buckingham Fountain, and west of Columbus Parkway east of the Illinois Central Railroad between Jackson and Congress, around the wildflower garden and tennis courts of the Daley Bicentennial Park, and around the lawns and gardens at the Shedd Aquarium.

Here's how you might want to start your birding hour in Grant Park: From Michigan Avenue, walk north to Randolph Street (100 N). Walk east along Randolph for about 1 block until you see the downhill ramps to Daley Bicentennial Park on the south side. At the extreme north end of the Park at 337 East Randolph is a Chicago Park District building, which has maps of the Museum Campus, and restrooms. You'll enjoy fairly good birding among the shrubs, hedges, and trees in the plaza area, as well as around the centrally located wildflower garden and the four sets of tennis courts. Nearby fruit-bearing trees and a prairie-like area attract sparrows and thrushes.

Continue south to the next street, which is Monroe Street. Cross at either Lake Shore Drive or Columbus Drive. Take either of two paved paths. One parallels Lake Shore Drive, the other parallels Columbus and is quieter. Bird for the next few blocks until you reach Jackson Street. Between here and Balbo Avenue, about half a mile, you'll find more hedges, shrubs, and trees, plus some small flower gardens and the Buckingham Fountain, which sometimes attracts warblers to take a bath in May. You'll find restrooms and concession stands here. Take the paths going south, checking flower and hedge areas for migrants, kestrels, swallows, sparrows, thrushes, and warblers near the Illinois Central Railroad tracks. The weedy vegetation along the east edge of the railroad tracks from Jackson to Balbo can be chock-full of sparrows in October and November.

About half a mile south of Balbo, after walking past baseball fields, you'll arrive at the entrance to the underpass to the museum campus, which includes the Field Museum, Shedd Aquarium, and Planetarium. For a taste of what you might see between Buckingham Garden and the Museum Campus, here's an account by a birder who walked the area one lunch hour during migration in the middle of September: 21 species of warblers, including 52 Blackpoll Warblers and 355 Palm Warblers, a Yellow-breasted Chat, a Pine, and an Orange-crowned Warbler, 4 Connecticut and 4 Black-throated Blue Warblers; 2 Clay-colored, 2 Nelson's Sharp-tailed, and 24 Savannah Sparrows among 11 species of sparrows.

Search for warblers in the trees, and sparrows and thrushes on the ground and in shrubs along the edge of Soldier Field (where the Chicago Bears play—don't try birding there during football games). Also check the lawn and gardens near the aquarium for migrants. Numerous swallows, including the Purple Martin, can often be found here in season. From the north side of the aquarium you can check the breakwater in Monroe Harbor for gulls and terns as well as ducks, loons, and grebes.

Early in the morning, in spring and fall, before swimmers and dogs arrive, check the Twelfth Street Beach located between the Planetarium and Meigs Field for shorebirds. Birders have seen Black-bellied and Semipalmated Plovers, Pectoral Sandpipers, Dunlins, Dowitchers, Ruddy Turnstones, Willets, and an occasional Whimbrel here. The vegetation on the north and east sides of Burnham Harbor, west of Meigs Field, attracts many migrants, including Snow Buntings in fall and winter and Lapland Longspurs during fall.

Snowy Owl at Lake Michigan shoreline. KANAE HIRABAYASHI PHOTO

In winter drive to the Planetarium and Meigs Field parking area to search for Snowy Owls and ducks. To get there, take Lake Shore Drive to downtown from either north or south. Signs directing you to the Museum Campus from Lake Shore Drive are well placed and helpful. From southbound Lake Shore Drive, exit at Roosevelt Road, go west 1 block to Columbus Drive, then south 1 more block to McFetridge Drive. Northbound Lake Shore Drive has an exit directly at McFetridge Drive. Go east on McFetridge to the parking areas in the Museum Campus. To be closest to the best birding, park at Solidarity Drive at the large parking area near Meigs Field and Twelfth Street Beach. Check both Burnham Harbor behind Meigs Field and Monroe Harbor (especially the dikes) for ducks and unusual gulls. In winter you may find large rafts of scaups, mergansers, and other ducks, including scoters and Oldsquaws. They usually remain closer to shore earlier in the day. A scope is helpful.

Often, one or two Snowy Owls use the grassy areas and rocks east of Meigs Field for hunting and resting in winter. You can stay indoors and use the second-floor observation deck at Meigs, with a scope, and stay warm, too, while checking for the owls.

Searching for Peregrines: Due to the success of Midwest Peregrine Falcon recovery efforts, a number of pairs of peregrines breed regularly in the Chicago area. Peregrine aeries range from the south end of the city, with a resident pair near the University of Chicago's campus in Hyde Park, to a pair on the north side near

Broadway and Hollywood Streets. Peregrines have nested downtown in the past few years. The current longest occupied aerie (since 1987) is at the 125 South Wacker building, across from the Sears Tower. Keep an eye trained for the adults perched on buildings nearby to the aerie during the breeding season, from March to July. Other times watch for the falcons hunting or migrating along the lakefront parks. Call the Chicago Peregrine Restoration program of the Chicago Academy of Sciences, which monitors the falcons for updates on the peregrine status or to report a sighting.

General information: Hazards include city traffic, pedestrians, bikers, and in-line skaters. It is not a good idea to be birding alone in some of these high-crime areas. In Grant Park you'll find restrooms in the Park District building at Daley Bicentennial Park, near Buckingham Fountain, and at the museums. You can get a Museum Campus map at the Daley Bicentennial Park building or various other places along the way.

ADDITIONAL HELP

DeLorme IA&G grid: 29.
Contact: Chicago Audubon Society, Chicago Academy of Sciences (for peregrine information), Field Museum of Natural History (for Museum campus information).
Nearest gas, food, and lodging: Downtown Chicago.

4 Illinois Beach State Park

Habitats: Lake Michigan shoreline, sand dunes, sand prairie, sand savanna, sedge meadow, fen, and fragmented pine woods.
Key birds: Migratory loons, gulls, shorebirds, rails, raptors, owls, and songbirds; breeding Brewer's Blackbird.
Best times to bird: Fall migration (September through November) for hawks and owls; spring migration; and winter.

Directions: Travel north on U.S. Highway 41 nearly to the Wisconsin border. Turn east on Wadsworth Road, driving for 2 miles past Sheridan Road. Wadsworth Road leads into the park. Follow the signs to the interpretive center. You can park there to gain access to the Dead River Trail and shoreline.

Birding: The 4,160-acre Illinois Beach State Park encompasses 6.5 miles of sandy Lake Michigan shoreline, which provides habitat for 650 species of plants and at least 300 species of birds.

Birders, especially those who enjoy hawk-watching, consider fall the best season to visit Illinois Beach State Park. Virtually any species migrating south can occur here in the fall or in the spring. Because of the park's location along the lake's western shoreline, strong westerly winds push migrating birds nearer to birders.

On an October day when west or northwesterly winds follow an Arctic cold front, birders come here to watch hawks. On the right days, birders might catalog up to 14 species of hawks, including Sharp-shinned and Cooper's Hawks, Northern

44

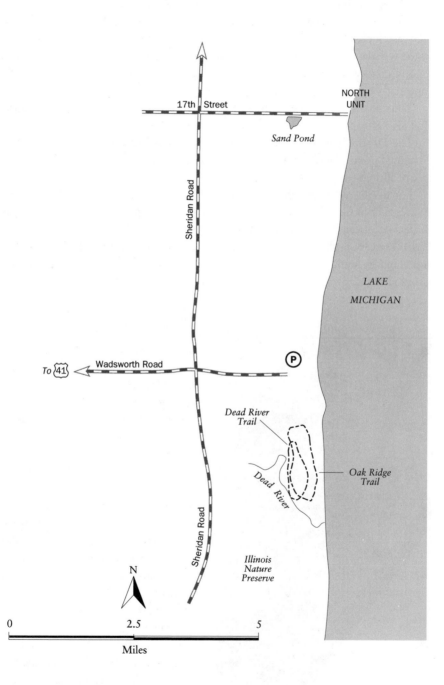

NORTH
UNIT

17th Street

Sand Pond

Sheridan Road

*LAKE
MICHIGAN*

To (41) ← Wadsworth Road

Ⓟ

*Dead River
Trail*

Dead River

*Oak Ridge
Trail*

Sheridan Road

*Illinois
Nature
Preserve*

N

| 0 | 2.5 | 5 |

Miles

45

Harriers, Ospreys, Merlins, Peregrine Falcons, American Kestrels, Broad-winged Hawks, Red-tailed Hawks, Red-shouldered Hawks, and on occasion Bald Eagles, and rarely, Goshawks, Swainson's Hawks, and Golden Eagles.

To watch for the hawks, park at the interpretive center, then walk east to the lake over a boardwalk. Find the highest point to stand on the shore, or walk south to the wooden tower where you can get an even better view. From here you have a good chance at seeing Northern Harriers, Bald Eagles, Ospreys, and falcons, raptors that aren't afraid to fly over the water.

You can also reach the shoreline via the Dead River Trail. Walking along this trail also affords you a better opportunity to see buteos and accipiters.

The Dead River, a stream blocked by sandbars much of the year, forms an elongated pond where you might see ducks and herons, and when the water level is low, shorebirds.

For ducks, walk the shoreline where you may find large rafts of wintering species such as Greater and Lesser Scaups, Oldsquaws, and Common Goldeneyes. Birders occasionally find Barrow's Goldeneyes, too. Look for Great Black-backed Gulls, Thayer's Gulls, Glaucous Gulls, and occasionally an Iceland Gull plying the shoreline. In some years, winter finches such as Red Crossbills, White-winged Crossbills, and Evening Grosbeaks frequent the pines along the Dead River.

American Kestrel. KATHY ADE PHOTO

As early as March, large numbers of passerines fly overhead on their trek north. The peak of songbird migration occurs in mid-May to the end of May as oaks open and attract insects. Earlier in May you might check the deciduous woods as you enter the park after you cross the railroad tracks for songbirds; parking is limited here. A series of ponds within here attract birds.

The Dead River Trail is perfect for a migrant walk where you'll find thrushes, flycatchers, warblers, and other migrants. During fall these walks can yield hundreds of American Redstarts in various plumages. Early in the morning or at dusk in April and early May, you may hear various rails and possibly an American Bittern calling from the marshes.

An even better place to search for spring migrating land birds is the trail that leaves the interpretive center parking lot and goes through the center of the preserve. Here you'll walk through a stand of oak trees, that can be quite productive for warblers and other migrating songbirds in mid- to late May. When all the migrants have long left southern Illinois, you can still find some here at Illinois Beach State Park, in the oaks where insects attract hungry birds.

Birding during breeding season can be difficult because the beach is extensively used by humans for recreation, and because the best nesting areas are closed to the public. Still, you can enjoy birding in June and early July. South of the Dead River Trail is a group of pines and a sandy grassland area where Western and Eastern Meadowlarks, Brewer's Blackbirds, and Grasshopper Sparrows have bred. If you'd like to bird this area, call the state park for information on whether you can obtain permission to enter.

If you can't get to the area south of the Dead River Trail, you might find the Brewer's Blackbird feeding along the shoreline early in the morning before it gets crowded on the beach in May, June, and July. Look for a grackle-sized bird with a rounded tail like a Red-winged Blackbird's, and yellow eyes. The blackbirds also nested near the hawk tower one year.

To search for puddle ducks, you can go to the Northern Unit of the park. Go north on Sheridan Road for about 2 miles to Seventeenth Street. Turn east on the road into the park where you'll find various ponds with small parking lots. Check the ponds for ducks in March and April and from October into November. During dry times, mudflats become exposed and attract shorebirds.

General information: In the late 1600s, French explorers came to the northern Illinois Lake Michigan shoreline while surveying the Northwest Territory. Before Illinois became a state in 1818, hunters, trappers, and others lived along the sandy shores. The northern unit of the park, known as Camp Logan, was used as a Union prisoner of war camp during the Civil War and for military training during World Wars I and II. The state acquired the first land rights in 1948 of what was to become Illinois Beach State Park. In 1964, the Illinois Nature Preserves commission designated 829 acres of the park as a state nature preserve, meaning it can never be developed. The preserve contains rare, natural ecosystems where animals and plants that can adapt to the lakefront environment survive. The park is open from 5:30 A.M. until 8 P.M.

ADDITIONAL HELP

DeLorme IA&G grid: 21.
Contact: Illinois Beach State Park.
Nearest gas, food, and lodging: Camping and picnicking inside the park, concession open May through October; lodging also available at the 96-room Illinois Beach Resort and Conference Center, which includes a restaurant; also motels on Sheridan Road in Zion.

5 Waukegan Beach and Bowen Park

Habitats: Lake Michigan shoreline and harbors, wooded ravines, and uplands.
Key birds: Migratory gulls and shorebirds, including rarities such as Purple Sandpiper and Piping Plover; migratory hawks and passerines; wintering Snowy Owl and breeding Common Tern.
Best times to bird: Spring and fall migration.

Directions: To get to Waukegan Beach, from U.S. Highway 41, exit at Grand Avenue going east into the town of Waukegan. Drive about 3 miles to Pershing Road, just west of Lake Michigan. Turn south, driving to the first stop sign at the bottom of the hill, which is Clayton Street. Drive east 1 block to Seahorse Drive. Turn north and drive until you get to the last parking area. Seahorse Drive is a 1-mile-long U-shaped dead-end road. When you reach the farthest parking lot you will actually be at the south end of the beach.

To get to the two Waukegan harbors from Waukegan Beach, return to Clayton. Continue east to the North Harbor. To get to the south harbor, go south on Pershing Road to the new harbor entrance.

Bowen Park can be reached off Sheridan Road, which intersects Grand Avenue and is west of Pershing. To get to the north entrance, take Sheridan Road north of Greenwood Avenue. Turn east into the parking lot where you'll find the Jack Benny Center, and bathrooms if the center is open.

To get to the south entrance, go to the corner of Sheridan and Greenwood. Follow Greenwood east to the baseball diamond and pool area. Park in the south lot next to the baseball diamond.

Birding: Waukegan Beach and Bowen Park, situated on the western shore of Lake Michigan, offer a unique birding experience for those who love to watch migrating hawks, ducks, shorebirds, and passerines. Sometimes when the winds are right, birders watch passerines flying south in spring. Some local birders call this a type of "reverse migration."

Several miles of Lake Michigan shoreline along with some wooded areas and rocky terrain in northeastern Illinois offer birders a chance to see at least 200 species.

Starting at the far south parking lot on Waukegan Beach off Seahorse Drive in spring, check the pines for Pine Warblers, Cape May Warblers, and other migrants. Then check both piers for shorebirds and gulls. In April and May, birders almost always document Glaucous Gulls, Great Black-backed Gulls, and Laughing Gulls, as well as the more common Bonaparte's Gulls and Common, Caspian, and Forster's Terns. Something rare might be sitting on one of those piers, for instance, a Little Gull, so take your gull guides.

In fall, sit on the beach pier and look north for lines of shorebirds flying by, including the potential for hundreds of Dunlins. This is also the place to look for the rare and beautiful Purple Sandpiper. The Waukegan Beach Pier is probably one of the best places in the state to look for this bird. Nearly every year, birders document Purple Sandpipers here between October and November.

5   Waukegan Beach and Bowen Park

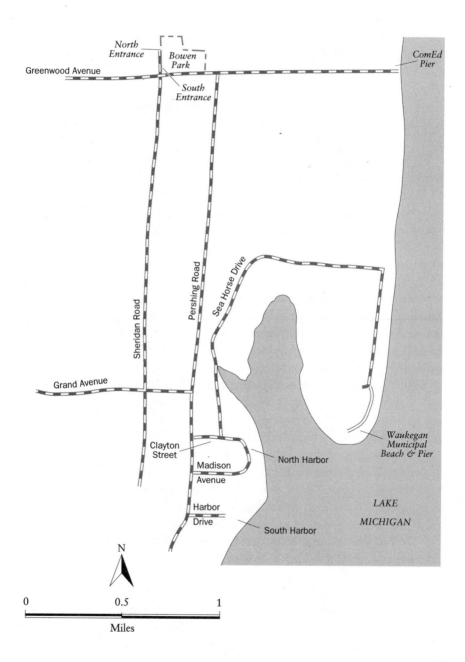

North
Entrance

Bowen
Park

South
Entrance

Greenwood Avenue

ComEd
Pier

Sheridan Road

Pershing Road

Sea Horse Drive

Grand Avenue

Clayton
Street

Madison
Avenue

North Harbor

Waukegan
Municipal
Beach & Pier

Harbor
Drive

South Harbor

LAKE
MICHIGAN

N

0   0.5   1

Miles

Walking the shoreline north from the pier in April and May will produce many shorebirds. You can walk 1.5 miles to Greenwood Avenue, where you'll find the ComEd Pier. Along the way, look for Ruddy Turnstones, Sanderlings, and Semipalmated Plovers in May, as well as the occasional White-rumped Sandpiper.

You'll see two Lake Michigan inlets as you walk. One or two Piping Plovers occur here almost annually in late April and May. This species formerly bred here, but no longer does due to habitat loss. Willets are more common, and someone almost always find a Whimbrel here in spring as well.

As you walk, you should easily see all five swallow species known to occur in northern Illinois—Barn, Tree, Cliff, Northern Rough-winged, and Bank. This is a good place in spring to learn the calls, flight patterns, and distinguishing characteristics of these swallows. As you near the ComEd Pier, look for Common Terns. This species breeds nearby on private property. The birds usually return in mid-May to begin breeding, and the young hatch sometime in late June or early July.

While you're walking the beach in spring, you might be surprised to see birds flying south instead of north. In spring, when southwest winds come, birds try to get on the east side of Lake Michigan, but then must fly back south again. Birders have seen Scarlet Tanagers and Western Kingbirds flying south at the end of May—the conditions have to be just right to watch this unique spectacle.

You can also walk along the shrubs and trees west of the lake to check for migrants in spring. The walking is tricky here as you meander through brambles, swales, beach grasses, and woods on the sand, so be careful. It's worth the walk, though, because you can catalog a diverse number of migrants, including Orange-crowned, Nashville, Magnolia, Pine, and other warblers, plus sparrows, sometimes including Nelson's Sharp-tailed in May. Least Bitterns and other wetland species also migrate along the lakefront.

In summer it's nearly impossible to find a place to park at the beach. But if you do, walk the shoreline in the morning before the crowds come, to search for Sanderlings, Semipalmated Plovers, and most other migrating shorebirds in August, and Black-bellied Plovers in September. Spotted Sandpipers and Killdeer also breed here.

In October, November, and throughout winter, check the Waukegan Harbor for Snowy Owls, wintering ducks, and Purple Sandpipers. To get to the harbor from the beach, return to Clayton Street and go east about 1 block to the yacht club. Turn south and drive to the harbor where you can look for Snowy Owls on the pier in winter as well as wintering ducks on the lake. You'll often find Common Goldeneyes, scaups, and mergansers here. Oldsquaws and Harlequin Duck are also possible, and during nasty winter weather, you can often find scoters in the lake. In spring, Pied-billed and Eared Grebes can be seen from this harbor.

Also check the south harbor, driving south on Pershing Road past Clayton Street to the harbor driveway. Turn east and park here to scan for Snowy Owls and all the wintering ducks mentioned above. This is also another place to look for Purple Sandpipers in October and November. Check the rocky riprap habitat for this bird.

The state's fifth record of an Arctic Tern, recorded at Waukegan Beach.
DAVID B. JOHNSON PHOTO

After visiting Waukegan Beach and Harbor, you might enjoy going to Bowen Park, where you can spend a few hours searching for migrating land birds in spring or hawks in fall.

Park at the north entrance next to the Jack Benny Center for the Arts for spring migrants. Walk north into the park where you can take an upland trail (called the Exercise Trail) or a ravine trail, both less than 1 mile long. In spring search for warblers and thrushes. Hairy Woodpeckers and Red-bellied Woodpeckers are rather abundant nearly year-round. A resident Cooper's Hawk has nested here.

The ravine trail is particularly good in spring for migrating warblers, which seek the water and protection in the ravine bottoms. Birders usually find Black-throated Blue Warbler every year in early to late May, along with many other migrating warblers, tanagers, and other passerines.

In fall go to the park's south entrance to watch migrating hawks. You'll be standing next to a baseball diamond. Look north-northeast for hawks that are flying by Illinois Beach State Park (see Site 4). This part of Bowen Park is on high ground compared to adjoining areas, making it a good vantage point to watch hawks as well as migrating Sandhill Cranes in fall. On the right day in October you might see hundreds of cranes flying in a kettle, giving their unique rattling calls.

When the hawks are moving, Bowen Park can be an excellent place to watch them. For your best chance at seeing large numbers of hawks, choose a day when southwest winds are changing to the northwest as a cold front moves over a warm area, and you may watch hawks trying to catch thermals and push on south before the winds change.

Between 9 and 10 A.M. on September 21, 1998, birders watched 8 Sharp-shinned and 2 Cooper's Hawks, an American Kestrel, and a Peregrine Falcon fly by. Then from noon to 1 P.M., they watched 88 Sharp-shinned, 4 Cooper's, 1 Red-shouldered, and 2 Red-tailed Hawks, as well as 1 Peregrine Falcon and 3 Broad-winged Hawks fly by.

Large kettles of Broad-winged Hawks as well as many single Sharp-shinned Hawks can be seen in September. In late October and November, you'll find more buteos and fewer accipiters here.

General information: The city of Waukegan is working to improve this area and has recently added a second harbor; however, certain areas in the town of Waukegan should not be visited after dark. Avoid the beach in summer; you won't find a place to park.

ADDITIONAL HELP

DeLorme IA&G grid: 21.
Contact: Waukegan Park District.
Nearest gas, food, and lodging: Waukegan for gas and food, Gurnee for lodging.

6 Wadsworth Savanna and Wetlands Demonstration Project

Habitats: Wetlands and savanna.
Key birds: Migratory waterfowl, shorebirds, and passerines; state-listed endangered breeding species, including Pied-billed Grebe, Sandhill Crane, Common Moorhen, and Yellow-headed Blackbird; also breeding Willow Flycatcher, Eastern Wood-Pewee, and Swamp Sparrow.
Best times to bird: Spring and fall migration and early in the breeding season.

Directions: The savanna and wetlands demonstration project are on the east side of U.S. Highway 41 near the town of Wadsworth, just south of the Wisconsin border. The savanna is north of Wadsworth Road; the wetlands project is just south of Wadsworth Road. Parking is available off Wadsworth Road, east of the highway.

Birding: Willow Flycatchers spit out *"fitz-bew, fitz-bew"* as you walk the Des Plaines River Trail at the Wadsworth Savanna in northeastern Illinois on an early June morning. Just across Wadsworth Road to the south, a series of wetlands meandering through more woods and savannas hosts a small breeding colony of the state-listed endangered Yellow-headed Blackbird.

More than 200 bird species have visited the Wadsworth Savanna and Wetlands Demonstration Project, at least 60 of which regularly breed here. Birders have

6 Wadsworth Savanna and Wetlands Demonstration Project

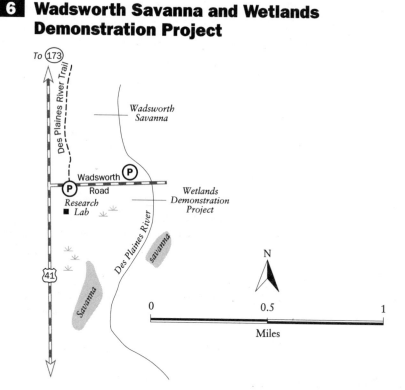

seen 15 waterfowl species during migration, as well as myriad warbler species and other passerines.

You'll find several miles of trails at both sites—the walks can get long, so bring water on warm days.

The Yellow-headed Blackbirds return sometime in April. To find them and other marsh species, park in a wetlands project pull-off just east of US 41 near the mobile biological station. Take the path directly northwest of the station.

Walk past one marsh on your left to the next marsh in front of you. Listen for the yellow-head's unusual rusty hinge-like call. Look here, too, for Common Moorhens, which breed in the marshes, as well as the Pied-billed Grebe.

You can continue walking the marsh trail to search for wading egrets and other birds. Eventually you'll reach a savanna where you'll find warblers during migration and nesting savanna species in summer.

To find shorebirds in spring and late summer, park in the main lot off Wadsworth Road. Then walk the 3-mile south trail loop. You will need a scope if you're searching for shorebirds. Depending on the time of year, the amount of rain, and the way the level at which the water is being maintained on a given day, you may find many shorebirds or none. On a good day in May, birders might find at least 10 different shorebird species in the middle of the afternoon. Birders have seen yellowlegs, Dunlins, sandpipers, and plovers. Late summer can also be a good time to search for shorebirds. Bring your field guides because many shorebirds will begin sporting their winter plumages.

To bird the Wadsworth Savanna, walk across Wadsworth Road to the trail entrance, which is part of the longer Des Plaines River Trail. The trail does not loop. Take the trail past wet meadows where Swamp Sparrows and Willow Fly-catchers breed, then past some fields where meadowlarks sing, and then through open woodlands where Eastern Wood-Pewees and other savanna birds nest.

Walk north for a mile until you reach a farm field east of the trail. Sandhill Cranes attempted to nest near here in 1996, and spent the summer feeding in the fields at about 5:30 or 6 A.M. Birders often find the cranes near this area in May through July.

You can also enjoy summer songs of Wood Thrushes, tanagers, and other species at this site. Plus, you can spot hosts of the last of the migrants, including dozens of species of warblers at the end of May as they head north to Wisconsin to breed. This is one of the last places migrating songbirds stop in Illinois before heading to the north country.

General information: The Lake County Forest Preserve District owns the Wadsworth Savanna, a state-dedicated nature preserve, and the land occupying the Wetlands Demonstration Project. A joint effort between the forest preserve, state of Illinois, and the federal government, the project is showing that restoring wetlands can help purify water, control flooding, and sustain wildlife populations, including birds. These groups are restoring a 2.8-mile stretch of the Des Plaines River. Six manmade marshes receive river water from pumps stationed on the land. Scientists monitor the water flowing into and out of these marshes to ensure that the project meets its goals of purifying water and controlling flooding. An exciting by-product of this project is the birding, which has improved tremendously since the project began. An avian biologist researching the wetlands found that two state-listed, the Least Bittern and the Yellow-headed Blackbird, began breeding after restoration.

The avian biologist also censused migrating waterfowl at the wetlands project. The number of individual waterfowl visiting the site increased by about 4,000 percent after restoration. The area today continues to attract migrating waterfowl and shorebirds in fall and spring, as well as warblers and other songbirds.

Meanwhile, the Wadsworth Savanna is being restored by the forest preserve district. It, too, contains some wetlands, which have attracted a pair of nesting Blue-winged Teals and several Soras. It's also one of the best places in northern Illinois to find rare butterflies.

ADDITIONAL HELP

DeLorme IA&G grid: 21.
Contact: Lake County Forest Preserve District.
Nearest gas, food, and lodging: Wadsworth.

7 Chain O' Lakes State Park

Habitats: Partially restored wet and dry prairie, bog, moraine hills, stand of white pines, upland forest, lakes, and streams.
Best times to bird: Spring and fall migration and early in breeding season.
Key birds: Breeding Forster's Tern, Sandhill Crane, Bobolink, Sedge and Marsh Wrens, American Redstart, Blue-gray Gnatcatcher, Cerulean Warbler, and migrating songbirds.

Directions: The main entrance is off Wilmot Road between Illinois Route 173 and U. S. Highway 12 in McHenry County. The Oak Point Day Use Area is accessed from IL 173 in Lake County. From Interstate 94/US 41, exit at IL 173 near the town of Rosecrans. Drive west 9 miles to the IL 173 entrance. To get to the Wilmot Road entrance, continue west on IL 173 past the Oak Point Day Use Area another mile to Lake Avenue. Drive north about a mile to Wilmot Road and then east into the park.

Birding: One of the best places in Illinois to find breeding Sandhill Cranes is at Chain O' Lakes State Park, which provides the unique habitat this bird needs—marshes adjoining upland oak woods. The park also provides habitat for one of the only two nesting colonies of Forster's Terns in the state. These rare Illinois birds along with some 200 other birds have been documented at Chain O' Lakes.

As you enter the park, check the prairie, which sometimes holds breeding Bobolinks as well as feeding Sandhill Cranes, especially during migration. Northern Harriers sometimes hunt here as well.

Next choose any of the trails that meander through the oak woodlands along the Fox River. You should have good luck in late April through May and again in late August through September finding warblers, thrushes, and vireos. Birders often choose the Gold Finch Trail for their migrant walk. The 1.7-mile trail starts by the headquarters building. Where the trail nears the Fox River you might find breeding Virginia Rails and Soras. Listen for breeding Blue-gray Gnatcatchers and American Redstarts.

Your best chance to see the Forster's Tern is to rent a canoe in early May through June. This species has nested on Grass Island, north of the boat and canoe rental concession at the Maple Grove launch. You may see the Forster's Tern as well as Black Terns foraging from the banks of the Fox River at the launch. Also listen for

7 Chain O' Lakes State Park

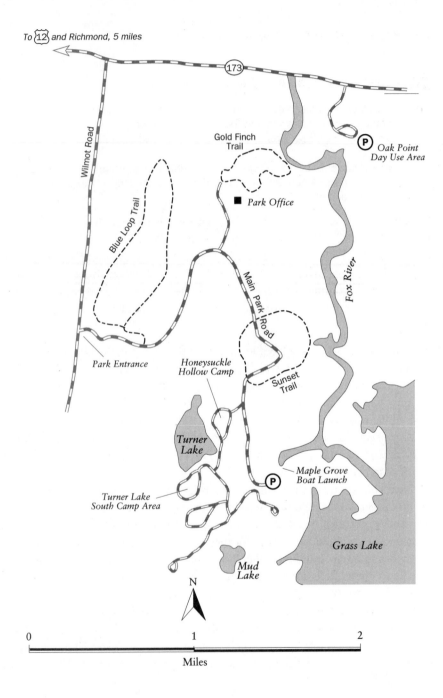

To 12 and Richmond, 5 miles

173

Wilmot Road

Gold Finch Trail

Blue Loop Trail

■ *Park Office*

Oak Point
Day Use Area

Fox River

Main Park Road

Park Entrance

*Honeysuckle
Hollow Camp*

Sunset
Trail

*Turner
Lake*

*Turner Lake
South Camp Area*

Maple Grove
Boat Launch

*Mud
Lake*

Grass Lake

N

0   1   2

Miles

the rattling call of the Sandhill Crane; four to five pairs breed annually in the park. You might also see the cranes if you come in the morning or close to dusk, and park by the headquarters where they are often heard or seen flying over the marsh.

Sedge Wrens breed at the southern end of Turner Lake by the Turner Lake South Camping Area and Marsh Wrens nest in the cattails along the Fox River and around Turner Lake. To view Turner Lake, go to one of the two floating docks in the park; one is near the Honeysuckle Hollow Camp Area and the other by the Turner Lake South Camp Area.

In some years Henslow's Sparrows breed in the field north of the horse trailer parking lot along the Blue Loop Trail, which starts from and returns to the horse trailer parking lot just inside the main entrance.

Sandhill Cranes breed at Chain O' Lakes State Park. DENNIS OEHMKE PHOTO

The Oak Point Day Use Area usually produces Cerulean Warblers in spring, some of which have remained to breed. Larger numbers of this rapidly declining neotropical migrant bred here in the past; fewer are counted each year. This is a good area to look for breeding Downy and Hairy Woodpeckers.

In January and February Great Horned Owls court and breed in the park. A visit at dusk will almost always provide good looks at them. Drive slowly along the main road and scan the tall trees along the way. The 1.7-mile-long Sunset Trail is a good place to walk while looking for owls. To search for roosting Long-eared Owls, check the pines northeast of the headquarters building.

General information: Chain O' Lakes became part of the Illinois state park system in 1945 and now totals 2,793 acres; an adjoining conservation area adds another 3,239 acres. The park borders Lake Marie and Nippersink Lakes and includes 44-acre Turner Lake, which is included on the Illinois Nature Preserves list of natural areas never to be developed.

The park is open daily except Christmas. Summer hours, May 1 through October 31, are 6 A.M. to 9 P.M. During the winter the park is open 8 A.M. to sunset. The park is closed for all activities except hunting, from the beginning of November until the end of the season in mid-December. Call for exact times and dates. Also, in summer, boating is popular, and birding can be hampered by the noise and amount of people. Canoes and paddle boats are available for rent.

ADDITIONAL HELP

De Lorme IA&G grid: 20.
Contact: Chain O' Lakes State Park.
Nearest gas, food, and lodging: McHenry; camping at the park.

8 Glacial Park and Vicinity

Habitats: Wetlands, including bogs, fens, and marshes; lakes, ponds, streams, woodlands, and prairies.
Key birds: Rare breeders, including Least Bittern, Sandhill Crane, Northern Harrier, and Upland Sandpiper; breeding Wild Turkey, Sedge Wren, and Dickcissel; wintering Short-eared Owl; migratory waterfowl and shorebirds.
Best times to bird: Year-round, early spring for waterfowl, midspring for shorebirds and songbirds, spring through early summer for breeders, late summer through fall for shorebirds, and fall through early winter for waterfowl migrants, and winter for owls.

Directions: You can reach Glacial Park off Illinois Highway 31 north of the town of McHenry. Turn west on Harts Road. One-half mile down the road is Parking Area 1; another 0.3 mile is the gravel road leading to Parking Area 2. To get to the Keystone parking and canoe launch site, take IL 31 north of Harts Road to Tyron Grove Road. Turn west to Keystone Road and proceed back south to the parking area.

Birding: Getting to some of the prime birding spots in this 2,806-acre gem in northern McHenry County requires a 1- to 1.5-mile hike in some instances. Be prepared with good hiking shoes, water, and some energy reserves.

Birders have recorded 100 breeding species here and more than 200 species total for the park.

You'll find five parking areas from which you can begin your birding. Drive 0.3 mile down Harts Road (the entrance road to the preserve), then pull over on the roadside to look at Lost Valley Marsh to the north for ducks in early spring and late fall. Greater White-fronted Geese have been seen in February. You'll need a scope. Listen for Sedge Wrens May through August; sometimes they are quite plentiful throughout the park.

The state-listed Least Bittern and Yellow-headed Blackbird have bred in the marshes nearby, but management practices have temporarily changed the water tables so that these birds have moved to other more suitable breeding habitats. As management strategies continue, these marshes should once again offer breeding habitat to some of the state's rarest marshland birds.

Lost Valley Marsh was once part of a vast marsh complex that stretched for miles north into Wisconsin. Thousands of ducks and geese, including Canvasbacks, Mallards, Northern Shovelers, and other species used the area as a major migratory resting spot. As restoration work continues, more ducks will return.

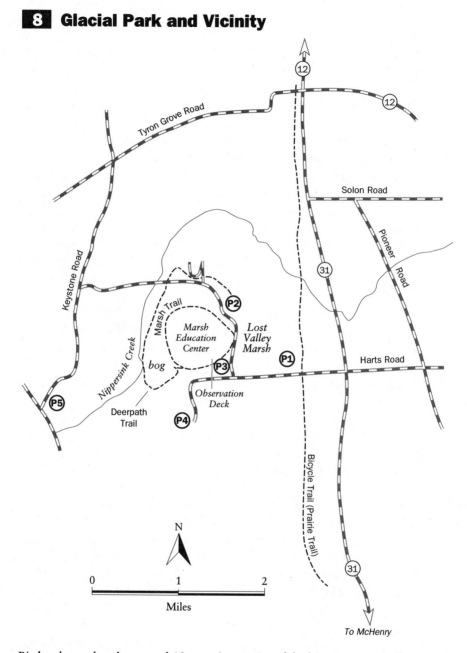

Birders have already spotted 12 or more species of ducks using Lost Valley Marsh during fall and spring migration.

Another 0.3 mile down Harts Road is a parking lot, labeled Parking Lot 1 on the map. Here you can either walk a prairie trail, which is a north-south bicycle route, or cross the street to walk an east-west horse trail. Neither are loops, so you'll have to backtrack to return to your car. If you take the horse trail, check the fields near the railroad tracks for breeding Dickcissels and other grassland birds in late May through August.

In spring along the prairie trail, you'll enjoy migrants on the shrubby edges and in the restored prairie and marshes. Some late migrants, including Alder Flycatchers and Yellow-billed and Black-billed Cuckoos frequent the edges. Orchard Orioles breed here. Earlier in spring at dusk you can hear Soras and Virginia Rails calling from the marshes. This bike path leads all the way to the Wisconsin border.

From Parking Area 1 drive to the next gravel road, about a quarter of a mile. Turn north and park at the top of the hill at Parking Area 2. You'll need a scope, but you can get a good view of the marsh and any birds using it from this point. Sandhill Cranes have bred near here and you might see them early in the morning or at dusk when they come to feed. A 1-mile walk down this gravel road takes you past an oak savanna where pewees and flycatchers breed, and to a good shorebird spot in August, September, April, and May. On a mid-August day, you'll likely find an assortment of Least and Semipalmated Sandpipers, a few Semipalmated Plovers, and perhaps a few Stilt Sandpipers, along with the typical Lesser and Greater Yellowlegs.

In winter Northern Harriers ply the grasslands by day, while Short-eared Owls come to feed at dusk. A family of Hooded Mergansers was seen in the nearby marshes along this trail in June. Eastern Bluebirds use well-kept manmade boxes to raise their young.

You may want to begin at Parking Areas 3 and 4 where you can find fields full of Bobolinks and possibly Grasshopper Sparrows May through July, and sometimes Henslow's Sparrows. Orchard and Baltimore Orioles also frequent this area. Parking Area 3 is about 0.3 mile west on Harts Road at the education center called the Weidrich Barn. The education center, which is open weekdays for limited times, has indoor restrooms. Parking Area 4, which as at the conservation district office, is just south of Parking Area 3.

At Parking Area 4, walk to the observation deck overlooking a marsh, and also walk a short distance around a bog and then up the Deerpath Trail, where you can gain access to the unique geological features of the park such as the camelback kames. Birders sometimes sit on top of the kames in October and watch Sharp-shinned Hawks and other raptor migrants fly by. The Deerpath Trail hosts woodland savanna species, including thrushes, gnatcatchers, Scarlet Tanagers, Blue-gray Gnatcatchers, and Wild Turkeys during breeding season. This is also a good place to bird during spring migration.

Another place to bird at Glacial Park is at the Keystone area canoe trail access point. Walk the trail north 1.2 miles and you'll be at the same spot as you were when you took the gravel road from Parking Area 5. Water and outdoor facilities are available. You can walk to the kames and along Nippersink Creek from this lot, and enjoy spring migrants along the way.

If you have a canoe, you might enjoy birding by boat along the Nippersink Creek, especially during spring migration.

General information: Glacial Park, owned and managed by the McHenry County Conservation District, features 330 acres of dedicated Illinois State Nature Preserve, and contains some of the state's most interesting geological features, including kames, kettles, and moraines created when glaciers left behind till and rocks more than 10,000 years ago. The series of marshes and other wetlands here are kettle holes created by glacial action. These contain habitat for 18 species of state-listed endangered and threatened plants and birds, as well as endangered mussels and rare fish. Because of its rare ecosystems, Glacial Park's entire acreage is not accessible to the public. But plenty of horse, biking, and walking trails exist to give you a flavor for the state's geological past and to enjoy the myriad bird species living here. To see some of the closed areas, you can join free guided walks given by the conservation district or local birding groups. Call the contact numbers in Appendix A learn when bird walks are scheduled here.

ADDITIONAL HELP

DeLorme IA&G grid: 20.
Contact: McHenry County Conservation District.
Nearest gas, food, and lodging: McHenry; primitive campsites at the park.

9 Moraine Hills State Park

Habitats: Wetlands, lakes, river backwaters, woods, prairie, and secondary growth.
Key birds: Breeding Pied-billed Grebe, Least Tern, Common Moorhen, Black Tern, Prothonotary Warbler, American Redstart, and Yellow-headed Blackbird; spring and fall migrants, including ducks and songbirds.
Best times to bird: March through October.

Directions: Moraine Hills State Park is 3 miles south of McHenry, Illinois. The. McHenry Dam, on the Fox River, is on the park's western border. To reach this area from Interstate 294, exit at Illinois Highway 176. Go west about 10 miles through the towns of Libertyville, Mundelein, and Wauconda to River Road. Turn north and drive about 2 miles to the main entrance of the state park. The entrance to McHenry Dam is another 0.5 mile north.

Birding: Observers have recorded more than 100 species of birds, including the state's rarest wetland breeders, at this 1,690-acre state park, filled with wetlands and lakes. You'll find more than 10 miles of trails at the park's main entrance; most are surfaced with crushed limestone for easy walking. The color-coded trails wind through hills, valleys, and wetlands. Start early in the morning in April or May at Pike Hills Marsh. Walk the short boardwalk trail, listening for Common Snipes winnowing in the air while Soras whinny from the cattails. Migrants, including warblers, feed on insects in the trees nearby. Least Bitterns have bred here, too.

9 Moraine Hills State Park

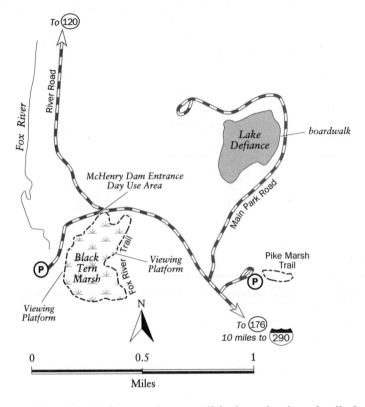

To (120)

Fox River

River Road

Lake
Defiance — boardwalk

Main Park Road

McHenry Dam Entrance
Day Use Area

Fox River Trail

Black
Tern
Marsh

Viewing
Platform

Pike Marsh
Trail

(P)

(P)

Viewing
Platform

N

To (176)
10 miles to (290)

0   0.5   1

Miles

Next, park at Lake Defiance, where you'll find another boardwalk that leads around the lake and where fishermen often congregate. Walk around the lake June through August and listen for Sedge Wrens, which breed here in the nearby wet meadows. You should also find bluebirds, rough-winged swallows, Barn Swallows, and other breeding birds here. You can also walk a 3-mile trail here to explore gently rolling hills meandering through wetlands.

One-half mile north of the main parking lot on River Road is the McHenry Dam Day Use Area, where birders often go in the morning to search for the rare breeding marsh birds as well as songbirds.

Park at the far end of the dam near the concession stand and outdoor facilities. Take the path through a white pine grove, where Chipping Sparrows breed and nuthatches congregate in winter, to a T intersection. Take the left turn to the Black Tern Marsh lookout, less than 0.1 mile. Stand on the wooden deck, which overlooks the area where Yellow-headed Blackbirds, Black Terns, grebes, moorhens, and Least Bitterns (occasionally) have bred. Arrive here early in the morning for your best chance at hearing and seeing these birds, from late April through mid-July. You can also view migratory waterfowl here in spring and fall. Postbreeding herons and egrets also visit the marsh in August and September.

You can walk this entire 2-mile trail loop around several marshes, but if you only have a short time, walk back to the T intersection and head in the opposite direction to listen for Prothonotary Warblers, which nest in boxes erected in the Fox River backwaters. American Redstarts, Blue-gray Gnatcatchers, and other songbirds also breed along this corridor. Here's where you may also see Pied-billed Grebes and their young in July and August, as well as numerous migrants during May and September.

If you do walk the entire trail, you'll find another wetland lookout about halfway around. This is a good place to look for migrating waterfowl in March. Shovelers, teals, and other species dabble in the shallows searching for food. You'll also pass through some grassland areas where you'll often hear Field Sparrows, Song Sparrows, and other breeders in spring and summer.

General information: Moraine Hills derives its name from a geologic formation known as a moraine, an accumulation of boulders, stones, and other debris deposited by a glacier. As glacial ice melted here following the Wisconsin glaciation period, it left gravel-rich deposits called kames, which you'll note in the park's wooded hills and ridges. Glacial melt also created holes called kettles, which became marshes, bogs, and fens. These include the 48-acre Lake Defiance and the 115-acre Pike Marsh. The state of Illinois has been restoring some of the wetlands here that attract endangered plants and animals. You'll find concession stands (open seasonally), picnic areas, and outdoor restrooms at the McHenry Dam Day Use Area, and an interpretive center, and indoor restrooms in the main park at Lake Defiance. You can also rent boats and cross-country skis here.

ADDITIONAL HELP

DeLorme IA&G grid: 20.
Contact: Moraine Hills State Park.
Nearest gas, food, and lodging: McHenry.

10 Crabtree Nature Center, Palatine Marsh, and Vicinity

Habitats: Partially restored prairie, upland forest, wetlands, lake, and ponds.
Key birds: Migratory waterfowl; breeding Pied-billed Grebe, Great Blue Heron, Common Moorhen, Hooded Merganser, Willow Flycatcher, and Bobolink; breeding Swainson's Hawk.
Best times to bird: Spring and fall migration and early breeding season.

Directions: The nature center entrance is off Palatine Road between Barrington Road on the east and Illinois Highways 68/59 on the west in the town of Barrington, Illinois. Palatine Marsh is on Palatine Road southeast of the nature center entrance road. Park along the road and be careful of the traffic.

10 Crabtree Nature Center, Palatine Marsh, and Vicinity

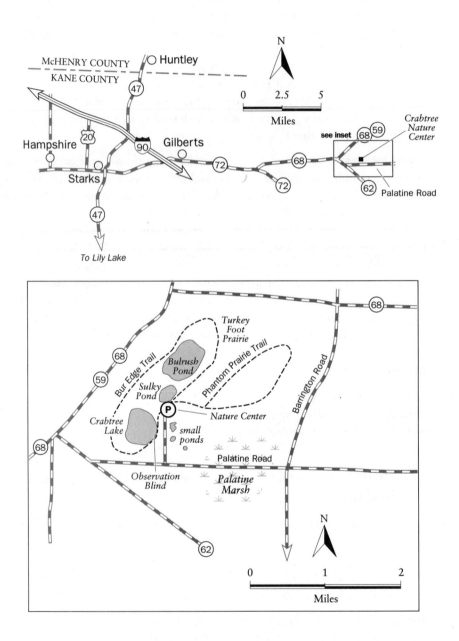

To find the Swainson's Hawks, starting from the intersection of IL 68/59, travel west on IL 68 for 5 miles until it ends at IL 72. Continue west on IL 72 for 9.5 miles to IL 47 in the town of Starks.

Birding: Crabtree Nature Center, with its diverse habitats, including ponds, marshes, woodlands, and restored prairie has attracted 260 bird species, including 80 confirmed breeders. Birders usually come to Crabtree searching for migrating waterfowl and the rarities that occur nearly every year.

The main entrance road to Crabtree, which is in the northwest Chicago suburb of Barrington, runs along partially restored prairie that has attracted Bobolinks, Eastern and occasionally Western Meadowlarks, and Song and Savannah Sparrows to breed. Watch for Northern Harriers hunting this field, too, and for migrating Sandhill Cranes that may stop to feed here.

In the spring, park in the main lot and walk to the visitor center. Watch for ducks in the small ponds as you walk the sidewalk to the center, and for warblers, thrushes, and vireos in the trees. When you reach the visitor center, the sidewalk ends and the 1.3-mile-long Bur Edge Trail begins. This trail circles Sulky and Bulrush Ponds, the marsh between the two ponds, a stand of bur oak trees, and parts of the prairie.

Take the path to your right and walk past some woods and Bulrush Pond on your left. Scan here in October and November and in March and April for dabbling ducks, including Mallard, American Black Duck, American Wigeon, Northern Shoveler, Green and Blue-winged Teals, Northern Pintail, and Gadwall. Also, many herons and egrets, which breed in a rookery at nearby Baker Lake (see Site 11), feed at Crabtree. Look for Great Egrets, Black-crowned Night-Herons, Great Blue Herons, and Double-crested Cormorants spring through early fall. Green Herons also feed in this pond. The east side of Bulrush Pond attracts good numbers of warblers and other passerines in spring and fall.

Continue around Bulrush Pond as the trail swings into the Turkey Foot Prairie where grassland birds breed. The trail then reenters the forest and comes to an area of old orchard and fields where woodland-edge birds can be observed. Look for Willow Flycatchers in breeding season. Here, you'll also find an elevated observation platform, which is a good spot to observe raptors, Sandhill Cranes, swallows, and other migrants in the fall.

Continue walking the trail until you reach the Crabtree Lake observation blind, which is close to the end of the loop. Diving ducks, geese, and swans prefer the larger open waters of Crabtree Lake, and a Neotropic Cormorant was seen here once. American Black Ducks have wintered here and are frequently seen on the Christmas Bird Count. Regular migrants include Snow, Greater White-fronted, and Canada Geese, as well as scaups, Buffleheads, Ring-necked, and Ruddy Ducks, and all three mergansers. Tundra Swans occasionally stop at Crabtree Lake, too.

As you return to the visitor center, look in the meadows for breeding Eastern Bluebirds, orioles, vireos, and swallows.

A Pied-billed Grebe on nest at Crabtree Nature Center.
ANNALEE FJELLBERG-FISKO PHOTO

For grassland birds, take the 1.7-mile Phantom Prairie Trail, which winds through a partially reconstructed tallgrass prairie. Here you may find Bobolinks, Eastern and possibly Western Meadowlarks, Song and Savannah Sparrows, Northern Harriers, American Kestrels, and Red-tailed Hawks.

Nearby Palatine Marsh attracts Hooded Mergansers, Wood Ducks, Common Moorhens, and Pied-billed Grebes. Also check the tall dead trees of the south side for a small rookery of Great Blue Herons and Double-crested Cormorants. Park on the side of Palatine Road and be careful; traffic can be heavy during peak travel times. Weekends are better for checking the marsh, which also provides habitat for dabbling ducks during migration.

A small population of the state-listed endangered Swainson's Hawk breeds about 15 miles west of Crabtree. Virtually all Illinois summer and breeding records for this species have occurred since the early 1970s in a relatively small area of extreme south-central McHenry County and the extreme northwestern corner of Kane County. Birders have recorded up to 12 birds and 5 nesting pairs in this region one summer, although recently they have found only one to two nesting pairs.

The hawks arrive to breed in Illinois sometime in early April and depart in late August through early September. The best place to look for these birds is along IL 47 in Kane and McHenry Counties. Search within the boundaries of the towns of Lily Lake, Hampshire, Huntley, and Gilberts. The area just west of IL 47/72 seems to be the most reliable. Sometimes the birds can be seen perched in trees along the roadside.

Although you could expect to see the Swainson's Hawk almost anywhere in migration in Illinois, the species prefers open savanna-like areas with large, open, grassy fields interspersed with patches of woods during the breeding season. Since most of this type of habitat is now gone from the state and has been replaced by row-crop agriculture, the species is now confined to the few open savannas in northeastern Illinois.

General information: In the 1960s, the Forest Preserve District of Cook County began acquiring 1,182 acres, much of it farmland and a privately owned nature preserve, in what is now Crabtree Nature Center. The forest preserve district converted the land to grasslands and woodlands, and preserved wetlands. The trails are open March through October from 8 A.M. to 5 P.M., and November through February from 8 A.M. to 4:30 P.M. The center is closed on Thanksgiving, Christmas Day, and New Year's Day.

ADDITIONAL HELP

DeLorme IA&G grid: 19 and 20.
Contact: Crabtree Nature Center.
Nearest gas, food, and lodging: Palatine and Barrington.

11 Baker's Lake and Ron Beese Park

Habitat: Shallow 165-acre lake with small heron rookery island, city park with fields, and woodland and shrubby edges.
Key birds: Migratory waterfowl in spring and fall, including thousands of coots, as well as numbers of grebes, ducks, herons, and egrets and occasional shorebirds and loons; breeding cormorants, Great Blue Heron, Black-crowned Night-Heron, Great Egret, Double-crested Cormorant, and occasionally Herring Gull; and breeding shrub and grassland birds.

Directions: From Interstate 90, exit at Barrington Road. Go north about 6 miles to Hillside Avenue. Go west 1 mile to the parking area on your left, which is just before Illinois Highway 14.

To get to Ron Beese Park, turn east off Barrington/Hough Road onto Princeton Street, which is 5 blocks south of Hough. Continue east, about 6 blocks, to the parking area.

Birding: To view the ducks and the rookery at Baker's Lake in the northwest Chicago suburb of Barrington, you'll need a scope. To protect the nesting birds, no one is allowed on the island. The best view of the rookery island is from the parking lot on the corner of Hillside Avenue and IL 14. The herons, egrets, and cormorants begin arriving in late March or early April, depending on the winter's severity. You can search for migrating waterfowl in March and April. Thousands of coots

The Black-crowned Night-Heron traditionally has bred at Baker's Lake, but its numbers have declined. Land managers are working to restore the habitat for this bird.
JOE B. MILOSEVICH PHOTO

11 Baker's Lake and Ron Beese Park

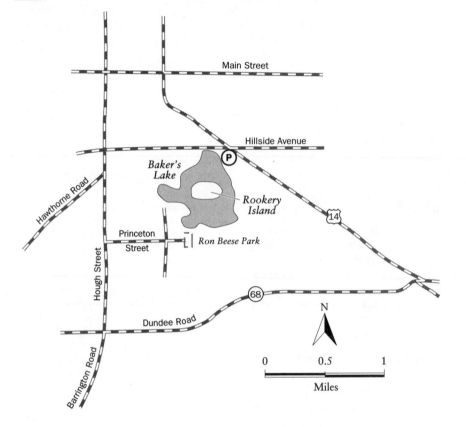

rest on the water at one time. Also look for Pied-billed Grebes, Horned Grebes, Common Loons, Ring-necked Ducks, Wigeons, Buffleheads, scaups, Gadwalls, Northern Shovelers, and Blue-winged Teals, and an occasional Canvasback.

Viewing the rookery from April through July can be exciting as the herons, egrets, and cormorants court, build nests, and feed young. If you're here in May, you can also search for warblers in the wooded area west of the lake on Hillside Avenue. In fall search for migrant songbirds as well as ducks, sometimes lingering into December.

You'll find grassland and shrubby areas at nearby Ron Beese Park. During migration and breeding season, you'll often find Bobolinks, Eastern Meadowlarks, Common Yellowthroats, Yellow Warblers, and various sparrows and catbirds. Rusty Blackbirds also visit the park during migration.

Birders can easily visit Baker Lake as well as nearby Crabtree Nature Center within the same day. See Site 10 for details.

General information: Baker's Lake, a natural wetland/island complex has held breeding herons and egrets for at least 30 years. It is partly owned by the village of Barrington, the U.S. Fish & Wildlife Service, and the Forest Preserve District of

Cook County, all of which have worked to manage the site as nearby development, natural erosion, and wind damage has degraded the rookery. At one time, the preserve held 220 Black-crowned Night-Heron nests. In 1998, this state-listed endangered bird has not successfully bred at the preserve. Forest preserve staff have erected manmade structures to attract the herons and egrets to breed. The forest preserve district has recently hired a consultant to help them with the task of improving these nesting structures.

ADDITIONAL HELP

DeLorme IA&G grid: 20.
Contact: Crabtree Nature Center and the Barrington Park District.
Nearest gas, food, and lodging: Barrington and Palatine.

12 Ryerson Conservation Area and the Des Plaines River Corridor

Habitats: Mixed deciduous woodlands, river bottomland, and northern flatwoods.
Key birds: Migrating passerines, including Black-throated Blue, Hooded, Mourning, and Connecticut Warblers; breeding raptors, including Cooper's and Red-shouldered Hawks and Great Horned Owl; breeding songbirds, including Veery, Wood Thrush, Great Crested Flycatcher, Eastern Wood-Pewee, Ovenbird, Rose-breasted Grosbeak, Scarlet Tanager, and Baltimore Oriole.
Best times to bird: May, June, and September.

Directions: Ryerson Conservation Area, known as Ryerson Woods, is easily accessed off Interstate 94 (Tri-State Tollway). Exit at Illinois Highway 22, about 15 miles north of Chicago. Turn west. Proceed 0.5 mile to Riverwoods Road, then go south 1 mile to the entrance.

Birding: In May, a plethora of warblers, sometimes up to 25 or more species in one day, descend on Ryerson Woods, a 500-acre hotspot in north suburban Chicago. Nearby Wright Woods and Half Day Forest Preserves offer similar birding experiences—all are along the Des Plaines River corridor, an important songbird migrating region. At least 200 bird species have been identified in this rich riverine habitat.

The best time to bird these areas is in late April through early June. Study your bird songs before coming to Ryerson Woods, especially in the latter part of May and into June when the trees are so lush that it's difficult to see all the birds. Besides, this place is so lively with song in May that it would be a shame not to know exactly what you are hearing.

In spring, start at the Ryerson Woods Visitor Center's parking lot just after dawn. North of the center is a row of shrubs and trees where the sun stirs insects

12 Ryerson Conservation Area and the Des Plaines River Corridor

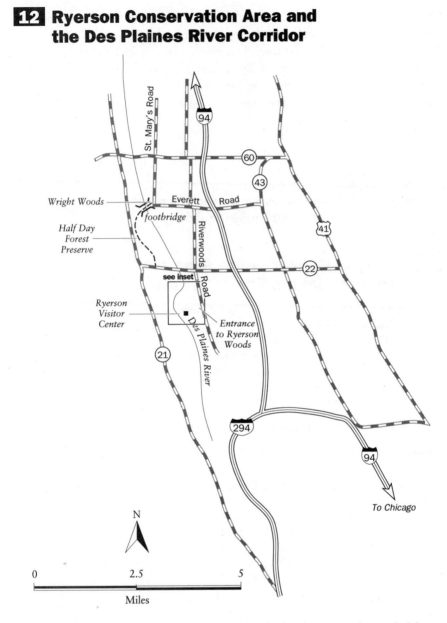

N

0   2.5   5

Miles

in the morning, and in turn, the migrating birds that have just descended from a night's trip or are resting for a few days before heading north. This is one of the best places to listen for the Hooded Warbler that has appeared here in early to middle May for many years. This is the extreme northern end of the breeding range for this species, but birders find at least two singing males each spring. In late May you can often hear the Hooded Warbler singing at Ryerson Woods when most other warbler species have left.

12 Ryerson Conservation Area and the Des Plaines River Corridor (Detail)

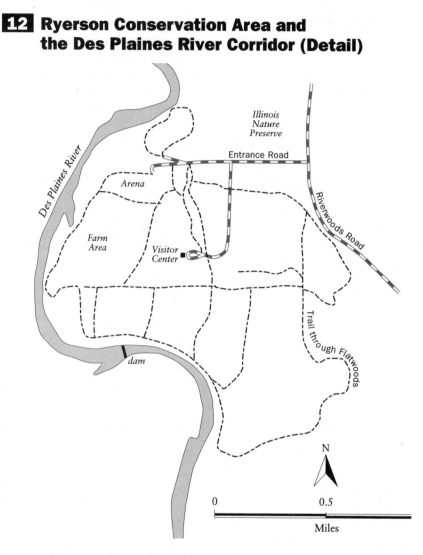

Next take any of the trails that lead to the river, where hundreds of migrants sing and feed. Palm and Yellow-rumped Warblers come through first in late April followed by Black-throated Green, Blackburnian, an occasional Prothonotary, and other warblers. The last to arrive are the Mourning, Canada, and Bay-breasted. The Black-throated Blue Warbler, one of my favorite warbler species, has appeared here on May 10 for at least six consecutive years. Listen for singing Scarlet Tanagers and Rose-breasted Grosbeaks, too. Watch for nesting Wood Ducks near boxes along the river, plus Belted Kingfishers perched on a snag overlooking the Des Plaines.

The rare Connecticut Warbler passes through Ryerson in late May nearly every year, finding a wet spot reminiscent of its boggy breeding site farther north. Check low, wet, tangly areas for this bird.

The far western trail near the farm area can be particularly rewarding during migration. The trees along the shoreline aren't as tall as they are in the deep woods and flatwoods areas, affording you easier looks at the migrants. This trail can get quite wet in spring, so wear appropriate footgear. Species encountered here include Ruby-crowned and Golden-crowned Kinglets in early spring, followed by Wilson's, Connecticut, and Mourning Warblers, plus several species of flycatchers later in spring.

Listen for the call of the Red-shouldered Hawk, plus Wood Thrushes and Veeries, as you walk the preserve's perimeter. Up to six or more pairs of Eastern Bluebirds breed here in boxes near the visitor center and farm area. A volunteer keeps the boxes clean, repaired, and free of House Sparrows and starlings.

To find breeding Veeries and Ovenbirds and—sometimes—Broad-winged Hawks, Acadian Flycatchers, and Tufted Titmice, walk the flatwoods on an early June morning. The flatwoods is south of a small restored prairie. You should hear pewees and Great Crested Flycatchers, too.

Northwest of Ryerson Woods is Wright Woods, another migrant hotspot. Any migrating warbler or vireo you didn't find at Ryerson Woods you have a good chance of seeing here. From Ryerson Woods, take Riverwoods Road north about 1 mile to Everett Road. Turn west after 1 mile to St. Mary's Road. The preserve is at the intersection of St. Mary's and Everett Roads.

Take the trail along the river where migrants typically congregate. You can walk this trail in the early evening before the sun sets to look for Nashville, Golden-winged, and other warbler species in spring.

One of the trails here is part of the Des Plaines River Trail and leads south to the Half Day Forest Preserve. The bridge on the way to Half Day is a good spot to search for migrants, including Prothonotary Warblers, sometimes seen in early to mid-May.

Parking is available off Milwaukee Road at Half Day, but it's just as easy to park at Wright Woods, then walk south. As you enter Half Day, you'll encounter some wet prairie habitat where dozens of swallows hawk insects in spring and summer, and Eastern Bluebirds nest in boxes.

Fall migration is a good time to visit these three preserves as well. Though the warblers are donning winter plumage and it's difficult to see them among all the leaves, you can still enjoy the migration and practice identifying warblers and other songbirds.

General information: Ryerson Woods, surrounded by suburban development, remains one of the largest undisturbed tracts of woods in northern Illinois. Nearly one-half of the preserve is listed as a state-dedicated nature preserve. Though surrounded by lands that once were prairies, Ryerson Woods retains its woodland feature because of its position next to the Des Plaines River. The river stopped the spread of prairie fires, saving white oaks, walnuts, maples, and other trees. Edward L. Ryerson, who owned a steel company in Chicago, built a cabin on what is now Ryerson Woods, which he enjoyed in summers with his family. He eventually

Birding at Ryerson Conservation Area. SHERYL DEVORE PHOTO

built a Greek revival–style home on the property, which now serves as the visitor center. Ryerson also helped found the Lake County Forest Preserve District, which owns Wright Woods, and Half Day Road Forest Preserve.

Rapid development, non-native species, and deer overbrowsing threaten the ecological balance of these preserves, especially Ryerson Woods. A land-management practice includes culling the deer herds, using volunteers to remove alien species, and reintroducing fire into some of the wooded areas, which will encourage more oak growth and maintain a balance between oaks and maples. Each spring, the Friends of Ryerson Woods and the Lake County Forest Preserve District sponsor a series of workshops and free bird walks during the heart of migration.

You can picnic at Wright Woods and Half Day, but not at Ryerson Woods. Facilities are available at all three preserves. Ryerson Woods is open from 6:30 A.M. to dusk. Wright Woods and Half Day are open from sunrise until sunset.

ADDITIONAL HELP

DeLorme IA&G grid: 21.
Contact: Ryerson Conservation Area and the Lake County Forest Preserve District.
Nearest gas, food, and lodging: Deerfield and Northbrook.

13 Chicago Botanic Garden

Habitats: Small lakes and lagoons, restored prairie, oak forest, specialized garden areas, local and foreign ornamental plants and conifers.
Key birds: Migratory waterfowl and songbirds; breeding woodpeckers, swallows, and orioles.
Best times to bird: Fall and spring migration.

Directions: The Chicago Botanic Garden entrance is off Lake-Cook Road, 1 mile east of U.S. Highway 41 in the town of Glencoe. You'll find six parking lots on the garden's northeast corner.

Birding: In this small birding spot, 385 acres, birders have documented more than 251 bird species, including 27 waterfowl, 14 raptors, 36 warblers, and 16 sparrows. Up to 74 bird species breed at the botanic garden in the Chicago suburb of Glencoe.

The garden features 75 acres of lagoons, 9 islands, 6 miles of shoreline, 15 acres of prairie, and 100 acres of woods.

For waterfowl birding, go in early March through April or October through December. Look for Canvasback, Redhead, Merganser, and Ruddy Ducks among others on the northeastern lakes, or lagoons as birders call them.

The duck life changes as the season progresses. For example, one year in late November, a botanic garden birding consultant recorded 2 Redheads, 9 Common Goldeneyes, 31 Buffleheads, 4 Ruddy Ducks, 24 Northern Shovelers, 15 Gadwalls, 57 Mallards, 2 Red-breasted Mergansers, 2 American Coots, and numerous geese using the lagoons. The same year on an early December day, the Bufflehead numbers had increased to 44, the Gadwall had decreased to 6, and the shovelers had decreased to 9. In mid-December, 31 Buffleheads and 21 Gadwalls used the lagoons, and 1 Common and 2 Hooded Mergansers arrived along with 4 Trumpeter Swans. Geese numbers rise to 600 or more during fall and early winter when the lagoons are not frozen. You can often see some duck life even through the coldest part of the year, because the garden staff keeps a few of the water bodies open to protect water lilies.

For land birds, walk from the Gateway Center east along the road just south of parking area 1. Follow this road, checking under the shrubs for sparrows, and the willows on the south for migrants. Search the trees along both sides of the road for migrants, especially warblers and vireos in May.

The 1-mile McDonald Woods Nature Trail, in the far northeastern section of the garden winds through a spring ephemeral demonstration plot and over a few from bridges where a small creek attract Northern Waterthrushes, Common Yellowthroats, Mourning Warblers, and other migrants in late April through May and again in August and September. As the sun rises, you'll notice more bird life here, and from 9 to 10 A.M. a flurry of song and warbler activity often begins. A pair of Great Horned Owls has nested in baskets placed in the northern section of McDonald Woods.

13 Chicago Botanic Garden

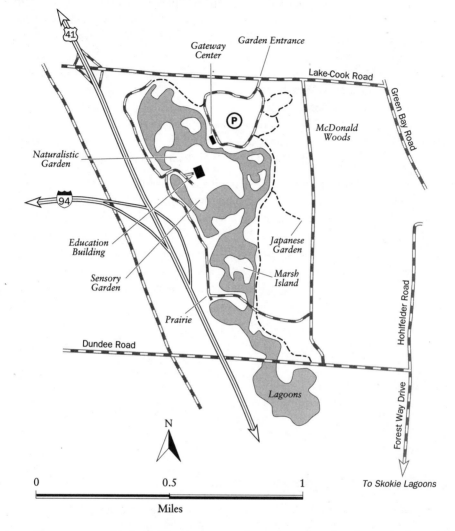

For more songbird migrants, return to the main trail and walk south along the creek listening for Winter Wrens in April and thrushes and warblers in May. When you reach the opening to the paved road (also a bicycle path), walk south 2 blocks to the group of trees surrounding the green maintenance barn to search for more migrants. In the morning the sun will be at your back at the maintenance barn plantings, affording you a good look at the migrants, which could, if you're lucky, include the rare Townsend's Warbler. Birders discovered this western species here several years ago. More typically they find Northern Parula, Black-throated Green, Magnolia, and Blackpoll Warblers here in spring and fall.

Also explore the restored prairies on the garden's south and west sides. You'll find the hike quite long but worthwhile. Check for swallows and ducks in the wetlands near the restored prairie. Then check grassland areas for breeding and migrating Eastern Meadowlarks and Savannah Sparrows. In May, birders find Clay-colored and Nelson's Sharp-tailed Sparrows as well as Orchard Orioles near the prairies. Look to the sky in spring and fall for migrating Ospreys and hawks, including Broad-winged and Cooper's.

A boardwalk near the wet prairie attracts rails, snipes, and other wet habitat birds in April and May. Nearby is the Skokie River, where migrating swallows, shorebirds, and hawks congregate.

The Dwarf Conifer Garden attracts winter finches and nuthatches, and the Sensory Garden, southwest of the education building, attracts warblers, sparrows, and other migrants, as well as good view of ducks in spring and fall.

General information: The Chicago Horticultural Society carries out its mission to collect, do research, and offer educational programs through the Chicago Botanic Garden, which opened in 1972 and is owned by the Forest Preserve District of Cook County. The garden includes 23 garden areas as well as native habitat featuring rare Illinois plants and offers programs including early morning bird walks. Hours are from 8 A.M. to sunset every day except Christmas, Thanksgiving, and New Year's Day. A wheelchair-accessible tram tour is available. An entry fee is required.

ADDITIONAL HELP

DeLorme IA&G grid: 21.
Contact: Chicago Botanic Garden.
Nearest gas, food, and lodging: Deerfield and Northbrook; the garden's Food for Thought Café in the Gateway Center is open for breakfast and lunch; designated picnic areas.

14 Skokie Lagoons

Habitats: Open water, marsh, woods, fields, meadows, and shrubs.
Key birds: Migratory songbirds; breeding Wood Duck, hawks, woodpeckers, flycatchers, and swallows.
Best times to bird: Spring and late summer into fall.

Directions: From Interstate 94, known as the Edens Expressway, exit at Willow Road east. Almost immediately after you exit, you'll notice a small parking area entrance on the north side of Willow Road.

Birding: Birders have documented more than 210 species of birds at the 540-acre Skokie Lagoons in the north Chicago suburb of Winnetka. These include 70 that breed or use the area during summer. Confirmed nesting species include Wood Ducks, Broad-winged Hawks, Red-tailed Hawks, American Kestrels, Eastern

14 Skokie Lagoons

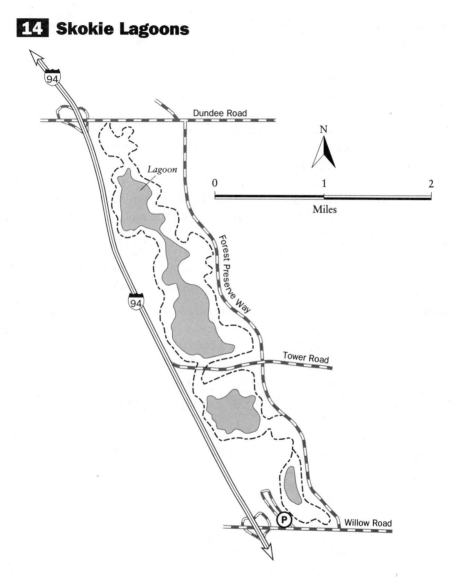

Screech-Owls, several species of woodpeckers; and flycatchers; and swallows. Black-billed Cuckoos, and Green Herons also probably breed here. The potential for finding a rarity or a straggler such as a late Yellow-bellied Sapsucker exists during migration.

The best birding is done from sunrise to 11 A.M. Drizzly or rainy days in May and September often produce good looks at migrating songbirds (as well as hungry mosquitos).

A series of long narrow lagoons extend for 4 miles into the Chicago Botanic Garden (see Site 13). You can walk along the lagoon banks or follow the bicycle trail to search for migrants. Be careful; some bicyclists speed through this area.

You might also want to walk the horse trail along the creek's western boundary. The wider, open nature of the trail offers good looks at migrants.

Each season, birders generally find all the warblers that regularly migrate through Illinois, including the less common Kentucky, Hooded, and Prothonotary Warblers in early to mid-May, and the Mourning and Connecticut Warblers in late May. The fall warbler migration runs from late August to late September.

Fields hold various migrating sparrows, including Clay-colored and Lincoln's in late April through early May, and again in mid-September through mid-October. Yellow-crowned Night-Herons sometimes feast on crayfish here during breeding season.

You'll notice abundant swallows, including Cliff Swallows, flying over the lagoons. You may find the Cliff Swallows nesting underneath a bridge on Tower Road in the lagoons.

The Evanston North Shore Bird Club has led traditional spring bird walks at the lagoons for years, and birders consider this one of the best spots in Chicagoland for spring migrants. If you're there when the walks begin, you're welcome to join.

General information: Once a shallow peat marsh, the Skokie Lagoons flooded regularly until the Civilian Conservation Corps, in the 1930s, created the present-day area by hand-digging the lagoons and constructed a series of spillways. The corps also built a water-control dam north of Willow Road to prevent downstream flooding. Water levels fluctuate dramatically throughout the year, sometimes creating potential hazards for birders, and preventing them from reaching certain areas after heavy rainfalls or spring snowmelt. Recently, the Forest Preserve District of Cook County drained the lagoons and dredged the silt that was depleting oxygen for the resident fish. Shoreline erosion caused the siltation of the lagoons.

Chicago Audubon Society volunteers and others are replanting the shoreline to curb the erosion. These plantings will provide excellent feeding habitat for waterfowl. The future for birding at the Skokie Lagoons seems good.

Somewhat primitive outdoor facilities only are available here; fishermen use the lagoons extensively.

ADDITIONAL HELP

DeLorme IA&G grid: 21.
Contact: Chicago Audubon Society, Forest Preserve District of Cook County, Evanston North Shore Bird Club.
Nearest gas, food, and lodging: Northbrook.

15 Gillson Park and Evanston Landfill

Habitats: Lake Michigan shoreline and surrounding green areas.
Key birds: Migrating water birds, including loons, grebes, gulls, terns, jaegers, and ducks; specialties, including Harlequin Duck, Red-necked Grebe, Black-legged Kittiwake, and scoters; migrating hawks and owls, including Merlin and Short-eared Owl; wintering ducks, including Oldsquaw, Common Goldeneye, and mergansers; winter gulls, including Glaucous and Thayer's; and migrating passerines.
Best times to bird: October through May.

Directions: To get to the reclaimed landfill, from Interstate 94 (Edens Expressway), exit at Dempster Street. Go east 5 miles to Chicago Avenue. Drive north for less than a mile until Chicago Avenue meets Sheridan Road. Continue north on Sheridan Road for 1 mile to Lincoln Street. Turn east, following the road a short distance to the lake and the landfill.

To reach Gillson Park, from I-94 (Edens Expressway), exit at Dempster Street. Go east 5 miles to Sheridan Road. Drive 3 miles on Sheridan Road to the Gillson Park entrance.

Birding: When Wilmette residents wistfully say goodbye to summer and stop frequenting the beach at Gillson Park, the birders come, dressed not in bathing suits but in warm attire to stave off the winds coming from Lake Michigan. Scope at the ready, these birders are looking for the hardy sea ducks such as scoters and the occasional Harlequin Duck, Red-necked Grebe, and jaeger, plus large flocks of wintering mergansers.

Take a scope and walk to the beach to search for water birds. Depending on weather conditions, beginning in October, you might have a chance to see a fly-by jaeger. Identifying the three species, Pomarine, Parasitic, and Long-tailed is difficult, especially since these birds fly by quickly, but you're more apt to see a Pomarine or a Parasitic Jaeger here.

Other fly-bys you may see in fall include White-winged, Black, and Surf Scoters and Common Loons. Also look for dozens of Horned Grebes, wigeons, Redheads, and mergansers either flying by or sitting in the water. American Tree Sparrows winter here, and you may find them in scrubby fields west of the beach. Snow Buntings are also possible.

In November, you may have a chance at finding a Harlequin Duck or the rare Red-throated Loon, a species that birders report once every year or so, as well as the rare Black-legged Kittiwake. At this time of year, you might see 800 or more mergansers on the lake, dozens of loons, and as the weather turns colder, the hardy Oldsquaws may return.

Look in November through January for wintering gulls, including Glaucous and Thayer's along with the much more common Ring-billed and Herring Gulls.

Spring migration can also be productive. For example, one recent day in the middle of May, birders reported four Thayer's Gulls, two Lesser Black-backed

15 Gillson Park and Evanston Landfill

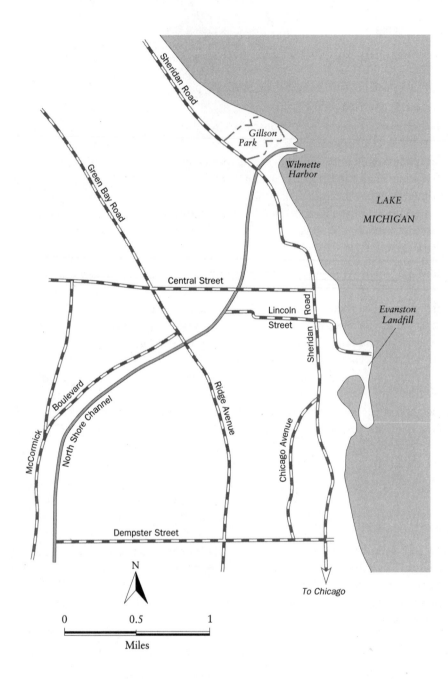

Sheridan Road

Gillson
Park

Wilmette
Harbor

LAKE

MICHIGAN

Green Bay Road

Central Street

Lincoln
Street

Sheridan Road

*Evanston
Landfill*

McCormick
Boulevard

North Shore Channel

Ridge Avenue

Chicago Avenue

Dempster Street

N

To Chicago

0   0.5   1

Miles

Gulls, and a Glaucous Gull. Also look for beach-combing shorebirds here, including Willets and Sanderlings in May and in September. An uncommon Illinois migrant, the Whimbrel, has also been seen at Gillson Park, 15 of them on one day at the end of May; several American Avocets, a western United States species, were seen at Gillson Park at the end of October.

The greenery west of the beach attracts migrating songbirds, so especially in May and in late August through September, check these areas. You've got the chance to see many warblers and flycatchers in spring and fall, plus large numbers of kinglets, including both Golden-crowned and Ruby-crowned in fall. Owls and hawks also migrate along the lake in fall—look for Short-eared Owls, Peregrine Falcons, and Merlins, among others.

The nearby old Northwestern University landfill in Evanston attracts similar water birds, but a different complement of land birds. A few scattered fields with much less green cover than Gillson Park sometimes attract migratory Nelson's Sharp-tailed, LeConte's, and Clay-colored Sparrows, and more commonly White-throated and White-crowned Sparrows in fall.

General information: Parking at Gillson Park, which is on Wilmette Park District property, can be difficult if you're not a Wilmette resident with a village sticker, but plenty of side streets exist near the park. You'll have to lug your scope to the beach. Contact the Chicago Rare Bird Alert to learn of the latest sightings here.

ADDITIONAL HELP

DeLorme IA&G grid: 21.
Contact: Chicago Rare Bird Alert.
Nearest gas food, and lodging: Wilmette for gas and food; Evanston for gas, food, and lodging.

16 O'Hare Post Office Ponds

Habitats: Mudflats, pond, and meadow.
Key birds: Migratory shorebirds.
Best times to bird: Mid-April through early October.

Directions: From Interstate 294, take the O'Hare International Airport exit, then immediately look for Mannheim Road. Proceed south less than a mile to Irving Park Road. Turn west. Drive for 1.5 miles to O'Hare Cargo Area Road. Turn north and you'll immediately see the mudflats and ponds, plus the O'Hare Post Office just northeast of Irving Park Road. Use caution when birding this busy location. Heavy truck traffic is common.

Birding: Who would have thought that a small area with mudflats and a pond would exist right near one of the busiest airports in the world? A local birder, who has been in charge of the Chicago Rare Bird Alert hotline for many years, discovered

16 O'Hare Post Office Ponds

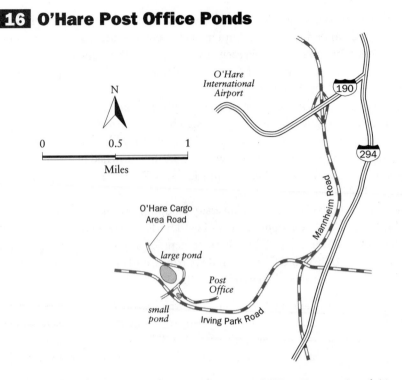

this secret shorebird spot in Chicago adjacent to O'Hare International Airport six years ago when delivering a letter to the post office for his wife. He saw 9 species of 114 shorebirds in the middle of May. Since then he and other birders have been exploring this new little hotspot and tallying nice lists of shorebirds, especially in May, and late July through September.

Birders can park at the O'Hare Post Office parking lot or along O'Hare Cargo Area Road, which is north of the mudflat. Late morning through midafternoon on weekdays and weekend mornings are the least busiest times, as far as traffic goes, to look for shorebirds.

In April, Killdeer and Common Snipes return, followed by Pectoral Sandpipers in late April, and Least and Semipalmated Sandpipers and Semipalmated Plovers in May. You should also see some Dunlins, Spotted Sandpipers, and yellowlegs in May. Look for the uncommon Wilson's Phalarope in middle May and the even rarer Baird's Sandpiper in late May.

In July Least Sandpiper numbers begin in the single digits, then rise to perhaps 50 or more in the middle of the month. A Red-necked Phalarope is also possible in July. Late August, you should find Semipalmated and Pectoral Sandpipers fairly easily. Mid-August is a good time to search for the rare Marbled Godwit, which was seen here on August 18 in 1998. Mid-September is a good time to search for Semipalmated Plovers. In late September and early October, you may find Black-bellied Plovers.

Mid-September is also about the right time to search for the rare White-rumped Sandpiper, and the rare Baird's Sandpiper. Lucky birders find one or two of these species annually, but be aware these are two of the rarest migratory shorebirds in Chicagoland.

General information: The O'Hare ponds exist because of the runoff water coming from nearby O'Hare International Airport. Water levels fluctuate depending on the season and rainfall. Local birders suggest you park at the post office and walk to the ponds. If you park your car off the highways and leave it unattended, you could get ticketed or towed by O'Hare airport security or Chicago Police.

ADDITIONAL HELP

DeLorme IA&G grid: 21.
Contact: Chicago Audubon Society.
Nearest gas food, and lodging: Bensenville and Schiller Park.

17 Morton Arboretum

Habitats: Meadow, forest, ponds, and pine plantation.
Key birds: Spring and fall migrants, including ducks and songbirds; breeding Eastern Bluebird; wintering Northern Saw-whet Owl, Cedar Waxwing, Red Crossbill, and other finches.
Best times to bird: Spring, fall, and winter.

Directions: Exit Interstate 88 (East–West Tollway) at Illinois Highway 53 in DuPage County. Go north less than 1 mile to the entrance.

Birding: The 1,500-acre Morton Arboretum in northeastern Illinois provides a year-round oasis for birds because of its variety of vegetation. Woods, fields, meadows, a restored prairie, streams, a river, and several small lakes and marsh areas provide habitat for some 276 bird species that have plucked the fruits, berries, insects, and other food off some of the 3,000 plant species growing here.

Park in the lot near the entrance, which gives access to the east side, or drive under a bridge to get to the west side. The east side contains native woods and plantings, whereas the west side includes meadows, edges, and various evergreens.

The Arboretum spans 3 miles, and you can walk or drive through nearly all of it as well as park at 25 separate pull-outs where you can walk through varied habitat. Examples include meadows (and bluebird boxes) for Eastern Bluebirds; forest edges for thrashers, yellowthroats, and other warblers; pine and spruce trees for crossbills and saw-whet owls, and small lakes for ducks and geese.

In spring and fall, starting at the east side, walk from the Visitor Center to Crabapple Lake to search for field birds and ducks, and then follow the Illinois Trees Trail Loop, a 2-mile walk to search for warblers, towhees, and other passerines. You'll pass Reed Marsh, which attracts migrating warblers when it's wet, as well as some fields where sparrows and towhees feed.

17 Morton Arboretum

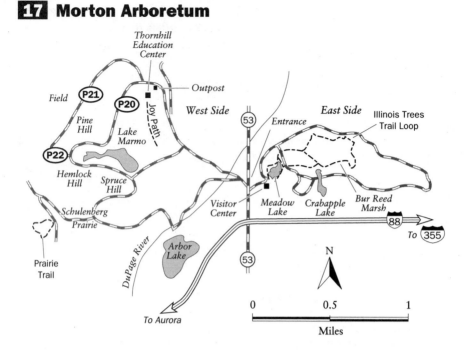

Visit Arbor Lake, where various migrating ducks, including American Black and Ring-necked, arrive the last week in March and during October.

To search for migrating warblers on the west side, stop at parking areas 18 and 20. Parking area 22 on the west side attracts migrating sparrows, and the woodlands west of Parking area 21 attract various songbirds.

The Joy Path near the Thornhill Education Center was Joy Morton's favorite place to walk, and on a spring day you should find many migrants, including Rose-breasted Grosbeaks, Scarlet Tanagers, and various warblers.

Walk to the Outpost behind the education center to search for winter finches in the fruit-bearing trees. Birders have observed Pine Grosbeaks, Bohemian Waxwings, Varied Thrushes, and Townsend's Solitaires along the ravine north of the Outpost. These are all rare winter visitors, not seen every year. More often you'll encounter wintering Brown Creepers and resident Great Horned Owls.

The evergreens near Lake Marmo attract Northern Saw-whet Owls in winter, and birders generally find at least one of this small, seemingly tame species each year. Look for whitewash at the base of trees and small pellets. Then look up to see if an owl is staring back at you. Be patient and be careful not to disturb the owl.

Hemlock Hill and Spruce Hill near Lake Marmo have attracted crossbills. In years of great pine cone production, flocks of dozens of White-winged and Red Crossbills can be found in winter.

The most common winter visitor to Morton Arboretum is the Cedar Waxwing, which travels from fruiting tree to shrub as the seasons progress. Ask at the visitor center which species are fruiting. Then visit those areas to search for Cedar Waxwings and other wintering birds. Also check the alder plantations along the DuPage River for Common Redpolls and Pine Siskins in winter. A walk through the alders and conifers at the arboretum in winter is quiet and peaceful and can often be productive for birding.

General information: Joy Morton, the founder of the Morton Salt Company, established the arboretum in 1922 as an outdoor museum of plants from various parts of the world that could grow in northern Illinois. The arboretum's main mission is to establish, care for, and gather research about these plants. Secondary to the mission is to provide habitat for birds.

Recently the arboretum has rededicated its mission to focusing solely on plants, but it still remains one of the best places in northern Illinois to go birding as well as a coveted spot for doing Christmas and Spring Bird Counts.

The Arboretum opens at 9 A.M. daily, but in spring, birders may enter as early as 7 A.M. A fee is charged, but if you belong to a horticultural society or another public garden, your membership card might get you in free.

ADDITIONAL HELP

DeLorme IA&G grid: 28.
Contact: The Morton Arboretum.
Nearest gas, food, and lodging: The arboretum has a restaurant overlooking one of the ponds, plus a gift shop and indoor restrooms. Hotels and motels are available in Lisle and Wheaton.

18 Blackwell Forest Preserve

Habitats: Restored prairie, meadow, wetlands, 60-acre lake, woods, and Mount Hoy, a capped landfill.
Key birds: Migrating waterfowl, raptors, and shorebirds; breeding Pied-billed Grebe, American and Least Bitterns, Virginia Rail, Sora, and Yellow-headed Blackbird.
Best times to bird: Fall for migrating raptors; spring and fall migration for passerines and waterfowl; early summer for breeding marsh birds.

Directions: Blackwell Forest Preserve is in DuPage County, east of Illinois Highway 59 and west of Winfield Road. The southern boundary is IL 56 (Butterfield Road) and the north boundary is Gary's Mill Road. It is bisected east and west by Mack Road.

The entrance to Mount Hoy is off IL 56 just west of Winfield Road. The McKee Marsh parking lot is off Mack Road 0.1 mile east of IL 59.

Birding: One late September day, several birders stood atop Mount Hoy some 30 miles southwest of Chicago and waited for the fog to lift from the surrounding hills. As the cloudy mist dissipated, a Cooper's Hawk flew out of a tree, followed

18 Blackwell Forest Preserve

by a Peregrine Falcon, and then another and another raptor speeding over their heads. Another time, birders counted 1,000 Broad-winged Hawks flying in thermals over Mount Hoy on a single day.

In autumn, Chicago area birders who have hawks on their minds, also have Mount Hoy on their minds. Mount Hoy is not a mountainous anomaly in the midst of flat Chicagoland. It's actually a 150-foot-tall capped landfill, making it the best spot in DuPage County, if not the whole Chicago region to watch hawks. Mount Hoy overlooks Blackwell Forest Preserve, where another birding gem can be found, the McKee Marsh where state-listed endangered marsh birds breed annually.

To watch hawks at Mount Hoy, choose a day in mid- to late September or early October when the winds are from the north. Bring a lawn chair, picnic lunch, and warm clothes and drive to the Blackwell Forest Preserve entrance off Butterfield Road (IL 56), just west of Winfield Road. Follow the road to the parking lot at the north side of Mount Hoy, then walk the path to the top. Midmorning and midafternoon are peak times for watching hawks.

Broadwings come through beginning in middle September, their numbers diminishing by the beginning of October. Eagles, buteos, accipiters, Ospreys, Sandhill Cranes, and Turkey Vultures fly over Mount Hoy in fall, and occasionally, perhaps once every one to two years, someone discovers a Northern Goshawk. Northern Harriers are fairly common during migration, so watch for this species' soaring or gliding manner of holding its wings in a slight dihedral, and its unsteady rocking in strong winds.

Silver Lake also attracts migrating waterfowl. All inland duck species as well as loons and swans have stopped here, except for scoters, in spring and fall. Check the northeast end of Silver Lake near the campground for migrating songbirds.

For more spring and fall migrants as well as breeding wetland species, visit the forest preserve's McKee Marsh, a manmade lake with marshy borders, small woodlots, and grasslands. From the parking lot walk north on the crushed gravel path through the prairie about 200 yards to the marsh. You'll find well-maintained paths going east or west on this 2-mile loop trail.

To view the east side of the lake, leave the main trail and walk the narrow grass trail. Walking here provides good opportunities to see Virginia Rails and Soras on the floating reeds in spring and early summer. This area also has attracted American Bitterns to breed. Listen for the *"oogalunk"* call of this bird in April and May early in the morning or at dusk. The best place to look for Least Bitterns is the cattail stand near the spillway at the southwest corner. This state-listed threatened bird has bred at the preserve. A sunrise walk on a May or June day will often be accompanied by the *"kidick kidick"* call of the Virginia Rail, the whinny of the Sora, the loud, maniacal laughter of the grebe, the rusty-hinge-like call of the Yellow-headed Blackbird, and the rapid typewriter-like sound of Marsh Wrens. Also during the postbreeding season, look for wandering Little Blue Herons. Birders have observed rarities, including Ruffs and Willets, species typically associated with lakefront migration, and not commonly found inland.

Return to the main trail, walking east away from the marsh and through a partially restored prairie that attracts grassland birds such as Bobolinks, Song Sparrows, Eastern Meadowlarks, Eastern Bluebirds, Tree Swallows, and occasionally Dickcissels and Grasshopper Sparrows. McKee Marsh is fairly reliable for finding migrating Nelson's Sharp-tailed Sparrows in September, too.

Catbird Trail (0.8 mile) branches off to the west of the main trail, proceeds through a woods and shrub area, and rejoins the main trail heading east. Birders spend time on this trail in fall and spring to search for migrating warblers, orioles, flycatchers, thrushes, and vireos.

General information: Purchased in 1960 by the Forest Preserve District of DuPage County, Blackwell Forest Preserve consists of 1,311 acres with 8 miles of trails, including a multipurpose Regional Trail that connects to the Illinois Prairie Path. While excavating McKee Marsh for restoration in 1977, workers uncovered a well-preserved woolly mammoth skeleton that is now displayed at the Fullersburg Woods Environmental Education center in Oak Brook, Illinois.

Mount Hoy was created from a landfill after large quantities of low-permeable clay were discovered while excavating the gravel pit that is now Silver Lake. You can picnic, fish, camp, rent boats, and exercise your dog at the preserve, which opens an hour after sunrise and closes an hour after sunset.

ADDITIONAL HELP

DeLorme IA&G grid: 28.
Contact: Forest Preserve District of DuPage County.
Nearest gas, food, and lodging: Camping at Silver Lake; hotels and motels in Warrenville.

19 Fermilab National Accelerator Laboratory

Habitats: Upland forest, floodplain woods, oak savanna, restored grasslands, pasture, cropland, lakes, streams, and wetlands.
Key birds: Migrating loons, grebes, waterfowl (including Ross's and Greater White-fronted Geese), and sparrows; Northern Harrier; Northern Shrike; rare nesting grassland species; wintering owls.
Best times to bird: Year-round, but especially spring and fall migration; winter for owls and northern visitors and early summer for breeding species.

Directions: The main entrance to Fermilab is on Pine Street in Kane County near Batavia. From Interstate 88, exit Illinois Highway 59. Drive north 1.5 miles to Butterfield Road. Turn west and drive 4 miles to Kirk Road. Drive north 2 miles to Pine Street, then back east 1 mile to the entrance.

Birding: Fermilab contains nearly all of the major ecosystems that once dominated the Midwest, and that varied habitat attracts unusual geese, shorebirds, grassland birds, shrikes, and wintering owls, not to mention the countless migrating sparrows and warblers. Birders have confirmed at least 262 avian species here, 83 of which breed on this 6,800-acre site. Recent rarities include Red-necked Grebes, Black Scoters, King Rails, Willets, Glaucous Gulls, Common Terns, Yellow-throated Warblers, Prothonotary Warblers, and Lark Sparrows. Though much of the site is closed to the public, plenty of accessible areas exist so that a birder can spend an entire day adding new species.

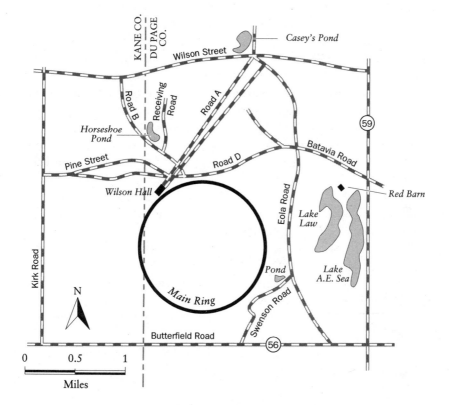

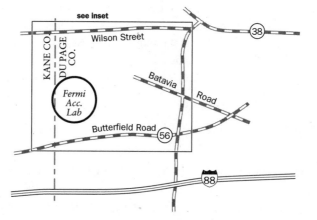

If you limit your birding to the areas described here, you should encounter no problems with Fermilab security. However, be careful not to enter the restricted areas without permission. Before birding you may wish to check with the Site Security office in the basement of Wilson Hall.

In any season, start with the lakes on the east side of Fermilab. To reach these lakes from the main entrance, drive east on Pine Street past the turnoff to Wilson Hall, a tall building. The road name then changes to Road D, which takes you past the bison pasture to the intersection of Batavia and Eola Roads. Drive east on Batavia Road past two lakes. You can park by the red barn on Sauk Drive, just south of a stop sign. Two trails lead to the lakes and grasslands. In winter search for Long-eared Owls and Red-breasted Nuthatches in the nearby pines off the first trail near the red barn. In early spring and late fall, use a scope to view the migrating waterfowl, loons, and grebes on the two lakes. You have an excellent chance of seeing nearly all inland duck species that migrate along the Mississippi Flyway, including Canvasbacks and Redheads. Shorebirds also congregate in shallow areas. Scan the shorelines carefully. You may discover a Pectoral Sandpiper or a Black-bellied Plover in the appropriate season.

Check the hedgerow at the south end of Lake Law for unusual sparrows in middle to late fall, including Harris's, LeConte's, or Nelson's Sharp-tailed. Look for various terns, including Caspian and Black, and listen in spring and early summer for Virginia Rails, Soras, and Marsh Wrens.

Nearby grasslands provide breeding habitat for Bobolinks, Grasshopper Sparrows, and sometimes Dickcissel.

At the intersection of Batavia Road and Eola Road, grasslands attract Northern Harriers and Short-eared Owls in winter. The harriers scope the grasslands by day, the owls come at dusk.

For shorebirds and waterfowl, check the fields along Eola Road when spring is particularly wet. Ephemeral ponds here have attracted Wilson's Phalaropes and other unusual shorebirds as well as Bonaparte's Gulls. Also check the permanent pond at the intersection of Eola and Swenson Roads for gulls and ducks.

Your best chance at finding a Northern Shrike in winter at Fermilab is to scout the scrubby areas near Casey's Pond where Eola Road ends at Wilson Street and Road A.

In spring park at Wilson Hall and walk to the oak woodlands northwest, searching for migrating warblers. Even better for warblers is Horseshoe Pond at the intersection of Receiving Road and Road B.

General information: Farmers living in a small village called Weston once owned the land that is now Fermilab. In the 1960s, the state of Illinois purchased the land and then donated it to the federal government for particle physics research. Today Fermilab, funded by the U.S. Department of Energy, houses the world's highest energy particle accelerator called the Tevatron. Volunteers have been restoring hundreds of acres on site to native prairies and savanna that provide a home to 45 reintroduced bison. In 1989 the Department of Energy designated Fermilab as one of six National Environmental Research Parks, permanent laboratories available for studying ecological issues.

The only facilities available are at Wilson Hall, open to the public every day from 8:30 A.M to 5:30 P.M. Visitor gate passes are available from 6 A.M. to 8 P.M. for birders who want to get an early start or search for owls at dusk. Observe off-limit signs and obey the instructions of the security officers.

ADDITIONAL HELP

DeLorme IA&G grid: 28.
Contact: Fermilab National Accelerator Laboratory.
Nearest gas, food, and lodging: Batavia. Restrooms are inside Wilson Hall when it's open.

The Palos Preserves, Sites 20–26: Birders have documented more than 290 species at the 14,000-acre Palos Preserves complex of woods, sloughs, and lakes, carved thousands of years ago by the advance and retreat of glaciers.

The Forest Preserve District of Cook County maintains 150 miles of trails in these preserves, more than 80 percent of which have been kept in a wild or semi-wild state. The preserves contain 87 miles of shoreline along rivers, creeks, ponds, lakes, sloughs, and many woodlands. They exist mostly in Palos Township, which encompasses the communities of Orland Park, Palos Park, Palos Hills, and Palos Heights. Most birders consider the Palos Preserves to include the holdings from Archer Avenue south to 143rd Street and from 86th Avenue west to Bell Road.

What follows are the most productive birding areas within these boundaries. You certainly cannot explore all of them in one day, and though many birders spend a great deal of time in the Preserves, not one of them has yet covered every square mile. Choose your spots based on the season and the birds you'd like to see.

Birders recommend that you call the Forest Preserve office to obtain a map of the Palos and Sag Valley Divisions before embarking on your birding.

The woodlands, which are located close enough to visit in one or two days, come first, followed by several sloughs that attract waterfowl in early spring and late fall.

▮**20** Conkey Woods

Habitats: Wooded creek.
Key birds: Migrating songbirds, including Winter Wren, and at least 29 species of warblers; breeding Broad-winged Hawk, Belted Kingfisher, and Red-headed Woodpecker.
Best times to bird: Late April and May.

20 Conkey Woods

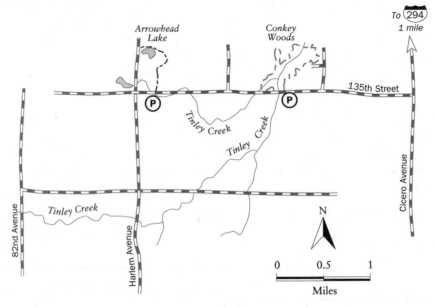

Directions: From Interstate 294, exit at Cicero Avenue. Go south 1 mile to 135th Street, and west 1 mile to the parking lot.

Birding: One May morning after an evening of southeast winds, several years ago, a birder discovered 29 species of warblers at Conkey Woods. Since then other locals have discovered this 20-acre migratory hotspot. The trails, if you can call them that, are quite muddy, but it's worth a stop if you're on a quest to find warblers, vireos, tanagers, and other songbirds in spring. Wear boots and be prepared for mosquitos and occasional poison ivy.

Begin at the parking lot where you might hear phoebes and gnatcatchers singing in late April immediately after you get out of your car. Tinley Creek flows through here, attracting migratory songbirds April through early June, and again in September. During breeding season, check the muddy embankments for a Belted Kingfisher. This species carves a hole into a bank in which to build a nest.

Then take what's locally know as the Girl Scout Trails. These are actually muddy, narrow pseudo-trails. Listen for singing Winter Wrens in late March and early April, as well as the two-syllable shriek of the Broad-winged Hawk, which has bred in these woods. In early April, birders discovered 150 Golden-crowned Kinglets, 70 Brown Creepers, and 11 Winter Wrens just by walking along the creek. Other species you might find include Wood Ducks, Green Herons, and Great Blue Herons. In early May you could encounter at least one huge pocket of warblers. Downy, Hairy, Red-headed, and Red-bellied Woodpeckers as well as Northern Flickers have bred here.

Tinley Creek meanders through the woods, then west to meet some small lakes and ponds in several other forest preserves. If you want to search for migrating ducks, you can continue west on 135th Street past Conkey Woods about half a mile to the Arrowhead Lake parking lot. A bicycle trail that goes west and then north takes you through woods and past the small lakes for additional birding. You can walk for quite a while here, so be prepared with hiking essentials.

General information: The Forest Preserve District of Cook County named this woods in the early 1900s to commemorate Elizabeth A. Conkey, a member of the board of commissioners. You'll find picnic facilities and metal pit toilets here. Call the Forest Preserve District to obtain a free Tinley Creek Division map.

Red-headed Woodpeckers breed at Conkey Woods.
PETER WEBER PHOTO

ADDITIONAL HELP

DeLorme IA&G grid: 29.
Contact: Forest Preserve District of Cook County.
Nearest gas, food, and lodging: Crestwood.

21 McClaughry Springs Woods

> **Habitats:** Woods, hilly terrain, and creeks.
> **Key birds:** Migratory and breeding songbirds; breeding Cooper's Hawk, Yellow-billed Cuckoo, and Barred Owl.
> **Best times to bird:** April through June.

Directions: From Interstate 55, exit at LaGrange Road (U.S. Highway 45). Go south 2.5 miles to Illinois Highway 83. Drive east 0.5 mile to Kean Avenue. Turn south and proceed 0.5 mile to the entrance, which is just before a bridge over the creek.

Birding: Local birders consider McClaughry Springs one of the Palos Preserves' premier birding sites during spring and fall migration. Birders have reported more than 120 species at this 250-acre preserve. Immediately as you exit your car from

21 McClaughry Springs Woods
23 Swallow Cliff Woods
24 Camp Sagawau
25 Saganashkee Slough

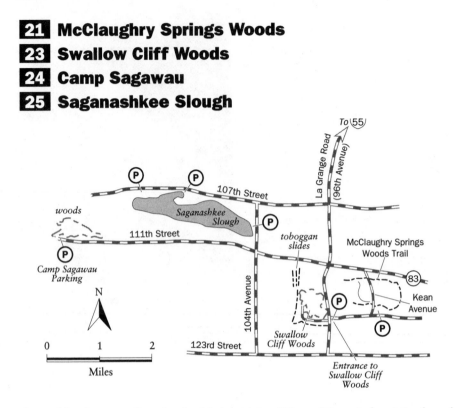

the parking lot, start listening for birds: singing Winter Wrens in late March and early April, Blue-gray Gnatcatchers in April, abundant warbler species in May, and Louisiana Waterthrushes, Scarlet Tanagers, and Tufted Titmice during May and June. Within the past three years, a Ruby-throated Hummingbird bred near the parking lot. Walk to Mill Creek near the parking lot to see these birds before embarking on the several miles of trails situated among hilly terrain. To see the most variety, walk the trail along the creek leading up a hill. Be prepared for a steep climb as well as mud and mosquitos.

As you walk along Mill Creek, you might hear 10 or more Winter Wrens singing in early April or view at least 21 species of warblers in May. Also listen for Louisiana Waterthrushes singing through June. As you walk up the hill, listen for calling Barred Owls, which have raised young in a tree overlooking the trail. Birders often get nice looks at the downy young when they are nearly ready to fledge.

Once you reach higher ground, listen for Yellow-billed Cuckoos, Cooper's Hawks, and woodpeckers, which breed here. Birders sometimes find the rarer warbler species during migration, including Hooded and Kentucky Warblers. Both species tend to be ventriloquial; be patient and stay on the trails. If the birds are there and you wait long enough, you should get nice views of them.

General information: The natural, cold, clear springs bubbling from areas such as this one attracted home-brewers during Prohibition, where they filled their jugs with water to make spirits. Though this and other preserves were marred by these activities as well as nearby dynamite blasting to widen the Calumet–Sag Canal, McClaughry Springs still attracts birds to its gentle, flowing waters.

ADDITIONAL HELP

DeLorme IA&G grid: 29.
Contact: Forest Preserve District of Cook County.
Nearest gas, food, and lodging: Hickory Hills or Palos Park.

22 Little Red Schoolhouse Nature Center and Nearby Sloughs

Habitats: Slough, fields, and woods.
Key birds: Migrating and breeding waterfowl, hawks, and songbirds.
Best times to bird: March through June and September through November.

Directions: From Interstate 55, exit LaGrange Road south 2 miles to 95th Street. Drive west 1 mile to the next stop sign, which is 104th Avenue or Willow Springs Road. Proceed south less than 1 mile to the parking lot. Buttonbush Slough is at the southwest corner of 95th Street and LaGrange Road. To get to Cranberry Slough, enter the Country Lane Woods parking lot on 95th Street, west of LaGrange Road. Take the trail southeast to the slough.

Birding: Birders confirmed 86 breeding species, including both cuckoos, Cooper's and Broad-winged Hawks, Hooded Mergansers, Blue-winged, Yellow, and Prothonotary Warblers, Cliff and Barn Swallows, and Orchard and Baltimore Orioles at this site.

An additional 15 species may also breed here, including Whip-poor-will, that often sing well into summer. On the right day in June, you might count nearly 100 species, and on the right day in May you should definitely make that your goal.

Start your birding in the parking lot, listening for the interesting catbird-like call of the Orchard Oriole, which has nested in the shrubby areas nearby. Then walk to Long John Slough behind the nature center. Search here for migrating puddle ducks, including American Black Ducks in spring and fall. You may also find Common Snipes and American Woodcocks in March and April. When water levels are sufficient, you may find Ruddy Ducks and Hooded Mergansers during breeding season. A Yellow-breasted Chat wintered near the beehives recently. Look near the orchard area, near the beehives or the open field immediately west of there in scattered trees and shrubs for nesting Orchard Orioles.

For migrants and breeders, walk the Farm Pond Trail that leads to the Black Oak Trail. As you walk past a pond and into a rather wooded area, search for migrating songbirds including Connecticut and Mourning Warblers, in middle to

22 Little Red Schoolhouse Nature Center and Nearby Sloughs

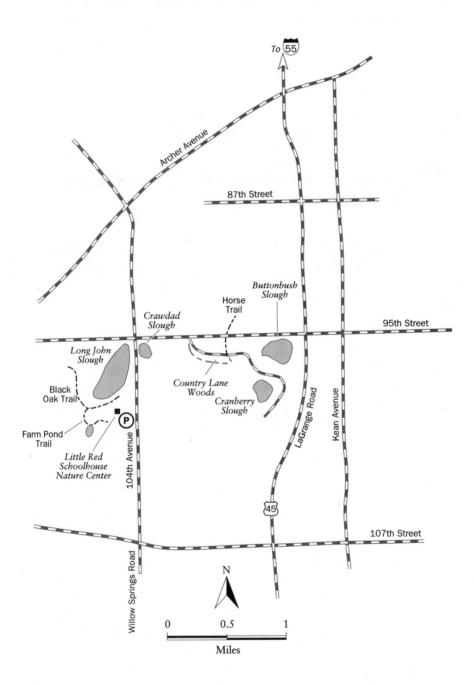

late May. Some birders consider this area to be one of the best places in northern Illinois for songbird migration in spring.

You'll soon reach a pond where a Pied-billed Grebe once fledged at least 10 young. The nearby brambles attract Winter Wrens in April.

Farther afield you'll enter what is locally known as the Nursery. Many breeding species use this area, including Marsh Wrens and Soras in the cattails, Sedge Wrens and Swamp Sparrows in the wet fields, and a host of edge and field birds, including Eastern Bluebirds, Cedar Waxwings, Field Sparrows, and Brown Thrashers. Look overhead for: Cooper's, Sharp-shinned, and Broad-winged Hawks; American Kestrels, and Turkey Vultures fly over during migration. All these except for the Sharp-shinned breed nearby; you may see one of them hunting here in mid-morning in May and June. Continue walking to a wooded area where the Wood Thrush often sings through May and June, and where you may encounter Cooper's Hawks.

In March and April you may want to stop at nearby Buttonbush and Cranberry Sloughs, where hordes of swallows snatch insects, and wading birds and dabbling ducks stop to feed.

Park at the 95th Street pull-out. You'll need a scope to search in March and April for migrating waterfowl. Egrets and herons visit these sloughs in late summer; shovelers, teals, and wigeons, in fall. Birders even discovered an Eurasian Wigeon, an Illinois rarity, here. Skeins of swallows are attracted to the slough in April, and Eastern Bluebirds have nested in natural cavity holes.

Soras breed regularly at Cranberry and Buttonbush Sloughs. Several birders confirmed breeding Whip-poor-wills at Cranberry Slough by finding two fledglings. Sandhill Cranes have also successfully bred at Cranberry Slough. Look for their return in April.

General information: A one-room log cabin served as a school for area children of local farmers 100 years ago. Today this cabin serves as a nature center for the Forest Preserve District of Cook County, as well as an entry point for birders who enjoy this site because of its diverse habitat. The nature center features special events, programs on falcons and other birds, and bird walks, including a morning owl prowl in winter. Free early morning bird walks are scheduled at 7 A.M. on Saturdays beginning in mid-April through the end of May. You can picnic here, too. Times and events can change, so call before coming.

ADDITIONAL HELP

DeLorme IA&G grid: 29.
Contact: Little Red Schoolhouse Nature Center.
Nearest gas, food, and lodging: Hickory Hills and Willow Springs.

23 Swallow Cliff Woods

See map on page 94

Habitats: Woods, savanna, and fields.
Key birds: Migrating and breeding songbirds, including woodpeckers, Great Crested Flycatcher, and Summer Tanager; wintering finches.
Best times to bird: Year-round, but especially in May and June.

Directions: Exit Interstate 55 at LaGrange Road. Travel south about 5 miles (past the toboggan slides) to the entrance, just north of 123rd Street. Several entrances exist for the preserve. This one is the southernmost entrance and provides access to all the trails.

Birding: Start at the parking lot of the southern entrance. Check the pines in winter for Pine Siskins, Red-breasted Nuthatches and winter finches. In spring and summer listen for the breeding songs of Indigo Buntings, catbirds, thrashers, and towhees at shrubby edges. Enter the savanna woodlands to listen for breeding Eastern Wood-Pewees, Great Crested Flycatchers, and Red-eyed Vireos. A loop trail here also reveals copious migrating warblers, tanagers, and flycatchers. Birders found a Yellow-throated Warbler here for four weeks one spring; this species could breed here.

For the Summer Tanager, take the long, steep climb up the north trail to the toboggan slide. The walk is about 2 city blocks long. Listen for Hairy and Red-bellied Woodpeckers year-round, and when you reach the top, hope for a reward of a Summer Tanager. Additionally, the Hooded Warbler has bred here.

General information: The Forest Preserve District is restoring savanna here and some birders fear that will reduce the habitat of their favorite species. The restoration is designed to provide a more viable ecosystem where some of the most rapidly declining birds in the Midwest, including Red-headed Woodpeckers and Great Crested Flycatchers can successfully raise young.

ADDITIONAL HELP

DeLorme IA&G grid: 29.
Contact: Forest Preserve District of Cook County.
Nearest gas, food, and lodging: Orland Park.

The Summer Tanager is a breeding specialty at Swallow Cliff Woods.
DENNIS OEHMKE PHOTO

See map on page 94

Habitats: Rock canyon and ravines.
Key birds: Migratory songbirds; breeding Louisiana Waterthrush.
Best times to bird: April through June.

Directions: Exit Interstate 55 at LaGrange Road (U.S. Highway 45). Travel south 5 miles to 111th Street. Drive west 4 miles to the entrance.

Birding: Walk along a creek at the bottom of a canyon at the 140-acre Camp Sagawau in Lemont on a spring day and you'll see luscious ferns growing along rock formations as warblers feed on the abundant insects. You can visit this rare treasure only by attending guided walks, many of which are free. More than 100 species of birds have been documented here at the only canyon in Cook County.

Typically naturalists lead two-hour bird hikes beginning at 7:30 A.M. Wednesday, Friday, Saturday, and Sunday from mid-April through May and on Saturday and Sunday in June. Often, you can just arrive at the site, park, and meet the leader, but since times and events change, you should call first before planning your trip. Since this is the lowest and wettest place in the Palos Preserves area, it also attracts the most mosquitos. Some of the rocky areas can be slippery. Wear appropriate shoes and clothing.

Go in April to see the early songbird migrants such as Winter Wrens and Hermit Thrushes. In May, particularly in the first and second weeks, you may see 20 or more species of warblers and many flycatchers. In early May, you'll probably find catbirds, House Wrens, White-throated, White-crowned, and Lincoln's Sparrows, as well as Northern Waterthrushes. You also have a good chance of finding a Black-throated Blue Warbler in early to mid-May and a Connecticut Warbler in middle to late May. In early June some migrants linger while the breeders are beginning their nest building. This is when you might hear singing Louisiana Waterthrushes at the bottom of the canyon.

General information: The Young Women's Christian Association of Chicago used the area that is Camp Sagawau for many years as a vacation and rest camp. These women left the preserve fairly well intact. The Forest Preserve purchased Camp Sagawau in 1952, vowing to maintain it as a geological and ecological museum. The preserve harbors species of ferns found nowhere else in the state. Because of the special nature of this preserve, the public cannot enter except during guided walks. A small nature center with nice restroom facilities is open periodically until about 3 P.M. on weekdays and sometimes on weekends when walks are led. Naturalist-led hikes include those pertaining to geology, fossils, butterflies, plants, birds, and other animals.

ADDITIONAL HELP

DeLorme IA&G grid: 29.
Contact: Camp Sagawau.
Nearest gas, food, and lodging: Palos Park and Hickory Hills.

25 Saganashkee Slough

See map on page 94

Habitats: Shallow edges and a large deep lake.
Key birds: Migrating waterfowl, including all three mergansers (spring or fall), and gulls.
Best times to bird: March and April, October and November.

Directions: From Interstate 55, exit LaGrange Road (U.S. Highway 45) and drive south 3 miles to 95th Street, then 1 mile west to 104th Avenue (Willow Springs Road). Drive south another 1.5 miles to a parking lot. Two other parking lots are west on 107th Street.

Birding: This large lake, not really a slough, attracts many ducks, fishermen, and birders. Nearly every dabbler and diver known to have occurred in Illinois have been recorded here. Birders have seen 19 species of ducks at the slough on a single day in fall. It's one of the most dependable spots in the Chicago area for seeing western duck species such as Canvasbacks and Northern Pintails. Birders found 47 Common Loons one October. Another time, 100 Franklin's Gulls sailed over the slough during fall migration at dusk. In addition, birders have documented 100 breeding bird species at the slough and bordering trees and shrubs.

To view ducks, park in 104th Avenue lot. The birding is easier in the mornings here when the sun is at your back. Take a scope to check for grebes, ducks, and other waterfowl in fall and spring. On a mid-March day you might find American Black Ducks, Northern Shovelers, Gadwalls, Common Goldeneyes, Hooded Mergansers, Ruddy Ducks, and courting Common Mergansers. Birders have the best chance of seeing Hooded Mergansers here in November.

In July you might see Black Terns snatching insects from the slough and immature Little Blue Herons and Snowy Egrets fishing from a stump. In late summer, look for cormorants drying their wings on some of the stumps, and herons and egrets feeding along the shorelines. If water levels are low, you may also enjoy birding along the slough's edges in late July and September. During the breeding season, you'll probably see Cliff Swallows feeding over the water. These birds nest beneath a bridge on 104th Avenue. Birders found 12 active nests on the east and west sides of the bridge in 1998.

You can also walk to a crude mile-long path along the southern edge of the slough. If you walk along the path in early summer, you may hear American Redstarts, Blue-gray Gnatcatchers, and Yellow-billed Cuckoos. Also watch along the shoreline for Spotted Sandpipers.

At the two 107th Street parking lots, look for breeding American Redstarts, Blue-gray Gnatcatchers, and Orchard Orioles. Check the shrubby areas for breeding Yellow-throated Vireos and Yellow Warblers.

Look for Bald Eagles in March and again in the fall, roosting anywhere in the trees on the south end of the slough. Also watch for Turkey Vultures overhead spring through fall.

General information: Saganashkee Slough was once a series of marshes and intermittent ponds that often became dry in summer. During the Great Depression of the 1930s, the Civilian Conservation Corps created dams and spillways at these sloughs. Saganashkee Slough may have been named after a Native American term, Ausagaunashkee, which meant slush of the earth.

ADDITIONAL HELP

DeLorme IA&G grid: 29.
Contact: Forest Preserve District of Cook County.
Nearest gas, food, and lodging: Hickory Hills and Willow Springs.

26 McGinnis Slough

Habitats: Lake, shoreline, and shrubby edges.
Key birds: Migrating ducks and shorebirds; breeding Pied-billed Grebe and Common Moorhen; postbreeding Little Blue Heron.
Best times to bird: Early spring, late summer, and late fall.

Directions: From Interstate 55, exit LaGrange Road (U.S. Highway 45). Go south 7 miles to just past 135th Street, where you'll find a parking area on the west side of the road.

Birding: One fall day 3,000 American Coots, 300 Ruddy Ducks, 100 Buffleheads, and 350 Double-crested Cormorants rested on the waters of 315-acre McGinnis Slough. Changing water levels attract migrating shorebirds, including some rare Illinois visitors. Confirmed breeders include the Pied-billed Grebe, Common Moorhen, Green Heron, and Yellow-breasted Chat, among 80 others. Migrating rarities have included Red-throated Loons, American White Pelicans, Greater White-fronted Geese, and Oldsquaws, a difficult water bird to find inland.

The best time to come is early in the morning.

Survey the slough, which looks like a large oblong lake, for ducks in March or October through November. In early spring look for all three species of mergansers, plus many other dabbling and diving ducks, including shovelers and Green-winged Teals. In late summer through fall immature Little Blue Herons in their white phase congregate. Look carefully at the small white heron-like birds; some may be Little Blues, others may be Snowy Egrets. Though difficult to distinguish, the Little Blues often have two-tone bills, and the Snowy Egrets have yellow feet and yellow lores. Use your bird identification books to help separate these two species during late summer. Neither of the species breeds here, but the young tend to disperse to other feeding areas in August and September.

In fall hundreds of Great Egrets sit in trees, taking their turns to pluck food from the waters. In April and May listen for the call of the Least Bittern and other breeding marsh birds.

26 McGinnis Slough

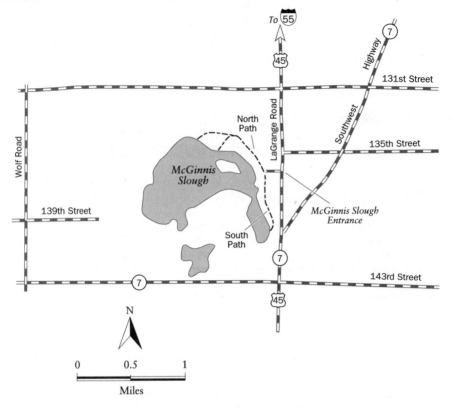

Next, walk the grassy path north to see the slough from another vantage point. Bring your scope. Along the way, look for numerous warblers and other songbirds during spring and fall migration. In breeding season, listen for singing Indigo Buntings and other edge dwellers.

When you reach the water's edge, if the water levels are right you may get close views of migrating shorebirds, including nice looks at Pectoral Sandpipers, sometimes numbering in the hundreds, and both yellowlegs, as well as an occasional view of the more unusual shorebirds seen here, including White-rumped, Baird's, and Stilt Sandpipers. Local birders have also recorded the rare Red-necked Phalarope and American Avocet, a western species.

General information: Another manmade slough, McGinnis once teemed with aquatic vegetation, including sedges and cattails that attracted migrating ducks and geese. Today the slough contains deeper water and fewer plants. The bird life here may be different than what was historically present, but the area still attracts abundant waterfowl and birders before the fishermen return in droves in spring.

ADDITIONAL HELP

DeLorme IA&G grid: 29.

Contact: Forest Preserve District of Cook County.

Nearest gas, food, and lodging: Palos Park.

27 The Bartel and Orland Grasslands

Habitats: Expansive grasslands, shrubby edges, and ponds.
Key birds: Breeders, including Marsh and Sedge Wrens, Brown
Thrasher, Common Yellowthroat, and Bobolink; Henslow's, Vesper, and
Grasshopper Sparrows; Eastern Meadowlark, Dickcissel, and Baltimore
and Orchard Orioles.
Best times to bird: Mid-May through mid-July, and winter.

Directions: The Bartel Grasslands, encompassing 3 square miles, is bordered on
the west by Ridgeland Avenue, the east by Central Avenue, the south by Vollmer
Road, and the north by Flossmoor Road. You can reach the grasslands via Interstate 57. Exit at Vollmer Road going west about a quarter mile to Central Avenue.
Go north about half a mile to Flossmoor Road. Turn left (or west) about a quarter
mile to the entrance to the Model Airplane Flying Field parking lot on the north
side of the road. The Bartel Grasslands is on the south side of Flossmoor Road,
but you'll find no sign denoting this as such.

To reach the Orland Grasslands from I-80 and U.S. Highway 45 (LaGrange
Road) south of Orland Hills, go north on US 45 1 mile to 179th Street, then west
1 mile to 104th Avenue. Turn south and park alongside 104th Avenue. The only
sign you may find for this grasslands is a small marker indicating that it is a forest
preserve.

Birding: If you love the Bobolink, visit the Bartel Grasslands in June. You'll likely
find 100 or more of this black-bellied, white-backed blackbird here, a species that
looks as if it were wearing a reverse tuxedo. You can easily observe the fascinating
behavior of this species.

Watch as several males pursue a female, singing as they fly just above your
head. Singing on the wing is a common grassland breeding behavior.

Bartel and Orland Grasslands near Flossmoor and Orland Hills in southern
Cook County together encompass more than 4 square miles. Here the grassland
bird lover can study and enjoy the songs and behaviors of Bobolinks, meadowlarks, and a host of sparrows as well as Common Yellowthroats, Brown Thrashers, Gray Catbirds, Eastern Towhees, and Baltimore and Orchard Orioles.

Birders have confirmed 33 breeding species at the Bartel Grasslands, including
the Bobolink, Grasshopper, Savannah, Henslow's, Field, and Song Sparrows, and
Eastern Meadowlarks. At the nearby Orland Grasslands, birders confirmed 44
breeding species, including Black-billed and Yellow-billed Cuckoos, Northern
Harriers, Sedge and Marsh Wrens, and Dickcissels. Vesper Sparrow and Ring-necked

27 The Bartel and Orland Grasslands

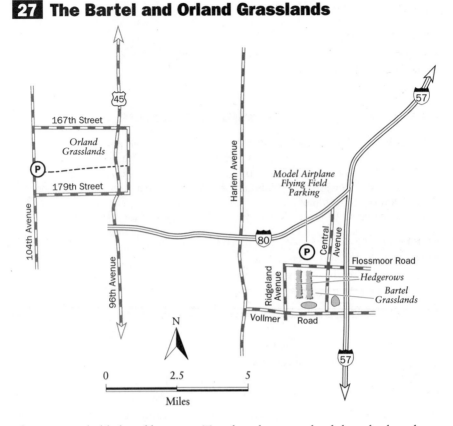

Pheasants probably breed here, too. Together, these grasslands have harbored more than 100 species of birds.

You can visit both places in a half day to enjoy many of the state's grassland breeders. Take a compass, water, and hiking boots.

Start your birding excursion at these grasslands early in the morning in late May or throughout June. Begin at the Model Airplane Flying Field, where you'll likely hear the *"see-you-see-see-you"* call of the Eastern Meadowlark and other more common grassland birds.

Then walk across Flossmoor Road and into the main grasslands. You'll see a "closed" sign hanging from two small iron posts; that's meant for automobiles. You can walk through the grasslands to your heart's content.

Walking west on an early summer morning, you will notice the changing grass heights and the variation of species. Savannah Sparrows prefer the shorter grasses and are more numerous here than at the Orland Grasslands. Bobolinks are often ubiquitous here in June. Continue west toward the edge of the property where a stand of woods exists. In front of these woods in the grasses you may find Henslow's Sparrows; this is the best spot for them. On your way back, walk along the shrubby areas to search for edge birds such as towhees, catbirds, and yellowthroats.

Brown Thrashers breed at the Orland Grasslands. DENNIS OEHMKE PHOTO

Grasslands change and bird life can be somewhat transient here.

The nearby Orland Grasslands is about half the size and takes less time to explore. Grasshopper Sparrows can be abundant here during right conditions, and depending on grass height and moisture, Henslow's Sparrows may also breed here.

An old concrete road slowly being filled by vegetation is a straight, fairly easy walk east through the grasslands. Follow this path to listen for meadowlarks, Bobolinks, and other birds. To find the Henslow's and get nice views of Grasshopper Sparrows, you may have to leave the makeshift trail and walk through the wet fields. Listen for the *"tslick"* call of the Henslow's and the insect-like trill of the Grasshopper Sparrow. You'll notice compass plants growing here and other grassland forbs that get quite tall in late July through September. These grasses tend to be taller compared with the Bartel Grasslands. Accordingly, you'll find a different complement of grassland species. Be careful as you walk not to disturb nest sites.

Before you leave, explore the shrubby edges and wetter areas for breeding Orchard Orioles, Brown Thrashers, Common Yellowthroats, and other species. A mid-June visit can yield dozens of young thrashers and yellowthroats begging for food.

General information: The Forest Preserve District of Cook County owns and manages the grasslands as natural habitats. Birders named this area after a beloved bird bander, Karl Bartel, who passed away several years ago. No picnicking is allowed, and only one outdoor restroom is available at the Model Airplane Flying Field. Check for ticks after you're done, and be prepared for tall, wet grasses and hot sun.

ADDITIONAL HELP

DeLorme IA&G grid: 29.
Contact: Cook County Forest Preserve District and the Chicago Audubon Society.
Nearest gas, food, and lodging: Orland Park.

28 Lake Calumet and Vicinity

Habitats: Marshes, lakes, and prairie.

Key birds: Large breeding colony of Black-crowned Night-Heron; breeding Least Bittern, Great Egret, Yellow-crowned Night-Heron, Common Moorhen, Sora, Virginia Rail, and Yellow-headed Blackbird; breeding colony of Ring-billed and Herring Gulls; migrating shorebirds in late summer and early fall; winter gulls.

Best times to bird: Late April through mid-June (Big Marsh, Indian Ridge Marsh, Hegewisch Marsh, and Powderhorn Marsh) July into mid-September (Deadstick Pond); December through February (Thomas J. O'Brien Lock and Dam).

Directions: You can access the Lake Calumet area from either 103rd Street or 130th Street off Interstate 94 on Chicago's far south side. Then follow the directions below to the specific sites.

Birding: The Lake Calumet region hosts one of the state's largest number of breeding Black-crowned Night-Herons. These and other endangered wetland species such as the Common Moorhen live tenaciously at this huge wetland complex surrounded by industry, a landfill, and a sewage treatment plant. More than 200 species of birds live or migrate through the Lake Calumet region, including 30 species of shorebirds and 25 state-listed endangered species. Birders have confirmed breeding for 72 birds and have documented an additional 33 birds that probably breed here.

You won't find this a picturesque place to bird. It has odorous landfills and industrial corridors, and some of the best birding areas are on private property. Nonetheless, it's a great place to bird if you're careful.

For those unfamiliar with the area, the best way to bird the region is by attending one of the many bird walks led by local organizations such as the Chicago Audubon Society and the Chicago Ornithological Society.

The following areas have been named by the local birders; you won't find markers indicating these spots. In some cases, you'll park along roadsides. Take care not to venture into areas marked private or no trespassing. Bring a scope, boots, and other appropriate clothing.

Private marsh tour—roadside viewing. Follow this route in spring through early summer and again in late July through mid-September to enjoy breeding wetland birds and migrating shorebirds and ducks.

Start at the 116th Street and Indian Ridge Marshes. From the 103rd Street exit off I-94, go east to Torrence Avenue, then south to 116th Street. Turn west and park alongside the road. The 116th Street Marsh is to the south. Check here for spring migrating shorebirds, including Dunlins and Stilt Sandpipers (when water levels are sufficiently low). At dawn or dusk, listen for calling Virginia Rails and Soras in spring and early summer.

Get back on Torrence Avenue, go south to 122nd Street, then go west for 0.25 mile. Park east of the railroad tracks. Look to the north at Indian Ridge Marsh

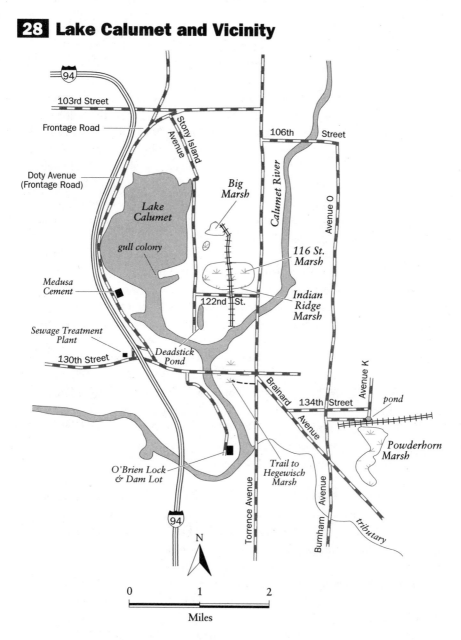

Lake Calumet and Vicinity map showing I-94, 103rd Street, Frontage Road, Stony Island Avenue, Doty Avenue (Frontage Road), Lake Calumet, gull colony, Big Marsh, Calumet River, 106th Street, Avenue O, 116 St. Marsh, Medusa Cement, Indian Ridge Marsh, 122nd St., Sewage Treatment Plant, Deadstick Pond, 130th Street, Avenue K, Brainard Avenue, 134th Street, pond, Powderhorn Marsh, O'Brien Lock & Dam Lot, Trail to Hegewisch Marsh, Torrence Avenue, Burnham Avenue, tributary, N, 0 1 2 Miles

into the cottonwood trees for postbreeding Black-crowned Night-Herons and Great Egrets in late summer. Yellow-headed Blackbirds and Common Moorhens have also bred here. You may find families of moorhens in late August. If you like enormous flocks of blackbirds, stop here in late fall when up to 18,000 starlings and Red-winged Blackbirds roost at night.

Next take 122nd Street west to Stony Island Avenue to visit Deadstick Pond, which is on the east side of Stony Island Avenue just south of 122nd Street. Park on the roadside; the pond is right there, although tall phragmites often block the view. Look for ducks, shorebirds, herons, and egrets, depending on the season and water levels. During spring migration, especially in March and April, you'll find many species of ducks, including Ring-necked, Bufflehead, Common Goldeneye, Lesser Scaup, Ruddy Duck, Redhead, Gadwall, and others. In late summer and early fall, birders have seen 23 species of shorebirds, including the Stilt Sandpiper and Wilson's Phalarope. On a late August day in 1998, birders recorded Buff-breasted, White-rumped, Western (very unusual for Illinois), Least, and Semipalmated Sandpipers, both yellowlegs, Wilson's Phalaropes, Short-billed Dowitchers, immature Little Blue Herons, Great Egrets, Great Blue Herons, Black-crowned Night-Herons, Semipalmated Plovers, Killdeers, Virginia Rails, and Soras.

About 1 mile north of Deadstick Pond on Stony Island Avenue is Big Marsh, considered one of the premiere birding spots of the Lake Calumet area. Park along the roadside. The marsh is on the east. Hundreds of Black-crowned Night-Herons have bred in the southeast part of the marsh. They return, along with other wetland breeders in middle to late April. You can often find them here loafing and feeding in nearby marshes and ponds throughout summer. The rookery sometimes contains about 400 nests, which aren't easily visible. However, at dusk you can see quite a few flying in the area to begin feeding. Be aware that the fluctuating water levels and other conditions have altered the breeding night-heron's habitat. For example, the night-herons did not breed at Big Marsh in 1999, but instead found a place inaccessible to birders to breed at Indian Ridge Marsh. Though they continue to nest in large numbers at this writing, their place here is tenuous.

You can also find migrating ducks in March and April, as well as some of the 23 species of shorebirds that feed and rest here in late summer and fall. The Big Marsh, owned by Waste Management, remains threatened by potential development.

Another privately owned marsh is Hegewisch Marsh. To get there, take 122nd Street east to Torrence Avenue, go south to the marsh, which is just past 130th Street. Park just south of the railroad tracks. Look for a gate on the west, then walk back into the marsh. You'll find this area somewhat more secluded than the other places described. Ruddy Ducks and Yellow-headed Blackbirds often breed here in summer. A pair of Redheads bred here once. More often you'll find breeding Pied-billed Grebes, Blue-winged Teals, and possibly shorebirds in July and August.

A huge colony of Ring-billed and Herring Gulls breed at Lake Calumet each year, numbering up to 12,000 pairs. To see the birds, park near the Medusa Cement Company gate, accessed by a frontage road. From 130th Street exit, go north onto the frontage road, east of I-94. Drive 1.8 miles to the Medusa Cement gate. Park and walk east to the gate; walk north to get to the lake's edge. Then look east across the lake, where you'll see the colony filled with thousands of birds breeding here from middle March into July. Please note that this is on private property; you will need permission to enter. Also, note that the colony is quite far from this vantage point. Bring a scope.

Also note the Metropolitan Chicago Water Reclamation District sewage treatment plant at 400 E. 130th Street, just west of I-94. Thousands of shorebirds feed in these mudflat ponds in late summer and fall, but you need permission to enter. Ask the guard at the gate if you can spend some time watching shorebirds. It's best to come in one car; large groups aren't permitted, and permission to enter is not guaranteed. If you are allowed inside, drive over the raised gravel hills to get to the ponds. Park on the gravel road and view the ponds below. On July 31, 1999, birders saw hundreds of shorebirds, including the following: 1 Buff-Breasted, 2 Baird's, 6 or more Semipalmated, 30 or more Least, 50 or more Pectoral, and many Spotted and Solitary Sandpipers as well as 2 Black-bellied Plovers. Rarities are always a possibility, and many have been recorded over the years.

Public Lands for Gulls and Marsh Birds. For winter gulls, visit the Thomas J. O'Brien Lock & Dam on the west side of the Calumet River. The entrance is off 130th Street, east of I-94 and west of Torrence Avenue. Search for Thayer's, Lesser Black-backed, and Glaucous Gulls on the landfill west of the entrance road. Restrooms are open during daylight hours. This is also a major swallow staging area in fall.

Nearby is the Powderhorn Lake Forest Preserve where Yellow-crowned Night-Herons have bred. Least Bitterns often breed here, too. You'll also find a nice prairie featuring meadowlarks, Savannah Sparrows, and other grassland breeders.

You have two choices, one which is the main parking lot, where birders say it is more difficult to find these birds, and another more circuitous route that sometimes is difficult to get into because of flooding.

1. Go east on 130th Street past Torrence Avenue to Brainard Avenue. Turn right (south) to the entrance, which is just past Avenue O. Brainard Avenue runs on an angle. Follow a grassy path north for about a mile, then listen for bitterns and watch for the herons in early morning from spring through summer.

2. Take Brainard Avenue southeast to 134th Street. Turn east and drive 1 mile past Avenue O to Avenue K. Turn south 2 blocks where Avenue O deadends at 136th Street. Park on the street. Follow the railroad tracks east just about a block to the second path that goes south along the lake toward the marshes. This path is difficult to negotiate.

General information: When the ice age glaciers began to retreat 12,000 years ago, they left behind a terrain ripe for the development of a relatively flat mosaic of wetlands in what is now Chicago. Shallow marshes and wet prairies spanning 22,500 acres thrived near the dunes, ridges, and shoreline at the south edge of Lake Michigan. Lake Calumet is a portion of the old Lake Chicago plain that developed after the last glacier retreated. When the industrial age arrived, the low-lying areas in the Calumet region were readily sacrificed and transformed to dumping grounds for industrial and municipal waste.

What's left today is a mere remnant of the area's ecological past, a maze of factories, landfills, and wetlands and prairies, much of it in private hands. Recognizing the need to protect these areas that held significant populations of rare breeding birds, local birders and environmentalists are working to preserve the remaining Lake Calumet marshes. They succeeded in halting the proposed Lake Calumet Airport, which would have destroyed or degraded hundreds of acres of wetlands and other natural areas, but their work is far from over.

Birding remains intriguing here, but the lands need to be protected if the Lake Calumet region is to continue providing habitat for some of the rarest avian species in the state.

This is a difficult place to bird for first-time visitors. You might wish to visit this area by attending one of the many guided walks.

ADDITIONAL HELP

DeLorme IA&G grid: 29.
Contact: Chicago Audubon Society.
Nearest gas, food, and lodging: Lansing, south of the Calumet region. Avoid the northern area.

29 Lake Renwick Heron Rookery Nature Preserve and Copley Nature Park

Habitats: Quarry lake with wooded islands and wooded shoreline.
Key birds: Breeding egrets, herons, and cormorants.
Best times to bird: May through July.

Directions: From Interstate 55, exit Route 30 and drive 1 mile northwest to Renwick Road. Turn right, driving 0.25 mile to the nature preserve entrance on the north side of the road.

Birding: On a sultry July day, hundreds of squawking young cormorants, herons, and egrets test their wings and their parents' patience on the protected islands in Lake Renwick at the state's largest most accessible heronry 35 miles south of Chicago. The Lake Renwick Rookery Nature Preserve, near the city of Plainfield, has been active since the 1960s, producing perhaps 1,000 or more young herons, egrets, and cormorants per year. Data from 1995 show this preserve provides 44 percent of the state's nesting areas for the Double-crested Cormorant, and nearly 100 percent for the Cattle Egret.

To provide peace for breeding herons and egrets, the preserve is open only from 8 A.M. to noon on Saturdays in May, June, July, and August, and on Wednesdays for a one-hour tour beginning at 10 A.M. Even with this limited schedule, you should be able to enjoy the birding here.

When you arrive, you will be able to study the interesting pattern in colonial breeders. Five species of birds breed at the rookery: Great Blue Heron, Great Egret,

29 Lake Renwick Heron Rookery Nature Preserve and Copley Nature Park

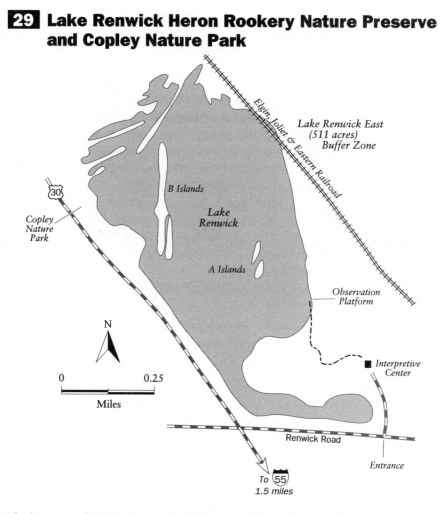

Black-crowned Night-Heron, Cattle Egret, and Double-crested Cormorant. These species occupy two colony areas within the nature preserve's boundary, the A islands, part of the original rookery site, and the B islands, the site of a more recent expansion. Within these areas these species form a rather predictable ordering of their apartment complex. Great Blue Herons and cormorants occupy the highest nest sites. Great Egrets build their nests midheight, and Black-crowned Night-Herons and Cattle Egrets remain low to the ground.

Populations at the site have changed dramatically. Great Blue Heron and cormorant numbers have increased, while the population of state-listed endangered Black-crowned Night-Herons has declined severely. Overcrowding at the A islands, plus natural loss of nesting trees, forced all five species to colonize the B islands, but these islands do not provide predator-proof nesting habitat. Land connections to the B islands have made mammalian predation a major problem for the ground nesters.

Double-crested Cormorants and Great Egrets at nest sites at Lake Renwick Heron Rookery Nature Preserve. JOE B. MILOSEVICH PHOTO

To solve this problem, the Forest Preserve District of Will County has purchased 511 acres adjacent to the preserve to provide nesting habitat. It also has installed more nesting platforms on the A islands, which these species readily use.

Either come during tour hours on Wednesdays and Saturdays when the forest preserve staff has set up scopes to enhance your viewing, or park along the gravel shoulder of Illinois Route 30. The highway is busy, so be careful, and do not climb over any fencing to view the birds.

You can also see a good variety of waterfowl from this stopover. Mostly you'll see teals, shovelers, and other common migrants, but this area has also produced its share of rarities, including Red-necked Grebes, White-winged Scoters, Snowy Egrets, and Little Blue Herons. Other rarities seen include Neotropic Cormorants, American White Pelicans, Tundra Swans, Greater White-fronted Geese, and Tri-colored Herons.

General information: In the late 1800s, the land that is now part of the Lake Renwick heronry was quarried for road gravel. Steamshovels unearthed fresh-water springs that filled the quarry with water. People swam here in 1914, and in winter used ice harvested from the lake to cool their refrigerators. By the mid-1940s, sewage runoff had polluted Lake Renwick so people could no longer use the lake. About a half-century ago, herons arrived. For seven years, birders and other conservationists battled to save this site from being developed. In 1990 the Forest Preserve District of Will County and the Illinois Department of Natural

Resources purchased the property to maintain habitat for nesting egrets and herons, including state-listed endangered species.

In August 1996, a real estate developer submitted a plan to the Board of Trustees of the village of Plainfield to build 21 townhomes on 3 acres just 200 yards west of the rookery. Local citizens, concerned for the future of the birds and their habitat, persuaded the developer to deter his plans while a campaign was mounted to create the Copley Nature Park on the land.

ADDITIONAL HELP

DeLorme IA&G grid: 28.
Contact: Forest Preserve District of Will County.
Nearest gas, food, and lodging: Plainfield.

30 Goose Lake Prairie and Heidecke Lake

Habitats: Native grasslands, wetlands, and power company cooling lake.
Key birds: Marsh and grassland and marsh breeders, including American Bittern, Common Snipe, King Rail, Henslow's and Grasshopper Sparrows, and Eastern Meadowlark; wintering ducks, gulls, and raptors, including Rough-legged Hawk, Short-eared Owl, and Northern Shrike.
Best times to bird: Late spring and early summer for prairie birds; late summer and fall for shorebirds; fall through early spring for gulls, ducks and other waterfowl; winter for raptors and shrikes.

Directions: From Interstate 55, exit at Lorenzo Road. Go west 3 miles and turn right at the Goose Lake Prairie entrance sign on Jugtown Road. Park in the lot by the visitor center. Do not park your car on Dresden or Lorenzo Road, or you may be ticketed by law enforcers.

Birding: Walk through this 2,370-acre grassland complex on an early summer's day and you should hear the fast, insistent *"tslick"* of the Henslow's Sparrow, the plaintive call of the Eastern Meadowlark, and possibly the low grunt of a King Rail. These birds and at least another 127 regularly visit the prairie, many of them breeders. Heidecke Lake, adjacent to the prairie, attracts gulls, shorebirds, and ducks—so the list approaches 200 when you combine these two areas.

Park at the Goose Lake Prairie Visitor Center and stop inside to obtain maps if it's open, then explore the well-marked 7 miles of trails. Stay on the trails to avoid being inundated with ticks and to avoid stepping on nests of ground-dwelling birds. If you want a closer look at these birds, bring a scope.

Tall Grass Nature Trail takes you through 3.5 miles of the largest stand of tallgrass prairie remaining in Illinois. You can feel the big bluestem, Indian grass, and switch grass, sway in the wind and smell the hot-buttered popcorn odor of the

30 Goose Lake Prairie and Heidecke Lake

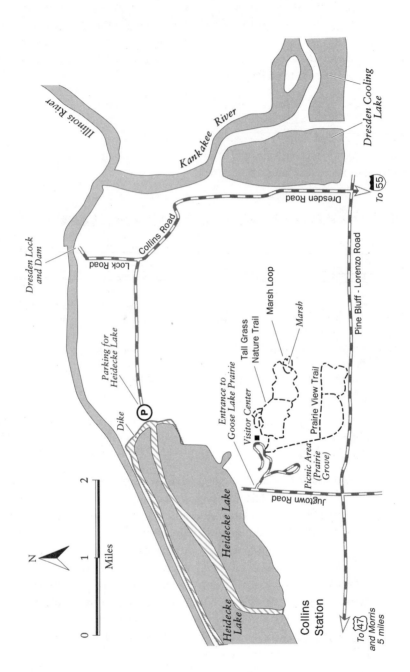

northern prairie drop seed. A 1-mile loop offers a hard-packed, barrier-free surface. You should find Eastern Meadowlarks as well as the ubiquitous Grasshopper Sparrow along this trail. Search for the rare Henslow's Sparrow in the dense, wet grassy areas.

Another favorite Henslow's Sparrow spot is the grasses where the Tallgrass and Marsh Loop Trails merge. The 0.5-mile Marsh Loop Trail takes you through the ponds and marshes that resulted when local farmers drained the lake in 1890. You'll find plenty of Red-winged Blackbirds, plus Belted Kingfishers, Great Blue Herons, Wood Ducks, Blue-winged Teals, and Mallards from spring through fall. In March and in October you may find many dabbling duck migrants, including Green-winged Teals and Northern Shovelers.

Check the fringes of the prairie potholes for King Rails and Common Snipes, which have bred here. Then check the cattail marsh for Soras, Virginia Rails, and American Bitterns, also documented as breeders. Look for Northern Harriers hovering over the wet fields from spring through fall.

In the wetter prairie areas, listen for Sedge Wrens singing—they are fairly common throughout the preserve. In spring and late summer the ponds and wet fields attract migrating Barn, Northern Rough-winged, and Tree Swallows.

Loggerhead Shrikes have bred near the prairie Grove Picnic Area and along Dresden Road. This species is more common the farther south you go in Illinois, and can be confused with the wintering Northern Shrike, so bring a field guide. Northern Mockingbirds have summered on Dresden Road, too. Check the Photo Blind Trail for Hooded Mergansers, which occasionally breed here.

Recent prairie restoration has removed much of the woody thickets and hedgerows that harbored Bell's Vireos, White-eyed Vireos, Orchard Orioles, and Yellow-breasted Chats on the preserve. But you may find these species along Dresden Road, which borders the northern boundary of Goose Lake Prairie and dead-ends into Heidecke Lake, a 2,000-acre cooling pond for Commonwealth Edison's Collins Station. The lake, which is managed by the state, offers fishing and hunting as well as good birding at certain times of the year.

Many areas are restricted, making this a difficult place to bird, but it is one of the best inland sites in the Chicago area to find species that typically remain along Lake Michigan. Sanderlings and Ruddy Turnstones regularly stop here during migration. Illinois birders love Buff-breasted Sandpipers, and this species often appears at Heidecke Lake from late August to early September. Birders have observed Oldsquaws, Sabine's Gulls, and Harlequin Ducks at this inland "pelagic" site.

Look for flocks of Bonaparte's Gulls in October; sometimes numbering in the hundreds. You should find teals, shovelers, mergansers, and other dabblers and divers at this lake in fall and spring. Large numbers of Common Mergansers, Mallards, and Common Goldeneyes regularly use the lake in winter. You may also find wintering gulls including Thayer's and Glaucous, as well as wintering Bald Eagles.

You'll pass the road to the Dresden Lock and Dam along the way. Turn north on Lock Road for a short distance to where it dead-ends at a visitor parking area.

Juvenile Buff-breasted Sandpiper at Heidecke Lake. JOE B. MILOSEVICH PHOTO

This facility has heated restrooms, which come in handy during the cold winters. Some of the winter birds you may see at the parking area include Thayer's Gulls, Iceland Gulls, and Bald Eagles.

Also check the Dresden Cooling Lake that parallels Lorenzo Road from the village of Lorenzo to Dresden Road. Look for Franklin's and Great Black-backed Gulls during migration. The extreme eastern end of the cooling lake once hosted a Ring-billed Gull colony. In winter, check the prairie and nearby fields to search for Short-eared Owls, Northern Harriers, Northern Shrikes, and Rough-legged Hawks. You should see the harriers during the day and the owls at dusk.

General information: Glaciers sculpted the land that is now Goose Lake State Natural Area, creating a relatively flat landscape and paving the way for the formation of the soils that harbored the various grasses and forbs indigenous to tallgrass prairie. At one time, nearly 60 percent of Illinois was covered with a mosaic of grasslands and wetlands. Bison, wolves, and prairie-chickens once roamed the land that is now Goose Lake Prairie. Native Americans hunted here and planted corn, squash, and beans, living with the land. European settlers came with different needs. They planted trees and drained a 1,000-acre area called Goose Lake for farmland. They also strip-mined the area, and even made pottery and fire brick from the clay beneath the soil.

In 1969 the state purchased 240 acres, many of which still contain native prairie remnants. The adjacent Heidecke Lake, used as a cooling lake by the local power company, offers respite for some of the ducks that no doubt once used the former Goose Lake during migration. More than half of Goose Lake Prairie is a dedicated nature preserve, protected by law from disturbance.

The visitor center has bathrooms, maps, and a nature display. Guided hikes and lectures are offered periodically. You'll find picnic tables, grills, water, and outdoor toilets at two picnic areas.

ADDITIONAL HELP

DeLorme IA&G grid: 36.
Contact: Goose Lake Prairie State Natural Area.
Nearest gas, food, and lodging: Morris.

31 Midewin National Tallgrass Prairie

Habitats: Grassland complex of tallgrass and medium grass prairie, shrubby grasslands, wetlands, and oak woods.
Key birds: Breeding Upland Sandpiper, Red-tailed Hawk, Short-eared Owl, Loggerhead Shrike, Belted Kingfisher, Sedge Wren, Bell's Vireo, Dickcissel, Bobolink, Eastern Meadowlark, Baltimore and Orchard Orioles, Henslow's and Grasshopper Sparrows, among others.
Best times to bird: March through November and especially during the breeding season from late May through late June.

Directions: The Midewin Visitor Center and tour meeting site is on Illinois Highway 53, 4 miles south of the Joliet Interstate 80 exit. Anyone interested in taking a tour of Midewin should call the center for further information and to make a reservation.

Birding: This is the first federally designated national tallgrass prairie, but don't think of it as one large land of 7-foot-high grasses. Instead, 21 natural communities from oak woodland to sedge meadow to tallgrass prairie exist in this 19,000-acre national park that supports 110 breeding species. Midewin (pronounced MID-DAY-WIN) is next to the 4,000-acre Des Plaines Conservation Area, making this a huge macro-site that offers breeding sites to some of the rarest birds in the Midwest. You'll find the state's largest breeding population of the endangered Upland Sandpiper here along with smaller populations of breeding Henslow's and Grasshopper Sparrows.

The large-scale size of this area is important because grassland species have specific requirements for breeding. For example, the Upland Sandpiper needs at least 100 acres of shorter prairie grasses to breed, while the rapidly declining Bobolink needs at least 100 acres of different grasslands for nesting and the state-listed endangered Henslow's Sparrow requires medium grasses. The Midewin National Tallgrass Prairie provides all these niches, and may be the last hope for some of these species to survive in Illinois. Because of its large size, this site also serves as a major migratory stopping place for grassland and wetland birds that will breed farther north or that are returning south to their winter homes.

31 Midewin National Tallgrass Prairie

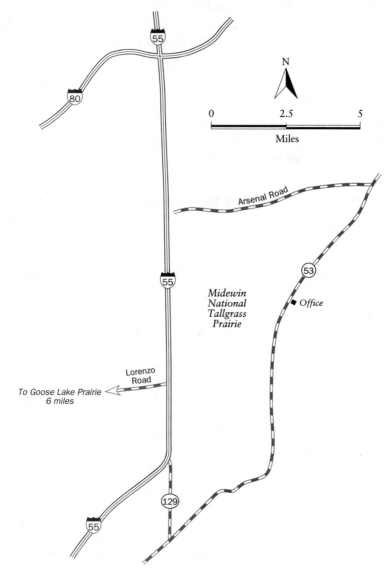

The Midewin National Tallgrass Prairie is occasionally open to the public for guided walks. As trails are constructed, the public will gain more access.

The best time for birders to visit is in late May through middle to late June. In a few years, trails and paths will be opened for more public access. By the time you read this, a picnic and camping ground with a few trails should be open to the public.

During spring and fall migration, large numbers of migrant grassland and shrubland birds use Midewin, and the small wetlands are important for migrating rails, snipes, Marsh Wrens, and Swamp Sparrows.

Upland Sandpipers can often be seen during breeding season from the roadside in the grasslands just north of the entrance along US/IL 53. Grazing cows keep the grasses to the height these birds prefer; the native bison, which once roamed the midwestern grasslands, may be introduced later. You'll find no facilities. Bring water, sunscreen, and insect repellent. Wear a hat. Check for ticks when you're done birding.

During breeding season—from late May to about June 20—you'll almost assuredly hear and see Dickcissels and Grasshopper and Savannah Sparrows in the shorter grass areas, Henslow's Sparrows and Sedge Wrens in the taller grasslands, Bell's Vireos and Loggerhead Shrikes in shrublands near the tall grasses, Bobolinks in hayfields, feeding herons and egrets in wetlands, and soaring Red-tailed Hawks throughout the park. Fourteen pairs of Redtails bred at Midewin in 1998. In winter, raptors including Long-eared and Short-eared Owls, Rough-legged Hawks, and Northern Harriers hunt the fields.

On a three-hour tour in a van at 8 A.M. in late June, a group of 65 birders saw Eastern Kingbirds, Tree Swallows, Turkey Vultures, Savannah Sparrows, Brown Thrashers, Baltimore and Orchard Orioles, Grasshopper Sparrows, Henslow's Sparrows, Red-tailed Hawks, Dickcissels, Eastern Meadowlarks, Eastern Phoebes, Upland Sandpipers, Sedge Wrens, Belted Kingfishers, and more.

General information: In 1940 the U.S. military purchased some 40,000 acres of land near Joliet, Illinois, southwest of Chicago. Called the Joliet Arsenal, this land was one of 60 facilities built during World War II. The government needed sites near urban areas to secure labor, near water because it takes a lot of water to make dynamite, and away from the East or West Coast, a strategy supported by the military. In the 1940s, employees made 5.5-million tons of dynamite at the arsenal each week during World War II. Workers also produced ammunition during the Korean and Vietnam Wars. Technology changes virtually shut down the arsenal, although a few items were still produced here until September 1998.

Although the land was owned by the federal government, much of it remained unused or farmed. Biologists gained permission, though not easily at first, to research the flora and fauna here. The discovery of nesting Upland Sandpipers encouraged the biologists to continue their research and to urge the federal government to protect this land. In 1996 President Clinton signed a bill giving Will County 455 acres for a landfill and local industry 3,000 acres. The government retained 1,000 acres for a national veterans cemetery, and the American people received the remaining 19,000 or so acres as a natural area to preserve native ecosystems.

State and federal employees are cleaning some of the polluted sites, growing grassland plants, converting cropland to prairie, and monitoring flora and fauna as well as conducting periodic controlled burns to foster the grasslands' integrity. A dedicated corps of local volunteers helps with grassland seed collecting and planting. Four creeks wind through Midewin. Though once heavily polluted, the creeks are slowly recovering and now contain nice populations of fish and native

The state-listed endangered Upland Sandpiper breeds at Midewin National Tallgrass Prairie. JOE B. MILOSEVICH PHOTO

mussels, food for the birds, and indeed for the entire ecosystem. The government expects some 4.5-million people to visit Midewin annually when it officially opens in several years.

ADDITIONAL HELP

DeLorme IA&G grid: 36.
Contact: Midewin National Tallgrass Prairie. Website includes updates on public access.
Nearest gas, food, and lodging: Joliet and Wilmington.

32 Kankakee River State Park, Momence Wetlands, and Sod Farms

Habitats: River and adjacent woods, backwater sloughs, and sod farms.
Key birds: Migrating ducks, shorebirds, including Buff-breasted Sandpiper and songbirds, including Winter Wren and Brewer's Blackbird; breeders, including Barred Owl, Prothonotary Warbler, and American Redstart.
Best times to bird: April, May, and June; November.

Directions: To get to Kankakee River State Park from Interstate 57, exit Illinois Highway 17 and go west 1 mile to U.S. Highway 45. Go north 2 miles to IL 102, which frames the park on the north. Follow the signs to the park.

For the wetlands, exit IL 17, but drive west 7 miles on IL 114. Continue east another 6 miles to State Line Road (County Road 1800E). Turn north onto this evenly graded gravel road.

The sod farms are south of the wetlands.

Birding: Kankakee River State Park includes 4,000 acres of riverine habitat in an area 6 miles northwest of Kankakee, and nearby area backwaters known as the Momence Wetlands. Birders have recorded more than 200 species of birds in these areas.

Begin your birding in April, May, or June at the Momence Wetlands on State Line Road. Drive slowly, roll down your windows, and listen at the shrub edges for catbirds and yellowthroats calling. When you reach the backwaters, park along the roadside and walk.

In April, listen for Winter Wrens, Rusty Blackbirds and other early migrants. In May, listen for House Wrens, Warbling Vireos, Great Crested Flycatchers, and American Redstarts calling in the silver maples and river birches. You'll also hear scolding gnatcatchers and vireos, and possibly, the Prothonotary Warbler, which breeds in tree cavities. Barred Owls have nested here. You can walk for at least 1 mile, scouting the backwaters until the wetlands merge into farm fields near a bridge that traverses the Kankakee River.

32 Kankakee River State Park, Momence Wetlands, and Sod Farms

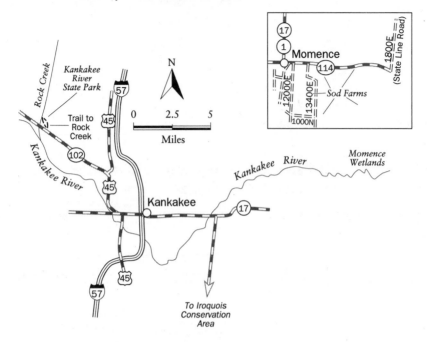

In August and September visit the Momence Sod Farms, 1 mile away from the wetlands. Some reliable places include the sod farms along CR 13400E just south of IL 114. On the right day in mid-July through late August you might find closely mowed grassy fields alive with sandpipers and peeps, along with flocks of American Golden-Plovers.

One day, three birders counted 19 species of shorebirds in the sod farms spanning a few square miles. Typically, Upland Sandpipers arrive in mid- to late July, followed by Pectoral Sandpipers and fewer numbers of Buff-breasted Sandpipers and Black-bellied Plovers. You'll count many more Killdeer and Horned Larks than the sandpipers and peeps. Pectoral and Least Sandpipers and both yellowlegs are fairly common. A Marbled Godwit and Whimbrel, both rarities, have been seen foraging here. Also watch for Cliff Swallows flying over; they nest beneath a bridge over the ditch along 13400E.

As you drive, listen for singing Western Meadowlarks, scattered among the more common Easterns. Vesper and Savannah Sparrows also breed here, and in early spring during migration, you may find Lapland Longspurs and maybe a small group of Smith's Longspurs in the fields.

To bird Kankakee River State Park, avoid weekends when it's crowded. It's easy to bird this long, narrow park along the river by hiking or canoeing. Canoeists can contact the park regarding rentals. Park staff will tell you where to retrieve your canoe, which is at Bird Park in Kankakee.

Drivers have several well-kept parking areas from which to choose along the river. From here you can take several hiking trails. The 3-mile route along Rock Creek treats you to scenic views of limestone canyons and a small waterfall. You can hike along narrow dirt-to-mud paths that meander along the river. Some can be a bit rocky and slippery when wet.

In March, search for dabbling ducks floating along the river. In April, search for early migrants such as Winter Wrens, kinglets, and Yellow-rumped Warblers flycatching along the river. In early May, look for tanagers, grosbeaks, orioles, and dozens if not 25 or more species of warblers in one day. Come November you'll find creepers and woodpeckers in the woods, and Red-breasted Mergansers, goldeneyes, and other ducks along the river.

General information: Potawatomi Indians hunted along the Kankakee River in the 1760s, finding abundant migrating waterfowl, beavers, and other animals to sustain their tribe. Europeans next came to the area to farm along the river. By the early 1900s, the area that is now part of the park hosted numerous summer cottages. In 1938 a Chicago resident donated 35 acres of land for a state park. Commonwealth Edison turned over another 1,715 acres to the state in 1956. With the company's additional grants in 1989, the park now roughly totals 4,000 acres, suitable for hunting, fishing, and birding.

In the 1990s the U.S. Fish & Wildlife Service worked to designate some 26,000 acres near the park as the Grand Kankakee Marsh National Wildlife Refuge in the Kankakee River watershed in northwestern Indiana and northeastern Illinois. The refuge lies within the 3.3-million-acre Kankakee River Watershed, which provides respite for migrating and breeding waterfowl and songbirds. The Kankakee watershed once contained one of the most important freshwater wetlands in the world, rivaling Florida's Everglades in the diversity of fish and wildlife it supported. Only remnants of the marsh remain. The establishment of the national wildlife refuge will help ensure the restoration of habitats that attract rare native plant and animal species, including many birds.

You'll find a concession stand, bike rentals, canoe rental information, picnic areas, and clean, well-kept washrooms in the state park.

You can easily combine these areas with the nearby Iroquois County Conservation Area (see Site 47), which is just a few miles away from the Momence Sod Farms and Wetlands. Hunting is allowed in fall and winter.

ADDITIONAL HELP

DeLorme IA&G grid: 36 (state park) and 37 (wetlands and sod farms).
Contact: Kankakee River State Park and Kankakee Audubon Society.
Nearest, gas, food, and lodging: Kankakee and Bourbonnais; camping at the park.

Henslow's Sparrow drawing by Denis Kania.

Northwestern Region

Tucked in the northwestern corner of Illinois is the driftless area, the only place where the last glaciers that inundated most of the state did not pass. The glaciers carved the northeastern part of the state into gentle, undulating terrain. As you drive west from Winnebago County toward the Mississippi River, you enter the driftless area, where the topography gradually gets steeper until you reach the scenic bluffs of the Mississippi Palisades State Park. Many migrants use the Mississippi River to get their bearings, while bald eagles, gulls, and ducks use available open water to find food in winter.

Birders and nonbirders make trips to northwestern Illinois to watch the eagles snatch gizzard shad from the icy waters, and to learn how to identify various plumages of this impressive bird.

Starved Rock State Park is Illinois' Grand Canyon, where visitors can enjoy spectacular waterfalls while birding. Nearby Lowden-Miller State Forest offers habitat for some of the state's rarest breeding warblers. It is the only place, so far, that the Black-throated Green Warbler has been confirmed as breeding in the state.

Where the glaciers began to do their work in the northwestern region, you'll find prairie/wetland complexes, including the Nachusa Grasslands. The steep sandstone outcrops descending into rocky meadows and streams provide places for Bell's Vireos, Orchard Orioles, and Henslow's Sparrows to breed.

33 Shabbona Lake State Recreation Area and Forest Preserve

34 Sugar River Forest Preserve and Alder Tract

35 Pecatonica River Forest Preserve

36 Rock Cut State Park and Keiselburg Forest Preserve

37 Mississippi Palisades State Park

38 Savanna Army Depot

39 Mississippi River Corridor

40 Starved Rock and Matthiessen State Parks

41 Castle Rock State Park and the George B. Fell Nature Preserve

42 Lowden-Miller State Forest

43 Nachusa Grasslands and Franklin Creek State Natural Area

44 Green River Conservation Area

45 Woodford State Fish and Wildlife Area

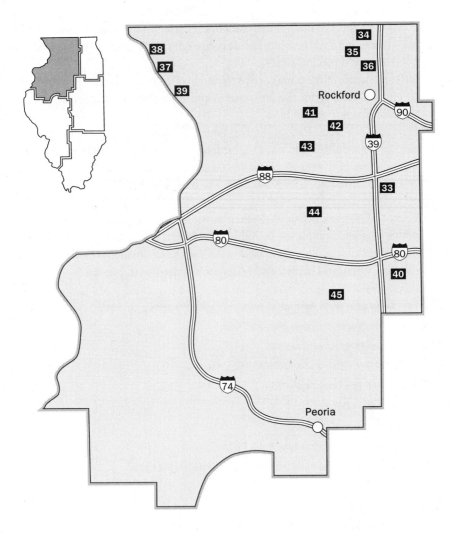

33 Shabbona Lake State Recreation Area and Forest Preserve

Habitats: Manmade lake surrounded by rolling hills, upland and bottomland woods, open fields, and restored prairies.
Key birds: Migrating grebes, dabbling and diving ducks, geese, swans, shorebirds, and passerines; postbreeding Little Blue Heron; possible Gray Partridge; breeding Hooded Merganser, Wood Duck, Red-headed Woodpecker, Sedge Wren, Bobolink, Orchard Oriole, and Savannah Sparrow.
Best times to bird: March through May; early fall before October 1.

Directions: From Interstate 88, exit at U.S. Highway 30, and drive about 13 miles west to Illinois Highway 23. Drive south for less than 1 mile to Forest Preserve Road, then follow the signs to the entrances to either the forest preserve or state recreation area.

To get to Afton Forest Preserve, follow the above directions, but turn north on IL 23 for 3 miles to McGirr Road. Go east 1 mile to Crego Road, and north 2 miles to the forest preserve entrance.

Birding: A bird flying over the northern Illinois farm fields has few places to refuel during migration; one of these is the 1,550-acre Shabbona Lake State Recreation Area, southwest of DeKalb in northern Illinois. An oasis in the middle of row crops, this park, though built to serve boaters, fishermen, and hunters, also attracts birds, especially during migration. It is connected to the 88-acre Shabbona Forest Preserve, northeast of the park.

A convergence of several habitats throughout the forest preserve and park has attracted more than 200 species of birds. This is also one of the best places in the state to search for the elusive Gray Partridge, a coveted species that has yet to make the list of many Illinois birders.

Start at the Shabbona Forest Preserve parking lot, listening at the grove edges on the entrance road for spring migrants. Walk to the woods behind the picnic tables to search for breeding Red-headed Woodpeckers, a declining Illinois species. Walk southwest toward a 7-mile snowmobile loop trail that winds through woods, woodland edges, and around the 300-acre lake. Here you are on the east side of Shabbona Lake. In March, April, and May, for the hardy soul (with lots of water and stamina), walking a good portion of the mowed trail can be a spectacular birding adventure. Along the trail you will find a pond that during dry seasons when shorebirds are migrating can be productive. In May, look for Barn, Tree, and Northern Rough-winged Swallows, and perhaps a Wood Duck nesting in a box.

To bird the state recreation area, drive slowly along the entrance road, stopping periodically to check the various ponds for waterfowl, wading birds, shorebirds, and marsh birds, depending on time of year and water levels. Birders once recorded an American and Least Bittern side-by-side at the first pond beyond the

33 Shabbona Lake State Recreation Area and Forest Preserve

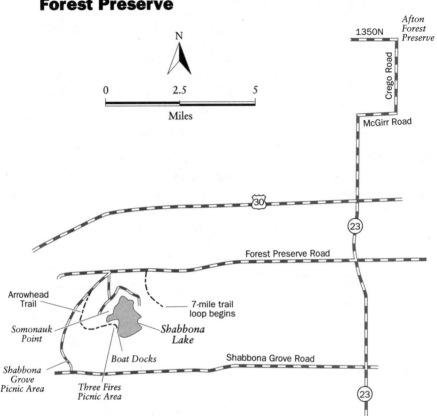

entrance. You should find egrets and herons feeding here, especially in late summer after the breeding season.

Check the fields for Sedge Wrens which sometimes nest here beginning in May. In April at dusk, you might want to park along the road and listen for the *"peenting"* of the American Woodcock, then watch as the male displays in the air. In winter, you may enjoy close-up views of birds partaking of seeds in strategically placed feeders along the drive.

You'll find the headwaters of Shabbona Lake along this drive where dispersing Little Blue Herons, often in their white phase, wade after August 1. Young Hooded Mergansers have also been seen in June.

Check for waterfowl at the Three Fires Picnic Area. Typically, 30 species of waterfowl stop annually, beginning with the spring break-up of ice in May and again in fall. Come on weekdays in March and April when the water is open except for a rim of ice at the edge, which keeps away the fishermen and gives the ducks some peace.

To look for migrating passerines in spring and fall, drive to the Somonauk Point parking lot. Dozens, if not 20 or more, warbler species flit among black cherries, hawthorns, and little leaf lindens. Walk the trail along the lake. It connects to Arrowhead Trail, where you can take a longer walk to search for more migrants and get a good view of the lake.

For another waterfowl migration spot, visit the Shabbona Grove Picnic Area. Park and walk to the dam to search for ducks, geese, grebes, and loons. Bring a scope. At the dam search for diving ducks such as Ruddy Duck and Common Merganser, occasional scoters (all three species have been seen here), Common Loon (April and even sometimes into May), and other migrants.

In late spring and through summer, listen for Sedge Wrens in the wet ridges, Bobolinks in the short grasses, and Orchard Orioles in the trees along the edge of the lake. You can also walk southeast below the dam to a series of wetlands to search for other interesting species; and if you want to try for the Gray Partridge, a bird that has sporadically been seen here, walk the fields.

You can also bird the nearby Afton Forest Preserve, owned by the DeKalb County Forest Preserve District. When you're on Crego Road, roll down your windows and listen for Western Meadowlarks, a species that typically breeds farther west than Illinois. You might also check the roadside ditches for the elusive Gray Partridge, which has been seen here by local birders. Afton Forest Preserve includes a prairie restoration, which hosts a variety of grassland birds, and a wetland mitigation project, which has produced shorebirds and wading birds. You should also see Ring-necked Pheasants and you may hear singing Savannah Sparrows during breeding season. Look in the north edge of the preserve for a Bobolink colony in May and June.

General information: Native American chief Shabbona and his tribe once lived in this rich area, which was mostly prairie and occasional tree groves. Europeans settled here in the 1830s, naming what is now the south part of the preserve Shabbona Grove. They farmed the rich soil, and lived beneath the shady trees. In 1965, the state acquired land to create a 3,000-foot dam to form a lake. The state is also restoring a prairie here. Half of the Shabbona Lake State Park is closed beginning October 1 through the end of hunting season in winter. Call first before planning trips during these times.

ADDITIONAL HELP

DeLorme IA&G grid: 26.
Contact: DeKalb County Forest Preserve District, Illinois Department of Natural Resources.
Nearest gas, food, and lodging: Camping at the Shabbona State Recreation Area; hotels and motels in DeKalb.

34 Sugar River Forest Preserve and Alder Tract

Habitats: Mature upland mixed deciduous/coniferous woods, river bottomlands, and sand prairie.
Key birds: Migratory songbirds; breeding Red-shouldered Hawk; Acadian Flycatcher, Yellow- throated and Cerulean Warblers, Lark Sparrow, and other grassland birds.
Best times to bird: April through September.

Directions: Exit Interstate 90 north of Rockford at Illinois Highway 75. Follow the road south and west to Rockton Road. Go 7 miles west, passing through the town of Rockton, to Forest Preserve Road. Continue west into the main parking area of the Sugar River Forest Preserve.

Birding:. The Yellow-throated Warbler is a specialty at Sugar River Forest Preserve in Winnebago County, but you'll also find many other breeding songbird species here that typically aren't found in northern Illinois.

Four rivers cut through the small dells and gentle rolling hills of farm country in Winnebago County. These rivers, the Kishwaukee, the Pecatonica, the Sugar, and the Rock, provide plentiful habitat for birds, as well as a scenic backdrop for viewing these colorful creatures. Birders tallied at least 300 bird species in the past century in Winnebago County, which includes 34 preserves situated in more than 7,000 acres.

The best birding spots in the county include Sugar River Forest Preserve, in the northwest part and the Pecatonica River and Pecatonica Wetlands Forest Preserves in the west-central part (see Site 35).

At the intersection of IL 75 and Winslow Road, drive north 2.4 miles on Winslow Road, which makes a 90-degree right turn headed east. From this turn, go 0.4 mile to the bridge that crosses the Sugar River. Pull over and check this area from the road and bridge. You might hear the *"kleeyur"* call of the Red-shouldered Hawk in May through July. You can also find Prothonotary, Cerulean, and Kentucky Warblers, along with Acadian Flycatchers during migration and breeding season, and resident Pileated Woodpeckers. In spring and fall, walk the road for 0.25 mile on both sides of the bridge. This is a productive spot, but do not leave the roadway. The neighbors here are reasonably friendly, but permission to enter their land is a must. Avoid entering the gun club.

After birding around the bridge, drive east 0.3 mile across the river to the intersection of Winslow and Hauley Roads. Turn north on Hauley. Drive 0.3 mile to the top of a small grade where you can stop in May and June to look and listen for Bobolinks, Dickcissels, Grasshopper and Savannah Sparrows, meadowlarks, and hawks on both sides of the road in the hay fields.

Continue north on Hauley for 1 mile to Forest Preserve Road. Turn west, noting that Hauley jogs to the right or north about 150 feet after you turn left. You will come back to that road if you want to go to Sugar River Alder Tract. For now, go straight for 0.5 mile to the entrance to Sugar River Forest Preserve. The campground entrance on the right attracts wintering owls, including Long-eared, as well as Red-breasted Nuthatches.

From May through July, as you enter the mature, upland hardwood forest, listen for the songs of Eastern Wood-Pewees, Cerulean Warblers, and Tufted Titmice. Park by the Sand Bluff shelter and listen for singing Yellow-throated Warblers, which frequent the white pines. Walk the paved short loop road, listening for Cerulean Warblers, Pileated Woodpeckers, Acadian Flycatchers, and Barred Owls. Mosquitos abound, so be prepared. Even on a hot day at the end of May at high noon, we heard several Yellow-throated Warblers at least six Acadian Flycatchers, and at least four Cerulean Warblers singing, plus a Northern Parula, a Black-throated Green Warbler, and an Ovenbird. One year, 15 Acadian Flycatchers

The Barred Owl breeds at Sugar River Forest Preserve. JOE B. MILOSEVICH PHOTO

defended territories in the preserve. Recently, several pairs of Kentucky and Hooded Warblers have been present in summer.

During migration the area bursts with warblers and other songbirds. Look to the sky for migrating Broadwinged and Red-shouldered Hawks. Check the pines behind the outdoor facilities across from the Sand Bluff Shelter in winter for Northern Sawwhet Owls.

You can also bird the Sugar River by canoe. On an early June morning, as you quietly paddle the narrow river, you can enjoy the serenades of Prothonotary, Yellow throated, and Cerulean Warblers, orioles, tanagers, and Great Crested and Acadian Flycatchers.

If you wish to go to Sugar River Alder Tract to locate Lark and Grasshopper Sparrows and other birds, retrace your route on Forest Preserve Road, but turn north on Hauley Road 0.4 of a mile east of the Sugar River entrance. Take Hauley north 2.4 miles, where it makes an S curve. The east/west part of the S is the Wisconsin/Illinois state line. When the road curves north, you will be on Roy Road and in Wisconsin. In 0.6 mile, you'll come to a stop sign at St. Lawrence Road. Turn west. Drive 0.5 mile to Beacon Light Road, then turn south or left on Beacon Light, and drive 0.4 mile to the entrance to Sugar River Alder Tract Forest Preserve. Look for Eastern Bluebirds and Dickcissels on Beacon Light Road. Once you park, listen in early spring for American Woodcocks *"peenting"* at dusk and for Whip-poor-wills and Barred Owls calling. Birders also heard Chuck-will's-widow here in May of 1995. A trail loops around a prairie where you might find Grasshopper and Lark Sparrows during the breeding season and Wild Turkeys year-round. Sandhill Cranes have nested in the wet meadows southwest of the prairie.

If you're here during shorebird season (April and May and July through August), you might want to check the flooded fields between Rockton Road and IL 75. From the intersection of Hauley and Yale Bridge Roads, turn east on Yale Bridge, driving 1.5 miles to Boswell Road. Turn south, then drive for 2 miles to Shirland Road. Turn east for 1 mile to Meridian Road, then drive south over the Pecatonica River for about half a mile. Search the flooded fields on both sides of the road.

General information: Original land surveys show Winnebago County consisted of 30 percent forest and 70 percent prairie. The forests grew along the rivers, where fires that swept the prairies were kept at bay. Most of the forested land has since been timbered, most of the prairies have been converted to grow crops and raise cattle, and many of the rivers, creeks, and marshes, have been channeled. In 1922, the people of Winnebago County established the forest preserve system, partially to ensure they had a quiet place in nature to picnic with their families. Today, county residents are working to restore these areas and to add choice properties that will maintain a greenway for the rich bird life. The Winnebago County Forest Preserve provides critical habitat for 21 animals and 60 plants on the Illinois endangered and threatened species list. Several other area preserves are worth checking, including Severson Dells and Kishwaukee Forest Preserve, both good for migrating birds. Call the forest preserve district for free maps of these areas before you go.

ADDITIONAL HELP

DeLorme IA&G grid: 18.
Contact: Winnebago County Forest Preserve District and the North Central Illinois Ornithological Society Birding Hotline.
Nearest gas, food, and lodging: Camping at Sugar River Forest Preserve and Rock Cut State Park; gas, food, and lodging in Rockford, Rockton, and Loves Park and South Beloit, Wisconsin.

35 Pecatonica River Forest Preserve

See map on page 131

Habitats: Mature upland mixed deciduous/coniferous woods and river bottomlands.
Key birds: Migratory shorebirds and songbirds; breeding Barred Owl, Pileated Woodpecker, Acadian and Willow Flycatchers, and Cerulean and Prothonotary Warblers.
Best times to bird: April through September.

Directions: From Interstate 90, take the U.S. Highway 20 exit, south of Rockford. Drive west about 20 miles to Pecatonica Road. Proceed north to Brick School Road and then west to the main entrance to the Pecatonica River Forest Preserve.

Birding: Pecatonica River Forest Preserve provides habitat for one of the rarest breeding warblers in the state, the Cerulean. Its fast *"zray-zray-zray-zray-zee"* call echoes in the bottomland woods on warm June days. Walking along the river oxbows and marshes will also provide you with good looks at spring migrants, as well as the breeding Prothonotary Warbler, almost a given in May and June.

Start at the intersection of US 20 and Pecatonica Road. Drive north 2.6 miles on Pecatonica Road to Blair Road. Turn west for 1.1 miles, where Blair Road turns off to the left, and another road, Best Road, continues north. Turn left and continue on Blair Road for 0.25 mile. You will come to a pull-out on the left that gives a good view of an oxbow lake and swamp. Across the road, you'll see a small upland woods where you can find numerous migrants in May as well as breeding Acadian Flycatchers. In August and September, shorebirds often feed along the edges if the water is low.

Continue west on Blair Road for another 0.2 mile to a locked silver gate on the left. This is part of the new forest preserve holdings. You are allowed to enter here, but park your car completely off of the road, and don't block the gate. Beyond the gate is an old farm lane. Follow it into the woods. It winds through oxbow swamp and river bottomwoods, paralleling the river for a while. It does not loop, so you will have to go out the way you came in. Listen and look for Cerulean Warblers, Acadian Flycatchers, and Barred Owls during breeding season and many migrants in April and May as well as in August and September. A pair of Brown Creepers bred here in 1997.

Now return to Pecatonica Road. Drive north to Brick School Road. Go east 1.6 miles to the main entrance gate of the forest preserve. Pass this gate and park by the locked silver gate 0.3 mile ahead on the right. Park here (don't block the gate, but you can park on the edge of the grassy drive that approaches the gate), pass through the gate, and walk the 1.5-mile trail that begins immediately behind the gate. This loop trail winds through habitat that attracts a host of migrant warblers and vireos in spring and fall, as well as breeding Cerulean and Prothonotary Warblers, Barred Owls, and Pileated Woodpeckers. You may also find the Barred Owl and Pileated Woodpecker in winter, particularly on sunny days with northerly winds. The area affords protection from the wind and often harbors flickers and sapsuckers in winter.

This loop trail meets another longer loop trail that takes you out to the road where you will have to walk back to your car. Either trail provides good birding, but if you get off the main loop, you'll have to walk farther.

Walk the trail counterclockwise and you'll discover an open fallow field that attracts Field and Song Sparrows, Indigo Buntings, Yellow Warblers, and Common Yellowthroats. You might also hear the Willow Flycatcher singing *"fitz-bew"* through June and July.

Soon the trail begins to parallel the river. When you reach a bridge that crosses a small stream, continue along the river to the bottomwoods. The river will be on your right and an oxbow lake and swamp on your left. About 500 feet after entering this woods, the trail will fork. Take the left hand trail (don't go straight ahead, or you will be on the long loop).

The trail gently winds through the bottoms and between several oxbows. When you come to a small footbridge, listen for the loud one-syllable chant of the Prothonotary Warbler, a bird that has bred here in the holes of dead trees. Farther along, the trail ascends to good vantage points for eye-level views of spring migrants. After passing the observation deck that overlooks the west end of the oxbow, follow the trail left through a honeysuckle thicket, and then to the right where you will be just south of the silver gate where you started.

In the winter, cross the road by the silver gate toward the maintenance sheds on the road's north side. A path leads to the environmental education center in the refurbished barn. Check the feeders since unusual birds sometimes appear in winter, including Evening Grosbeaks.

For some nearby shorebirding, visit the Winnebago Ponds, as dubbed by local birders. The best times to check are in spring when the oxbow is full of water or after wet summers. From the silver gate at Pecatonica Preserve, Brick School Road curves left. Drive 1.6 miles north to Trask Bridge Road (IL 70). Turn east and in 1.3 miles you will pass the Howard farm on your south. This is a hotspot for geese in March to May and October through early January. Check for Snow, Ross's, and Greater White-fronted Geese among the hundreds to thousands of Canadas. You'll find several places where you can pull off the road far enough to park.

Continue another 2.5 miles on IL 70 to Winnebago Road. Turn south and check the edges of the oxbow marsh for shorebirds in April, May, August, and September. In dry years the oxbow is plowed and planted. Shorebirds are present only after wet summers or a period of heavy rain during fall migration. This area almost always holds water in spring.

General information: Pecatonica River Forest Preserve and Wetlands is being developed for easier access by birders at this writing. Some of the gates and pull-outs mentioned may be further improved when you arrive. For the most up-to-date information, call the Winnebago County Forest Preserve District for current maps. See the Sugar River Forest Preserve entry (Site 34) for more information on the forest preserve district's work to protect these areas.

ADDITIONAL HELP

DeLorme IA&G grid: 17.
Contact: Winnebago County Forest Preserve District and the North-Central Illinois Ornithological Society Birding Hotline.
Nearest gas, food, and lodging: Camping at Sugar River Forest Preserve, Seward Bluffs Forest Preserve and Rock Cut State Park; hotels and motels in Rockford.

36 Rock Cut State Park and Keiselburg Forest Preserve

Habitats: Rolling plains, two manmade lakes, restored prairie, woods, and sedge fen.

Key birds: Migrating ducks and songbirds, including at least 36 species of warblers; breeding Yellow-billed and Black-billed Cuckoos, Sedge Wren, Eastern Bluebird, Acadian and Willow Flycatchers, Cerulean, Kentucky, and Hooded Warblers, Ovenbird, Yellow-breasted Chat, Grasshopper Sparrow, and Dickcissel.

Best times to bird: March through early December.

Directions: To reach Rock Cut State Park's south entrance from the Riverside Boulevard, exit off Interstate 90, just north of Rockford. Take Riverside Boulevard 0.75 mile west to MacFarland Road, then north 1.5 miles to Harlem Road, then back east for 1 mile to the entrance. To get to the north entrance, exit Riverside west 1 mile to Perryville Road. Turn north for 3.5 miles to Illinois Highway 173. Drive east for 1.5 miles to the north entrance. Note that an exit off I-90 at IL 173 may be constructed, which will make access easier to the north entrance.

To get to Keiselburg Forest Preserve from the Rock Cut State Park north entrance go west on IL 173 for 0.8 mile to Mitchell Road, then north another 1.7 miles, to a stop sign at Swanson Road. Go west 0.3 mile to the preserve entrance.

Birding: *"Bee bzzz." "See you-see-see-yer." "Bouncing ping pong ball." "Lispy trill." "Tee der der." "Witchety-witchety."* I was barely out of the car at Rock Cut State Park in northern Illinois near Rockford and I had already heard a Blue-winged Warbler, Eastern Meadowlark, Field Sparrow, Grasshopper Sparrow, Baltimore Oriole, Common Yellowthroat, and more birds singing from their territories at the park's north entrance.

If you want a good day's list of birds in a picturesque setting, you'll find that at this state park, composed of varied habitats that attract good numbers of migrants and nesters. Nearby Keiselburg Forest Preserve, which is part of the Winnebago County Forest Preserve District, features a rare sedge fen, teeming with unusual plants and attracting Sedge Wrens to nest, as well as Dickcissels and other birds in the drier grasslands.

Birders can walk 10 miles of trails through woods and prairie, and use scopes to view diving and dabbling ducks at two manmade lakes on this 3,092-acre state park and the 211-acre Keiselburg preserve. Birders have recorded more than 230 species of birds at Rock Cut State Park alone. Most recently, local birders added the Mississippi Kite and Purple Sandpiper to the park's bird list as well as breeding Cooper's and Broad-winged Hawks.

Starting at the IL 173 (north) entrance, park in the first lot at the north edge of the restored tallgrass prairie to listen for singing breeders in late May and June. Listen for Grasshopper Sparrows as well as Eastern Bluebirds, which use the boxes provided for them.

36 Rock Cut State Park and Keiselburg Forest Preserve

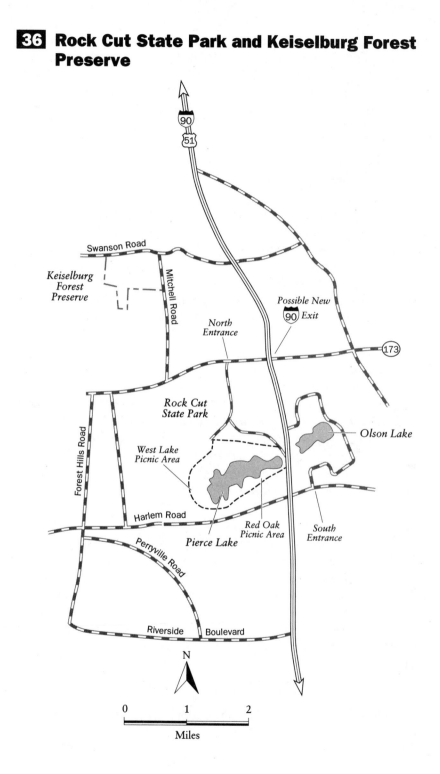

Then drive south past the prairie toward the dam. Go slowly—keep your windows rolled and listen for migrating and breeding birds in May and June. As you approach a shrubby area, listen for Alder Flycatchers, Willow Flycatchers, Yellow Warblers, and Yellow-breasted Chats. The Willow Flycatcher, Yellow Warbler, and chat have bred here; the Alder sometimes lingers into June, then flies north to breed.

Continue your drive south past a grove of trees where the breeding woodland birds start singing—Ovenbirds, Veeries, Red-throated Vireos, Yellow-throated Vireos, Scarlet Tanagers, and others.

During fall and spring migration, park by the dam near the lake and walk the bike path west along Turtle Creek to search for migrating songbirds. This can be a terrific hotspot when the weather is windy and cool. A 30 to 40-year-old forest populated with black walnuts attracts Yellow-billed and Black-billed Cuckoos. American Redstarts breed here. This 4-mile hike takes you over the creek and around Pierce Lake. You can also take footpaths off the main bike trail to explore shrubby niches, especially during migration. If you take the path all the way around, you will encircle Pierce Lake, going west at first, but then going east. Follow the trail signs.

A trail south of the dam will take you to a limestone ravine where Acadian Flycatchers, Hooded Warblers, and Kentucky Warblers have often bred. The Cerulean Warbler has also bred here somewhat regularly.

To watch ducks, view the expanse of Pierce Lake at the dam. Most of the diving ducks use this lake because it provides good fishing and clams. You should find Canvasbacks, Redheads, scaups, and even Common Loons here in spring or fall. Scoters sometimes use the lake in late fall. A small rock island—we're talking very small here—in the lake near the dam has attracted some unusual shorebirds, including American Avocets (single record), Willets, and Purple Sandpipers (single record).

Once you've finished viewing the ducks, drive to the West Lake and Red Oak Picnic Areas. Park, then walk toward the lake to get a different vantage point. Two Common Loons remained at Pierce Lake one year until early June.

In March and April search for the dabbling ducks such as shovelers and teals at Olson Lake on the east part of the park The entrance is off Harlem Road, or you can drive the park's main road from the IL 173 entrance to get to Olson Lake. In late summer and early fall when water levels recede, exposed mudflats attract shorebirds, including Greater and Lesser Yellowlegs, Semipalmated Plovers, Black-bellied Plovers, and Least, Semipalmated, and Pectoral Sandpipers.

You can spend an entire day at Rock Cut State Park, but you're so close to the Keiselburg Forest Preserve that you may wish to drive there as well to search for breeding Dickcissels, chats, and occasionally Bell's Vireos. It's a small, easily walked area. Park in the first lot and walk the trail. From May through July you may find and hear Dickcissels, Sedge Wrens, Orchard Orioles, occasional Bell's Vireos and chats, as well as Grasshopper and Savannah Sparrows. Walk the path around the perimeter of the shortgrass prairie, listening for these grassland songsters. The Dickcissel and sparrows tend to stay on the east side of the path. Walking toward the pines, you'll find the sedge meadow on the east side of the prairie by the boardwalk. Listen for Sedge Wrens and chats here in spring and summer. In winter, birders often find Long-eared Owls in the pine plantations, though not every year.

General information: Native Americans once settled along the Rock River in what is now Rock Cut State Park. Later, Scots, Canadians, and New Englanders settled here, a railroad was built, and the limestone rocks were blasted. Today the park is owned and managed by the Illinois Department of Natural Resources. Restorationists have worked to convert scrubby boxelder fields into grasslands, attracting prairie birds such as Eastern Meadowlarks as well as the rarer species, including Grasshopper Sparrows. Bluebird boxes attract breeding Eastern Bluebirds and Tree Swallows.

Rock Cut State Park features a campground, picnic areas, and clean restrooms. It also attracts fishermen and boaters in summer and snowmobilers and cross-country skiers in winter. For a quieter birding experience, you may wish to avoid weekends. The park opens at 8 A.M. November through middle April and 6 A.M. the rest of the year. You'll find a bait shop and concession stand here, too.

Keiselburg Forest Preserve, owned by the Winnebago County Forest Preserve District was acquired to protect its rare sedge fen and grasslands. Extensive prairie restoration is under way. See Sites 32 and 33 for details on the Winnebago County Forest Preserve District and how to acquire maps.

ADDITIONAL HELP

DeLorme IA&G grid: 18.
Contact: Rock Cut State Park and the Winnebago County Forest Preserve District.
Nearest gas, food, and lodging: Rockford, camping at Rock Cut State Park.

37 Mississippi Palisades State Park

Habitats: Mature upland and bluff forests, small prairie restorations, and limited scrub/shrub habitat.

Key birds: Migrating American White Pelican, Snow and Canada Geese and ducks, including Northern Pintail, Northern Shoveler, Gadwall, American Wigeon, Canvasback, Common Goldeneye, Bufflehead, and Common Merganser; migrating Osprey, Bald Eagle, Northern Harrier, Cooper's Hawk, Northern Goshawk, Red-shouldered Hawk, Broad-winged Hawk, Red-tailed Hawk, Golden Eagle, Merlin, and Peregrine Falcon; 35 species of migrating warblers; breeding herons and egrets, Wild Turkey, Turkey Vulture, Whip-poor-will, Ruby-throated Hummingbird, Hairy and Pileated Woodpeckers, Yellow-bellied Sapsucker, Eastern Wood-Pewee, Veery, Scarlet Tanager, Rose-breasted Grosbeak, Indigo Bunting, Eastern Towhee; wintering Purple Finch, Red and White-winged Crossbills, Common Redpoll, Pine Siskin, and Evening Grosbeak.

Best times to bird: All year, but particularly during spring and fall migration and the breeding season; plus winter during invasion years.

Directions: The Mississippi Palisades State Park's two entrances are about 2 miles north of Savanna, Illinois, along Illinois Highway 84.

Birding: In a typical year, you can find 180 to 190 species of birds within the Mississippi Palisades State Park and adjacent river areas. Nearly 100 breed here. One main paved loop road through the park links the north and south entrances. At the north end, additional paved roads wind through the various campgrounds. You can choose from nine hiking trails, totaling 13 miles. The five north trails are fairly easy to traverse. The four south trails are moderate to difficult for hiking.

During March and April and again in October and November, look for some of the 27 species of waterfowl and other water birds that rest here during migration in the side channel and backwater habitats. You can view these ducks from any of the five overlooks (Lookout, Oak, Louis', Ozzie's, and High), but a spotting scope is necessary.

Some of the waterfowl you might find include Pied-billed Grebes, American White Pelicans, Double-crested Cormorants, Tundra Swans, Snow and Canada Geese, Wood Ducks, American Black Ducks, Mallards, Northern Pintails, Gadwalls, American Wigeons, Canvasbacks, Lesser Scaups, Common Goldeneyes, Buffleheads, and Common Mergansers.

The five overlooks are also good for observing migrant raptors. As many as 15 species of diurnal raptors can be observed during migration, including Ospreys, Bald Eagles, Northern Harriers, Sharp-shinned Hawks, Northern Goshawks, Rough-legged Hawks, Golden Eagles, Merlins, and Peregrine Falcons.

In April, May, September, and October, look for myriad neotropical songbirds migrating through the park, including 7 species of woodpeckers, 7 species of thrushes, 6 species of swallows, and 8 species of flycatchers, including Olive-sided and Yellow-bellied. You can also find 5 species of migrating vireos, and 34 warbler species, including the less common Connecticut and Mourning, plus 10 species of

37 Mississippi Palisades State Park

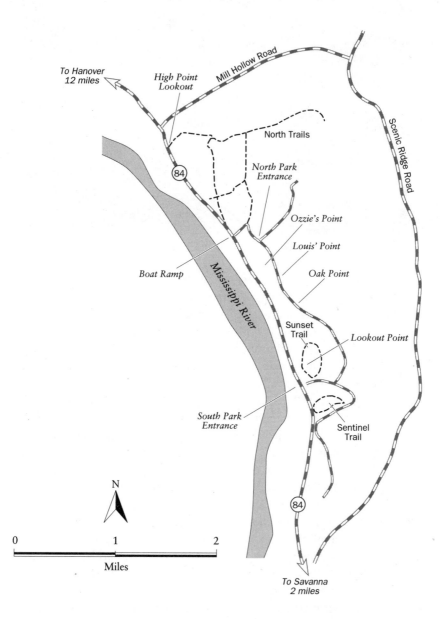

To Hanover
12 miles

High Point
Lookout

Mill Hollow Road

Scenic Ridge Road

North Trails

84

North Park
Entrance

Ozzie's Point

Louis' Point

Boat Ramp

Mississippi River

Oak Point

Sunset
Trail

Lookout Point

South Park
Entrance

Sentinel
Trail

N

0   1   2

Miles

84

To Savanna
2 miles

Mississippi Palisades State Park. STEVEN D. BAILEY PHOTO

sparrows, including Clay-colored. Try one of the many hiking trails or just bird by car along the paved roads during migration.

During summer check the river adjacent to the park for Pied-billed Grebes, Double-crested Cormorants, Great Blue Herons, Great Egrets, and Green Herons. Look overhead for Turkey Vultures, Bald Eagles, and Red-tailed Hawks soaring above the bluffs. Within the mature forest, Cooper's Hawks and at least one pair of Broad-winged Hawks breed.

A large population of Wild Turkeys lives throughout the park. Look for them in the early morning or evening foraging alongside the roads or in the mowed fields or picnic areas. Listen for Whip-poor-will calling from the wooded slopes in the morning or evening.

Forested trails along the river offer opportunities to find the common Pileated Woodpeckers and Yellow-bellied Sapsuckers. Listen for the sapsuckers calling and drumming here in summer; this is at the south end of their breeding territory.

Birding the parking and pavilion area at the south entrance will usually yield a territorial male Yellow-throated Warbler, as well as nesting Eastern Phoebes. Immediately south of the pavilion you'll find a wooden footbridge, over a creek, which joins a spur of the Sentinel Trail. This wooded creek bottom and adjacent bluff attract Acadian Flycatchers, Blue-gray Gnatcatchers, Veeries, Wood Thrushes, Northern Parulas, Black-and-white Warblers, Louisiana Waterthrushes, Kentucky Warblers, Scarlet Tanagers, and Rose-breasted Grosbeaks. Take the paved road south of the loop to the parking area at the south trail system trailhead to find Veeries, Wood Thrushes, Cerulean Warblers, Ovenbirds, Hooded Warblers, Scarlet

Tanagers, Rose-breasted Grosbeaks, and Eastern Towhees. Where this road ends at a scrubby/shrub habitat, you may find Black-billed Cuckoo, Blue-winged Warbler, Yellow Warbler, Chestnut-sided Warbler, Indigo Bunting, and Orchard Oriole.

The north trail system attracts breeding Yellow-billed Cuckoos, Carolina Wrens, Blue-gray Gnatcatchers, Veeries, Wood Thrushes, Yellow-throated Vireos, Warbling Vireos, Red-eyed Vireos, American Redstarts, Ovenbirds, and Scarlet Tanagers.

The park is open in winter and provides superb birding opportunities. On the river, you can see large numbers of Bald Eagles and an occasional Golden Eagle. Within the woods and pine stands, you may find Red-breasted Nuthatches and Brown Creepers, while Winter Wrens frequent the wooded creek bottoms. Several species of winter finches spend the season here during invasion years, including Purple Finches, Red and White-winged Crossbills, Common Redpolls, Pine Siskins, and Evening Grosbeaks.

General information: This park is open all year, except during the firearms deer hunting season. The entrances usually open at 7 A.M. Many facilities are available at this park such as water, restrooms, showers, picnic areas, and a small convenience store (not always open) near the park headquarters. Good hiking footwear is essential. Protect yourself from mosquitos and ticks in the summer, and wear warm clothes and boots in the winter. Maps of the park's road, trail, and campground facilities can be obtained from the office at the headquarters near the north entrance.

ADDITIONAL HELP

DeLorme IA&G grid: 15.
Contact: Mississippi Palisades State Park.
Nearest gas, food, and lodging: Trailer and tent camping in the park. Savanna, Illinois, and Clinton, Iowa.

38 Savanna Army Depot

Habitats: Upland sand prairie, oak savanna and upland forest, bottomland floodplain forest, and wetlands.

Key birds: Migrating waterfowl and songbirds, including 30 species of warblers; breeding Great Blue Heron, Black-crowned Night-Heron, Northern Harrier, Upland Sandpiper, Black-billed Cuckoo, Short-eared Owl, Willow Flycatcher, Western Kingbird, Wood Thrush, Northern Mockingbird, Brown Thrasher, Loggerhead Shrike; Bell's, Blue-headed, Yellow-throated, and Red-eyed Vireos; Yellow-breasted Chat, Prothonotary Warbler, American Redstart, Cerulean Warbler, Scarlet Tanager, Blue Grosbeak, Dickcissel, Vesper, Lark, and Grasshopper Sparrows, Bobolink, Eastern and Western Meadowlarks, Orchard Oriole, and Pileated Woodpecker; postbreeding dispersal of Little Blue Heron and Cattle Egret.

Best times to bird: All year, but especially during migration and the breeding season.

Directions: The Savanna Army Depot is 7 miles north of Savanna along Illinois Route 84, and adjacent to Mississippi Palisades State Park. A sign marking the Savanna Army Depot entrance is about 7 miles north of the town of Savanna along IL 84.

Birding: The Savanna Army Depot, owned by the federal government until the year 2000, provides habitat for a diverse array of birds during migration and summer, some of which are difficult to find anywhere else in the state. Between the floodplain and uplands, birders can find 200 species in a given year at the depot, with at least 100 of them breeding. The U.S. Fish & Wildlife Service will receive ownership of the site in the year 2000. After then, the public may be allowed to access parts of this ecologically rich site to bird, but it may take several years to develop a trail system and open the site for birding.

The following information, provided by Kelly McKay, gives you an idea of how you may be able to bird the area after it is open to the public. PLEASE NOTE: Public access will be determined in the year 2000—you MUST call first before coming to see if any roads have been opened to bird the depot.

Birders may be able to travel the main road into the depot, then drive down some of the smaller gravel roads to bird the uplands. Or they may be able to bird the bottomlands, via a boat, probably a canoe. A good ramp facility exists along the road immediately adjacent to the river. Sloughs, backwater bays, and other wetlands bisect the floodplain.

During March and April as well as October and November, birders should find a large number of waterfowl, including 23 species of swans, geese, and ducks. Some of these include Tundra Swans, Snow Geese, Wood Ducks, Green-winged Teals, Northern Shovelers, Gadwalls, American Wigeons, Canvasbacks, Ring-necked Ducks, Hooded Mergansers, Common Mergansers, and Ruddy Ducks. Migratory songbirds use the floodplain forest in April and May, as well as in September and October. The list includes all 7 of the state's woodpeckers and

38 Savanna Army Depot

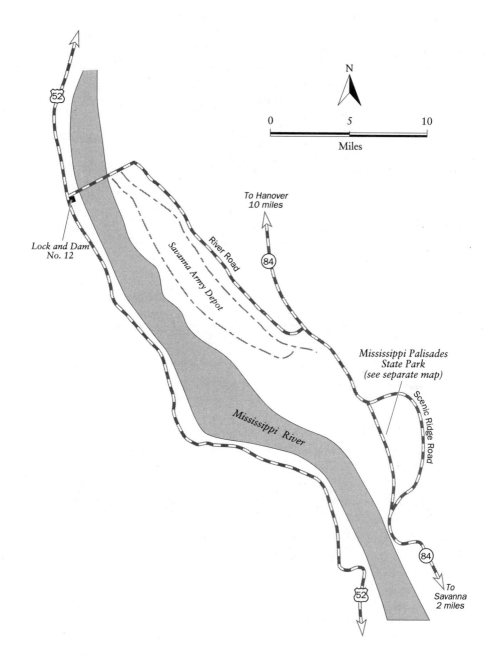

N

0   5   10

Miles

US 52

Lock and Dam
No. 12

River Road

Savanna Army Depot

To Hanover
10 miles

US 84

Mississippi Palisades
State Park
(see separate map)

Scenic Ridge Road

Mississippi River

US 84

To
Savanna
2 miles

US 52

thrushes, all 6 swallows, and 8 species of flycatchers. Additionally, about 30 species of warblers use these forests as migration corridors, along with several species of vireos, Scarlet Tanagers, and various grosbeaks, sparrows, blackbirds, orioles, and finches.

The floodplain forest/backwater wetland complex of the Savanna Army Depot is also important in terms of breeding birds. A rookery contains over 100 pairs of breeding Great Blue Herons, along with several Black-crowned Night-Herons and Green Herons, some of which you might see foraging while on your boat trip. Two to three pairs of Bald Eagles also nest here annually, in addition to at least one pair of Red-shouldered Hawks.

At the extreme upper end of the depot's floodplain is Lock and Dam 12. A long levee and spillway connecting the dam to the depot creates a large shallow-water bay immediately upstream. This bay serves as brood habitat for several species of waterfowl and water birds, including Wood Ducks, Blue-winged Teals, Pied-billed Grebes, and Double-crested Cormorants. Access the levee from the upland road immediately adjacent to the river at the extreme upper end of the depot.

The bottomland forest provides breeding habitat for many species of songbirds, including Yellow-billed Cuckoos, Pileated Woodpeckers, Carolina Wrens, Veeries, Yellow-throated Vireos, Warbling and Red-eyed Vireos, Northern Parulas, Cerulean Warblers, American Redstarts, Prothonotary Warblers, Scarlet Tanagers, Rose-breasted Grosbeaks, and Baltimore Orioles.

The upland area of the depot is dominated by several thousand acres of short-grass sand prairie, with smaller patches of oak savanna. A wide array of migratory songbirds can be found in the upland forest and oak savanna habitats during spring and fall, including many species of flycatchers, thrushes, vireos, and warblers. However, the avian community of the grassland habitat is most impressive during the breeding season.

Driving the three parallel paved roads and the many secondary and gravel roads that crisscross the large grassland during late spring and summer might yield grassland birds such as Turkey Vultures, Northern Harriers, Upland Sandpipers, Common Nighthawks, Eastern Kingbirds, Horned Larks, Eastern Bluebirds, Loggerhead Shrikes, Dickcissels, Vesper Sparrows, Lark Sparrows, Grasshopper Sparrows, Bobolinks, Eastern and Western Meadowlarks, and Orchard Orioles. Most of these species occur in relatively large densities. Especially numerous are the meadowlarks and Grasshopper Sparrows.

Additionally, species ordinarily rare in northwestern Illinois, including the Western Kingbird, Northern Mockingbird, and Blue Grosbeak, often breed in the depot's grasslands.

Scrub habitat bordering the savannas provides nesting habitat for species such as the Black-billed Cuckoo, Willow Flycatcher, Brown Thrasher, Bell's Vireo, Yellow-breasted Chats, and Indigo Bunting.

The upland forest also attracts breeding Pileated Woodpeckers, flycatchers, thrushes, Yellow-throated and Red-eyed Vireos, Northern Parulas, American

Bald Eagle. DENNIS OEHMKE PHOTO

Redstarts, Ovenbirds, Scarlet Tanagers, and Rose-breasted Grosbeaks. Interspersed wetland areas hold several wading bird and waterfowl species, including Great Blue Herons, Great Egrets, dispersing Little Blue Herons, Cattle Egrets, Green Herons, and Wood Ducks.

General information: This facility will be turned over to the U.S. Fish & Wildlife Service and Illinois Department of Natural Resources in the year 2000. Until then it is closed to the public. Staff is working on plans for hiking trails.

You'll find limited primitive restroom facilities and no fresh water. A hunting policy might be established, so call first before making the trip. You'll need plenty of water, insect repellent, hat, sunscreen, long pants and boots, and stamina; walking the area can be physically challenging.

ADDITIONAL HELP

DeLorme IA&G grid: 15.

Contact: Illinois Department of Natural Resources.

Nearest gas, food, and lodging: Savanna and the Quad Cities; camping at Mississippi Palisades State Park.

39 Mississippi River Corridor

> **Habitats:** Forested islands and tree-lined shorelines of the Mississippi River, open backwaters and tailwater areas below locks and dams.
> **Key birds:** Bald Eagle, occasional Golden Eagle, plus wintering or migrating loons, ducks, and other waterfowl; wintering gulls, including Mew, Thayer's, Lesser Black-backed, Great Black-backed, and Iceland.
> **Best times to bird:** November through March

Directions: The tour begins at Illinois Highway 84 near the town of Fulton.

Birding: In winter, Bald Eagle viewing along the Mississippi River from Fulton, Illinois, to New Boston, Illinois, can be quite productive. Some 300 to 600 birds, and occasionally more than 1,000 Bald Eagles can be found within this stretch— anywhere the birder can gain access to the riverfront should yield eagles. See Map 1 for areas from Lock and Dam 13 south to the Hampton River Front. See Map 2 for areas from Hampton west to Sunset Park near Lock and Dam 15 Visitor Center. See Map 3 for the area near Lock and Dam 16.

Traveling north a few miles out of Fulton on IL 84 will lead you to Lock and Dam 13. An excellent elevated viewing platform exists in the Lock 13 visitor parking area.

The islands downstream of Lock 13, as well as the Illinois shoreline, often maintain a large population of foraging Bald Eagles. Lock and Dam 13 serves as a staging area for south migrating eagles, with as many as 400 birds occasionally

39 Mississippi River Corridor, Map 1

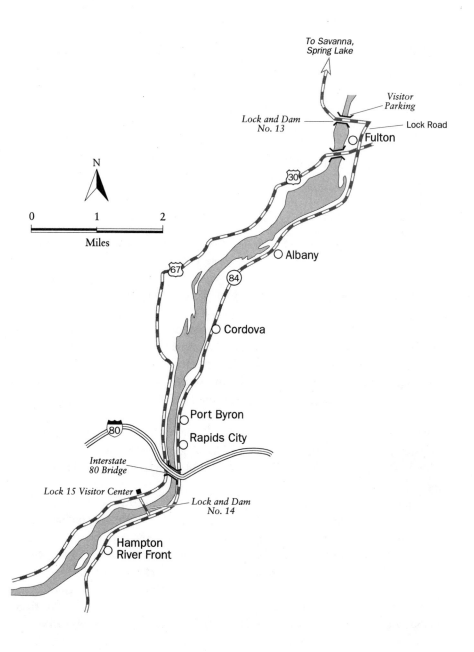

To Savanna,
Spring Lake

Visitor
Parking

Lock and Dam
No. 13

Lock Road

Fulton

30

N

0   1   2
Miles

67

84

Albany

Cordova

Port Byron

Rapids City

80

Interstate
80 Bridge

Lock 15 Visitor Center

Lock and Dam
No. 14

Hampton
River Front

39 Mississippi River Corridor, Map 2

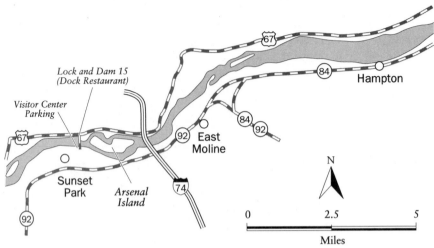

congregating here for no more than a couple of weeks in December. This location does maintain a large population throughout the winter when enough ice cover is present. During winters with little ice cover, sport fishermen can access the river from Fulton, Illinois, or Clinton, Iowa. In these situations, few eagles remain below Lock and Dam 13.

The lower end of Spring Lake, immediately upstream of Lock and Dam 13, is one of the best locations for observing migrating and wintering waterfowl, gulls, and other water birds. This is especially true during mild winters when less ice cover and more open water is present on Spring Lake. Some of the interesting species to be seen include Common Loons, Horned and Eared Grebes, Trumpeter and Tundra Swans, Snow Geese, Gadwalls, American Wigeons, Canvasbacks, Ring-necked Ducks, Oldsquaws, Black and White-winged Scoters, Common and Red-breasted Mergansers, Ruddy Ducks, Golden Eagles, and Franklin's, Bonaparte's, Ring-billed, Herring, Iceland, Thayer's, Lesser Black-backed, Glaucous, and Great Black-backed Gulls.

Traveling south on IL 84 takes you through the river towns of Fulton, Albany, Cordova, Port Byron, and Rapids City. Albany and Cordova often maintain large populations of wintering Bald Eagles. The Cordova riverfront also hosts large populations of wintering diving ducks such as Ring-necked Ducks, Lesser Scaups, Common Goldeneyes, and Common and Red-breasted Mergansers.

Continuing on IL 84 south of Rapids City brings you to Lock and Dam 14 just north of Hampton, Illinois, where you may find up to 100 wintering eagles. To get to the Lock 14 parking area, cross over the I-80 bridge 1 mile north of Lock 14 Cross the bridge and proceed south on IL 67 in Iowa to get to the Lock 14 visitor parking area. This location provides some of the best eagle photographic opportunities in the Midwest, as long as you remain in your vehicle. The birds are so close

39 Mississippi River Corridor, Map 3

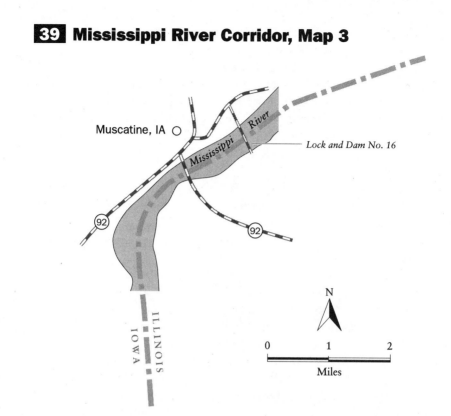

Muscatine, IA

Mississippi River

Lock and Dam No. 16

92

92

N

ILLINOIS
IOWA

0 1 2
Miles

that if you attempt to get out of your car, they will definitely be disturbed and fly. This causes the eagles to waste valuable energy reserves and may become extremely dangerous to their survival, particularly during cold weather.

Open water areas, which normally persist each winter above Lock 14, serve as wintering sites for many waterfowl and gulls, including Trumpeter Swans, Canada Geese, American Black Ducks, Mallards, Canvasbacks, Ring-necked Ducks, Lesser and Greater Scaups, Common Goldeneyes, Buffleheads, Hooded and Common Mergansers, Ruddy Ducks, Ring-billed, Herring, Mew, Thayer's, and Glaucous Gulls.

The Hampton, Illinois, riverfront along IL 84 usually yields 25 or more Bald Eagles. Driving along IL 92 near East Moline can also offer good birding. You'll find several pull-outs giving you access to the river. Eagle numbers here are generally relatively low, but it is an excellent location for viewing waterfowl and gulls. A large number of Mallards winter here as well as fewer numbers of American Black Ducks, Green-winged Teals, Wood Ducks, Northern Pintails, Northern Shovelers, Gadwalls, and American Wigeons. This stretch of river also holds large numbers of diving ducks, including Canvasbacks, Ring-necked Ducks, Lesser Scaups, Common Goldeneyes, Common Mergansers, and Ruddy Ducks. In the evening, the river serves as a roosting site for gulls, whose numbers often exceed 5,000. Search for rarities, including Franklin's, Bonaparte's, Ring-billed, Mew, Herring,

Thayer's, Iceland, Glaucous, Slaty-backed, Lesser Black-backed, Great Black-backed, Black-legged Kittiwake, and even Sabine's Gull.

South on IL 92, you'll find an information sign to Arsenal Island. Once on the island, follow the road until it comes to another bridge that crosses the remainder of the Mississippi River into Iowa. Just before crossing the river, make a right and then immediately a left turn into the U.S. Army Corps of Engineers Visitor Center parking area. From the observation platform observers can often view a large number of Bald Eagles foraging below Lock and Dam 15 on the lower end of Arsenal Island.

The best eagle viewing at Lock 15 is available on the Iowa shoreline. Cross the Arsenal Bridge and take the first left turn in Iowa, followed by the next available left. Make a right turn at the stop sign and go 1 block. Turn left into the parking lot of the Dock restaurant. From this parking area, birders can look across the river at the lower end of Arsenal Island, where often 50 or more Bald Eagles forage. During warm periods, a large number of sport fishermen congregate below Lock and Dam 15, and then the eagles leave.

Sunset Park on IL 92 also offers good eagle viewing. Scan across the river from this park and look downstream on the Illinois shoreline for eagles.

The next Bald Eagle site is 25 to 30 miles south of the park on IL 92 at Lock and Dam 16 on the Iowa side. Just before crossing the IL 92 bridge into Muscatine, Iowa, take the gravel road (Lock Road) north for 2 miles to Lock and Dam 16. The Lock Road downstream and upstream of the dam provides excellent Bald Eagle viewing and photographic opportunities. The large oaks, cottonwoods, and silver maples along the shoreline are usually heavily used as foraging perches by as many as 25 to 75 eagles. These trees are immediately next to the road and the birds within them provide excellent subjects for photographers. A word of caution, however: Observers along the road must remain within their vehicles to avoid disturbing the Bald Eagles present.

At the Lock and Dam, an elevated viewing platform allows observers to see not only most of the eagles on the Illinois shoreline, but also the birds perching on the Iowa side. The number of Bald Eagles using the Lock and Dam 16 area varies greatly from year to year. During a typical year, both sides of the river combined may harbor anywhere from 50 to 150 Bald Eagles.

When enough open water exists to keep the Muscatine boat ramps open, a large number of sport fishermen heavily utilize the Lock 16 tailwaters. During these times, few Bald Eagles remain in the Lock and Dam 16 vicinity. When little ice cover is present, the upstream side of this dam maintains a fairly large number of wintering diving ducks and gulls.

General information: Apart from Alaska, Illinois hosts the nation's largest Bald Eagle wintering population. The birds are attracted to rivers and locks and dams. Besides binoculars, a spotting scope and camera will make your eagle-watching trip a much more satisfying and memorable experience. Also, observers should always bring enough warm clothes and footwear. Even if the temperature seems fairly pleasant, it always feels much colder when on the riverfront.

Please follow proper eagle etiquette. Remain at least 200 meters away from foraging and resting birds when possible and stay inside your vehicle. Bald Eagles are easily disturbed and will flush from perches when people step outside their vehicles. Automobiles actually serve as blinds, which allow you to approach eagles while minimizing disturbance to them.

ADDITIONAL HELP

DeLorme IA&G grid: 15, 22, 23 and 30.
Contact: Kelly McKay or Tom Stalf.
Nearest gas, food, and lodging: Anywhere along the river route.

40 Starved Rock and Matthiessen State Parks

Habitats: Canyons, forested 125-foot-tall sandstone bluffs, and restored grasslands.

Key birds: Migratory waterfowl, shorebirds, and songbirds; migratory American White Pelican; breeding Red-shouldered Hawk, American Woodcock, Wild Turkey, Acadian Flycatcher, Louisiana Waterthrush, Scarlet Tanager, and grassland birds; wintering Bald Eagle, wrens, and finches.

Best times to bird: Spring and fall migration and early in the breeding season.

Directions: Visitors coming from the west can get to the Starved Rock area off Illinois Highway 178 via Interstate 80. IL 178 is east of Interstate 39 and west of IL 23. Drive south on IL 178 to IL 71 to begin your exploration of the Starved Rock and Matthiessen State Parks. Visitors coming from the east (Chicago area) should exit at IL 23 near Ottawa, drive south to the Illinois River bridge, turn west on IL 71 at the south end of the bridge, and then drive 6 miles to the Lone Point Shelter parking area on the north side of the road.

Birding: Like Dorothy in the *Wizard of Oz,* you might enter Starved Rock State Park along the Illinois River just south of Utica and exclaim, "I have a feeling we're not in Illinois anymore." This state park filled with bluffs and 18 stream-fed canyons along the Illinois River is the state's Grand Canyon, beckoning more than 1 million visitors each year to walk the 15 miles of well-marked trails.

More than 225 bird species have been recorded at Starved Rock State Park and nearby Matthiessen State Park. You can spend a fruitful day nearly any day of the year exploring these parks, gathering a nice-sized bird list, and enjoying the spectacular scenery. Be prepared with good hiking shoes, water, a hat, insect repellent, and a picnic lunch.

40 Starved Rock and Matthiessen State Parks

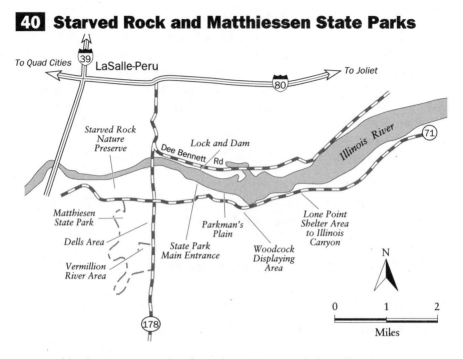

Local birders recommend making the Lone Point Shelter–Illinois Canyon area at the far east end of the park off IL 71 your first priority when visiting the site year-round. This area, along the Illinois River, has attracted all of the state's migrating waterfowl, including occasional Mute and Tundra Swans, Greater White-fronted and Snow Geese, Common Loons, and, sometimes scoters. You may also find migrant Ospreys and lingering Bald Eagles, plus numerous gulls and terns of the predictable species and the occasional rarity such as Great Black-backed or Laughing Gulls. Check the flats around the offshore islands for small numbers of migrant shorebirds, including rarities such as godwits, Willets, and Avocets. In spring 1997, nearly 400 American White Pelicans rested here for a few weeks; time will tell if this becomes a regular occurrence.

In late summer and early fall, search this area for returning shorebirds, numerous terns, and large flocks of Great Egrets and Great Blue Herons along with an occasional vagrant Snowy Egret or Little Blue Heron. In winter, if water is open, large flocks of Common Mergansers and scaups with other waterfowl remain, and you can often see feeding Bald Eagles.

The woods around the Lone Point Shelter provide the best migrant birding in the park. All the warblers, vireos, and flycatchers (including Alder and Olive-sided) may be found there in spring and fall.

Migrant birding at the Illinois Canyon is also productive, and may be better than at the point if it's windy. A diligent birder might find Mourning, Connecticut, Kentucky, and, rarely, Worm-eating Warblers in the woods surrounding the parking lot. The trail into the canyon provides an opportunity to view thrushes and

Winter Wrens, and possibly Summer Tanagers. Besides the expected woodland species, Illinois Canyon regularly hosts breeding Acadian Flycatchers, Louisiana Waterthrushes, Scarlet Tanagers and Wild Turkeys. In fall and winter you may often find Carolina and Winter Wrens, Brown Creepers, Golden-crowned Kinglets, Red and White-breasted Nuthatches, and Tufted Titmice.

To watch displaying woodcocks in the twilight, drive 1 mile west of the Illinois Canyon parking lot to a small parking area along IL 71.

Another 1.5 miles west on IL 71 will bring you to the Parkman's Plain parking area on the north side of the road. The lower river trails out of the lot lead to typical woodland birding, which are best explored during migration. The upper trail leads to an overlook platform that is a good place to scope the river for waterfowl during migration and winter.

Drive 2 miles farther and you will be at the park's main entrance, about a mile east of IL 178. Drive north on the entrance road to the river parking area at the bottom of the bluff. Turn into the parking area entrance, then drive as far west as possible through the picnic grounds. Where the road loops back east you will be paralleling a rather foreboding floodplain forest. If the mud and nettles aren't too bad, this is a good place to find nesting Barred Owls, Red-shouldered Hawks, Brown Creepers, and sometimes Pileated Woodpeckers.

West of IL 178, between IL 71 and the river, you'll find a large tract of bottomland forest designated as the Starved Rock Nature Preserve. This undeveloped and rarely birded preserve attracts woodland birds, including Prothonotary Warblers, Louisiana Waterthrushes, Pileated Woodpeckers, and Red-shouldered Hawks. In summer, birders sometimes find Yellow-crowned Night-Herons. To access the area, inquire at the park visitor center.

Nearby Matthiessen State Park is worth exploring. The Vermillion River Area entrance, with its extensive prairie restoration, hosts breeding Dickcissels, Grasshopper Sparrows, Eastern Meadowlarks, Northern Bobwhites, Eastern Bluebirds, and in some years, Sedge Wrens. Northern Mockingbirds and Summer Tanagers have been found in the shrubs and woodland edges. To get here from the Illinois Canyon parking lot, drive west on IL 71 for 5 miles to IL 178. Then drive south another 2 miles to the

Acadian Flycatcher at nest.
JOE B. MILOSEVICH PHOTO

entrance. If you'd like to take another canyon hike, you can drive back north on IL 178 to the Dells Area entrance and park at the picnic area. You can walk to the canyons and back here in about an hour—it's a mini-version of Starved Rock State Park, and sometimes is quieter and less populated. At the canyon's top, you may see Cliff Swallows, as well as Scarlet Tanagers and Cedar Waxwings feeding on the berries of northern honeysuckle and serviceberry.

If you walk atop the bluffs through oaks and hickories, you should hear nuthatches, chickadees, and woodpeckers. At the moist canyon floor, you may hear and see the ubiquitous Carolina Wren and possibly Winter Wren during early spring migration, as well as pockets of migrants in spring and fall.

No guide to Starved Rock would be complete without mentioning the Army Corps Visitor Center at the Starved Rock Lock and Dam. It's directly across the river from Starved Rock and provides excellent Bald Eagle viewing in the winter and early spring. Look in winter for vagrant winter gulls, and bring a scope.

General information: Glacial meltwater and stream erosion formed the canyons and bluffs that are the hallmark of the park. Glacial action also formed moraines and rivers where sparkling waterfalls flow today amid moss-covered sandstone and other lush vegetation. Several thousand years later, a warming period made way for the creation of upland prairies, some of which have been saved at the 2,000-acre Matthiessen State Park, just a few miles from Starved Rock. This park features forested canyons and restored grasslands. You'll find a small visitor center at Starved Rock State Park; the state plans to build a larger center soon. Duck-hunting season starts in October or November and continues for several months, so plan your outing accordingly or call the park for more information.

ADDITIONAL HELP

DeLorme IA&G grid: 34.
Contact: Starved Rock State Park.
Nearest gas, food, and lodging: Starved Rock Lodge (reservations necessary) or Country Inn near Matthiessen State Park; nearby motels in Ottawa; restaurants in Utica.

41 Castle Rock State Park and the George B. Fell Nature Preserve

Habitats: Dry-mesic forest, upland ridges, mesic ravines, small fen, scattered forest edge and successional areas, Rock River, and its associated floodplain forest.

Key birds: Migrating waterfowl, terns, and raptors, including Osprey and Bald Eagle (along the Rock River and nearby bluffs); breeding birds, including Cooper's Hawk, Wild Turkey, Barred Owl, both cuckoos, Whip-poor-will, Pileated Woodpecker, Least and Acadian Flycatchers, Veery, Wood Thrush, Rose-breasted Grosbeak, and at least 15 species of warbler, including Prothonotary, Blue-winged, Golden-winged, Black-and-white, Cerulean, Chestnut-sided, Kentucky, Canada, Hooded, Worm-eating, American Redstart, Louisiana Waterthrush, and Ovenbird.

Best times to bird: Summer for uncommon-to-rare warblers and other passerines.

Directions: From Interstate 39/U.S. Highway 51, exit west at the Illinois Highway 64 interchange. Proceed 14 miles to the town of Oregon. Just after crossing the Rock River, turn south in town onto IL 2, then drive south 2 miles to the park entrance, where you can obtain a map and other information. Lowden–Miller State Forest (Site 42) is just across the river and another good place to bird in the early summer. Nachusa Grasslands (Site 43) is also nearby, and yet another early summer birding hotspot.

Birding: Along with Lowden-Miller State Forest (see Site 42) immediately across the Rock River, this area hosts an amazing variety and combination of rare breeding warblers and other passerines. The park encompasses more than 2,000 acres of one of the largest significant natural areas found in northern Illinois, including spectacular rock formations, deep ravines, and several unique plant communities. The best birding area is the George B. Fell Nature Preserve (686 acres) with additional surrounding forested areas, including a small floodplain forest along the Rock River.

State biologists did intensive bird research here in 1993 and 1994 and found small nesting populations of several bird species either rare or absent from much of the state. Parking access to the area is fairly limited and the more adventuresome birder has two choices. Take IL 2 (running parallel to the Rock River) south past the main entrance of the park to the parking lot on the east side of the highway (Wayside Area), or park at the Castle Rock Scenic Overlook parking lot.

In spring and summer you should see or hear Eastern Kingbirds, Baltimore Orioles, and many Cedar Waxwings near the open parklike area adjacent to the overlook parking lot. Climb to the sandstone bluff overlook where you might see soaring Turkey Vultures. After enjoying the panoramic view of this pristine stretch of the Rock River, explore the floodplain forest immediately south and west of the overlook, between the river and the highway. Although traffic whizzes by, you should find a dozen or more pairs of nesting American Redstarts in some of the

41 Castle Rock State Park and the George B. Fell Nature Preserve

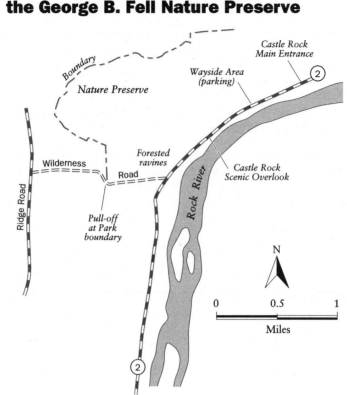

smaller trees in the area. Least Flycatchers and Prothonotary Warblers have also bred here, as well as Cerulean Warblers in the large oak trees right over the highway.

Just across the highway to the west, the mouth of a fairly large ravine system, empties via a tiny fen-fed stream. Although no trails exist, you can explore this forested ravine system, provided you do not disturb this fragile area. During summer you should find many interesting breeding species. In 1994, just inside the forest a short distance from the highway, in and around the fern-choked woodland fen and surrounding forested ravine, researchers found breeding or otherwise summering Acadian Flycatchers, Veeries, Carolina Wrens, Blue-gray Gnatcatchers, American Redstarts, Louisiana Waterthrushes, and Kentucky and Canada (pair carrying nest material and food for young) Warblers. Just down the road, in a small patch of successional habitat, a female Golden-winged Warbler was found with a male. Canada and Golden-winged Warblers typically breed farther north, so Castle Rock can be thought of as a little piece of southern Canada in northern Illinois

You may want to return to your car at this point and continue south and west just a short distance, being alert for an unmarked road (known as Wilderness Road on park maps) going west up a fairly steep incline and through the heavily forested ravines with scattered successional openings of the nature preserve.

Continue to the top, and just before the road makes a sharp jog to the north at the park boundary, park your vehicle at a small pull-out on the south side of the road. Explore the woods on the north or south side of the road (with a good compass and insect repellent) or for the less adventurous, simply walk Wilderness Road east the way you came. Either way you are likely to add several species to your list, including Broad-winged and Cooper's Hawks, Wild Turkeys, Barred Owls, Whip-poor-wills, Pileated Woodpeckers, Tufted Titmice, Wood Thrushes, Rose-breasted Grosbeaks, Yellow-throated and Red-eyed Vireos, Ovenbirds, and if you're lucky, Chestnut-sided or Hooded Warblers.

General information: The area has a rich history of occupation by Native Americans, including the Sauk and Fox tribes, from 1730 through 1832. The famous Sauk chief Blackhawk returned to Illinois after being forced west, and led his tribe in a series of battles known as the Blackhawk Indian Wars until his capture in 1832. Local residents proposed making this area a state park as early as 1921, but it wasn't until 1964 that a nonprofit natural lands preservation group known as the Natural Lands Institute conducted a public fundraising campaign to preserve the area. Today much of the acreage in the park is listed as state dedicated nature preserve property, protecting it from development. The park features several picnic areas, including scenic ones along the river near the main entrance. Trails are limited. New camping facilities may be added soon.

ADDITIONAL HELP

DeLorme IA&G grid: 25.
Contact: Castle Rock State Park.
Nearest gas, food, and lodging: Primitive canoe camping within the park, and other camping in nearby Lowden State Park near Oregon (not to be confused with Lowden-Miller State Forest, which does not offer camping facilities). Motels and restaurants in nearby Oregon.

42 Lowden-Miller State Forest

Habitats: Deciduous and coniferous forest at various stages, including former clearcuts and evergreen nursery.
Key birds: Breeding Whip-poor-will, Least Flycatcher, Brown Creeper, Golden-crowned Kinglet, Veery, Wood Thrush, Red-eyed Vireo, 20 species of warblers, including Hooded, Blue-winged, Yellow-throated, and Black-throated Green (only confirmed place in state where this species breeds), and Vesper Sparrow.
Best times to bird: Late May and June.

Directions: You'll find Lowden-Miller on Flagg Road east of the Rock River, between the towns of Oregon and Dixon. From Interstate 88 (East–West Tollway), take Illinois Highway 251 north 2 miles past IL 38 to Flagg Road. Travel about 15

42 Lowden-Miller State Forest

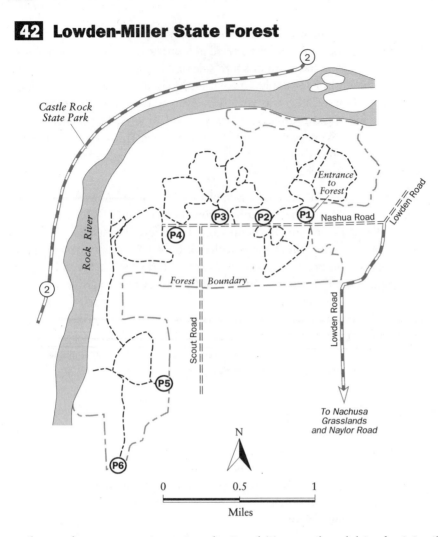

miles to a four-way stop sign at Lowden Road. Turn north and drive for 3.8 miles to the road leading to Lowden-Miller State Forest. Follow the signs to the entrance.

Birding: Dr. Scott Robinson, the Illinois Natural History Survey scientist noted nationally for his work on breeding neotropical migrants, discovered this little-known area in 1994 when he conducted a breeding bird census. The 2,225-acre Lowden-Miller State Forest near Oregon contains Illinois' most unusual and surprising breeding bird community, a blend of northern and southern species found nowhere else in the Midwest.

Robinson and his team recorded 100 species breeding or defending territories, among them 20 species of warblers, more than breed in the entire 260,000-acre Shawnee National Forest in southern Illinois. They also discovered the state's first two Black-throated Green Warbler nests here in a white pine plantation, as well as 15 other Black-throated Green Warbler territories.

As you enter the forest, listen for singing Vesper Sparrows in the fields. They often perch on tops of trees along hedgerows. Then begin at parking lot 3, where you can traverse several habitats to get a flavor of just how many different species can be seen, actually heard more often than seen, in early summer. You'll find well-marked trails here and at the other five parking lots scattered in the forest.

At parking lot 3, you enter a grove of red and white pines where the Yellow-throated Warbler has bred. This species breeds either in sycamore or old pine plantations in Illinois, and you'll find both habitats at the forest. Listen, too, for Ovenbirds, Veeries, Wood Thrushes, and Red-eyed Vireos, which are more typically associated with hardwood instead of coniferous forests. Chipping Sparrows are abundant here.

Next you'll pass a shrubby secondary growth area where Yellow-breasted Chats and Blue-winged Warblers have bred. As the habitat changes, so does the bird life. For example, recent clearcuts less than three years old contained small numbers of Canada, Mourning, and Golden-winged Warblers, which are extremely rare breeders in Illinois. Some of the older clearcuts attract White-eyed Vireos, Yellow-breasted Chats, and Black-and-white Warblers. As these clearcuts grow, the bird life will change, and these species may leave.

Another satisfying birding experience at Lowden-Miller is at parking lot 2 where you'll hear Whip-poor-wills singing at dusk in spring and early summer.

If you're up for more exploring, try walking the other trails. Though they are well marked, they can be long and it can be hot, so come with good walking shoes, mosquito repellent, and water.

General information: Before it was sold to the state of Illinois, the forest was part of the Sinnissippi Tree Farm. Here extensive white and red pine plantations are interspersed with selectively logged oak-hickory forests and floodplain forest along the Rock River.

The area is open to the public for nature-watching and hunting. Sometimes the area is closed during the morning in May or during fall for hunting. Call first before going so you won't be disappointed if you can't get in. You'll find only one small outdoor restroom here, at parking lot 1.

This birding hotspot is 5 miles away from Nachusa Grasslands (see Site 43), where you'll find some rare grassland species during the breeding season. You can visit both places in a day, though you might want to stay here for a few days to experience morning and dusk in early summer at the grasslands and Lowden-Miller.

ADDITIONAL HELP

DeLorme IA&G grid: 25.

Contact: Castle Rock State Park.

Nearest gas, food, and lodging: Primitive canoe camping within the park; other camping in nearby Lowden State Park just east and north of Oregon (not to be confused with Lowden-Miller State Forest, which does not offer camping facilities). Motels and restaurants in nearby Oregon.

43 Nachusa Grasslands and Franklin Creek State Natural Area

Habitats: Prairie, fen, marsh, creek, savanna, and sandstone outcroppings.

Key birds: Rare or endangered breeding grassland birds, including Northern Harrier, Upland Sandpiper (declining in numbers), Bobolink, Grasshopper, Henslow's, and Lark Sparrows; breeding Whip-poor-will and Bell's Vireo; fall sparrows; wintering owls; migratory songbirds at nearby Franklin Creek State Natural Area.

Best times to bird: May through late June, late fall and winter.

Directions: You'll find the grasslands on Flagg Road, east of the Rock River, between the towns of Oregon and Dixon, Illinois. From Interstate 88 (East–West Tollway), take Illinois Highway 251 north 2 miles past IL 38 to Flagg Road. Travel about 15 miles to a four-way stop sign at Lowden Road. Turn south and drive for 1.8 miles. On the west side of the road will be the grasslands and a parking area for about eight cars next to a Nature Conservancy sign.

Birding: At the Nachusa Grasslands south of Oregon, you can wander through a rolling landscape consisting of a mosaic of 11 natural community types, including dry prairie, tallgrass prairie, bur oak savanna, sand savanna, fen, sedge meadow, and streamside marsh. Scattered among old corn and soybean fields, these high-quality natural areas provide a unique opportunity to restore Illinois' original landscape, and in the process, provide nesting habitat for some of the state's rarest birds.

You'll hear the rollicking, buzzy, whistle-like tones of at least 90 species of breeding birds. Indulge your sensory pleasures by listening to bird song and enjoying the muted brown, yellow, and green hues of the prairie landscape.

The only request: Take special care not to disturb the rare and endangered grassland birds that find perfect habitat to raise their young.

Before beginning your birding excursion, be prepared. You'll encounter heat and tick invasions during breeding season; bring plenty of water; wear a hat to block the sun, long-sleeved, light-colored clothing, and good hiking shoes.

43 Nachusa Grasslands and Franklin Creek State Natural Area

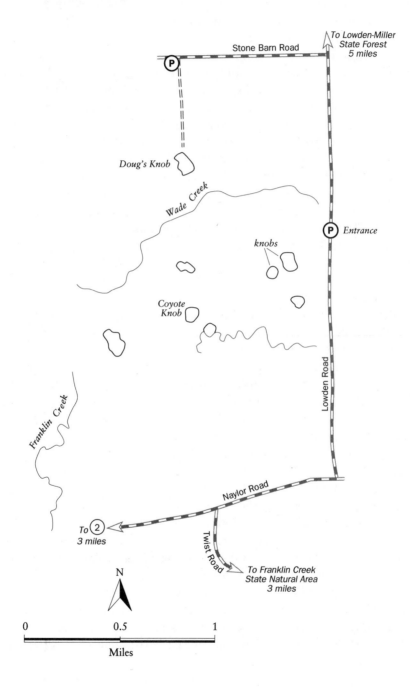

Stone Barn Road

To Lowden-Miller
State Forest
5 miles

Doug's Knob

Wade Creek

knobs

Entrance

Coyote
Knob

Lowden Road

Franklin Creek

Naylor Road

To 2
3 miles

Twist Road

To Franklin Creek
State Natural Area
3 miles

N

| 0 | 0.5 | 1 |

Miles

Begin at the main parking area and check the kiosk for a posted map to help get your bearings. Walk southwest toward the main knobs, groups of hills. First-time visitors might wish to hike southwest to Coyote Knob, one of the far west knobs. As you walk, listen in mid-May through late June for the *"pit-up-zee"* call of Grasshopper Sparrows, the fast two-syllable call of the Henslow's Sparrow, as well as the Dickcissel announcing its name. Sedge Wrens are also quite common in the wet meadows. Look in this area, too, for the Upland Sandpiper. As of this writing, only one nesting pair of Upland Sandpipers remained at Nachusa.

Just west of Coyote Point you'll find a seep and fen ecosystem that attracts breeding White-eyed Vireos, Yellow-breasted Chats, and Blue-winged Warblers, as well as a host of spring migrants.

Listen for the Lark Sparrow, which prefers sandy soils between the knobs. Bobolinks and Horned Larks use the crop fields, which are being converted to prairie. The larks will move to shorter grasses as the restoration continues.

Check the many thickets on the knobs for breeding Bell's Vireos, Yellow-breasted Chats, and Willow Flycatchers, and search the bur oak areas for breeding Orchard Orioles. Next walk to Wade Creek, which is beyond a fence. Perhaps you'll hear a Veery or observe Eastern Bluebirds nesting in tree cavities.

Walk south of the creek for a while, listening for Vesper Sparrows. Then look for the high ridge that will take you back northeast to where you parked. Here's your best chance to find the state-listed endangered Northern Harrier, which has nested, though not every year, and to find a Northern Mockingbird that sometimes frequents the area.

You may also wish to explore Nachusa Grasslands at the Stone Barn Road entrance. To get there, head north on Lowden Road to Stone Barn Road, then go west to the Nature Conservancy sign. You'll find a place to park a few cars here. Walk south along a farm road that bisects the main complex of knobs. Listen, as you begin walking, for Grasshopper Sparrows, Sedge Wrens, and Upland Sandpipers, all of which have been seen and heard here. You'll be walking toward Wade Creek.

Sometimes Sedge Wrens sing or nest in the wet fields just north of the creek. This area is known as Doug's Knob. Explore the savanna area west for Great Crested Flycatchers and Eastern Towhees, then head back to walk along Wade Creek to search for White-eyed Vireos and Scarlet Tanagers. If you sit quietly beneath a tree in the savanna at dusk, you might hear Whip-poor-wills calling, Great Horned Owls hooting, and coyotes howling.

Nearby Franklin Creek State Natural Area offers a cool respite from the hot grasslands. To get there from Nachusa Grasslands, go south on Lowden Road 1 mile to Naylor Road, which is the next road south of Stone Bard Road. Go west for 0.5 mile to Twist Road. Follow this winding and sometimes hazardous road to the entrance.

You may find singing Acadian Flycatchers, Northern Parula Warblers, and Cerulean Warblers here in late May through June, as well as Broad-winged Hawks and Veeries. It's a nice place to watch migrating songbirds while enjoying the blooming Virginia bluebells and other wildflowers that proliferate along an easy boardwalk.

If you're really adventurous, the unpaved roads in the vicinity are worth a look. Look for various sparrows and Western Meadowlarks. The Gray Partridge is also within reason, and Long-eared Owls once bred here.

Also, note that Lowden–Miller State Forest (Site 42) is extremely close. You might wish to spend a day at Nachusa and Franklin Creek and the next day at Lowden–Miller State Forest.

General information: Steep sandstone outcrops descending into rocky meadows and streams made Nachusa Grasslands difficult to farm, so much of it was spared from the plow. Even so, had it not been for the foresight of two prairie enthusiasts, Doug and Dorothy Wade, and the Illinois Nature Conservancy, the Nachusa Grasslands could easily have become another distant memory in the state's ecological history. In the 1960s, the Wades heard the wolf-whistle call of the Upland Sandpiper (then called the Upland Plover) and discovered bits of native prairie throughout farmland and pastures. Keen botanists and prairie flower nurserymen, they alerted The Nature Conservancy to the presence of several extremely rare plant species still thriving here.

In 1986, The Nature Conservancy purchased the core of the preserve 15 minutes before the beginning of a land auction that would have turned the area into a sea of 5-acre homesites. Today, the conservancy owns and manages 1,000 acres, and plans to purchase 1,500 more adjoining acres of old fields that can be restored to healthy grasslands. The conservancy also hopes to raise enough funds to protect additional high-priority lands and link with the nearby 515-acre Franklin Creek State Natural Area. You'll find facilities at the natural area, but not at the grasslands.

ADDITIONAL HELP

DeLorme IA&G grid: 25.
Contact: The Illinois Chapter of The Nature Conservancy.
Nearest gas, food, and lodging: Oregon.

44 Green River Conservation Area

Habitats: Restored and remnant prairies, scrub land, forest, sedge/wet meadow, cattail marsh, pine plantations, and hedgerows.
Key birds: Breeding scrubland and grassland birds, including Bell's Vireo, Yellow-breasted Chat, Bobolink, Orchard Oriole, and Lark Sparrow; wintering sparrows; migrant bitterns and rails.
Best times to bird: May through summer, and winter.

Directions: From Interstate 88 near the town of Dixon, exit Illinois Highway 26. Go south about 14 miles to Maytown Road. Turn west to reach the main entrance

44 Green River Conservation Area

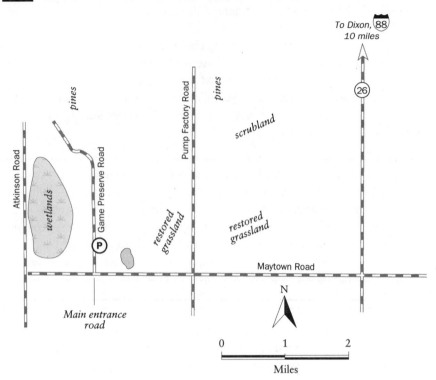

to Green River Conservation Area, which is on the north side of the road. Park in the lot and explore the area on your own.

Birding: Birding Green River area requires a rather adventurous spirit; no real trails have been designated for hikers, but you can walk through these habitats quite easily listening to Bobolinks, Savannah Sparrows, and other grassland species singing amid blazing stars and coneflowers.

The scrubland located sporadically through the site contains good concentrations of Bell's Vireos, Orchard Orioles, Yellow-breasted Chats, and Willow Flycatchers from spring through the breeding season. Visit the area along the east side of Pump Factory Road for your best chance at finding these birds.

Restored prairies at the intersection of Pump Factory and Maytown Road provide habitat for Bobolinks and Lark, Grasshopper, Savannah, and Field Sparrows, as well as the occasional foraging Northern Harrier. Lark Sparrows use this site because it contains a sand prairie, their preferred breeding habitat.

Fragmented forests throughout the site contain Wood Thrushes, Veeries, and Cooper's Hawks during breeding season and good numbers of migrants in spring and fall. In mid-May, the forests, especially the wetter forests, can be full of migrants. Birders have often counted more than 20 species of warblers on one day in May.

The once-productive marsh is now choked with cattails, but a shallow pond on the south part of the conservation area contains breeding Pied-billed Grebes and Hooded Mergansers. Also check for bitterns and rails.

Reed canary grass dominates the site's center, but some sedge areas attract Marsh and Sedge Wrens, Willow Flycatchers, and Swamp Sparrows to breed.

You'll find two large pine plantations that support Red Crossbills and Long-eared Owls some winters. Check the north edge of the site along Pump Factory Road for these birds.

You'll also find hedgerows, which attract migrating sparrows. The hedgerow along the main road into the site has contained such rarities as the Harris's Sparrow. This is the site where a Golden-crowned Sparrow, an accidental species in Illinois, was found in two consecutive years. You'll have a better chance searching for the Harris's Sparrow. Look through flocks of White-crowned Sparrows during October and November for this western species. White-crowns flush more readily than Harris's, so be patient.

General information: Originally set aside as a wildlife refuge for the federally listed endangered Greater Prairie-Chicken, the area now is managed for game hunting. The prairie-chickens have not bred here since the 1960s. A new regime to restore a remnant Illinois prairie should improve the population of many grassland species. Check for the hunting schedule and either avoid the area during those times or wear bright clothing and be careful.

ADDITIONAL HELP

DeLorme IA&G grid: 25.
Contact: Illinois Department of Natural Resources.
Nearest gas, food, and lodging: Dixon; private camping area near Amboy.

45 Woodford State Fish and Wildlife Area

Habitats: Mixed deciduous river bottomland woods and sometimes, flooded fields; large lake, manmade fishing channels.
Key birds: Wintering Great Blue Heron, gulls, Bald Eagle, and Brown Creeper; breeding birds, including five swallow species, Great Egret, Great Crested Flycatcher, Red-headed Woodpecker, Eastern Wood-Pewee, Prothonotary Warbler, and Baltimore Oriole; migratory birds, including most Illinois waterfowl, ducks, grebes, geese, and Double-Crested Cormorant; American White Pelican in April.
Best times to bird: September through February for herons, eagles, gulls, and wintering passerines, including Brown Creeper and Eastern Bluebird; April through May for migrating songbirds.

Directions: From the intersection of Interstates 80 and 39, drive south on I-39 for 18 miles to Illinois Highway 17. Turn west and drive 18 miles to the town of Lacon, which is along the Illinois River. Turn south on IL 26 for 9 miles to the Conservation Area Access Road.

45 Woodford State Fish and Wildlife Area

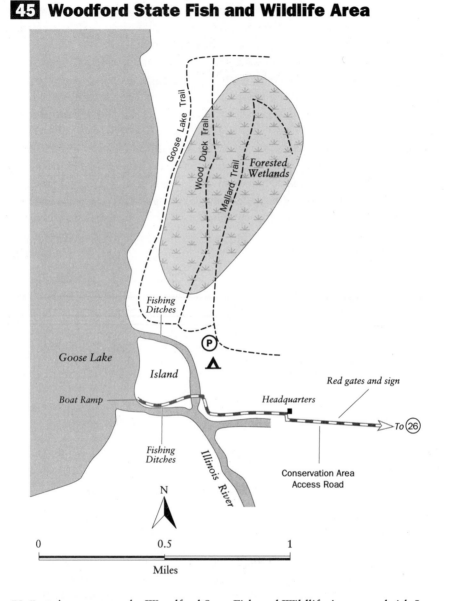

Birding: As you enter the Woodford State Fish and Wildlife Area on a brisk January morning, you may hear the rattling call of a Belted Kingfisher on a low sycamore branch or the chatter of a Brown Creeper, Black-Capped Chickadee, Tufted Titmouse, and White-Breasted Nuthatch flitting in cypress trees in their winter flocks. Near the river, hundreds of gulls soar in search of dying gizzard shad, accompanied by Bald Eagles. All this happens in winter, when bird life is surprisingly active at this conservation area, 20 miles north of Peoria.

Begin your birding at the brown sign for the wildlife area on the Conservation Area Access Road. Look for wintering Eastern Bluebirds on the telephone lines and birds of prey on the telephone poles as well as Horned Larks on the roads, and after a snowstorm, Lapland Longspurs. The fields often flood in spring, attracting various waterfowl, including dabblers such as Blue- and Green-winged Teals.

As you reach the red gates and a wooden sign, you'll learn immediately if you can enter. If this area is flooded, the gates are locked, but most of the time the area is open. Drive the short distance to the area headquarters, listening in summer for calling Northern Bobwhites in the fields, and Winter Wrens in fall and spring in wooded tangles, as well as passerines, including Brown Creepers, feeding in the cypress trees in winter.

Bird the fishing ditches off the main paved road. If water is low enough during winter, artesian wells keep the ditches free of ice, offering prime habitat for eagles and gulls. You might see as many as ten Bald Eagles sitting in one tree. Look out on the river for eagles sitting on the ice and flying over, as well as wintering Great Blue Herons. The gulls and eagles are hunting for dying gizzard shad. During a good shad year you may view thousands of gulls here. Birders found an immature Glaucous Gull for three days in February. In April, look for flocks of American White Pelicans migrating overhead. During summer, swallows hawk insects over the ditch. Opposite the ditches you'll find woodlands where Pileated Woodpeckers congregate in winter. In summer, especially in June, listen for the calls of Yellow-Billed Cuckoos.

The campground site offers woodland and wetland birding from three trails, the Goose Trail, the Mallard Trail, and the Wood Duck Trail. To offer peace for resting waterfowl, these trails are closed in fall. But you can walk them in spring to search for large numbers of migrating Wood Ducks as well as migrating warblers that feed near the water's edge. Watch for a Pileated Woodpecker flying over the path in front of you, or listen for its loud flicker-like call. Listen for calling Barred Owls, which breed here. In late spring and through summer, listen for Eastern Wood-Pewees, House Wrens, Great Crested Flycatchers, Scarlet Tanagers, and other woodland birds. Search for various woodpeckers on the dead snags. Redheaded Woodpeckers are easy to see during the breeding season. Brown Creepers sometimes winter and sometimes breed here. They may be heard singing through the heat of the summer. If the river is low enough in August, the shallow waterways support several species of shorebirds.

General information: The ditches east of the Illinois River were constructed 75 years ago for fishermen. Birders have recently discovered this interesting site. Hunting season begins in fall and lasts through part of winter; call before coming at these times to learn whether you can enter the area. Spring flooding can also close the conservation area. Trails are closed in fall to protect waterfowl.

ADDITIONAL HELP

DeLorme IA&G grid: 41.

Contact: Woodford State Fish and Wildlife Area; Illinois Department of Natural Resources.

Nearest gas, food, and lodging: Camping available, but closed during flooded periods. Nearest hotels in Peoria.

East-Central Region

Some call the east-central region of the state a "corn and soybean desert." But within this desert are oases for birds and for birders, including manmade lakes and natural areas that foresighted individuals saved from destruction. For example, more than 230 species of birds have visited the 1,800-acre Forest Glen Preserve, where several rare orchids grow and where one of the most sought-after warblers, the Worm-eating, breeds. Nearly every breeding warbler in Illinois has been confirmed breeding in this mosaic of wooded ravines, marshy areas, grassy meadows, old fields, ponds, and old-growth beech-maple forest.

Birders have come from New York, Canada, and even Great Britain to the east-central region of Illinois to see a coveted species, the Smith's Longspur. Annual spring treks through cornfields where foxtails grow, produce close views of these migratory birds as they flash white wing patches in the prairie sky.

Lake Shelbyville and Lake Clinton, both manmade lakes, and the surrounding marshes and grasslands, give birders excellent chances to see large numbers of loons, grebes, herons, egrets, and other waterfowl; migratory shorebirds, raptors, and songbirds—especially sparrows and longspurs.

46 Banner Marsh and Rice Lake State Fish and Wildlife Areas

47 Iroquois County Conservation Area

48 Middle Fork State Fish and Wildlife Area

49 Kickapoo State Park

50 Kennekuk County Park

51 Forest Glen Preserve and the Harry "Babe" Woodyard State Natural Area

52 Moraine View State Park

53 Clinton Lake

54 Lake Springfield and Washington Park

55 Carpenter and Riverside Parks

56 Lake Shelbyville and Arcola Marsh

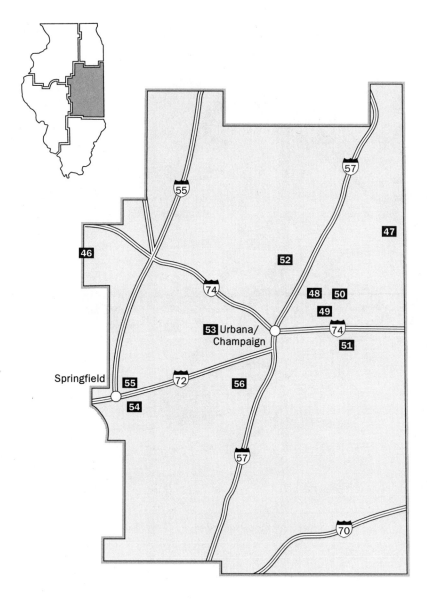

Springfield

Urbana/
Champaign

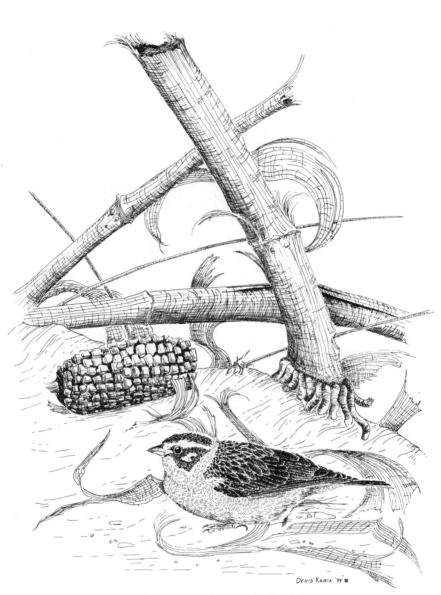

Smith's Longspur drawing by Denis Kania.

46 Banner Marsh and Rice Lake State Fish and Wildlife Areas

Habitats: Wetlands, forest, scrubland, sedge meadow, open water, grasslands, and reclaimed pasture at Banner Marsh; floodplain forest and backwater lakes at Rice Lake.

Key birds: Migratory waterfowl, including occasional rarities; migratory American White Pelican; breeding wetland and grassland birds, including Least Bittern; wintering Rough-legged Hawk, Short-eared Owl, and sparrows; Eurasian Tree Sparrow.

Best times to bird: Late summer, winter, and spring.

Directions: Three entrances are well marked off U.S. Highway 24 south of the Peoria/Pekin area.

Birding: Restored strip mines along the Illinois River at Banner Marsh south of Peoria include acres of diverse habitat that offer birders a chance to see many different bird species, some of which can be rare for the area. One of the specialties is the American White Pelican, which can often be seen soaring along the river in spring.

Although most roads are closed to the public, three main roads lead to good, accessible birding areas.

The north entrance off US 24 takes you through several habitats. As you turn onto the road, check the feeders, which often attract White-crowned, White-throated, and Fox Sparrows in winter. The small ponds and sloughs along this road and throughout the marsh provide good areas to find waterfowl. Follow the north entrance road for about a mile until you reach a lower area that is often flooded in spring, attracting myriad waterfowl. Also check the forest fragments along the road for singing Great Crested Flycatchers, Warbling Vireos, and Baltimore Orioles in spring and summer.

You'll see a marsh along the south edge of the road where the Least Bittern stops during migration, and sometimes remains to breed. Banner Marsh has probably attracted the highest concentration of Least Bitterns in central Illinois. Search for these birds early in the morning or at dusk when they are most active. Also look for Pied-billed Grebes, Common Moorhens, and King Rails.

When you reach a T intersection in the road, you'll notice a gate that is often closed. But you can park and walk the road past the gate. Walk south along this road, noticing a slough to the east that occasionally contains Double-crested Cormorant and breeding Hooded Mergansers and Blue-winged Teals.

On the west side of the road, you'll notice scrubland, which has attracted Bell's Vireo, Orchard Orioles, and occasionally Blue Grosbeaks.

The middle entrance to Banner Marsh leads to a boat launch. If the open water beyond the launch is not frozen in winter, large numbers of waterfowl, including ducks and geese congregate.

46 Banner Marsh and Rice Lake State Fish and Wildlife Areas

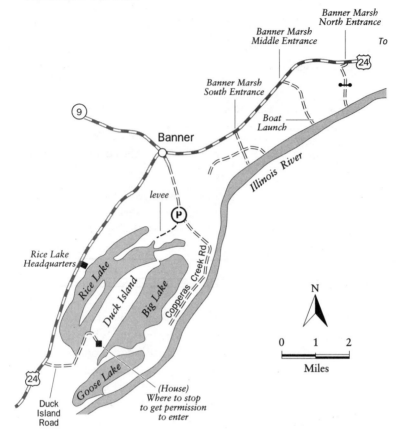

The south entrance is perhaps the most interesting to bird. A large shallow pond along the road provides great habitat for waterfowl, terns, and shorebirds in spring and fall. As you drive this road, take the first crossroad south to a pasture and wetland. Search here for Henslow's Sparrows, Bobolinks, and Sedge Wrens from late April through July. Short-eared Owls and Rough-legged Hawks often feed in these grasslands in winter, as well as throughout the Banner Marsh area.

After birding Banner Marsh, you might enjoy stopping at nearby Rice Lake Fish and Wildlife Area, a large floodplain lake surrounded by floodplain forest, just south of the town of Banner. You'll find the main headquarters off US 24, and you can stop here to search for waterfowl, but two other areas provide much better birding opportunities.

The first area is located along Copperas Creek Road, a road that meets US 24 in the town of Banner and goes south to a boat launch on the Illinois River. Take the road for 2 miles until you reach a pullout where you can park. Take the trail leading south along a levee, that takes you to the north side of Rice Lake. From this vantage point, you should find many waterfowl species, including dabbling and diving ducks in fall and spring, and during low-water season, many shorebird species. Birders have documented Piping Plovers here; you'll more likely see Semi-palmated and Least Sandpipers and other common peeps.

The floodplain forest along Copperas Creek Road and surrounding most of the lake provides good habitat for breeding Prothonotary Warblers, American Redstarts, Warbling Vireos, Pileated Woodpeckers, and Eurasian Tree Sparrows. Some rarities that have been seen here include Mississippi Kites and Golden Eagles.

The south entrance to Rice Lake also leads to the second lake called Big Lake. Duck Island, a private hunt club and quarry, separates these two lakes. To enter this area follow US 24 south of the headquarters to Duck Island Road. Turn east and follow the road to a quarry. Be careful since large trucks use this area. The owners of the area welcome birders, but recently they have charged a fee for birders. Stop by their house before entering.

The best area to bird is along the road east of the quarries where you'll see Rice Lake through a small row of trees. Take any of the beaten paths to the lake, where you can get good views. This south part of the lake has been excellent for rarities in the past few years. Here's a partial list: Ruff, Sabine's Gull, Black-necked Stilt, White Ibis, White-faced Ibis, and California Gull. Even if you don't find the rare one, you're sure to see many interesting shorebirds; nearly every shorebird species recorded in central Illinois has visited this spot either in spring or in summer when mudflats get exposed.

You might also find large concentrations of egrets, herons, cormorants, and ducks. The waders gather in August and September, followed by the ducks in October and November.

The quarries provide a good habitat for shorebirds and terns, including Ruddy Turnstones and Sanderlings in summer and early fall. Also look for terns foraging in the quarry pits.

Past the house where you received your permit is a road running the length of Big Lake. This road is rough and off-limits during hunting season. However, if you are able to bird here, you may find large concentrations of shorebirds, egrets, herons, swallows, and ducks in the appropriate season.

Please keep in mind this south access to the lake is private and that all courtesies should be taken to ensure it remains open to birders.

General information: Banner Marsh provides a good example of how an environmentally devastating activity can be mitigated into a productive area. Once a strip mine, this area, managed by the Illinois Department of Natural Resources, provides recreational activities for birders, hunters, and fishermen. Call ahead for hunting season times; you may wish to avoid the area then. Also, weekends can be busy with fishermen.

ADDITIONAL HELP

DeLorme IA&G grid: 40 and 50.
Contact: Illinois Department of Natural Resources.
Nearest gas, food, and lodging: Pekin and Peoria.

47 Iroquois County Conservation Area

Habitats: Black oak sand savanna, wet flatwoods, upland forest, sedge meadow, cattail marsh, sand prairie, pine plantations, and shrubby successional areas.
Key birds: Breeding Least Bittern, King, Virginia, and Sora Rails, Northern Bobwhite, Broad-winged Hawk, Whip-poor-will, Red-headed Woodpecker, Sedge Wren, Veery, White-eyed and Bell's Vireos, and Grasshopper, Swamp, Henslow's, and Lark Sparrows; migrating sparrows including LeConte's and Nelson's Sharp-tailed; possibly Blue Grosbeak.
Best times to bird: Spring migration and breeding season.

Directions: From Interstate 94, exit at Illinois Route 394, near the town of Lansing. Go south approximately 8 miles until IL 394 merges with IL 1. Continue south through the town of Momence to County Road 3300N, 2 miles past the town of St. Anne. Follow this road east to the entrance.

Birding: As you drive along IL 1, some 65 miles south of Chicago, you notice an interesting and seemingly sudden change from the cornfields and occasional river backwaters that people associate with north-central Illinois. Clay soil gives way to sandy soil and on a windy day, you feel you've entered a new state, perhaps even a new country. Probably because of its seeming anonymity and being off of most birders' well-beaten paths, this underappreciated site receives little visitation by anyone other than hunters. However, birders can find several highly sought-after species that are either near the southern (Virginia Rail, Common Snipe, Swamp Sparrow) or northern (Northern Mockingbird, White-eyed Vireo, Summer Tanager, Blue Grosbeak) edge of their breeding ranges, or are rarely found anywhere in the state as a breeder. Summer records exist for Long-eared Owls, Blue-headed Vireos (a pair with nest material in oak savanna), and Cerulean, Hooded, and Chestnut-sided Warblers.

If you're a birder, you immediately realize you are in Lark Sparrow country when you enter Iroquois County. Lark Sparrows love the sandy soil—and you should find this bird fairly easily if you're here in May or June. This is wild, untamed country—it's also a hunter's heaven. Time your trip properly and you can have a fascinating birding excursion at the conservation area and the nearby town of Pembroke.

While driving the road to the conservation area, check the fields west along 3200N for Rusty Blackbirds in March, and April for breeding Vesper Sparrows as well as Northern Bobwhites. You might also see a Wild Turkey.

47 Iroquois County Conservation Area

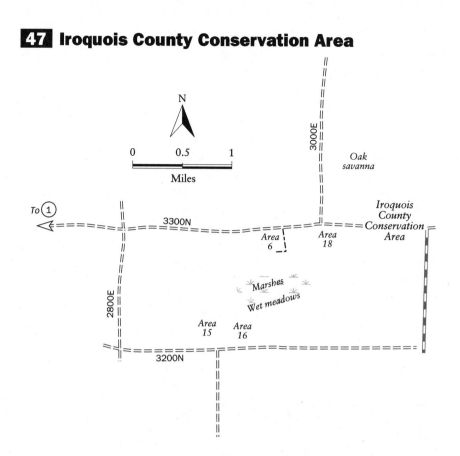

The conservation area features 16 parking areas. What follows are some of the best places to park to search for birds. Park in the first lot and walk along the sandy roads searching for Northern Mockingbirds, Orchard Orioles, and possibly Blue Grosbeaks in spring and summer. You should also see Lark Sparrows easily along the roadside.

Parking areas 15 and 16 feature wet grass prairie habitat. This area can be flooded with water or hot and dry depending on the season and the amount of rainfall during the year. With the right conditions, you can enjoy a chorus of Sedge Wrens and Swamp Sparrows from mid-April through July. Yellow-breasted Chats often chatter in spring and summer.

In late April and early May, listen for Common Snipes winnowing at dusk, though they may also winnow during the day at the height of the breeding season. Soras, Virginia Rails, and Least and American Bitterns have been flushed from the tall grasses and cattails in this area during spring. Some remain to breed. Look east for a potential glimpse at a Northern Harrier, another breeder, scouting the wet fields for prey. You may find Short-eared Owls during migration in early spring, and some have spent the summer. If you look carefully, you may even stumble upon migrating LeConte's and Nelson's Sharp-tailed Sparrows near this area in late April through May or from middle September through late October.

To enjoy a nighttime chorus, arrive an hour before sunset, sit in your car, and listen for Barred Owls and Whip-poor-wills. Parking area 6 on CR 3300 N just west of CR 3000 is a good spot for these active night birds.

To hear the nighttime songs of several other species, walk the Prairie View Trail from this parking area, north and west to a vast expanse of wet meadow/shallow marsh stretching to the south and west all the way to CR 3200N. On a still, moonlit night you should add American Woodcock, Sedge Wren, and Henslow's Sparrow to your list and with any luck you might hear one or more of the peculiar calls of a Least and/or American Bittern as well as a Sora and Virginia Rail. This area is one of the state's finest and most extensive sedge meadows, and it's highly likely that as birders begin to come here more often they may discover the coveted Black and Yellow Rails, at least in migration. The shear size of the area as well as a dearth of birders have made this difficult to verify. This was once the southern extension of the Grand Kankakee Marsh, historically a breeding area for Black Rails, and perfect habitat for them and for migrating Yellow Rails.

To find Lark Sparrows, drive to parking area 8 near the oak savanna. You'll often find them during May and into breeding season. A nice complement of Tufted Titmice, nuthatches, and four species of woodpeckers call from the woods. This is also probably the best place to bird during spring migration. The oak trees, teeming with insects, attract hungry songbirds. Wander the area to search for other less common species, such as Summer Tanagers and perhaps a Blue Grosbeak; both have summered here. Follow a path leading south to the edge of a prairie where you might find Henslow's Sparrows if the grasses are the right height and the area is not too wet.

General information: Driving this area can be treacherous on the sandy washboard roads. Be prepared. Also note that hunting season begins in fall. Call ahead to learn the times and dates if you want to avoid birding at this time. Deer flies and mosquitos can be bothersome in summer. The Iroquois Conservation Area is close to the Momence Wetlands and Sod Farms. See Site 32 for more information.

ADDITIONAL HELP

DeLorme IA&G Grid: 45.
Contact: Iroquois County Conservation Area.
Nearest gas, food, and lodging: St. Anne and Momence.

48 Middle Fork State Fish and Wildlife Area

Habitats: Upland oak-hickory-maple forest, upland and bottomland (sandy) fields, including restored and native prairie remnants, fallow and cultivated fields, cedar glades, small pine plantations, and wetlands, including seeps, bogs, swamps, and forested river floodplain.

Key birds: Spring and fall migrants, including the potential for 10 flycatcher, 36 warbler, 7 vireo, and 16 sparrow species; breeding Whip-poor-will, Pileated Woodpecker, Acadian Flycatcher, Carolina Chickadee, White-eyed and Bell's Vireos, Yellow-throated, Prothonotary, and Kentucky Warblers, Louisiana Waterthrush, Yellow-breasted Chat, Summer and Scarlet Tanagers, and Vesper, Lark, Savanna, and Grasshopper Sparrows; migrating Ruby-throated Hummingbird; wintering Long-eared, Northern Saw-whet, and other owls.

Best times to bird: Spring and fall migration for hawks and passerines, breeding season especially for warblers, winter for hawks and owls.

Directions: Exit Interstate 74 near Danville at Oakwood/Potomac. Go north for 8 miles on this road (County Road 900E) to CR 2250N. Turn east, driving 1 mile to the main entrance. To access a visitor center with restrooms, a public phone, and maps, continue north along CR 900E another 1.5 miles to CR 2400N and go east a short distance to the site headquarters.

Birding: Birders have more than 35 miles of marked trails and 2,700 acres of woods and fields to wander at Middle Fork. By visiting this and Kickapoo State Park (see Site 49), you could easily find 100 species in a single day at the right time of year; more than 200 species of birds have been listed at these two parks.

The Middle Fork River acts as a magnet, attracting hordes of migrating and breeding birds winging their way north in spring and south in fall or looking for an acceptable place to raise their young. The north-south orientation of the river with its low-lying forested bluffs creates a natural migration corridor as well as a lush environment for breeding species.

For a chance to see the most variety of habitats and build a large bird list, choose a day in early to middle May or in mid-September and hike along the Middle Fork wildlife area's entrance road. Begin at the first parking lot you en-counter at the south entrance. Listen here beginning in late April through early May in the breeding season for Whip-poor-wills and Barred Owls that call at dusk and dawn. The Barred Owl will sometimes call during the day.

Next, walk north along the old cinder road that meanders the scenic Middle Fork River for 2 miles. (Remember, you'll have to retrace your steps to return to your car, so bring plenty of water and energy.) Along the way, you will see scrubby overgrown fields with scattered groves of red cedar or planted pines. Listen for the strange gurgles, clacks, and popping calls of the Yellow-breasted Chat in spring and early summer, as well as singing White-eyed and Bell's Vireos, and Blue-winged Warblers. These species prefer scrubby overgrown areas for breeding.

48 Middle Fork State Fish and Wildlife Area

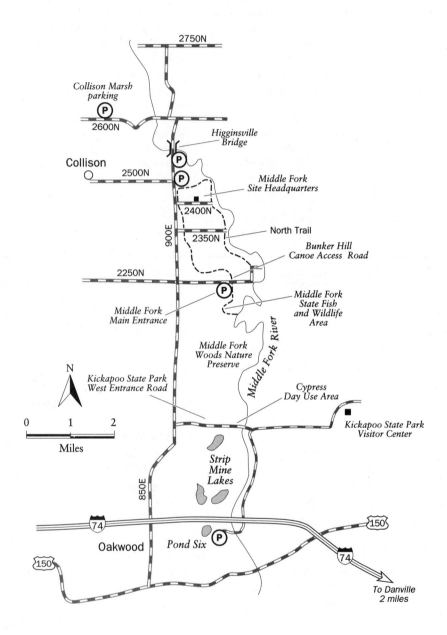

2750N

Collison Marsh
parking
℗

2600N

Higginsville
Bridge

℗

Collison

2500N ℗

Middle Fork
Site Headquarters

2400N

900E

2350N

North Trail

Bunker Hill
Canoe Access Road

2250N

℗

Middle Fork
Main Entrance

Middle Fork
State Fish
and Wildlife
Area

Middle Fork
Woods Nature
Preserve

Middle Fork River

N

Kickapoo State Park
West Entrance Road

Cypress
Day Use Area

Kickapoo State Park
Visitor Center

0   1   2

Miles

850E

Strip
Mine
Lakes

74

150

Oakwood   Pond Six ℗

150

74

To Danville
2 miles

During spring and fall migration, you should find more than 25 species of warblers here on a single day, along with vireos, grosbeaks, and other neotropical migrants. Also, listen for the sounds of Bank Swallows buzzing overheard. This species nests in steep, eroding banks along the river. Throughout the region, you'll find scattered areas with pine plantations and cedars, good places to search for Long-eared, Short-eared, and Northern Saw-whet Owls in winter. One of the best places to search for the Long-eared Owl is at parking area 6, driving north on CR 900E, where an old cedar grove grows. Birders also occasionally find Short-eared and Northern Saw-whet Owls as well as resident Barred Owls in the nearby deciduous woods. Also search this area in winter for lingering Winter and Carolina Wrens, kinglets, waxwings, Purple Finches, and Fox and White-throated Sparrows.

To search for grassland species, park at parking area 7, which you'll find just before the Higginsville Bridge over the Middle Fork River. Fields south along the river for about a mile often hold breeding Lark Sparrows as well as Vesper, Savannah, Grasshopper, and Field Sparrows. Occasionally Henslow's Sparrows have been found as well.

The Collison Marsh complex at Middle Fork (at the park's northwest corner) can be rewarding for birders. This area features a large bog, seeps, and a marsh that provide habitat for some botanical treasures, including jewelweed, blue-flag iris, bottle gentian, skunk cabbage, and marsh marigold. The marsh parking area is north of the town of Collison on CR 2600N.

The habitats here attract some of the state's rarer species, including Yellow-crowned Night-Herons, Red-shouldered Hawks, and breeding Black-billed Cuckoos, Brown Creepers, and Veeries. One particularly impressive ornithological attraction of this area is the large concentration of Ruby-throated Hummingbirds. Sometimes as many as 75 hummingbirds feed at a large jewelweed patch, west of the old railroad bed and north of the parking lot, from early August to early September.

General information: Most of the land that now encompasses the Middle Fork State Fish and Wildlife Area as well as Kennekuk County Park (see Site 50) and parts of Kickapoo State Park (see Site 49) was purchased in the late 1960s and early 1970s by the state of Illinois in anticipation of building a dam across the Middle Fork River forming a 3,300-acre reservoir. After a long battle, environmentalists, with the help of a tiny, state-listed endangered minnow called the blue-breasted darter, prevailed in securing this site for conservation. In 1986, the state legislature designated a 17-mile stretch of the Middle Fork River as Illinois' first State Scenic River, followed in 1989 by its designation as a National Wild and Scenic River.

The Middle Fork State Fish and Wildlife Area as well as the adjacent Kennekuk County Park, Kickapoo State Recreation Area, and land owned by Illinois Power (but leased by the state and county) form an almost unbroken stretch of more than 10,000 acres of public parklands from just east of the town of Oakwood (on the

The Long-eared Owl sometimes winters at the Middle Fork State Fish and Wildlife Area.
KANAE HIRABAYASHI PHOTO

south end) to just a few miles south of the town of Potomac (on the north end), a stretch of more than 12 miles.

Middle Fork is open to hunting, in season and used for horseback and bicycle riding, fishing, mushrooming, canoeing, dog trials, snowmobiling, hiking, and camping. Call ahead during hunting season to learn where you can and cannot bird.

ADDITIONAL HELP

DeLorme IA&G grid: *55.*
Contact: Illinois Department of Natural Resources and the Middle Fork State Fish and Wildlife Area.
Nearest gas, food, and lodging: Camping at Middle Fork. Gas and food in Oakwood; lodging in Danville.

49 Kickapoo State Park

See map on page 180

Habitats: Woodlands, deep strip-mined lakes, and reclaimed strip-mined hills covered with shrubs and trees.
Key birds: Migrating waterfowl, shorebirds, and songbirds; breeding Yellow-throated, Northern Parula, Prothonotary, and Cerulean Warblers, and Scarlet and Summer Tanagers; resident Carolina Chickadee and Carolina Wren.
Best times to bird: Spring and fall migration.

Directions: Exit Interstate 74 at Oakwood/Potomac. Drive north 1 mile, then turn east at the brown park sign and proceeding to the park's west entrance. Follow this road east to access the two parking areas and to get to the visitor center.

Birding: Birders can explore 2,800 acres of open parkland, dense scrubby thickets and open water at this state park. If you want to add the Prothonotary Warbler to your list as well as search for some marsh and water-loving birds, visit Kickapoo State Park. You won't find marshy edges, and fishermen are here from ice-out to ice-up, but you should still be able to find herons, egrets, and shorebirds, as well as songbirds.

During migration and breeding season, park at the lot just west of the bridge over the Middle Fork River called the Cypress Day Use Area, or at the Pond Six parking lot. On a May morning, you are almost assured of hearing the songs of the Yellow-throated, Northern Parula, Prothonotary, and Cerulean Warblers, as well as American Redstarts and Louisiana Waterthrushes near these two parking areas. All these species have bred here, and you don't have to walk far to see them.

The 83-acre Middlefork Woods Nature Preserve, just north of the parking lot at the west entrance, is an especially rich area for uncommon woodland wildflowers such as shooting stars and bloodroots as well as forest-interior bird species such as Summer Tanagers and Acadian Flycatchers. In the summer, expect to see all six woodpeckers, including Pileated, plus Carolina Chickadees, Carolina Wrens, Wood Thrushes, Red-eyed and Yellow-throated Vireos, Scarlet Tanagers, Kentucky and Cerulean Warblers, and perhaps an Ovenbird or Louisiana Waterthrush. Explore this area, but be careful not to trample the vegetation.

A canoe trip down the river from Higginsville Bridge to Kickapoo State Park in the breeding season will almost certainly net the more adventurous birder such fairly common species as Green Herons, Wood Ducks, Belted Kingfishers, Bank Swallows, Barred Owls, Blue-gray Gnatcatchers, and, in the numerous tall sycamores, cottonwoods and silver maple trees, singing Yellow-throated Warblers and Northern Parulas.

General information: A former turn-of-the-century strip-mined area, Kickapoo State Park has 22 deepwater ponds and lakes ranging in size from 0.2 to 57 acres, providing water for human recreation and wildlife. Activities include boating, scuba diving, cross-country, running, and bicycling.

Restrooms, pamphlets, and public phones are available at the visitor center.

You can visit the nearby Kennekuk County Park (see Site 50) and the Middle Fork State Fish and Wildlife Area (see Site 48) as well as Kickapoo State Park in one to several days.

ADDITIONAL HELP

DeLorme IA&G grid: 55.
Contact: Illinois Department of Natural Resources.
Nearest gas, food, and lodging: Camping at Kickapoo State Park; gas and food in Oakwood; lodging in Danville.

50 Kennekuk County Park

Habitats: Wooded ravines, scattered cedar groves and pine plantations, scrubby/successional areas, restored marshes, grassy meadows and tallgrass prairie, large lake, small ponds, river bottomland fields, and forest.

Key birds: Migratory waders, including American and Least Bitterns; migratory waterfowl and raptors, including Osprey and Bald Eagle; migratory American Golden-Plover; wintering Long-eared and Northern Saw-whet Owls; breeding Wild Turkey, American Woodcock, Whip-poor-will, Pileated Woodpecker; Acadian and Willow Flycatchers, Carolina and Sedge Wrens, White-eyed and Bell's Vireos, and 14 species of warblers.

Best times to bird: Year-round, but especially spring and fall for migrants, summer for uncommon breeding species, and winter for northern irruptive and owl species.

Directions: To reach Kennekuk County Park, exit Interstate 74 at Martin Luther King Drive (also U.S. Highway 150) on the west edge of Danville. Bear right, heading east on US150, to the first stoplight. Turn north onto Henning Road and proceed 4.7 miles to the park entrance along the west side of the road.

Birding: This 3,000-acre site is a birder's "park for all seasons." A quiet hike through the numerous small conifer plantings or cedar glades in winter may reward the patient observer with winter finches or the wide-eyed glare of a diminutive Northern Saw-whet Owl. On an early spring morning you can hear *"peenting"* woodcocks, the almost deafening calls of dozens of Whip-poor wills, sometimes accompanied by a cacophony of calling coyotes, and if you hurry to the wet meadows, you can listen for the maniacal laughter of the Pied-billed Grebe, the *"oogalunk"* of the American Bittern and the *"ticket- ticket"* call of the Virginia Rail.

Once a group of nine juvenile Mississippi Kites spent three weeks here feasting on the abundant emerging periodic cicadas.

Birders might find 10 flycatcher, 5 wren, 7 vireo, 36 warbler, and at least 16 sparrow species annually in spring and fall. Kennekuk is also known for its long and impressive list of breeding birds, including many uncommon or rare species for this part of Illinois. Local birders conducted the state's breeding bird atlas project from 1986 to 1991, and discovered breeding Pied-billed Grebes, Least Bitterns, Cooper's and Sharp-shinned Hawks, Northern Harriers, American Coots, Black-billed Cuckoos, and Yellow-bellied Sapsuckers (extremely rare anywhere in the state). In all, 107 species were confirmed as breeding species in this one area, with 4 more possibly breeding, more than any other quadrant in the state, including the Chicago area.

Birding begins immediately as you pass through the park gates. During the breeding season, you'll see Eastern Meadowlarks and Eastern Bluebirds, and occasionally you might hear the Henslow's Sparrow's peculiar two-syllable insect-like call as you drive the fields to the visitor center. This species' numbers are declining in Illinois.

50 Kennekuk County Park

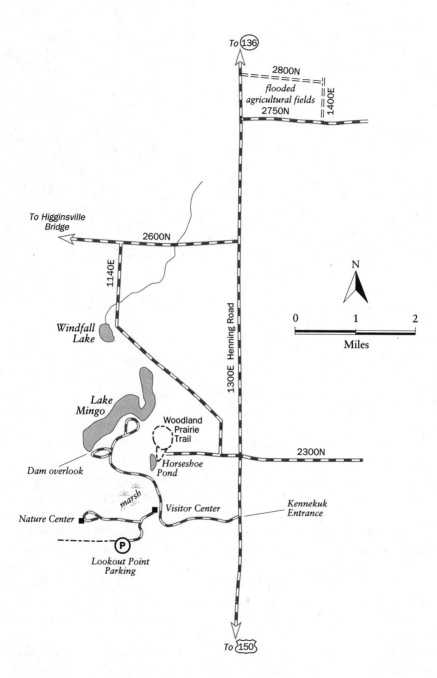

American Golden-Plovers migrate through Kennekuk County Park in fall. JOE B. MILOSEVICH PHOTO

Just west of the visitor center, check the shrubby hedgerow for a potential Bell's Vireo during breeding season. If the visitor center is open, you can obtain park maps and ask about local bird sightings. Then drive to the Lookout Point Picnic Area, listening on your way along road edges for migrating flycatchers, vireos, and warblers.

Take a trail west to Lookout Point through forest and shrubland where you might find Wood Thrushes, Carolina Wrens, and Scarlet Tanagers in spring and summer, as well as more migrants in spring and fall. Fields along the trail have also attracted breeding Lark Sparrows, and Blue-winged Warblers.

When you reach the bluffs overlooking the Middlefork River, you can view migrating hawks in fall. In spring and summer you may also hear singing Northern Parula, Cerulean, and Yellow-throated Warblers, which breed in the treetops.

To find marsh birds, park at the lot by the nature center. Put on your boots and walk north along a gravel road to the marsh complex east of the road. In mid-April, birders find dozens of Soras here, fewer Virginia Rails, and almost always Least and American Bitterns. You can also find up to 18 species of ducks in March as well as 6 swallow species in April and May.

To search for wintering birds, park at the Horseshoe Pond lot. Take the Woodland Prairie Trail to the small red and white pine plantation where you might find Short-eared and Long-eared Owls from late fall through early spring. Accipiters also hunt and roost here.

For ducks and gulls, check Lake Mingo from the Dam Overlook. Bald Eagles and Ospreys perch in the large trees along the lake's edge during migration. You might also find Pied-billed and Horned Grebes, up to 20 species of ducks, Black-crowned Night-Herons, Bonaparte's Gulls, and Caspian and Forster's Terns on the lake during spring migration. Ducks peak in March and gulls peak in April or May.

A few areas lying just outside of the park—all on private property—are worth visiting. Bring spotting scopes and respect people's privacy. Windfall Lake (also known as Indian Springs Farm) is a privately owned rural residential area just north and adjacent to the park's northern boundary. This lake has attracted an amazing variety of water-loving birds over the years. All three species of swans (including some of the reintroduced Trumpeters) have overwintered as well as Greater White-fronted and Snow Geese, and most of the common dabbling and diving ducks. Great Egrets, Black-crowned Night-Herons, and Little Blue Herons occasionally stop on migration. Ospreys sometimes fish during migration, and shorebirds sometimes visit in the fall when the water level is low enough at this rather shallow lake. Swallows swarm over the lake in spring and fall. Also listen for Red-headed Woodpeckers in the large oak trees.

Flooded and fallow agricultural fields to the north and northeast of the park, especially north of the intersection of County Roads 2750N/1400E (use care and common sense in traveling down the dirt CR 1400E during or after wet weather) have hosted open-country, waterfowl, and shorebirds during migration after heavy rains. Birders have recorded such uncommon-to-rare species as Tundra and Trumpeter Swans, Greater White-fronted Geese, Cinnamon Teals, Bald Eagles, Sandhill Cranes, and 28 shorebird species, including Black-bellied Plovers, American Avocets, Willets, Ruddy Turnstones, Sanderlings, Baird's, White-rumped, and Buff-breasted Sandpipers, Dunlins, both dowitchers, and Wilson's and Red-necked Phalaropes.

This is one of the best places in central Illinois to find flocks numbering in the thousands of both American Golden-Plovers and Lapland Longspurs, as well as fewer numbers of American Pipits and Smith's Longspurs. Listen for the golden-plovers' plaintive, thin whistles echoing across the barren Illinois cornfields as they travel to their tundra breeding grounds in the high Arctic.

General information: Initial land acquisition in what was to become Kennekuk Cove County Park (later changed to Kennekuk County Park) began in the late 1970s. After plans for the proposed Middle Fork Reservoir fell through, a land exchange between the county and the state allowed for separate parks to be developed on each side of the Middle Fork River, Middle Fork State Fish and Wildlife Area on the west side of the river, and Kennekuk on the east. Kennekuk's visitor center houses an interpretive display of Native American and natural history. You can rent boats at Lake Mingo and picnic on the grounds.

ADDITIONAL HELP

DeLorme IA&G grid: 55.

Contact: Vermilion County Conservation District.

Nearest gas, food, and lodging: Camping in nearby Kickapoo State Recreational Area and the Middle Fork State Fish and Wildlife Area; hotels, motels and restaurants in nearby Danville.

51 Forest Glen Preserve and the Harry "Babe" Woodyard State Natural Area

Habitats: Wooded ravines, marshy areas, grassy meadows, old fields, ponds, Vermilion River corridor, savanna, several pine plantations, and old-growth beech-maple forest.

Key birds: Spring migrants, including 36 warbler species; breeding birds, including Red-shouldered, Broad-winged, and Cooper's Hawks, Wild Turkey, American Woodcock, both cuckoos, Whip-poor-will, Pileated Woodpecker, Acadian and Willow Flycatchers, Brown Creeper, Veery, Wood Thrush, Carolina Wren, Sedge Wren, Bell's and White-eyed Vireos; Worm-eating, Yellow-throated, Blue-winged, Cerulean, Kentucky, and Prairie Warblers; Louisiana Waterthrush, American Redstart, Ovenbird, Northern Parula, Yellow-breasted Chat, Rose-breasted Grosbeak, Scarlet and Summer Tanagers, Orchard Oriole, Henslow's, Grasshopper, Swamp, Vesper, and Savanna Sparrow, and occasionally wintering Long-eared, Short-eared, and Northern Saw-whet Owls.

Best times to bird: Migration and summer.

Directions: To get to Forest Glen from Interstate 74 and IL 1 interchange, go south 6 miles to the town of Westville. Turn left at the stoplight (County Road 1200N) and follow the signs south and east 8 miles to the park entrance, which is off CR 900N. To get to "Babe" Woodyard, instead of turning at Westville on CR 1200N, continue south several miles on IL 1 to the town of Georgetown. Turn left on Mill Street, which becomes Mill Road. Drive east on this curving road 6 miles to CR 650N; by this time, you are heading southeast. Turn west on CR 650N and drive 0.5 mile to park at the headquarters, where the road ends.

Birding: More than 230 species of birds have visited the 1,800-acre Forest Glen Preserve, where botanists have discovered rare plants, including several types of orchids. One of the most coveted Illinois warblers, the Worm-eating, breeds here. What's really astounding, though, is that nearly every breeding warbler in Illinois has either been confirmed breeding here or heard and seen on territory throughout the summer. Yellow, Blue-winged, Kentucky, Prairie, Cerulean, and Worm-eating Warblers, Common Yellowthroats, Louisiana Waterthrushes, and Yellow-breasted Chats are confirmed breeders. Northern Parulas, Yellow-throated Warblers, American Redstarts, and Ovenbirds are summer visitors.

51 Forest Glen Preserve and the Harry "Babe" Woodyard State Natural Area

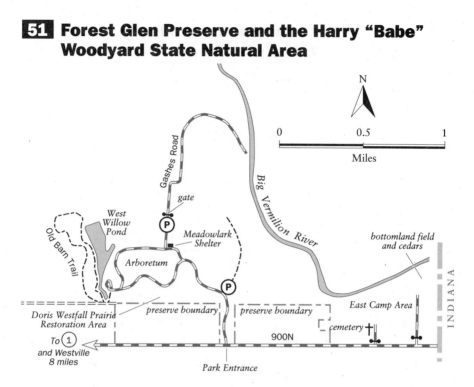

Locate the East Camp area at the southeastern extremity of the park, near the Indiana border. You can park at one of the two gated roads. Check the large open fields for breeding Ring-necked Pheasants, Northern Bobwhites, Eastern Kingbirds, Sedge Wrens, White-eyed Vireos, Yellow-breasted Chats, and Prairie and Blue-winged Warblers. Walk north toward an old cemetery and some fine oak-hickory woods, where you should find more breeding warblers. Continue walking toward the Vermilion River and Illinois/Indiana state line to a large bottomland field that has become extremely overgrown with hundreds of red cedars. Search these trees for roosting sparrows, finches, accipiters, and the occasional Long-eared and Northern Saw-whet Owl in winter.

The Big Woods Trail, north of the park entrance, takes you through an old-growth beech-maple forest and to a 72-foot-high observation tower that overlooks the wooded Vermilion River Valley. As you walk the trail, listen for Ovenbirds, Kentucky Warblers, and Louisiana Waterthrushes, especially in the wetter areas and slopes. Cerulean Warblers have nested in the large white oaks at the base of the tower. Worm-eating Warblers have nested in the ravines just below and beyond the tower.

If you're here during spring migration, you might want to take the Old Barn Trail, which park naturalists use during guided bird walks. You'll walk through or next to meadows, wetlands, ponds, and upland and bottomland forest. In the bottomland forest, listen for the Pileated Woodpecker, fairly common year-round. In meadows listen for singing grassland species, and in the wetlands you might

51 Forest Glen Preserve and the Harry "Babe" Woodyard State Natural Area

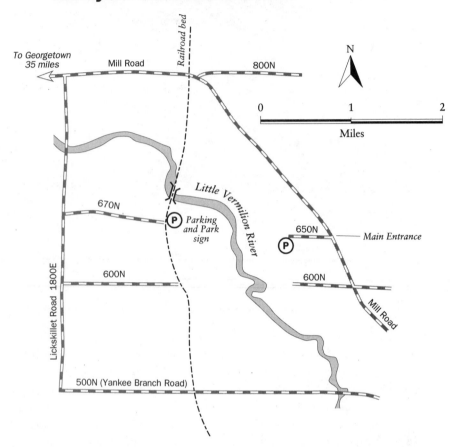

hear Virginia Rails and Soras. The potential also exists to see Little Blue Herons and Cattle Egrets, as well as Black-crowned and Yellow-crowned Night-Herons. On good days you'll encounter pockets of warblers, vireos, tanagers, and other migrants feasting on insects rising from the wetlands or hiding in the trees.

To see many of the park's breeding birds as well as numerous migrants in spring and fall, walk along Gashes Road. This unimproved road begins just west of the Meadowlark Shelter and goes north for more than 1 mile to the banks of the Big Vermilion River. Migrants funnel along the tree rows parallel to the road. Past the locked gate you'll find old field habitat where Blue-winged and Prairie Warblers and Yellow breasted Chats have bred. Check the numerous small red cedars in winter for Northern Saw-whet Owls. In brushy thickets and successional areas along the way, you might encounter White-eyed Vireos, Eastern Bluebirds, and Orchard Orioles. As the road cuts its way through a good stretch of forest with steep-sided ravines, be alert for Scarlet and Summer Tanagers, Pileated Woodpeckers, Wood Thrushes, Carolina Wrens, Louisiana Waterthrushes, and the occasional

Veery and Worm-eating Warbler. Feel free to dip down into the wooded ravines along the way. If you make it all the way to the river, you should be rewarded with Acadian Flycatchers, Blue-gray Gnatcatchers, Northern Parulas, and Yellow-throated Warblers.

An early summer stroll along this road (with flashlight handy) on a quiet moonlit night could yield Barred, Great Horned, and Eastern Screech-Owls as well as Whip-poor-wills, and rarely, Chuck-will's-widows. In March and April, American Woodcocks *"peent"* in the old fields just beyond the gate.

To find open-field birds, visit the Doris Westfall Prairie Restoration Area (Illinois' first restored habitat to be dedicated a state nature preserve, with an outstanding example of a long list of native prairie plants, all propagated from seed collected only in Vermilion County) just east of the park nature center. This is an excellent spot to look for Northern Harriers, Short-eared Owls, rails and LeConte's Sparrows in migration and breeding Sedge Wrens and Savannah, Vesper, Grasshopper, and Henslow's Sparrows as well as many other common open-country birds, in season.

If you've got a sense of adventure, you can visit the nearby Harry "Babe" Woodyard State Natural Area. Wild Turkeys abound and Northern Parulas and Yellow-throated Warblers sing from the tops of the many large sycamore trees along the river. Park off the road near the park sign along the area's west boundary, and walk the old railroad bed heading north toward the river and a nice section of bottomland forest; you'll get a fantastic view looking down into the river from an old stone arch railroad bridge. Work your way down the steep hillside on the east side of the railroad bed and meander along the north side of the river, exploring the wet bottomland fields, thickets, and forested area that stretches for several miles. In winter, Long-eared Owls have roosted in cedar trees in old field habitat along the river.

To search for more woodland birds, including migrants and breeders, park at the end of the main entrance road, then walk west to the river, along the old farm access roads, which are being turned into trails.

General information: In February 1966, ten residents of the Vermilion County area in east-central Illinois got a referendum passed to establish a county conservation district. In 1968, the first parcel of land they purchased was the Forest Glen Preserve. In 1975, the group acquired Kennekuk Cove (Site 48), 8 miles northwest of Danville at Henning Road, a 3,000-acre park of wooded ravines, fields, meadows, and prairies along the Middle Fork River. The conservation district has established these two preserves to be enjoyed quietly and slowly—no horseback riding or motorized vehicles are allowed. You can enjoy the birding, then picnic, fish, or camp. You can rent canoes here. You'll find picnic tables, playgrounds, and a restored pioneer homestead. You can also enjoy the Michael J. Reddy Arboretum and tree research area.

The Harry "Babe" Woodyard State Natural Area was just recently purchased and dedicated in honor of a noted local political figure. The park is mostly

The Red-shouldered Hawk breeds at Forest Glen Preserve. DENNIS OEHMKE PHOTO

undeveloped, but old roads are being converted to hiking trails. The Department of Natural Resources will also build a small lake on this 1,000-acre site. The stretch of the Little Vermilion River that flows through the area was identified by the Illinois Natural Areas Inventory as one of the cleanest, high-quality stream segments left in the state, providing habitat for rare, threatened, and state-listed endangered species, including mussels, sedges, fish, the federally listed endangered Indiana bat, and Yellow Lady's Slipper orchid.

ADDITIONAL HELP

DeLorme IA&G grid: 55 and 65.
Contact: Vermilion County Conservation District and the Illinois Department of Natural Resources.
Nearest gas, food, and lodging: Danville; primitive and family camping at the park.

52 Moraine View State Park

Habitats: Deep lake, upland and bottomland forest, restored prairie, agricultural fields, stream, cattail-willow marsh, and reclaimed fields.
Key birds: Migrating loons, grebes, ducks, hawks, and songbirds; migratory Smith's Longspur and American Golden-Plover; wintering hawks, Snow Bunting, Lapland Longspur, and sparrows.
Best times to bird: Late August to late May.

Directions: From Interstate 74, exit at LeRoy. Drive north 5 miles to the entrance.

Birding: The most obvious feature of the park is Dawson Lake. Its large distance from other bodies of water coupled with an unusually deep bottom for such a small lake attract myriad water birds. Birders have confirmed nearly 200 species of birds in the park and adjacent fields. These include rarities such as Red-necked Phalaropes, Red-throated Loons, Red-necked Grebes, Surf Scoters, and a drake Eurasian Wigeon.

52 Moraine View State Park

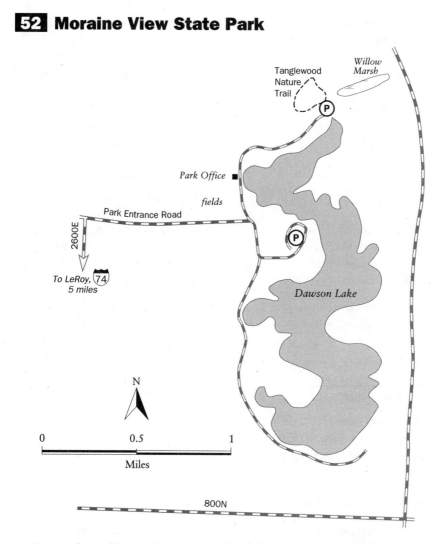

Start at the park's west entrance, searching for Northern Bobwhites year-round. You may hear them calling their name before you see them.

Then check Dawson Lake for water birds, including ducks and sometimes gulls and terns. If winter is mild open water may remain on the lake, attracting some waterfowl. Canvasbacks, American Wigeons, Mallards, and Greater White-fronted Geese have wintered on Dawson Lake. Ducks may number close to 1,000 in March.

The Tanglewood Self-Guided Nature Trail and surrounding areas have hosted rails, Marsh Wrens, Green Herons, and Black-crowned Night-Herons in spring. Also look for migrating and summering Pied-billed Grebes. In late April and May and again in September, migrating warblers and vireos feed in tangles and willows on the Tanglewood Nature Trail and in the tall oaks just south of the dam. During breeding season, you may find various woodpeckers, Wood Thrushes, Veeries, and Whip-poor-wills in the woods.

Suitable habitats in the park (scrubby willow thickets and reclaimed fields) may be your best bet for finding Bell's Vireos and Yellow-breasted Chats during breeding season as well as wintering Fox, White-throated, White-crowned, and American Tree Sparrows. Bluebirds also breed in nest boxes.

An amazing migration spectacle occurs in April and May when thousands of American Golden-Plovers arrive on their staging grounds before they depart for the Arctic. As you bird, look to the sky for what appear to be clouds of smoke on the horizon. It could be a flock of hundreds of golden-plovers. Also search the nearby flooded fields to find the plovers as well as other shorebirds.

The cornfields surrounding the park also attract Smith's Longspurs in March and April. These birds prefer fields with foxtail grass. Look between the rows of cornfields for the longspurs; bring a scope and remember to stay off private property. Rough-legged Hawks, Snow Buntings, Lapland Longspurs, Northern Harrier, and Short-eared Owls also use the fields during winter and into early spring.

General information: During deer season, wear blaze orange if you plan on venturing off the roads or trails. Although the park is open all hours all year, the gates to the southern half are locked at sunset in winter and at 10 P.M. in summer. The gates reopen at sunrise or 8 A.M.

ADDITIONAL HELP

DeLorme IA&G grid: 53.
Contact: Moraine View State Park.
Nearest gas, food, and lodging: LeRoy and Bloomington; camping in the park.

53 Clinton Lake

Habitats: Deep lake, deep and shallow marshes, grassland, upland woods, old fields, pine and alder plantations, cultivated fields, and pastures.
Key birds: Migratory loons (including Red-throated and Pacific) and grebes (including Western, Red-necked, and Eared); all regularly occurring migratory waterfowl, including rarities; migratory shorebirds, raptors, and land birds; migratory and wintering gulls, including rarities; wintering finches.
Best times to bird: Year-round.

Directions: Reach the Clinton Lake area off Interstate 74 west of Champaign and southeast of Bloomington. Exit at Illinois Highway 54, heading south to the north end of Clinton Lake. The headquarters for the state recreational area is about 13 miles south. You can access any of the other areas listed from IL 54.

53 Clinton Lake, East

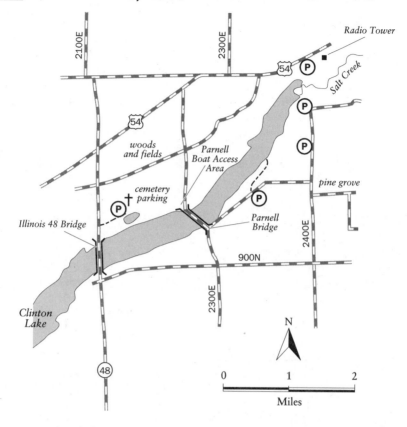

Birding: Birders have recorded 25 species of waterfowl in one day as well as 5 species of grebes at this 10-square-mile manmade lake 30 miles west of Champaign in central Illinois.

The following descriptions of lake areas start from the east end and suggest which birds you can see at which times of year. In addition, in late fall, winter, and early spring, drives through the surrounding countryside can result in rewarding looks at raptors and longspurs.

Begin at the east end of Clinton Lake (see Clinton Lake east end map), which features an expansive wet meadow and marsh. During a normal to wet spring, this area hosts large concentrations of waterfowl, although they will often be hard to see unless flushed. Bring boots or waders. Park along IL 54, east of County Road 2300E. Look for a small lane near a radio tower. From here, a short hike takes you to a wet meadow and marsh where you can view the lake.

You can see the opposite shoreline by parking in two lots along CR 2400E. Waterfowl, rails, sparrows (including Nelson's Sharp-tailed and LeConte's during migration), wrens, and raptors frequent these two areas. Birders often see Greater White-fronted Geese during migration. During dry periods, the water may recede

53 Clinton Lake, Central

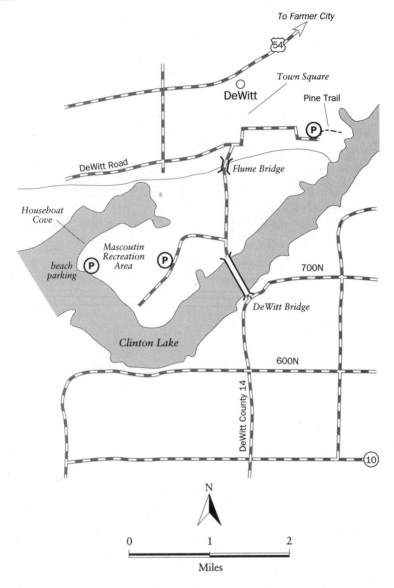

drastically, attracting shorebirds in fall. Check the wildlife plantings between the two parking lots and the lake for sparrows and finches. Huge flocks of blackbirds roost here during migration, including Brewer's Blackbird.

Nearby, you'll find another parking lot near an old pine grove on the south side of the lake. A trail offers several vantage points for viewing the lake that are otherwise inaccessible. Check the lake views for migrating waterfowl and raptors. Birders have found the rare Gyrfalcon and Prairie Falcon. Also, look for land birds along the trail. Birders have documented LeConte's Sparrow during migration.

53 Clinton Lake, West

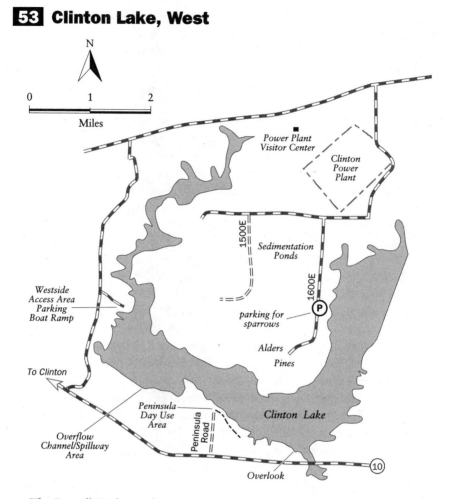

N

0   1   2
Miles

Power Plant
Visitor Center

Clinton
Power
Plant

1500E

Sedimentation
Ponds

1600E

Westside
Access Area
Parking
Boat Ramp

parking for
sparrows

(P)

Alders

Pines

To Clinton

Peninsula
Day Use
Area

Peninsula
Road

Clinton Lake

Overflow
Channel/Spillway
Area

Overlook

(10)

The Parnell Bridge and access parking lot is a good spot to view waterfowl, gulls, and terns. When there is a shelf of ice, waterfowl often cluster around the edge. Birders have documented a jaeger once, along with Lesser Black-backed and Little Gulls, and Ross's Goose.

While checking these sites for waterfowl and land birds, you might want to comb the nearby fields for raptors and for waterfowl during wet seasons. You might find thousands of ducks and geese feeding in the fields. A nearby farmer's pond once harbored a Eurasian Wigeon.

The Illinois 48 bridge is on a busy highway, but you'll find wide shoulders at both ends and you can get excellent views of two basins from here. In early spring, numerous waterfowl and gulls sit on the ice or in open water nearby. Birders have discovered Barrow's Goldeneyes and several Oldsquaws at the Weldon Access parking lot at the south end of the bridge.

Just past the north end of the IL 48 bridge, you'll find a cemetery with a lane leading to a small parking area. From this parking area, a trail leads east through some small woods, fields, and an old pond. Downstream from the pond, you'll find a beaver dam marsh at the end of an inlet of the lake. This area provides habitat for migrating and wintering sparrows, gamebirds, and raptors. The pond and beaver dam marsh harbor waterfowl and herons at the right season. Birders have also recorded Northern Goshawks, Common Redpolls, and Northern Mockingbirds here.

A nearby upland woods attracts migrating songbirds as well as some that overwinter. A trail through the woods leads to an area where you can view the warm-water outlet from the power plant. In winter, thousands of ducks congregate here. Birders also discovered a Red-throated Loon here recently.

Farther south, the busy DeWitt Bridge (see Clinton Lake map central) can be scanned from either end. You can view gulls as well as waterfowl and the occasional shorebird. An observer spotted a Red Phalarope once.

If waterfowl are present, go to the bridge over the power plant flume, a long east–west discharge canal. During hunting season and in winter, especially, most of the ducks on the lake concentrate on the flume. A Eurasian Wigeon was once found along the flume on a Christmas Bird Count.

Past the town square in DeWitt you'll find a road heading east that dead-ends at a parking area. Walk through the cedar, pine, and alder plantations to search for winter finches, sparrows, and accipiters, including the occasional goshawk. The cove at the end of the trail often harbors numerous waterfowl not visible from any other vantage point.

Mascoutin State Recreation Area contains large open meadows, some old fields, and a small fragmented woods. It attracts sparrows, Orchard Orioles, upland game birds, and raptors. The Bell's Vireo has bred in the shrubby areas. The beach often holds large concentrations of gulls and terns, including the occasional Laughing and Franklin's Gulls. You can often see loons from the beach during fall and especially in spring. Some springs, there are large concentrations of geese in the basin off the beach. Included among them one spring was a Brant. The trail leading northwest through the woods ends at Houseboat Cove, a large hidden arm of the lake that often holds large concentrations of waterfowl.

Along the south shore of the lake, opposite Mascoutin, pay attention to the alder plantations that provide excellent habitat for small finches; more than 200 Common Redpolls were seen in these alders. You'll also find several places to view the lake where loons and gulls have been recorded in good numbers. Birders documented Little and Black-headed Gulls here.

The most famous, and most difficult to find, part of the lake is known locally as the Overlook (Clinton Lake West map). Birding is best in the late afternoon through dusk or early morning. Parking is best where the shoulders are wide, just west of an inlet that crosses IL 10. If you want to bird here, you'll have to hack through the brush along the inlet's edge to stay on public property. You'll reach a fairly open area overlooking the lake. Several cement blocks offer unique seating for birders. In the late fall and early winter, virtually all the birds on the lake gather at dusk in the center of the large basin off the overlook. Birders have seen three loon species, five grebe species, four geese species, all scoter species, Oldsquaws and all the common ducks. Rarities include Mew Gulls, Little Gulls, Black-legged Kittiwakes, and jaegers. Hawks and eagles are often seen at close range.

Sometimes, birders find the Peninsula Day Use Area even better than the Overlook. Seating is a bit more comfortable, too. You can sit in the picnic shelter and view the entire basin to the east of the peninsula. In addition, you'll find a trail leading east from the circle before going into the day use area. Birders have found the rare California and Black-headed Gulls while walking this trail. You may find it useful to go back and forth between the picnic shelter and trail area to get good views of all the birds. The Peninsula Day Use Area also allows access to the west side of the basin next to the dam. An old overgrown trail leads to the peninsula's tip. This walk can yield looks at migratory land birds, including interesting sparrows and Northern Saw-whet Owls. It can be cold and windy at the end of the peninsula, but you may be rewarded with rarities such as a Little Gull or a Western Grebe. Look up as birds fly over the peninsula. Hike southwest across the field next to the parking lot to reach a rise overlooking a small cove where birds often concentrate. During low water periods, many shorebirds feed here.

To find bitterns, rails, and sparrows, check the overflow channel or spillway area, which has become a large marsh with wet grass and cattails interspersed. Virginia Rails breed here. You have the best chance out of any of the mentioned sites to find LeConte's and Nelson's Sharp-tailed Sparrows during migration. Hard-working, diligent birders have found Yellow Rails here during fall and spring migration.

The West Side Access Area has a large parking lot and a boat ramp that offer great views in the afternoon of the lake basin by the dam, where gulls abound at times. Rarities include kittiwakes, Thayer's Gulls, and Little Gulls.

Near the power plant visitor center off US 54, look for gulls and waterfowl. When water is low, look for shorebirds. During winter, gulls often stand on the ice. The Great Black-backed Gull has been seen and Gyrfalcons have harassed gulls and waterfowl in three different years.

Follow the road on the east side of the power plant south from IL 54 (looking for Northern Shrikes in winter) until coming to a road that leads west on the south edge of the power plant. The Illinois Power Company owns all this land except for the roads and the private residences. The company allows no one in the fenced areas, but the public can enter the other areas from February through October. Look along the Illinois Power fence in the summer for Blue Grosbeaks. In the winter, look for Northern Shrikes.

The following areas are excellent for birding, but be aware that they are sometimes closed for all use except hunting.

On CR 1500E, look for the observation deck where you can scan the sedimentation ponds. The ponds harbor huge concentrations of waterfowl and occasionally have a number of shorebirds. Gulls and terns also frequent the ponds. Harriers can sometimes be observed hunting the edges and the dikes at the appropriate time of year. Nearby fields, when wet, can harbor shorebirds. Birders once discovered 28 American Avocets. North of the main east–west road are some fields and woods that are excellent for sparrows, rails, and snipes.

The best area on the lake for sparrows is where CR 1600E dead-ends at a parking circle. Search for numerous sparrows in the brush. Harris's Sparrow is found here almost regularly in fall. Warblers are often abundant during migration. The open fields of corn stubble with mixed foxtail attract Smith's Longspurs in the spring. One spring, a birder found a Yellow Rail in a wet ditch through the field.

Where the lane extension of CR 1600E turns west, note that an overgrown lane also continues south, to the lake This offers a good view of the lake from the north side, and a Pacific Loon has been seen from this side of the lake that could not be picked out from the overlook. The alder plantations attract wintering Pine Siskins and Redpolls. The several pine plantations and large cedar plantation to the west provide good habitat for Long-eared and Northern Saw-whet Owls. In winter the pines and cedars hold lingering land birds.

General information: The state owns a number of fish and wildlife areas, including Mascoutin State Recreation Area and smaller access areas around the lake. The Illinois Power Company also owns much of the shoreline as well as some upland areas. Many of these areas are open to the public for portions of the year. All of these areas offer excellent year-round birding.

Be careful about trespassing on private holdings. The Illinois Power Company allows public access to some of its land, but has fenced areas that are closed.

Hunting is allowed during certain times of year in portions of this land. Be prepared by calling ahead and wearing blaze orange while birding during hunting seasons.

This is a huge area with many winding country roads. Using *Illinois Atlas & Gazetteer* by DeLorme Mapping should help you find your way.

ADDITIONAL HELP

DeLorme IA&G grid: 52 and 53.
Contact: Champaign County Audubon Society.
Nearest gas, food, and lodging: Picnic areas at all of the Department of Natural Resources day use areas and at Mascoutin State Recreation Area; camping at Mascoutin and nearby Weldon Springs State Park; motels, restaurants, and convenience stores in Farmer City and Clinton.

54 Lake Springfield and Washington Park

Habitats: Manmade lake, shoreline edges, and wooded parks.
Key birds: Migratory and wintering waterfowl, migratory gulls and songbirds, Eurasian Tree Sparrow.
Best times to bird: Spring and fall migration and winter.

54 Lake Springfield and Washington Park

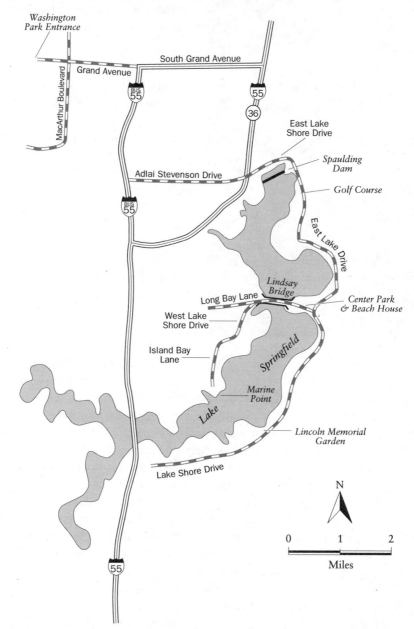

Washington Park Entrance

South Grand Avenue

Grand Avenue

MacArthur Boulevard

BUS 55

55

36

Adlai Stevenson Drive

BUS 55

East Lake Shore Drive

Spaulding Dam

Golf Course

East Lake Drive

Lindsay Bridge

Long Bay Lane

West Lake Shore Drive

Center Park & Beach House

Island Bay Lane

Springfield

Marine Point

Lake

Lincoln Memorial Garden

Lake Shore Drive

N

0   1   2

Miles

55

Directions: You can reach Lake Springfield via Interstate 55 from Exits 88, 90, or 94. To get to the East Lake Shore Drive, exit at Adlai Stevenson Drive, going east to Spaulding Dam.

To get to Washington Park, exit at South Grand Avenue and drive west 3 miles to MacArthur Boulevard. Turn north to find one entrance to the park, just about

The Least Flycatcher. DENNIS OEHMKE
PHOTO

half a mile down the road. The other entrance is on South Grand Avenue, just west of MacArthur Boulevard.

Birding: In Sangamon County, smack dab in the middle of Illinois, exists the relatively shallow manmade 4,300-acre Lake Springfield with 40 miles of shoreline, much of it bordered with houses, but enough areas to provide good waterfowl watching. Abraham Lincoln Memorial Gardens, a 90-acre informal garden features rolling terrain populated with trees, shrubs, ground cover, woods, meadows, and marshes, attracting migrating passerines.

More than 330 bird species have been documented in and around Lake Springfield and nearby habitats. (This list includes Carpenter and Riverside Parks—see Site 55.)

Depending on the time of year, you'll see different birds on the lake. In early February, for example, birders often observe hundreds of Greater and Lesser Scaups and Greater White-fronted Geese, with fewer numbers of Northern Pintails, a species that more frequently uses other flyways rather than the Mississippi Flyway. In late April, you may find a Least Bittern at the north end of Lake Springfield, and often Smith's Longspurs west of the lake in cornfields. On a mid-May day, hundreds of Cliff Swallows and dozens of scoters may fly over the lake. Come October, you should see grebes, mostly Pied-billed, with some Horned, and possibly an Eared, plus 10 or more species of ducks, including Redheads, wigeons, and Ruddys. Birders may find 15 to 17 species of ducks in one day on the lake. If you're there at the right time, you have the chance to find deepwater species such as loons, grebes, cormorants, ducks, gulls, terns, swans, and occasionally pelicans as well as all three scoters, and Oldsquaws. Some rarities include the Harlequin Duck and King Eider.

Begin your Lake Springfield birding excursion by driving east on East Lake Shore Drive to the Spaulding Dam. You can park on both ends of the dam, but be careful of traffic. In early spring, especially in February and March, you'll find abundant waterfowl in the deeper part of the lake (bring a scope). Common Loons, grebes, and terns also use this lake during migration.

Follow East Lake Drive Shore Drive south as it winds around the lake's east side. You'll pass a golf course and fishing area before you reach Lincoln Memorial

Gardens, about 5 miles from Spaulding Dam. Park in the garden lot, and walk any of the trails; they all lead to the lakeshore. Along the way you may find breeding Yellow Warblers and Eastern Towhees. Migrating warblers, including Blackpoll, Golden-winged, and even Connecticut can be found at the forest edge in May. You'll also enjoy nice views of Lake Springfield where you might often find ten or more species of ducks, Snow Geese, and cormorants in spring and fall.

The west side of lake offers several access points for viewing waterfowl. From Spaulding Dam, go east, then south on East Lake Shore Drive until you reach the Lindsay Bridge, which is north of the Lincoln Memorial Garden. Go west through Center Park and stop at the Beach House to view the lake. Continue west over the bridge, taking the left fork, which is West Lake Shore Drive. Follow this road southwest to Island Bay Lane. Turn south and drive to the end, which is Marine Point, where you can view the lake and islands here. Bring your scope when you visit these access points.

You'll find land birds at nearby Washington Park, which is in the center of Springfield. Take any of the paths in spring to listen for singing thrushes and chattering warblers during migration, including Hermit Thrushes, Scarlet and Summer Tanagers, and Kentucky Warblers. At the woodland edges and into the woods, you might find Red-bellied and Red-headed Woodpeckers, along with Tufted Titmice and Carolina Wrens.

Also, while you're driving, check the corn stubble fields west of Lake Springfield in April for Smith's Longspurs. Year-round you might also find the introduced Eurasian Tree Sparrow along fence rows and barnyards west of Lake Springfield.

General information: In the 1930s, the city of Springfield dammed Sugar Creek and flooded nearby Lick Creek to be used for the city's water supply and recreation—but hunting is not permitted. The city has declared this area a wildlife refuge and planted trees such as sweetgums and cypresses in wet areas along with understory shrubs, including redbuds, dogwoods, and serviceberries along the lake edges and in nearby parks. The city dredged the west and south end of the lake, altering habitat that once attracted shorebirds and marsh birds, but Lake Springfield continues to be a good spot for finding a large and diverse number of migrating waterfowl, as well as songbirds that use the parks.

Arrive at Washington Park early and during the week to avoid the crowds. If you visit the park, you may wish to stop at the Illinois State Museum to view natural history displays, including those involved with birds.

ADDITIONAL HELP

DeLorme IA&G grid:: 60 and 61.
Contact: Illinois State Museum and city of Springfield.
Nearest gas, food, and lodging: Springfield.

55 Carpenter and Riverside Parks

Habitats: Upland and bottomland forest, sloughs, and prairies along the Sangamon River.
Key birds: Spring and fall migrants; breeding Hooded Merganser, Barred and Great Horned Owls, Pileated Woodpecker, Yellow-throated Vireo, Great Crested Flycatcher, and Scarlet Tanager.
Best times to bird: Middle to late spring and fall.

Directions: Carpenter and Riverside Parks are 2 miles north of Springfield on the Sangamon River. From Interstate 55, take the Sangamon Avenue exit. Go west 0.5 mile to the stop light, which is Dirksen Parkway. Turn north, following this angle road several miles to a T intersection at Peoria Road. Turn north on Peoria Road, from where you'll find the entrances to both parks. Riverside Park is just south of the Sangamon River and Carpenter Park is north of the river. Both are on the west side of the road.

Birding: Carpenter Park and Riverside Preserve north of Springfield in central Illinois include 700 acres of oak woods, river bottomland, steep ravines, and sand-stone outcroppings, providing picturesque viewing of migratory birds.

These relatively small sites feature easy-to-walk trails that on the right day result in great lists of migratory songbirds. Northern Illinoisans waiting for the warblers often look to these preserves as the signal that birds are heading their way. Search along the river, the railroad or in shrubby areas in both parks for migratory passerines. On an early April morning, listen for calling Barred and Great Horned Owls, both breeders in these parks. Also listen for singing Winter Wrens, Eastern Phoebes and early warblers such as Yellow-rumped, Palm, and Black-and-white.

In midspring the parks resound with songs of insectivorous warblers and vireos as they snatch food from the shrubs and trees. Early in the morning, check the parks' open edges where the sun shines on trees, stirring the insects and attract songbirds.

In late spring search for Tufted Titmice, various vireos, and warblers, including the Northern Parula and Yellow-throated. Search the river backwaters for Prothonotary Warblers. Yellow-throated

A Great Horned Owl and young.
DENNIS OEHMKE PHOTO

55 Carpenter and Riverside Parks

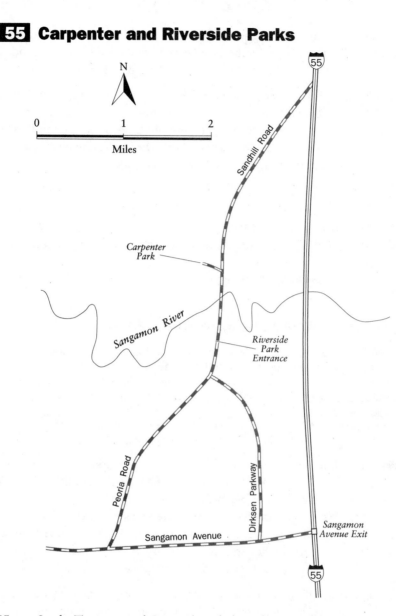

Vireos, Scarlet Tanagers, and Great Crested Flycatchers are also common during migration. The tanager and flycatcher remain to breed. Sometimes even in the middle of the day in June you might hear the buzzy *"three-eight"* call of the Yellow-throated Vireo.

You also may be lucky enough to discover broods of Hooded Mergansers, which have bred near Riverside Park, and are already parading their young in early May. At least 82 species of birds breed within the two parks, including the Pileated Woodpecker.

In fall, often beginning in August, the warblers return. Peak warbler migration is usually in early to middle September; you've got a fairly good chance of finding a Black-throated Blue Warbler at either park in mid-September.

General information: The Springfield Park District purchased Carpenter Park in 1922. In 1979, the Illinois Nature Preserves Commission designated 322 acres at this site as a state nature preserve, affording it the highest protection in Illinois. The gates usually open by 7 A.M. Be there early for the best spring birding and to avoid crowds. The city of Springfield owns Riverside Park.

ADDITIONAL HELP

DeLorme IA&G grid: 61.
Contact: Springfield Park District for Carpenter Park, and the city of Springfield for Riverside Park.
Nearest gas, food, and lodging: Springfield.

56 Lake Shelbyville and Arcola Marsh

Habitats: Manmade lake, sub-impoundments, marshes, old fields, fragmented upland, and bottomland hardwoods.
Key birds: Migratory loons, grebes, herons, egrets, and other waterfowl; migratory shorebirds, raptors, and songbirds, especially sparrows and longspurs
Best times to bird: Spring, late summer (when herons and egrets are dispersing and early shorebirds are migrating), and fall.

Directions: Exit Interstate 57 at Illinois Highway 16 (Mattoon). Drive west for several miles to IL 121, then northwest 7 miles to the Lake Shelbyville area. You'll be at the northeastern end of the lake near the Kaskaskia River Unit.

To get to the Wolf Creek and Eagle Creek State Parks where IL 121 and IL 32 split just west of the town of Sullivan, drive south on IL 32 to the road leading to Findlay (west). Drive west to the entrance T road to Wolf Creek State Park, which goes south. The entrance to Eagle Creek State Park goes south from Findlay.

Birding: Lake Shelbyville contains more than 11,000 acres, providing various recreation opportunities, including birding. Along its shores, you'll find numerous access areas at Wolf Creek and Eagle Creek State Parks and the West Okaw River and Kaskaskia River Fish and Wildlife Management Areas.

Look for deepwater birds, such as loons, grebes, and diving ducks at the southern tips of Wolf Creek and Eagle Creek State Parks and the Findlay Bridge area. Gulls and terns tend to concentrate on the beaches near the dam, which also offers high vantage points for watching migrating hawks.

You might find birding at the two state parks hampered by the droves of tourists staying at the Eagle Creek resort and campsites, or using the boat launches. However,

56 Lake Shelbyville and Arcola Marsh

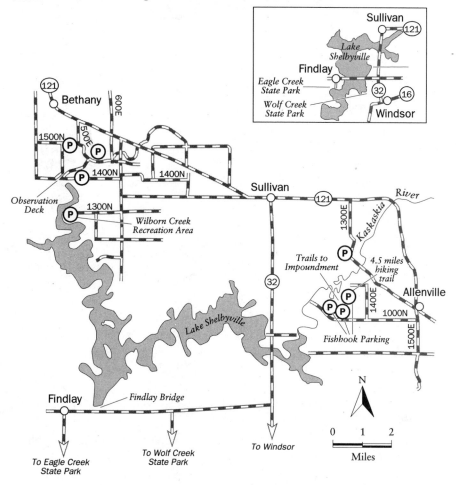

you can explore the nearby extensive old fields and emergent woodlands for such species as breeding Orchard Orioles and Bell's Vireos. During migration, almost any dead-end road through woods in a hunting area can turn into a little migrant hotspot on the right day.

The crown jewel for birding at Lake Shelbyville is the Kaskaskia River Fish and Wildlife Area, particularly the large impoundment near Allenville called Fishhook, which has several parking areas, accessed from IL 121.

Take the trail to the Fishhook impoundment where birders once found a Cinnamon Teal as well as Smith's Longspurs, when the marsh dried to a wet field.

Two parking lots are off County Road 1000N. The one marked Fishhook leads to the impoundment dike and offers another good vantage point. Many American White Pelicans stopped here in the spring of 1998. This species seems to be expanding its migratory range so that it stops at some of the large lakes in

56 Lake Shelbyville and Arcola Marsh

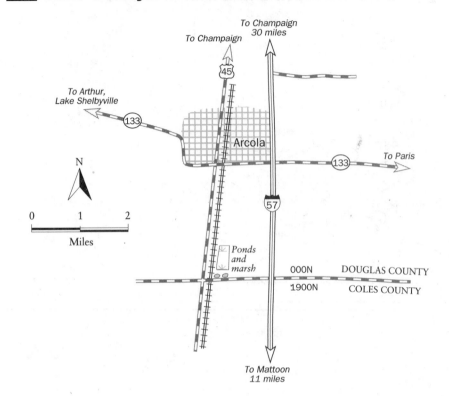

central Illinois. It's fairly easy to add this species to your Illinois bird list if you come here at the right time

A third parking lot off CR 1400E leads you to the northern part of Fishhook where shorebirds abound when mudflats appear. Herons also wade and feed here. When the water is higher, you'll find waterfowl more abundant. If the water level is too high, you won't be able to access the area.

For those who enjoy a good walk, you can take a 4.5-mile hiking trail that encircles most of the Fishhook impoundment. The trail, which leads through old fields and woodlands, can be wet and laden with mosquitos, so be prepared. Migrating songbirds abound in spring, and in fall you'll enjoy numerous sparrows where the woods, old field, and marshy habitats of the impoundment meet. Across the river from Fishhook you'll find another small impoundment that sometimes attracts shorebirds and Blue Grosbeaks. The area also hosts a heron rookery from April through mid- to late summer. You can reach it by taking CR 1300E south from IL 121 until it ends at the river. The diked area is immediately adjacent to a parking area.

Although the West Okaw River Fish and Wildlife Management Area doesn't have the reputation of the Kaskaskia unit, it can also offer good birding. Birders saw many American White Pelicans here in the spring of 1998, and two lingered into the summer. The area also attracts heron, egrets, migrating waterfowl, and shorebirds if the water levels are low.

Access this area south of IL 121. Take CR 600E south to the first lane west marked as Department of Natural Resources land, for one good spot. South of there, take the extension of CR 1400N west until it dead-ends. Park there to bird. A third parking area is near a lane that leads to an observation deck. Walk west from the deck to the wet area to search for shorebirds.

The Wilborn Creek Recreation Area offers a good view of the west arm of the lake, as do boat access points at dead ends of CR 1300N on either side of the lake. Birders have enjoyed white pelicans here, too, in good numbers, as well as waterfowl and gulls. Migrating songbirds use the extensive woods and old fields.

Just southwest of Lake Shelbyville is Arcola Marsh, one of the best and easiest to access places in east-central Illinois for waterbirds including shorebirds, ducks, and waders. The owner of Arcola Marsh welcomes birders as long as they are courteous and careful.

To get there on your way south along Interstate 57 to Lake Shelbyville, take the Arcola/Paris exit (Illinois Highway 133) west through the Amish town of Arcola to U.S. 45. Drive south on US Highway 45 for 2 miles to the Douglas–Coles county line, which is a road named 000N. Drive east over the railroad tracks, and immediately on the north you'll notice a small pullout at a locked gate. Park and walk north down the old gravel road up onto the grassy dike around the ponds.

Concentrate your birding around the large pond next to road 000N. Most of the marsh and open-water birds can be seen from the southern third of the large lake and marsh with a scope, or by walking the cattail edges along the top of the dike. Restrict your walking to the tops of the dike; it's extremely dangerous to venture into the marshy areas, which contain a thin layer of floating vegetative debris suspended over deep water and sanitation material dumped here by the city of Chicago years ago.

The best time to bird Arcola Marsh is spring and fall, but it's worth the quick stop any time of year. Late winter to early spring can produce large numbers of ducks and geese, including 20 duck species and good-sized flocks of Snow and Greater White-fronted Geese. From March through early May, search for Eared, Horned, and Pied-billed Grebes among the large groups of American Coots. In April look for LeConte's Sparrows. In April through early May, you should hear as well as see Soras (50 flushed in one day) and Virginia Rails as well as either or both American and Least Bitterns. From mid-April through early June, look for up to 25 shorebird species as well as Common, Forster's, Caspian, and Black Terns, and Marsh Wrens.

Check the flooded fields east of the ponds along the country roads. In April you should find flocks of American Golden-Plovers numbering in the hundreds, sometimes the thousands, as well as good numbers of Pectoral and other Sandpipers. Also search the willows and other trees and shrubs near the two small ponds south of the large main lake and marsh for warblers and other neotropical migrants after cold fronts in spring and fall.

During the breeding season, you may find the state-listed Common Moorhen and Least Bittern, as well as Ruddy Ducks.

Fall may be the best time to search for shorebirds, depending on water levels and how much of the cattails have been removed by the abundant muskrat population. The fewer the cattails, the easier to see the shorebirds.

Rarities are always possible. Some of them have included the Red-necked Grebe, American White Pelican, Little Blue Heron, Black-crowned Night-Heron, Ross's Goose, Osprey, Yellow, Black, and King Rails, Sandhill Crane, American Avocet, Willet, Hudsonian Godwit, Ruddy Turnstone, Red Phalarope, and Blue Grosbeak.

General information: Birders recommend you obtain a map from the U.S. Army Corps of Engineers to aid you while birding Lake Shelbyville. You can find a map at the visitor center by the east side of the dam. Most of the areas around the lake have good bathroom facilities, although you'll find the amenities around Fishhook more primitive and you'll find no facilities at the West Okaw unit.

ADDITIONAL HELP

DeLorme IA&G grid: 63, 64, and 71.
Contact: U.S. Army Corps of Engineers Visitor Center.
Nearest gas, food, and lodging: You can picnic at both state parks and at most of the Army Corps of Engineers recreation areas. The corps sites require day use fees, but these are primarily for fishermen launching boats. You can camp at Wolf and Eagle Creek State Parks. You'll find fast food in Shelbyville and Sullivan, and family restaurants in Mattoon.

American Golden-Plover drawing by Denis Kania.

West-Central Region

The Illinois River wends through the west-central part of the state, feeding one of the most important shorebird habitats in the Midwest, if not the country. Birders can count on seeing up to 27 species of shorebirds at Lake Chautauqua National Wildlife Refuge in August. Tens of thousands of shorebirds feed on the lake's shoreline, and upwards of 150,000 geese and ducks rest and feed during migration. A nearby oak-hickory forest tucked among cornfields holds breeding Wild Turkeys, Chuck-will's-widows, and Whip-poor-wills.

The soil in parts of the west-central region is sandy; this type of habitat attracts Lark Sparrows and Blue Grosbeaks to breed.

The Mississippi River hugs the west part of this region, and the bird life is a little different here than in the northwestern part of Illinois. At the Mark Twain National Wildlife Refuge, you'll find yourself in near-wilderness. You can traverse riverine backwaters, wooded bluffs, lakes, marshes, bottomland woods, fields, and moist soil units, while searching for many breeding Prothonotary Warblers, migrating American White Pelicans (a recent addition to the local avifauna), as well as waterfowl, shorebirds, hawks, and many herons and egrets. Only here and farther south will you find the breeding Mississippi Kite, the Eurasian Tree Sparrow, and some southern herons and egrets, including the Snowy Egret and Little Blue Heron.

57 Sand Ridge State Forest

58 Lake Chautauqua National Wildlife Refuge

59 Meredosia National Wildlife Refuge

60 Beardstown Marsh and the Sanganois Conservation Area

61 Siloam Springs State Park

62 Mark Twain National Wildlife Refuge—Keithsburg Division

63 Pere Marquette State Park and Mark Twain National Wildlife Refuge—Brussels District

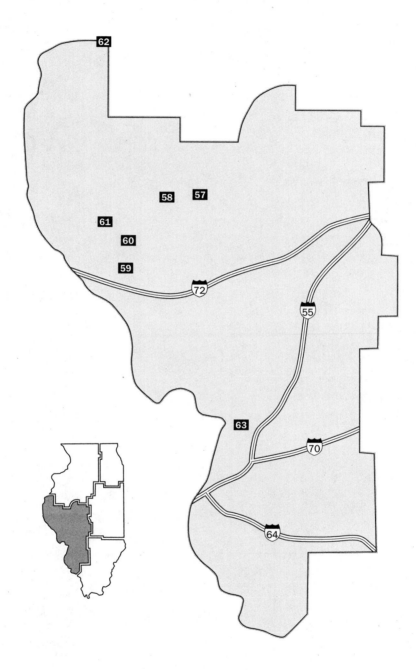

57 Sand Ridge State Forest

Habitats: Oak-hickory forest, pine plantations, open fields of grassland and wildlife plantings, sand prairie, and ponds.

Key birds: Migrating songbirds, including warblers; breeding Wood Duck, Wild Turkey, American Woodcock, owls, Chuck-will's-widow, Whip-poor-will, Blue Grosbeak, Lark Sparrow, Scarlet and Summer Tanagers; wintering crossbills and other finches.

Best times to bird: March through June for migration, late spring into summer from dusk to dawn, especially on moonlit nights for Chuck-will's-widow and Whip-poor-will; fall for migrant raptors; winter for winter finches.

Directions: A key highway for approaching the area from anywhere east, and all but northwest Illinois is U.S. Highway 136, which crosses central Illinois from the Indiana border to Keokuk, Iowa, on the Mississippi River. Once on US 136, proceed to Havana on the Illinois River. From Havana, take Manito Road north to Forest City and then follow the road identified by a Sand Ridge Forest sign to the forest. While several county and township roads lead to the forest, the first-time visitor should enter from Forest City, which will lead you to the Pine Campground and to forest headquarters. Birders from north and west of the Illinois River traveling on Interstate 74 should exit near Peoria at I-474 (the Peoria bypass), head to the junction with Illinois Highway 29, and travel south 5 miles to Pekin. Just south of Pekin at the federal correctional institution, take Manito Road through Manito 17 miles to Forest City.

Birding: Sand Ridge State Forest is a 7,500-acre forested island in the midst of central Illinois cornfields just east of the Illinois River. About 3,900 acres contain oak-hickory forest; 2,500 acres contain pines; and the remainder hold open fields and sand prairie. You can hike surrounded by panoramic vistas of sand ridges and valleys and ponds. The largest state fish hatchery, which is in the forest, attracts aquatic birds and their associates.

The annotated bird checklist and update, available at the forest headquarters, lists 208 species of birds found within Sand Ridge's boundaries. Of these, 90 have been confirmed or strongly suspected of breeding.

Before beginning your birding excursion, obtain a bird checklist and trail brochure at the forest headquarters. Be aware of prickly pear cactus, sand burrs, poison ivy, ticks, and insects. Hiking on the sand can be strenuous, but most trails are only moderately difficult. The longest trail loop is 17 miles and a real challenge. It includes most of the primitive tent sites in the forest. However, the best birding areas can be reached with only a short, relatively easy walk from a designated parking area. For example, a walk along Sand Ridge Road west from the forest headquarters can yield good views of spring migrants and nesting grassland birds, such as the Lark Sparrow. Birders observed the Henslow's Sparrow in the extensive grassy area in the spring of 1997.

57 Sand Ridge State Forest

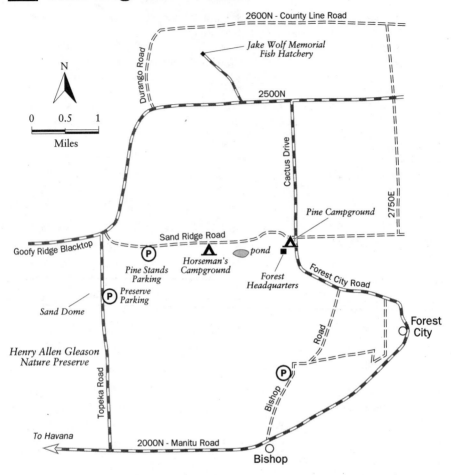

Find the parking area off Sand Ridge Road (an unpaved sand road) west of the forest headquarters. Follow the trail from the parking area about 200 yards to a pond, which has been productive for birders seeking Wood Ducks and neotropical migrants.

Search for Red Crossbills from fall through spring along Sand Ridge Road from the Pine Campground to the pine stands 2.5 miles west of the forest head-quarters (near the parking area before Sand Ridge Road connects with the Goofy Ridge blacktop). In some years, birders also see White-winged Crossbills in this area during winter. If you're here in the summer, look for the Red Crossbills, too, which may breed here.

One of the most productive birding sites during spring migration is the mesic forest region encountered along Bishop Road, an unpaved sand road at the extreme southern portion of the forest. Bishop Road can be reached from Forest City Road, the road you used to enter the site. Birders have documented 27 warbler species along this road, as well as 7 thrush species and Scarlet and Summer Tanagers during migration in late April through late May. You can park on Bishop Road, then walk to search for birds.

Neotropical migrants crossing the agricultural land surrounding the forest sometimes drop into this area in great numbers. Birders have counted as many as 150 newly arrived Rose-breasted Grosbeaks along a quarter mile of forested edge.

In the area just south of the Pine Campground, one or more Chuck-will's-widows often call from dusk to dawn beginning in late April through July, especially on moonlit nights. Sand Ridge is the most dependable place in central Illinois to find Chuck-will's-widows, a southern species. You may also be serenaded by numerous Whip-poor-wills in the area around the campgrounds, especially along oak margins.

Several osage-orange hedges in the forest along with wet thickets attract American Woodcocks, especially at dusk in the spring. Check along Sand Ridge Road, east and west of the forest headquarters.

Topeka Road, which joins the Goofy Ridge blacktop near the Sand Ridge Road junction, leads to the Henry Allen Gleason Nature Preserve. A sand dome in the preserve is one of the highest points in Mason County, offering panoramic views. It's a good place to look for migrating raptors following the Illinois River valley south in September and October.

Also check the 20-acre solar pond and the rearing ponds at the Jake Wolf Memorial Fish Hatchery, which attracts water birds and their associates. You might see a Wild Turkey in the nearby oak-hickory woodlands as well.

General information: The site remains one of the few places in Illinois that supports desert plants and animals. Receding floodwaters of the last ice age left a large desert-like expanse in this part of central Illinois. A period of extreme dryness followed, allowing plants and animals of the southwest to extend their range into much of the Midwest. Shifting winds sculpted 100-foot-high sand dunes in the glacial outwash evident today in the now-wooded ridges for which the forest is named.

In 1939, the state purchased 5,504 acres of forested tracts and run-down farmsteads to be managed by the Division of Forestry as an experimental forest. The Civilian Conservation Corps planted pine trees to control wind erosion and demonstrate the viability of growing a commercial tree crop on sandy soil. In 1971, the Division of Land Management took over management of the site, and the area became known as Sand Ridge State Forest. It is now a multiple-use recreational site. Check at forest headquarters regarding dates, sites, and times of hunting activity. Blaze-orange outerwear is recommended when birding during the hunting season, even when in areas closed to hunting.

ADDITIONAL HELP

DeLorme IA&G grid: 50.
Contact: Site superintendent, Sand Ridge State Forest.
Nearest gas, food, and lodging: Havana, plus camping at the forest.

58 Lake Chautauqua National Wildlife Refuge

Habitats: Floodplain forest, open water, upland terrain, and timber.
Key birds: Migratory ducks, geese, swans, shorebirds, gulls, and terns; migratory American White Pelican; breeding Bald Eagle, Pileated Woodpecker, Prothonotary Warbler, American Redstart, and Eurasian Tree Sparrow.
Best times to bird: Late July into September for shorebirds, fall and spring for waterfowl, winter for Bald Eagle; spring migration for warblers and water birds.

Directions: You'll find signs leading to the refuge off U.S. Highway 136 about 5 miles east of Havana. At the junction of US 136 and County Road 2130E, go north 4 miles to CR 2000N, west 2 miles to CR 1950E, then north 1 mile on CR 1950E to the refuge headquarters entrance sign.

Birding: Two birders stood along the Lake Chautauqua shoreline on a warm August day to estimate the number of shorebirds using the refuge: 20,000! Long-legged waders such as American Avocets and smaller peeps, including Buff-breasted and Pectoral Sandpipers ventured to the pools of water. Some of the shorebirds hid in the grasses, but flushed when a Northern Harrier flashed its white rump as it dipped into the marsh.

Situated along the Illinois River south of Peoria in Mason County is Lake Chautauqua National Wildlife Refuge, one of the state's crown jewels for shorebird watching. Indeed, the Western Hemisphere Shorebird Reserve Network has designated the refuge as a regionally significant site that provides critical habitat for shorebird species of international concern.

This 4,488-acre national wildlife refuge in north-central Illinois has attracted more than 254 species of birds, including 27 species of waterfowl and 27 species of shorebirds. During late summer, tens of thousands of shorebirds feed on the extensive shoreline touching 3,500 acres of open water; and in fall, 100,000 ducks and up to 40,000 geese stop to rest and feed.

Begin your birding at the refuge headquarters. When open, you can get a brochure, a map of the refuge, and the Birds of Chautauqua checklist.

View shorebirds and waterfowl from observation platforms overlooking the south Wasenza pool along a barrier-free nature trail beginning at the refuge headquarters parking area. In July and August you'll need a scope to view the thousands of peeps present. During spring migration the trail provides good views of neotropical migrants following the bluff along the east side of the lake.

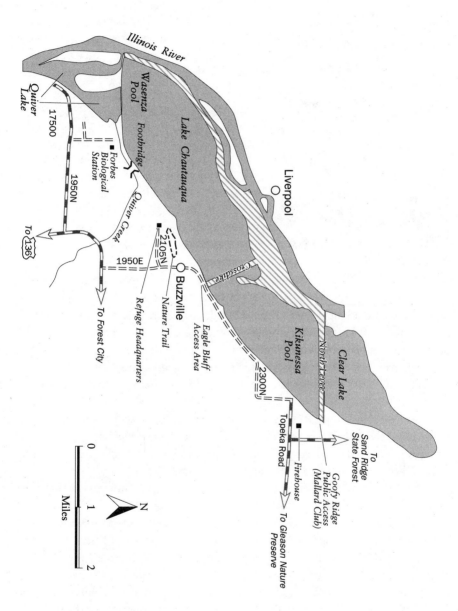

Pectoral Sandpiper migrates through Lake Chautaqua.
JOE B. MILOSEVICH PHOTO

A better place for viewing shorebirds and waterfowl is the Eagle Bluff access area. Birders may find up to 500 American White Pelicans during spring and fall. From an elevated platform on the east bluff, you can view a large portion of the south (Wasenza) pool and north (Kikunessa) pool, separated by a dike crossing Lake Chautauqua.

To get to the platform, walk the short trail leading from the south edge of the parking area. When construction is completed, you can drive the road near the boat-launching ramp as far as the gate at the east end of the crossdike where you'll find a second boat launching ramp. Birders discovered Marbled Godwits, American Avocets, Buff-breasted Sandpipers, and Red-necked Phalaropes, as well as 14 other species of shorebirds at this area in mid-August of 1998.

You may observe an active Bald Eagle nest in the drowned timber of the Melz Slough. You'll need a scope to see the nest. Eagles usually begin nesting in March or April.

Also check the Goofy Ridge public access area, a place worth visiting for waterfowl and shorebirds where a new water-control system has been placed. This site is adjacent to the north levee, which separates Lake Chautauqua from Clear Lake. A heron colony and another active Bald Eagle nest are on private land near here. At times, this area offers excellent viewing of waterfowl moving between the two lakes.

Goofy Ridge, an unincorporated community, is next to the Kikunessa pool of Lake Chautauqua. A sign near the Ridge Lake Fire House identifies the road to the refuge parking area at the back end of the community near the Mallard Club. A short trail leads from the parking area to the north levee.

You'll also want to search for neotropical migrants and waterfowl along the south levee, as well as Eurasian Tree Sparrows in shrubs along the roadway. To get to the south levee, drive to the Illinois Natural History Survey's Forbes Biological Station (open only on weekdays.) A tiny sign, easy to miss, marks the entrance. You'll find limited parking here.

Cross Quiver Creek on a footbridge that separates the Forbes station from the south levee. An automobile pull-out just south of the footbridge is a good place to use a spotting scope to scan for waterfowl in spring and fall, shorebirds during low water periods, and gulls and terns during migration, as well as loafing and courting Bald Eagles from October through March. Pileated Woodpeckers and Eurasian Tree Sparrows also frequent this area. During migration, birders have seen 27 species of warblers, including Connecticut, Mourning, Hooded, Canada, and Wilson's, along with breeding American Redstarts and Prothonotary Warblers.

General information: The area that now comprises the Chautauqua National Wildlife Refuge once provided sloughs, wetlands, and woods for millions of waterfowl and other birds that fed and rested while migrating to their southern winter homes. In the 1920s, agricultural development, including diking and draining, greatly disturbed the ecosystem. Aquatic plants and fish were deprived of oxygen as silt from development filled in the backwaters.

But in 1936 when the federal government purchased the Chautauqua Drainage and Levee District, things changed. Restoration work began, and today, birders, fishermen, and hunters can enjoy the area.

Chautauqua National Wildlife Refuge, one of four units comprising the Illinois River Fish and Wildlife Refuges, consists of open water and floodplains within the Mississippi Flyway along the Illinois River. The refuge links with 1,790 acres of the Cameron–Biullsbach Unit, 3,300 acres of the Meredosia National Wildlife Refuge (see Site 59), and 1,120 acres of the Emiquon National Wildlife Refuge, which will be accessible to birders soon. Together these refuges encompass 10,000 acres on 125 miles along the Illinois River. When acquisitions are complete, the Illinois River Refuges will include 32,000 acres of bottomland forest, backwater lake, floodplain wetlands, and prairies.

Management, including the modification of water level control at Lake Chautauqua, should solve a chronic flood and sedimentation problem and improve conditions for migrating waterfowl and shorebirds. A one-way automobile route atop the perimeter levee surrounding the Wasenza Pool is being considered and would have pull-outs for improved viewing during part of the year, although its use would be restricted by water levels and hunting season.

Be aware of poison ivy, ticks, and insects. As construction continues here and during hunting season, some sites might be closed. Call before you go for an update on construction status, water levels, and restricted sites, including hunting areas.

ADDITIONAL HELP

DeLorme IA&G grid: 50.
Contact: Chautauqua National Wildlife Refuge.
Nearest gas, food, and lodging: Havana, plus camping at nearby Sand Ridge State Forest.

59 Meredosia National Wildlife Refuge

Habitats: Large floodplain backwater lakes surrounded by floodplain forest, agricultural fields, fallow fields, sloughs, and moist soil units.
Key birds: Migratory waterfowl, including American White Pelican, migratory shorebirds and sparrows; breeding Double-crested Cormorant, floodplain forest birds, and Lark Sparrow; wintering Bald Eagle; Eurasian Tree Sparrow (year-round).
Best times to bird: Mid-March through mid-May and mid-July through December 1 for waterfowl; April through June and mid-July through October for shorebirds; mid-November through mid-March for eagles.

Directions: Take U.S. Highway 67/Illinois Highway 104 to the town of Meredosia, which is about 15 miles west of Jacksonville. Just after IL 104 splits from US 67, you'll see the sign declaring the entrance to Meredosia National Wildlife Refuge. This turnoff (from US 67) takes you to a T intersection where you'll find the main parking and information area for the refuge.

Birding: Standing at the main parking lot at Meredosia National Wildlife Refuge, you are less than 1 mile from sandy scrub grassland, open water, shorebird flats, savanna, and floodplain forest. These habitats provide respite for thousands of dabbling ducks plucking aquatic delicacies from flooded fields, dozens of Eurasian Tree Sparrows feeding in the shrubs, and hundreds of migrating American White Pelicans.

Located along the Illinois River, this 2,224-acre refuge (with an additional 3,000 soon to be purchased) and surrounding habitat, just north of the town of Meredosia, provides the first large complex of forest and wetland habitats for a northbound migrant since the area where the Illinois and Mississippi Rivers join at Pere Marquette State Park and the Mark Twain National Wildlife Refuge.

The backwater lake dominates the area, attracting birders, commercial fishermen, and hunters. Birders compiled a list of more than 200 species, and have often observed 100 species in a single day during migration.

Begin by checking the refuge's main parking area for Lark Sparrows and possibly Blue Grosbeaks, spring through summer. Then follow the path near the visitor center to the observation deck; here you'll see sloughs leading from the river to the lake. In spring and summer, you may see Prothonotary Warblers, egrets, herons, and an occasional Blue-winged Teal, plus possibly Snowy Egrets in late summer. Next, take Meredosia Bay Road north, or left, out of the main parking area to enter the lake basin. Sometimes the road is closed if water levels are too high, but when you can get through, you can search for birds in the floodplain forest adjacent to the lake. Park alongside the road in spring and summer to look for Black-crowned Night-Herons, Red-headed Woodpeckers, and Prothonotary Warblers.

Next, drive past the first bridge. In winter, you'll often find sparrows, including Fox and White-crowned. In all other seasons the area to the west past a row of trees is the best place to find American White Pelicans and shorebirds during normal to low water levels. Birders have observed large concentrations of pelicans,

59 Meredosia National Wildlife Refuge

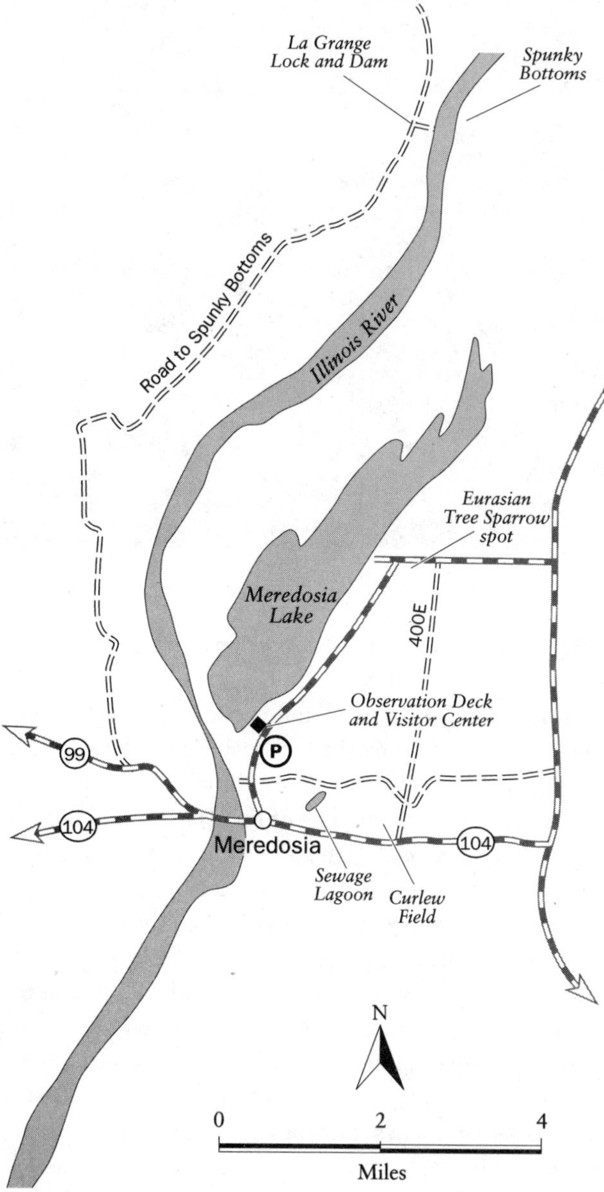

La Grange
Lock and Dam

Spunky
Bottoms

Road to Spunky Bottoms

Illinois River

67

Eurasian
Tree Sparrow
spot

Meredosia
Lake

400E

Observation Deck
and Visitor Center

P

99

104

Meredosia

Sewage
Lagoon

Curlew
Field

104

N

0   2   4

Miles

300 or more, at this south part of the lake. They have also recorded many shore-birds, including Buff-breasted Sandpipers and Willets, as well as the American Avocet and Western Sandpiper, both of which are more commonly found in the western United States.

The entire lake but particularly the south part is good for migrating terns and gulls. Also look for foraging Great Blue Herons, Double-crested Cormorants, and

Eurasian Tree Sparrow. DENNIS OEHMKE PHOTO

possibly Great Egrets, which breed in a rookery on a peninsula on the other side of the lake.

Continuing north along the road you'll encounter a community of summer homes, which has been acquired by the U.S. Fish & Wildlife Service. Large concentrations of waterfowl congregate here, and in winter if water is open you can easily see diving ducks even in the middle of the day. The dabbling ducks, which can number in the thousands, feed during the day in the surrounding agricultural fields and roost on the lake. Look for Bald Eagles in winter.

As the road continues north, you'll see a slough on the east and the lake on the west. This slough attracts ducks, and the Cinnamon Teal, another western species rarely seen in Illinois, has been observed between mid-March and early May.

To see Eurasian Tree Sparrows, follow Meredosia Bay Road to the point at which it turns east and crosses a large dike. These sparrows are common throughout the refuge but the brushy area along the road especially at this point has been a favorite roosting spot—birders sometimes see hundreds of them. The adult of this Old World species has a brown crown, black ear patch, and black throat, compared with the House Sparrow's gray crown and more extensive black throat.

Following the road over the dike you'll see large expanses of agricultural fields where in winter you can find dabbling ducks and geese, including the Greater White-fronted Goose, also an uncommon Illinois species. Take the first road, County Road 400E, to your left to view the refuge's eastern boundary, where the U.S. Fish & Wildlife Service is managing fields, wet soil units, and wildlife planting areas, which attract sparrows during migration as well as Northern Harriers.

Continue south along this road until you cross a leveed ditch. Just past this ditch on the west you'll find one of the best shorebird areas, if water levels are right. Locally know as the Curlew Field after birders discovered a very rare Long-Billed Curlew, this low area during wet years has attracted birds such as the federally listed endangered Piping Plover, and the rare Red Knot, plus many other more common species, including dowitchers, phalaropes, peeps, yellowlegs, sandpipers, and plovers, as well as occasional pelicans, terns, ducks, Cattle Egrets, and American Pipits.

Northwest of the field you'll find a sewage lagoon. Access is limited but you can still view the lagoon by going north from the main parking area to a trailer park, turning into the trailer park entrance, and taking the second road on your left. Follow the road through the park and along the refuge to the sewage lagoons. These lagoons are next to a grassland that during migration holds Bobolinks and Grasshopper and Savannah Sparrows. The lagoon is a good area for ducks and the occasional rarity such as a Surf Scoter and Cinnamon Teal.

Spunky Bottoms is a floodplain wetland complex recently purchased by The Nature Conservancy. This area between the lake and the Illinois River can be accessed by parking near locked gates and then walking.

The area is south of LaGrange Lock and Dam across the Illinois River from the Meredosia refuge. This area along the Illinois river can be accessed from LaGrange Lock and Dam Road. Spunky Bottoms and other nearby flooded fields have contained birds such as Tundra Swans, American White Pelicans, Eared and Horned Grebes, Wilson's Phalaropes, various peeps, summering Bald Eagles, and Prothonotary Warblers.

General information: The Meredosia refuge was established in 1973 to provide sanctuary for wildlife, primarily for waterfowl and other migratory birds. Land management programs promote migratory bird, fish, and resident wildlife habitat in the Illinois River basin. When acquisition and restoration are complete, the refuge will include a combination of high-quality backwater lakes, bottomland forest, upland forest, prairie, seasonal wetland, and permanent marsh habitat.

Duck-hunting season begins in late fall and lasts through early winter. Wear bright clothing and be cautious, or avoid birding during these times. For exact times and dates of hunting season, contact the National Wildlife Refuge system office. Some areas are closed to the public between October 16 and February 15.

ADDITIONAL HELP

DeLorme IA&G grid: 58 and 59.
Contact: Lake Chautauqua National Wildlife Refuge manager.
Nearest gas, food, and lodging: Jacksonville and Beardstown; camping at Siloam Springs State Park (see Site 61).

60 Beardstown Marsh and the Sanganois Conservation Area

Habitats: Deepwater marsh surrounded by upland fields and residential areas; three large lakes and smaller backwater lakes and sloughs, fallow fields, and floodplain forest.

Key birds: Migrating waterfowl and shorebirds, including King Rail, marsh birds, including breeding Pied-billed Grebe, Common Moorhen, and Least and American Bitterns; Loggerhead Shrike; Blue Grosbeak, Lark Sparrow, Western Meadowlark, and Eurasian Tree Sparrow (year-round).

Best times to bird: Year-round, but especially March through September.

Directions: Sanganois Conservation Area can be reached from Illinois Highway 78 just north of the Sangamon River. Take the paved road (County Road 150N/ 200N) west until you reach the conservation area entrance in about 10 miles. To get to the marsh, from the intersection of U.S. Highway 67 and IL 125, go east 1 mile to Boulevard Road. You'll find the marsh south of the intersection of IL 125 and Boulevard Road. Plans are being made to repave and widen Boulevard Road and even change its location, but following these directions should still get you to the heart of the marsh.

Birding: Drive through central Illinois amid the cornfields, and you might think no wetlands or forests exist for miles; that is, until you get to the Illinois River Valley, where backwater lakes, a deepwater marsh, and woods instantly break the monotony. The Illinois River Valley's most diverse birding area lies between Havana and Beardstown, where you'll find the Sanganois Conservation Area and Beardstown Marsh.

The Sanganois Conservation Area, north of Beardstown, encompasses a mosaic of habitats, including three major lakes (Chain, Steward, and Crane), and smaller lakes and sloughs.

Along the road (CR 150N) leading from IL 78 to the entrance to Sanganois, you'll find many fallow fields that provide ideal foraging area for sparrow, raptors, and finches. The sandy soil provides a breeding habitat favored by a few unusual species, including Lark Sparrows, Blue Grosbeaks, and Western Meadowlarks. In winter these fields support raptors such as Rough-legged Hawks, Northern Harriers, and occasionally Short-eared Owls. Also, scan power lines for Loggerhead Shrikes.

Once you reach the conservation area entrance, you'll drive the main road to the levee-bisecting Chain Lake, where two Wood Storks were seen one year, and where Mississippi Kites occasionally circle the sky in spring and summer. Stay on the main road; the side roads off this road are in poor shape.

The three large lakes, visible from the main road, attract many waterfowl, including tens of thousands of ducks. During migration you should see American White Pelicans, and Tundra and Trumpeter Swans. Bald Eagles forage here year-round; a few pairs nest in the area. In fall and winter, look for migrating Golden Eagles.

60 Beardstown Marsh and the Sanganois Conservation Area

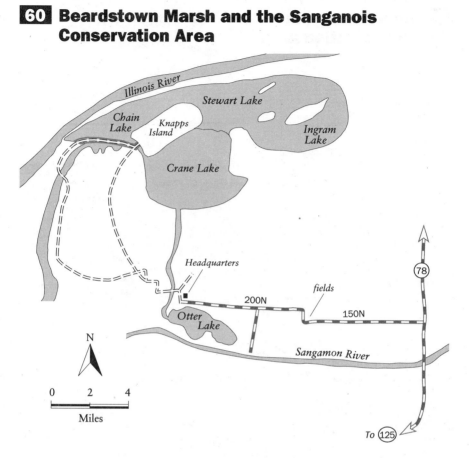

As with all floodplain lakes, water levels vary. When deep, they provide habitat for gulls, terns, and ducks. Sometimes the lakes are little more than mudflats providing excellent habitat for shorebirds and wading birds. The best times to view shorebirds are from late April through May and mid-August through September. You should find plenty of Pectoral and Least Sandpipers as well as Lesser Yellowlegs, along with fewer numbers of Semipalmated Sandpipers, Semipalmated Plovers, Stilt Sandpipers, dowitchers, Dunlins, and Greater Yellowlegs.

The forest along the main and secondary roads provides habitat for many breeding species, including Prothonotary Warblers, Yellow-throated Vireos, American Redstarts, Pileated Woodpeckers, Barred Owls, and Warbling Vireos. The forest also attracts spring warblers.

Search the roadsides for Eurasian Tree Sparrows, especially near the refuge headquarters, which is at the end of CR 150N. A Bewick's Wren, endangered in the state, bred in 1998.

Near Sanganois you'll find one of the largest cattail marshes left in Illinois on the southern edge of the river town of Beardstown at the intersection of IL 125 and Boulevard Road.

60 Beardstown Marsh and the Sanganois Conservation Area

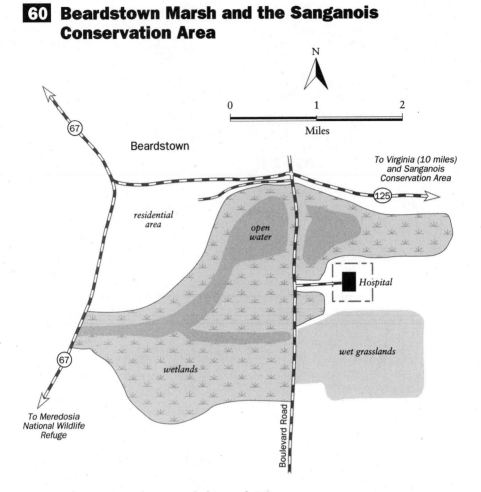

Beardstown Marsh, a rare habitat of 468 acres supports many uncommon breeding birds such as Pied-billed Grebes and Common Moorhens, which can often be seen in late summer tending to fledglings. The marsh also provides critical foraging areas for many migrants as well as occasional rare breeders, including King Rails, Yellow-headed Blackbirds, and American Bitterns. Rarities include White-faced Ibises and Great-tailed Grackles.

For migrating Soras and Virginia Rails, check the marsh along the west side of the road and on the east side of the road before the hospital. An impressive number of Soras use the area during migration in April and May. Common Moorhens, Pied-billed Grebes, and Least Bitterns have bred here. During low water level periods, shorebirds often cover all the open areas. Birders typically find Pectoral and Least Sandpipers as well as Lesser Yellowlegs to be the most abundant shorebirds. Other possibilities include Wilson's Phalaropes, both dowitchers, American Avocets, Black-necked Stilts, and Western Sandpipers, all documented. Check the ditches along the road for herons and egrets, including both Yellow-crowned and Black-crowned Night-Herons during migration or postbreeding dispersal in late summer. The open areas also provide habitat when the water is not frozen for migrating waterfowl, primarily Blue- and Green-winged Teals and Northern Shovelers.

Also, check the lawn areas of the hospital for migrating sparrows, including the less common species. Birders have recorded LeConte's and Nelson's Sharp-tailed Sparrows during spring and fall migration.

South of the hospital along the east side of Boulevard Road, a grassy pasture provides habitat for many grassland birds, including Ring-necked Pheasants, Northern Bobwhites, Eastern and occasionally Western Meadowlarks, and Sedge Wrens. The pheasants and bobwhites use the grounds nearly year-round. Sedge Wrens return in spring. Meadowlarks arrive in early spring, some of them overwintering.

General information: Several local residents own and maintain Beardstown Marsh. Birders are welcome as long as they remain on the roads. As with many other areas in the Illinois floodplain, high water levels and flooded fields can create phenomenal habitat in a matter of days. Even with limited access, Beardstown Marsh is easily explored by birders. If you're birding the Meredosia National Wildlife Refuge (see Site 59), consider stopping at Beardstown Marsh and Sanganois as part of your day's trip. Beardstown Marsh is listed on the Illinois Natural Areas Inventory, but is not protected as a state nature preserve. Birders and other conservationists hope to get this area protected. Wear bright clothing during hunting season, which usually begins in fall and lasts through early winter. Sanganois Conservation Area is surrounded by many hunt clubs that manage the region not only for ducks but also for other nongame species.

ADDITIONAL HELP

DeLorme IA&G grid: 49.
Contact: Sanganois Conservation Area and the Illinois Department of Natural Resources.
Nearest gas, food, and lodging: Jacksonville and Beardstown, state campground at Anderson Lake Conservation Area and at Site M, a state-owned recreation area east of Chadlerville.

61 Siloam Springs State Park

Habitats: Hardwood forest, scrubland, pasture grassland, and medium-sized lake.
Key birds: Migratory and breeding forest birds, including Cerulean and Worm-eating Warblers, Northern Parula and Louisiana Waterthrush; scrub and grassland birds, including Bewick's Wren and Loggerhead Shrike.
Best times to bird: Mid-March to mid-August.

61 Siloam Springs State Park

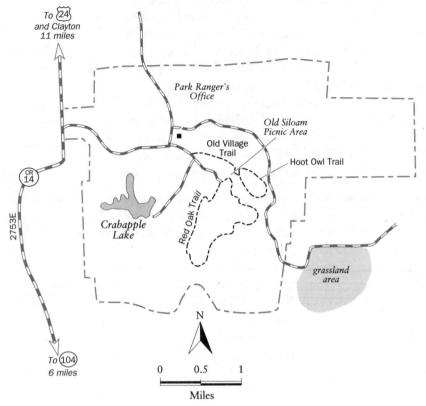

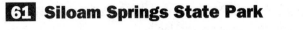

Directions: The park is halfway way between Quincy and Jacksonville along Illinois Highway 104. Take IL 104 to County Road 2873E and go north 6 miles to the main entrance.

Birding: This 3,323-acre state park set in the rolling hills of the western Illinois forests near Mt. Sterling contains many uncommon breeding birds and can be spectacular during migration. The well-maintained and accessible park serves as an example of what western Illinois forests looked like before settlement.

Hardwood forest covers most of the park, though the Illinois Department of Natural Resources manages some open area for game bird hunting. Private citizens have set aside grasslands as conservation reserves, and these areas attract breeding and migrating grassland birds.

At the scrub areas, of which the largest and best are around the hunters' check station office and park ranger's house, you'll occasionally find breeding Bewick's Wrens, Blue-winged Warblers, and Bell's Vireos. Look for the Bewick's Wren nesting in and around the hunting check station. A pair built its nest in a barbecue grill the summer of 1998! Migrants such as Clay-colored Sparrows and Connecticut Warblers also forage nearby early in the morning in middle to late May.

Choose nearly any camp site or road in the park and you can find plenty of migrants in spring and fall. One of the best of these areas is the Old Siloam Picnic Area, where you may find migrant and nesting warblers, vireos, flycatchers, and tanagers. Ovenbirds, Louisiana Waterthrushes, and Cerulean, Yellow-throated, and Kentucky Warblers, as well as Northern Parulas breed. Check the large sycamores along the road for Cerulean and Yellow-throated Warblers and Northern Parulas. Walk the paved road beneath the sycamores to find breeding and migrating songbirds.

Illinois birders are particularly fond of the Worm-eating Warbler, and Siloam Springs attracts these birds to nest in the deep ravines around the valley, even along many of the roadsides through the park.

Some other breeding species include Broad-winged Hawks, Pileated Woodpeckers, Summer and Scarlet Tanagers, Wood Thrushes; Red-eyed, Yellow-throated, and Warbling Vireos, and possibly Least Flycatchers and Black-and-white Warblers.

The Red Oak, Hoot Owl, and Old Village Trails provide the best opportunity to get into the heart of the forest and away from the picnic areas to search for these birds.

The pastures and set-aside fields around the park provide good habitat for Loggerhead Shrikes, and Henslow's, Grasshopper, and Lark Sparrows. These are some of the rarest breeding bird species in Illinois, and your best bet at finding them is at this park.

ADDITIONAL HELP

DeLorme IA&G grid: 58.

Contact: Siloam Springs State Park and the Illinois Department of Natural Resources.

Nearest gas, food, and lodging: Camping on site; reservations advised. The closest town with services is Mt. Sterling about 9 miles north. Other lodging in Quincy.

62 Mark Twain National Wildlife Refuge— Keithsburg Division

Habitats: Early successional floodplain bottomland forest interspersed with ample backwater slough and submergent wetland habitats. The entire refuge is separated from the river by a levee system. The main channel of the Mississippi River is immediately adjacent to the refuge.

Key birds: Migrating waterfowl, raptors, and songbirds, including American White Pelican and Greater White-fronted Goose, 25+ species of warblers, 12 species of sparrows, including Harris's Sparrow, and Rusty Blackbird; breeding Pileated Woodpecker, Yellow and Black-billed Cuckoo; Brown Creeper, Yellow-throated Warbler, and Eurasian Tree Sparrow.

Best times to bird: Spring migration and the breeding season; the refuge is closed to the public from September 15 to January 1 to provide migratory waterfowl a place for feeding and resting.

62 Mark Twain National Wildlife Refuge— Keithsburg Division

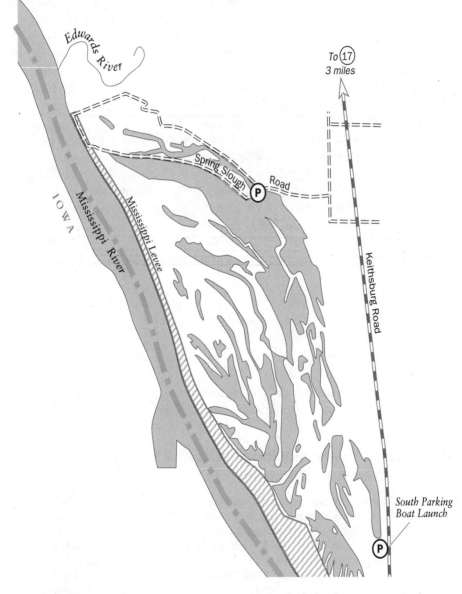

Directions: From Illinois Highway 17 at the town of Aledo, drive west 12 miles to Keithsburg Road. Go south 3 miles to the gravel entrance road leading to Spring Slough Road. This is the north entrance where you can park and walk. If you're birding by boat, go to the south entrance. Travel 4.5 miles from the intersection of IL 17 and Keithsburg. Turn west onto a gravel road that leads to the boat launch.

Birding: You'll find no roads upon which to drive within the Keithsburg Division, but you can bird either on foot or by boat. Boat access is at the refuge's south entrance, where you can traverse sloughs and shallow-water areas, as well as various-sized stands of young floodplain bottomland forest.

To bird by foot, park at the refuge's north entrance next to the permanently closed gate, then walk Spring Slough Road into the refuge. After walking about 1 mile, Spring Slough Road ends at the Mississippi River levee. At this point you can follow the Mississippi levee south for about 3.5 miles, where it intersects an old railroad levee. You'll then have to retrace your steps back to your car, so be prepared!

If you walk north at the Spring Slough Road/Mississippi levee junction, you can make a 2.5-mile loop that brings you back to your car. Both tours pass through backwater sloughs where you can view migratory or breeding waterfowl as well as woodlands that attract passerines.

In a typical year at least 180 species of birds visit the refuge, and at least 80 of them breed. Birding this refuge in March and April yields an incredible abundance and diversity (as many as 26 species) of migratory waterfowl. Some of the more interesting species include Pied-billed Grebes, American White Pelicans, Greater White-fronted Geese, Snow Geese, Wood Ducks, Green-winged Teals, American Black Ducks, Northern Pintails, Redheads, Lesser Scaups, Greater Scaups, Buffleheads, Hooded Mergansers, Red-breasted Mergansers, and Ruddy Ducks.

During March and April birders can also find as many as 12 species of sparrows and 13 species of diurnal raptors in migration. Some of the sparrow species include Fox, Lincoln's, Swamp, White-throated, White-crowned, and (rarely) Harris's. The sparrows concentrate in the heavy grass cover of the levees and at the bottomland woods along Spring Slough Road. Listen for migrating Marsh Wrens in the heavy grasses, too. Keep your eyes to the sky for migrating Ospreys, Bald Eagles, Sharp-shinned Hawks, Broad-winged Hawks, Rough-legged Hawks, Merlins, and Peregrine Falcons.

From late April through May Keithsburg serves as migration habitat for a wide array of birds, including 6 species of gallinaceous birds (Ring-necked Pheasants, Wild Turkeys, Northern Bobwhites, Virginia Rails, Soras and American Coots) and Sandhill Cranes. Most of the migratory species can be found foraging in the early successional forest.

Walking along Spring Slough Road and the levee system, or boating to the various stands of forest within the interior of the refuge will permit birders to observe 7 woodpecker and 7 thrush species, 6 swallow species, and 9 species of flycatchers in spring. Five species of vireos (Blue-headed, Yellow-throated, Warbling, Philadelphia, and Red-eyed) and more than 25 species of warblers have been identified at Keithsburg during migration.

During springs when water levels are very low, many of the shallow bays and sloughs dry, forming mudflats. These areas provide temporary habitats for many species of shorebirds such as Semipalmated Plovers, Greater and Lesser Yellowlegs,

White-rumped and Baird's Sandpipers, Dunlins, Stilt Sandpipers, Short-billed and Long-billed Dowitchers and Common Snipes.

In summer a small colony of Double-crested Cormorants breeds in a slough and bay area about halfway between Spring Slough Road and the railroad levee. A pair of Bald Eagles also breeds nearby. Other diurnal raptors using the refuge during the breeding season include Turkey Vultures, Cooper's Hawks, Red-shouldered Hawks, Red-tailed Hawks, and American Kestrels.

Many songbirds nest throughout the bottomland forest tracts and can be found either by boat or on foot. Search for Black-billed and Yellow-billed Cuckoos, Belted Kingfishers, Hairy and Pileated Woodpeckers, Eastern Wood-Pewees, Willow and Great Crested Flycatchers, Carolina Wrens, Blue-gray Gnatcatchers, Yellow-throated and Red-eyed Vireos, Yellow Warblers, American Redstarts, Prothonotary Warblers, Rose-breasted Grosbeaks, Indigo Buntings, and Baltimore Orioles.

Brown Creepers breed in the forest near the north entrance and Yellow-throated Warblers breed in a small grove of sycamores at the extreme north end of the refuge. A fairly large group of Eurasian Tree Sparrows can be found breeding along the Mississippi River levee from the intersection with Spring Slough Road all the way south to the railroad levee.

General information: This refuge is closed to the public from September 15 to January 1 for the benefit of migrating waterfowl. You'll find no water or restroom facilities. Bring plenty of water, insect repellent, sunscreen, and a hat. The refuge is open for squirrel hunting in late summer through sometime in fall. Hunting also occurs on the land bordering the refuge, so use caution when birding in the spring.

ADDITIONAL HELP

DeLorme IA&G grid: 30.
Contact: Mark Twain National Wildlife Refuge Headquarters.
Nearest gas, food, and lodging: Muscatine, Iowa.

63 Pere Marquette State Park and Mark Twain National Wildlife Refuge—Brussels District

Habitats: Riverine backwaters, wooded bluffs, lakes, marshes, bottomland woods, fields, and moist soil units.
Key birds: Migratory American White Pelican, waterfowl, shorebirds, hawks, including Mississippi Kite and songbirds; breeding Black-crowned and Yellow-crowned Night-Herons, Prothonotary Warbler, and Eurasian Tree Sparrow; postbreeding dispersal of herons and egrets; wintering Bald Eagle.
Best times to bird: Year-round, but especially at the peak of spring and fall migration, in winter, and early in the breeding season.

63 Pere Marquette State Park and Mark Twain National Wildlife Refuge—Brussels District

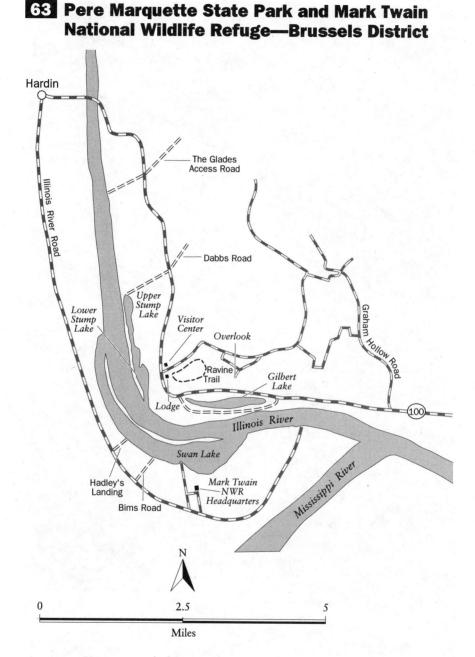

Directions: You can reach the Brussels Ferry or any of the various sites mentioned off Illinois Highway 100 (Great River Road) between the towns of Grafton and Hardin. To get to the park entrance on IL 100 from Interstate 55, exit at IL 16. Go west through Jerseyville to IL 100 and south to the park entrance. You'll pass the Brussels Ferry on your way. If the ferry is closed (which is seldom), you can drive

Yellow-crowned Night-Herons breed at the Mark Twain National Wildlife Refuge.
THOMAS JACKMAN PHOTO

north on IL 100 for 20 miles to the town of Hardin, where you can go west over a bridge to access the Illinois River Road and bird the refuge.

Birding: The Mississippi Flyway serves as one of the nation's major migratory paths for birds, and one of the key spots along the flyway is where the Illinois River joins the Mississippi River in southwestern Illinois near Pere Marquette State Park and the Brussels District of the Mark Twain National Wildlife Refuge. Together, the park and refuge total more than 16,000 acres.

Birders have recorded more than 250 species at these sites combined, and rarities occur yearly. You should plan several days to bird this area; water levels sometimes change daily, affecting the bird life. Also be aware that hunting season occurs typically from mid-October through mid-December, when many of these sites are closed, except to hunters with licenses.

You can access the following birding sites off IL 100 or the Illinois River Road after crossing the Brussels Ferry.

From the visitor center at the main park entrance on IL 100, hike the Ravine Trail, which leads to higher ground along a creek and woods. In spring, look and listen for Louisiana Waterthrushes, Ovenbirds, Northern Parulas, Yellow-throated Warblers, and other migrants. When the water flows, it attracts warblers and other songbirds. As you walk farther up the hill, you might find a Worm-eating Warbler singing the thin, buzzy breeding trill as it returns to breed in the park.

You can also drive the main park road into the park about half a mile to a mound and scenic spot overlooking Swan Lake. You can watch eagles here in winter, American White Pelicans during fall migration, and Turkey Vultures from March through October. They move in when the eagles move out. Occasionally, when the Bald Eagles are present a Golden Eagle joins them.

Also listen here in May and June for breeding Worm-eating Warblers and Northern Parulas, Eastern Wood-Pewees, and Yellow-billed Cuckoos, among other songbirds.

To look for more songbirds, continue on the main park road about 1.5 miles until you reach Graham Hollow Road at a junction. You can bird along this road, stopping in pull-outs and listening for Ovenbirds, chats, warblers, Summer Tanagers, White-eyed and Red-eyed Vireos, and other breeding songbirds. You can also reach Graham Hollow Road by driving north on IL 100, about 2.6 miles past the town of Grafton. The first Eastern Phoebes and Louisiana Waterthrushes return in March to Graham Hollow, a good full month before this species is typically seen in northern Illinois.

From the state park entrance, walk or drive across the road to the marina where you might see and hear Fish Crows in late April and May. To view Lower Stump Lake, walk north to the levee where you'll find scores of ducks in March and September and egrets and herons, sometimes numbering in the hundreds, in August and September. You'll find white-phase Little Blue Herons here. Be careful to separate them from the occasional Snowy Egret that stops by.

Search for immature Yellow-crowned and Black-crowned Night-Herons after the breeding season. The Yellow-crowns used to be more common in this area, but now Black-crowns seem to be more numerous. To separate these species in the juvenile plumage, note that the Yellow-crowned Night-Heron extends its legs farther when flying, compared with the Black-crowned. The Yellow-crowned also has a longer neck and stouter bill, and the Black-crowned's lower mandible is light colored.

From the state park entrance, drive south less than a mile to a spot birders call The Overlook. This is a small unmarked gravel road that parallels IL 101 for about half a mile. You can find this spot by noting the first sign that is marked Mark Twain National Wildlife Refuge. Sedge Wrens breed here, and sing even well into August.

The gravel Dabbs Access Road (County Road 450N), which is 2 miles from the state park entrance, takes you west through mudflats that attract sandpipers and other shorebirds at the right season. Birders call this area Upper Stump Lake, and in July you might find hundreds of sandpipers depending on water levels. In March, myriad waterfowl, including shovelers and other dabblers also use this flooded region.

When you reach the end of the gravel road at the boat launch, look to the shoreline for godwits, plovers, sandpipers, and yellowlegs, especially in late July and early August. Some of the less common shorebirds you might see include Wilson's Phalaropes. Rails and Least Bitterns have bred here, and are most often seen or heard in late April through May at dawn or dusk.

Farther north, 4 miles from the state park entrance or 2 miles from Dabbs Access Road, you'll find the Glades River Access Area road (CR 830N). Go west, checking near the entrance for migrating sparrows in April and October. When you reach the sloughs, you should find many singing Prothonotary Warblers in spring. You can drive along the Illinois River and park on the side of the road. Birders particularly like this spot in late April and through May and again in September for migrating warblers. Mississippi Kites sometimes fly along the Illinois River in May and June. Birders also expect the area to be good for watching waterfowl; state and federal agencies are creating berms here that will hold water during flooding. Check for terns, Ospreys, and gulls, including Bonaparte's and Franklin's during migration. Also look for Wood Ducks and listen for the loud call of the Pileated Woodpecker. Both these species are seen year-round in bottomland areas in the park and the wildlife refuge.

About 1 mile south of the state park entrance is the Gilbert Lake Access, one of the best places to bird in southwestern Illinois. Turn west on the gravel road, checking the entrance for Yellow-crowned Night-Herons in spring, early summer, and early fall. Not far after you enter the access road, you'll find a locked gate. Park on the roadside without blocking the gate, then walk west. This road continues for 3 miles, so bring plenty of water and wear good hiking shoes. You'll want your scope, but remember, as far as you walk one way, you'll have to go back.

Look for eagles sitting in trees in winter and egrets replacing them in the summer. Fish Crows have bred here in some seasons, as well as Barred Owls and Red-tailed Hawks. Also look for Wild Turkeys year-round, and for spring and fall warblers, as well as lingering Winter Wrens in December. Walk this corridor in May and June and you should hear singing Acadian Flycatchers, Prothonotary Warblers, and American Redstarts.

About 1.5 miles down the road, a place known locally as the Middle Woods, seems to be a hotspot for migrants. In addition, backwaters and mudflats on the south side of the road can hold many shorebirds. In July and early August, birders have seen thousands of Pectoral Sandpipers here. This area is closed during hunting season.

To bird the west side of the river, take the free five-minute Brussels Ferry off IL 101 just south of the Gilbert Lake Access road. The ferry operates year-round 24 hours unless the river becomes too icy. Immediately as you drive off the ferry, turn south on a gravel road to get to what birders call Calhoun Point, where Prothonotary Warblers breed. Follow this road along the river and listen for this warbler's loud, repeated, single-pitched song in late April through June.

When you're done birding Calhoun Point, return to the main road off the ferry dock, which is Illinois River Road. Drive 4 miles to the Mark Twain National Wildlife Refuge headquarters. Along the way, look in the fields for Northern Harriers, and stop at the pump station road, about 1 mile before you reach the refuge sign. This gravel road, sometimes closed, leads to Swan Lake. At the entrance check the fields in spring for migrating LeConte's and Nelson's Sharp-tailed Sparrows, and possibly, an American Pipit. Then drive east to the pump, and walk out to Lower Swan Lake, which is often ice-free throughout winter. This area attracts huge concentrations of Snow Geese from October 15 through March 15. Numbers peak at 20,000.

The lake also attracts migrating American White Pelicans beginning in August, though some pelicans have summered here. This species began migrating through the wildlife refuge about 12 years ago. No one is certain why, but the white pelican is now an easy species to add to your Illinois life list if you know where to find it. Also look in August for Green-winged Teals, Canvasbacks, and Northern Pintails, some of which remain throughout winter. This area is closed during hunting season

Next, visit the wildlife refuge headquarters to observe shorebirds in late summer at an observation deck overlooking several moist soil units. You'll need your scope. Search for Eurasian Tree Sparrows in the shrubs or in the cottonwoods along a gravel road leading to Swan Lake. Here, too, are bottomlands where Barred Owls and Brown Creepers live. At the lake, you may find up to 100 or more American White Pelicans beginning in middle August through early winter. Search in September, October, and March for various waterfowl, including teals.

You'll find one more place to view Swan Lake farther north along Illinois River Road. It's known as Bim's Road (CR 850N). Drive this gravel road east to the lake to view shorebirds and waterfowl in fall and spring. North of Bim's Road

239

is Hadley's Landing, a 2-mile gravel road off CR 1300N that leads east to Fuller Lake. Check the shrubs along the way for Eurasian Tree Sparrows. Mississippi Kites have also been seen flying over the river. Waterfowl and shorebirds frequent this area, too, depending on the time of year and water levels. More likely you'll see Pied-billed Grebe, but occasionally Eared and rarely Red-necked Grebes stop over.

General information: A product of an ancient shallow sea 350 million years ago and the last ice age 12,000 years ago, what is now the Pere Marquette State Park and adjoining Mark Twain National Wildlife Refuge attracted humans to enjoy its abundant wildlife at least 10,000 years ago. In 1673, missionaries including Father Marquette, for whom the park was named, landed at the confluence of the Illinois and Mississippi Rivers. Today the state park and wildlife refuge, established in 1958, are managed for hiking, fishing, hunting, and other activities. Birding is excellent, but you may want to avoid the area during hunting season. In fact, many of the areas described above are closed to all but those with proper hunting licenses starting sometime in October and ending sometime in December. Call before coming to find out hunting season dates and times. You may be able to bird these areas after 4 P.M. even during hunting season.

The Mark Twain National Wildlife Refuge headquarters office is open on weekdays only, from 7:30 A.M. to 3 P.M. The Pere Marquette State Park Visitor Center is open on weekdays only, from 9 A.M. to 3 P.M. You'll find restrooms in both locations. Call first to obtain more information and bird checklists.

ADDITIONAL HELP

DeLorme IA&G grid:

Contact: Mark Twain National Wildlife Refuge, Brussels District and Pere Marquette State Park.

Nearest gas, food, and lodging: Camping at the park; lodging at the Pere Marquette State Park Lodge (reservations often necessary); bed and breakfasts and restaurants in Grafton and Elsah. Note that no gas is available between Grafton and Hardin on the west side of the river.

Prothonotary Warbler drawing by Denis Kania.

Southern Region

It's a land of poisonous snakes, huge mosquitos, and poison ivy. It's also a land of natural beauty. To appreciate southern Illinois and the birding adventures it offers, you'll just have to go. Once you do, you'll want to return again and again. On a spring bird count day in southern Illinois, you can easily tally 30 or more warblers. During the breeding season, many of these warblers remain. This is the only part of the state where Prairie Warblers and Northern Parulas regularly breed. You can always find singing Hooded, Kentucky, and Worm-eating Warblers in southern Illinois if you know where to go. (This guide will help.)

In southern Illinois there are thousands of acres of bottomland swamps, with 200-year-old cypress trees creating an eerie backdrop to the sound of singing frogs and Louisiana Waterthrushes, as Black Vultures soar overhead.

The Purple Gallinule breeds in only one place in Illinois; that's at Lake Mermet, at the southern tip.

When you can't take winter anymore, drive to southern Illinois in springtime. In early to late April, the white blossoms of the flowering dogwood and the purple blossoms of the redbud cheer any birder's spirit. When these shrubs are blooming, the songbirds are returning. Acadian Flycatchers and Summer Tanagers, rare in northern Illinois, are plentiful. The Chuck-will's-widow, a true southern Illinois specialty, breeds here. You can even find breeding grassland species such as Henslow's Sparrows in southern Illinois—and the state-listed endangered Barn Owl and state-listed endangered Least Tern is possible only in the far reaches of the state.

64 Carlyle Lake and Eldon Hazlet State Park

65 Horseshoe Lake State Park

66 Prairie Ridge State Natural Area and Newton Lake State Fish and Wildlife Area

67 Rend Lake

68 Sauget Marsh

69 Crab Orchard National Wildlife Refuge

70 Giant City State Park

71 Union County Conservation Area and Associated Levees

72 Cypress Creek National Wildlife Refuge

73 Cache River and Heron Pond State Natural Areas

74 Horseshoe Lake Conservation Area

75 Pomona–Cave Creek

76 Atwood Ridge and Hamburg Hill

77 Trail of Tears State Forest

78 Pine Hills–LaRue Ecological Area

79 Oakwood Bottoms and the Big Muddy River Levee

80 Mermet Lake

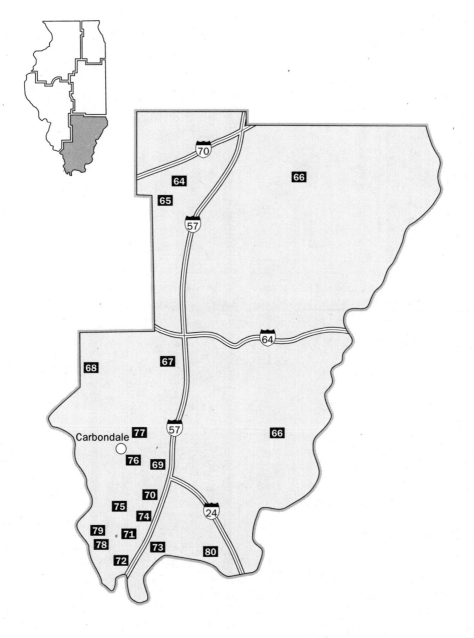

Carbondale

64 Carlyle Lake and Eldon Hazlet State Park

Habitats: Open water, flooded dead timber, agricultural fields, deciduous woodlands, grasslands, and some prairie; various wetlands.
Key birds: Waterfowl, shorebirds, gulls, owls, and neotropical migrants in fall and spring; American White Pelican, Double-crested Cormorant, Sabine's Gull, Bald Eagle, and Eurasian Collared-Dove.
Best times to bird: Year-round.

Directions: Access Carlyle Lake off U.S. Highway 50 from the east and west or Illinois Highway 127 from the north and south. Interstate 70 is about 15 miles to the north of Carlyle and I-64 is roughly 25 miles south.

Birding: Carlyle Lake includes 80 miles of tree-lined shores in southern Illinois, 80 miles south of Springfield and 50 miles east of St. Louis. Ross's, Snow, and Greater White-fronted Geese have increased their wintering numbers immensely in the past few years. Also, in late fall and early spring, American White Pelicans frequent the northernmost reaches of Carlyle Lake. You may find close to 1,000 of them at the lake in spring.

You'll also find the state's largest rookery of Double-crested Cormorants south of Chicago near Carlyle Lake. In 1998, birders counted 100 cormorant nests and sometimes 500 cormorants on the lake in summer. In fall, 5,000 to 10,000 cormorants stop by the lake.

Because Carlyle Lake is so large, gull concentrations can be large. Many different gull species appear; however, none attracts the birder more than the Sabine's Gull. Carlyle Lake may be the best inland lake in Illinois to see a Sabine's Gull. The best time is in late September into early October.

Shorebirds can congregate by the thousands if upper lake conditions are favorable. When lake levels are low, large expanses of mudflats become available, attracting various shorebirds, including the rare Whimbrel, Hudsonian and Marbled Godwits, all three phalaropes, Buff-breasted and Upland Sandpipers, Ruffs, and Red Knots.

Surrounding forested areas attract owls, including Short-eared, Long-eared, and Northern Saw-whets, and in the winter, sometimes even Snowy Owls.

Most birders start their day at the lake on the west side, accessing the area from IL 127/50. Drive north on IL 127 about half a mile to the lake access road, which goes east to the Dam West boat launch, just about half a mile down the road. Park here.

Many Ring-billed Gulls frequent the area year-round, and during winter other gull species can be seen roosting on the sandy beach south of the parking lot. During the cold months, waterfowl congregate toward the main dam when all other lake waters are frozen. In some years, Common Goldeneye and Common Merganser numbers are incredible. Scoters and Oldsquaws sometimes make an appearance.

64 Carlyle Lake and Eldon Hazlet State Park

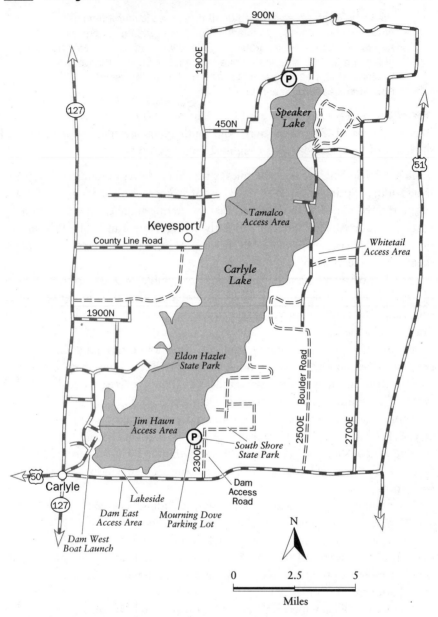

Next, take the north country road that you passed on your way to the boat launch. Keep your eyes open for any dove on the telephone poles and wires. You might spot the Eurasian Collared-Dove, a species that attempted to nest near the golf course in 1997, and is now on the Illinois state checklist.

Drive north about a mile to the Jim Hawn Access Area (formerly Honker's Point) sign. Turn east and drive for 0.5 mile to the parking lot and walk southeast to the lake. Search for cormorants, herons, egrets, and, if mudflats are available, shorebirds. Terns and gulls also frequent this cove during migration. Look especially for Common, Forster's, and Caspian Terns.

Check the pine trees to the north of the access road in winter for Long-eared Owls. To find these elusive birds, look on the ground for pellets or look for the whitewash on trees. Then look to an inner tree branch for a long, thin-looking owl sitting still and close to the trunk. Birders have counted as many as eight Long-eared Owls in one tree in some winters.

Return the half mile to the country road and continue north about 2 miles until the road curves east. Drive for another mile to the Eldon Hazlet State Park entrance.

You'll find many trails for hiking or biking as well as a campground and cabins at the park. Neotropical migrants, especially during the fall, are numerous.

The trails wind through deciduous forest, shrubs, and thickets where warblers, vireos, thrushes, orioles, and sparrows consume insects. You have a chance at listing 20 warbler species on a good fall day, including the Black-throated Blue Warbler, a rarity in southern Illinois.

One of birders' favorite trails is the Cherokee Nature Trail. As you access the park at a Y, go right 0.1 mile, then left and drive toward the park office. Go past the park office and continue to the stop sign. At the stop sign, turn left and then take an immediate right for about half a mile. You'll be facing east at a large parking lot. Once there, you can start the trail to the north, southeast, or southwest. All points connect so it's difficult to get lost.

Birders suggest taking the southwest trail into the small shrubby and grassy area to look in fall for migrating warblers, vireos, catbirds, thrashers, grosbeaks, and orioles. Spring migration can be rewarding, but the fallouts in fall seem to favor this trail. Flycatchers can be good in spring; birders often find Yellow-bellied, Alder, and Olive-sided Flycatchers in middle to late May.

Continue walking the trail until you reach a beautiful view of Carlyle Lake. In late September, with the afternoon sun behind you, this is the best spot to search for Sabine's Gulls. Look for a tern-like gull foraging in the lake. In recent years birders have found up to ten Sabine's Gulls at this point in middle to late September. You can also scan the lake for terns and Bonaparte's Gulls.

After Eldon Hazlet State Park you can travel the northern reaches of Carlyle Lake past the Keyesport area. Continue north on the county road that leads to Eldon Hazlet State Park. About 3 miles north, past the town of Keyesport, stop at the Tamalco Access Area. Turn east to access this area, where a pair of Bald Eagles has bred since the early 1990s.

You'll need a spotting scope to enjoy the breeding Double-crested Cormorants and all the other birds, including herons and egrets in spring through summer, American White Pelicans from fall through winter, and migrating gulls, terns, waterfowl, and shorebirds, depending on water levels.

The Sabine's Gull is a Carlyle Lake specialty. AL SEPPI PHOTO

Other access areas exist on the west side of the lake; however, many of these are also hunting areas, so you should check with the state or Corps of Engineers staff before entering. One such area is parking lot 3, which contains Speaker Lake. This Waterfowl Resting Area is off-limits to hunters and birders from early November through middle March. In fall, if mudflats exist, this area can hold numerous shorebirds, including such rarities as Marbled Godwits, Buff-breasted Sandpipers, and Red Knots.

The east side of Carlyle Lake also contains some rewarding birding areas. Travel south to the town of Keyesport and head west on County Line Road for 5 miles, out of town to IL 127.

Go south 10 miles on IL 127 to the town of Carlyle to US 50. Take US 50 east 2 miles to the Dam East Access Area. At the stop sign turn west, drive up the hill and down again, and turn right to the little fishing access area called Lakeside.

You'll have an excellent view of the lake, and in winter and early spring, you can get good views of waterfowl and gulls as well as loons and grebes.

Once you're done viewing this area, return to the stop sign and drive east on the Dam East Access Road for about 1.5 miles until the road bends to the left. Enter South Shore State Park. This park contains many small campground and access areas, which can be good for a quick drive-through with your windows open to listen for bird songs and chip notes. Excellent viewing of the lake exists on the west edge of South Shore Campground, where you can search in late fall and winter for gulls and waterfowl. Also check in late September for Sabine's Gulls. In fall, you may also find small pockets of migrants.

The road through the park (County Road 2200E) curves south back to US 50. Turn east for 1 mile to a blacktop road (CR 2300E). Go north 2 miles to the Mourning Dove parking lot, which is on the west side of the road. This area is mainly for dove hunting; however, birders have taken advantage of the good access and habitat to discover the Bell's Vireos, Willow Flycatchers, and Yellow Warblers that nest in the small trees near the ponds.

In wet springs, birders have flushed Pied-billed Grebes, coots, rails, and bitterns from the pond east of the parking lot. Walk the wet grasses in spring and you'll sometimes encounter lingering ducks and shorebirds.

You should find one more access area interesting, called the Whitetail Access Area (also referred to as Boulder Flats). Continue north on CR 2300E, which soon becomes CR 1500N. Drive east for 3 miles to a stop sign. Turn north on Boulder Road (CR2500E). Drive 2 miles north past the Boulder Access Area. The road curves east, crosses over railroad tracks, and then bends north. Continue another 2.5 miles to a wooded driveway on the left. Note the small access sign. You'll find a parking lot with room for six cars.

Walk the boardwalk to gain an overall view of the area. If conditions are right, the extensive mudflats and small pockets of marshy sloughs can be smorgasbords for shorebirds, herons, and egrets. Otherwise, you can walk north and search the system of small levees, exploring for shorebirds, herons, and other birds. Don your boots before blazing your own trail. Birders find the best shorebirds by sloshing through mud.

Some rarities have included Whimbrels, Red Phalaropes, Marbled Godwits, and Glossy and White-faced Ibises.

General information: The U.S. Army Corps of Engineers built Carlyle Lake, which lies in the Kaskaskia River basin, in 1967 to improve flood control and the area's water supply, as well as provide habitat for wildlife and recreational activities for humans. Archaeological studies show prehistoric Americans first entered the area 10,000 years ago. American Indians roamed the prairies and riverways along a natural ford on the Kaskaskia River. Settlers used the ford when traveling over land from the Ohio River to St. Louis. Founded in the early 1800s, the city of Carlyle (and later, the lake) was named after the British author, Sir Thomas Carlyle.

Lying like a giant teardrop in a northeasterly/southwesterly direction, Carlyle Lake's shoreline includes small creeks, coves and inlets, sandy beaches, picnic areas, boat launches, and boat rental facilities.

Eldon Hazlet State Park, owned by the Illinois Department of Natural Resources, opened in 1971.

Hunting seasons in fall include dove, squirrel, rabbit, pheasant, deer, and waterfowl. For more information, check with the U.S. Army Corps of Engineers, Lake Office, located on the west side of the lake near Dam West Access, or the Illinois Department of Natural Resources. Many areas of private property exist adjacent to federal and state property. Obey all signs.

ADDITIONAL HELP

DeLorme IA&G grid: 77 and 78.
Contact: US Army Corps of Engineers or Eldon Hazlet State Park.
Nearest gas, food, and lodging: Food and gas are available in Carlyle and other towns nearby. Lodging in Greenville and Salem. Camping and cabin rentals at Eldon Hazlet State Park.

65 Horseshoe Lake State Park

Habitats: Lake, emergent marsh, bottomland hardwood forests and upland forest, grasslands, agricultural fields, and borrow pits.
Key birds: Waterfowl, gulls, including Sabine's, shorebirds, owls, loons, grebes, American White Pelican, Eurasian Tree Sparrow.
Best times to bird: Winter for gulls and waterfowl.

Directions: Horseshoe Lake State Park is west of Illinois Highway 111, about 3 miles north of Interstates 55/70 in Madison County. From I-270, go south on IL 111 for about 7 miles. The western portion of the lake is just east of IL 203, also reached by driving I-55/70, then going north on IL 203 to Big Bend Road.

Birding: Birders have recorded more than 200 species here, including all the waterfowl, shorebirds, and egrets that migrate through the state. Perhaps the best time to bird Horseshoe Lake State Park is winter when large congregations of gulls gather around the lake and adjoining borrow pits to the south and west. Many of the rare gulls for Illinois have been recorded, including Great and Lesser Black-backed, Glaucous, Thayer's, Iceland, Laughing, and Sabine's. In spring large numbers of Common Mergansers, Ruddy Ducks, Gadwalls, Lesser Scaups, Northern Shovelers, teals, Redheads, and Canvasbacks frequent the lake. American White Pelicans, Double-crested Cormorants, Common Loons, and Pied-billed and Horned Grebes occur in good numbers. Rarities have included Red-throated Loons and Red-necked Grebes.

You can bird Horseshoe Lake from the west or the east. Those who like to bird from their cars should follow the east side, where the recently upgraded main entrance road provides a smooth and scenic drive along the shore. From IL 111 turn west into the park entrance and follow the road south. This drive goes past the state headquarters on your left about a quarter mile.

You'll soon enter a half-mile causeway, which has water on both sides. Fishermen abound here; however, if you park along the causeway you should get nice views of waterfowl in early spring and shorebirds in late August through October. At that time, pumping drains the lake area to the south exposing large mudflats for a brief period. Thousands of shorebirds rest and feed while hundreds of egrets and herons forage for the buffet of dead and dying fish.

After birding the causeway continue west until the road curves to the left and converts to gravel within 0.1 mile. This road leads to a campground and encircles a small tract of bottomland hardwoods. During spring migration you should enjoy watching neotropical migrants, including the Prothonotary Warbler, which often remains in summer to breed.

Just past the office headquarters is a curving 2-mile-long road that goes left or north paralleling the lakes' eastern shore. You'll find pull-outs along the way. Search on this road for Eurasian Tree Sparrows inhabiting the small trees along the lakeshore. In 1 mile you'll find another causeway of sorts that crosses the lake. The area to the east and northeast often attracts foraging waterfowl as well as herons and egrets, especially Black-crowned Night-Herons.

65 Horseshoe Lake State Park

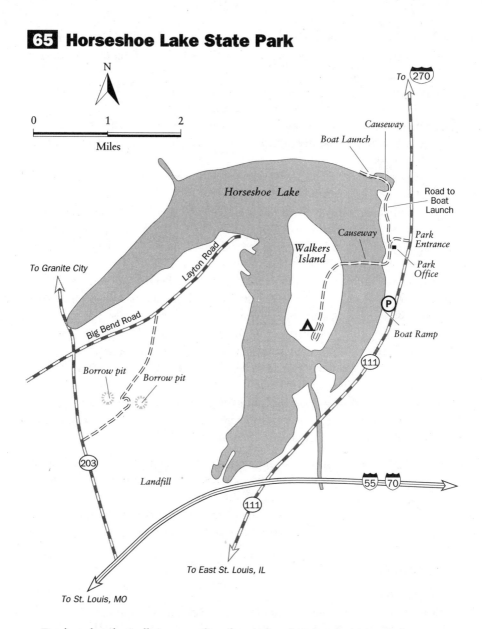

N

0   1   2

Miles

To 270

Causeway

Boat Launch

Horseshoe Lake

Road to Boat Launch

Causeway

Walkers Island

Park Entrance

Park Office

To Granite City

Layton Road

Big Bend Road

P

Boat Ramp

111

Borrow pit

Borrow pit

203

Landfill

55 70

111

To East St. Louis, IL

To St. Louis, MO

Farther ahead, small tree areas line the road and attract, in spring and summer, Bell's Vireos, Orchard Orioles, Gray Catbirds, Indigo Buntings, Warbling Vireos, Yellow Warblers, and at times, Blue Grosbeaks, and Eurasian Tree Sparrows.

The road ends at a boat launch, which can be a good spot to scan the lake for terns, pelicans, waterfowl, and the rare loon or grebe that may be out there. This is not a loop drive, so you'll need to retrace your steps back to IL 111.

To reach the west side of Horseshoe Lake, exit south on IL 111 until you reach I-55/70 westbound. Take I-55/70 west for about 4 miles until you reach IL 203 north (toward Granite City). The large landfill to the north hosts thousands of gulls during winter. Most of these gulls forage at the landfill by day and take the short flight to the west side of Horseshoe Lake in late afternoon, spending the night on the lake.

Also, explore the borrow pits, which change depending on landfill operations. One day you might find waterfowl and gulls, and the next, extensive mudflats may invite waders and shorebirds to dinner, including some rarities such as Piping Plovers, Red Knots, Sanderlings, Ruddy Turnstones, Laughing Gulls, and Tricolored Herons.

To get to the borrow pits, drive past the landfill entrance road, cross the bridge, then turn right at a gravel drive that leads east.

You can take this gravel drive back to Big Bend Road, which parallels the lake for about 4 miles, offering excellent views of gulls, cormorants, and waterfowl. Look to the largest trees bordering the road for wintering Bald Eagles. Also look for Eurasian Tree Sparrows.

After the railroad tracks, about 1.5 miles, Big Bend Road becomes Layton Road. At this point, you'll be driving southeasterly into grassland and agricultural areas. Check the shrubs and brushy areas for sparrows in winter. You should find good numbers of White-throated, White-crowned, Fox, Field, Song, and Swamp Sparrows, as well as an occasional Harris's Sparrow. In winter at dusk, Short-eared Owls and Northern Harriers often hunt the fields. Birders have observed good numbers of these species in winter.

Continue east on Layton Road until you get to the lake. This vantage point has been a good place to view rare loons and grebes, including Pacific and Red-throated Loons, and Red-necked and Eared Grebes.

General information: Waterfowl hunting season closes a portion of the lake each fall and winter. Call first to get public access closure dates. Camping is available at the campground. Mosquitos are numerous here. The west side of Horseshoe may have heavy traffic on race days at the Gateway International Motor Speedway. Expect large crowds. Plan your trip to avoid these races.

ADDITIONAL HELP

DeLorme IA&G grid: 75 and 76.
Contact: The Illinois Department of Natural Resources in Springfield.
Nearest gas, food, and lodging: East of Collinsville and north along IL 270 at Pontoon Beach.

66 Prairie Ridge State Natural Area and Newton Lake State Fish and Wildlife Area

Habitats: Grasslands, including meadows of introduced grasses and restored and remnant prairies, wetlands, and agricultural fields (Prairie Ridge); shrub areas, woodlands, and manmade cooling lake (Newton Lake).

Key birds: Migratory waterfowl, warblers, and sparrows; breeding grassland and shrubland birds, including Greater Prairie-Chicken, Northern Harrier, Short-eared Owl.

Best times to bird: March and April for Greater Prairie-Chicken, May and June for breeding birds, December through February for Northern Harrier and Short-eared Owl.

Directions: To reach the office of Prairie Ridge from Newton, go west on Illinois Highway 33 about 1.5 miles to the Bogota-Wakefield Road. Head south for 4 miles. At the curve to the west, turn east onto County Road 600N and go east 1 mile to CR 1000E, then south another 1.7 miles.

Birding: Grassland habitats come at a premium in Illinois, and so do many grassland birds. Prairie Ridge, tucked away in southeastern Illinois, is the best place to find many of these species. The main attraction is the group of displaying male Greater Prairie-Chickens in spring. Fortunately, the "booming ground" locations are predictable and visible from roadsides, so visitors from March to early May are not likely to leave disappointed.

Besides hosting the last populations of Greater Prairie-Chickens in Illinois, the state natural area also has the largest wintering and breeding populations of Northern Harriers and Short-eared Owls. Also breeding on the site are King Rails, American Bitterns, Upland Sandpipers, and a growing population of Henslow's Sparrows, all endangered in Illinois.

While the grasslands and marshes of Prairie Ridge are the most unique feature of this area, a wide variety of habitats is nearby, including shrubby areas, small woodlots, and Newton Lake, all surrounded by the ubiquitous croplands of central Illinois. Birders have listed about 250 species around Prairie Ridge and Newton Lake.

Begin at the Prairie Ridge office to determine where booming grounds are viewable from roadsides. Check before visiting for organized birding tours given to Audubon societies, The Nature Conservancy, and other groups. This is the best way to gain access to restricted areas.

Just past the southwest gate of the office yard is a wetland, often open in late winter and early spring when migratory waterfowl are at their peak. This spot is also good for wading birds such as Great Egrets, Black-crowned Night-Herons, and American Bitterns. The King Rail is present, but seldom seen.

To the northwest about 300 yards is a prairie-chicken booming ground. This is visible from within the yard when the grassland is closed. The birds display from first light until a few hours after sunrise. In April there is often a less intense

66 Prairie Ridge State Natural Area and Newton Lake State Fish and Wildlife Area

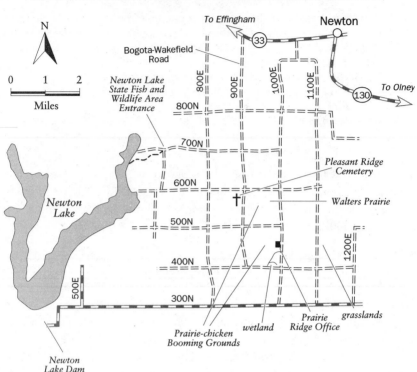

display period in the evening. DO NOT attempt to approach the booming grounds when birds are present.

This is also a winter roosting area for Northern Harriers and Short-eared Owls. During the breeding season, Grasshopper Sparrows, Eastern Meadowlarks, and Dickcissels are likely to be seen, with Sedge Wrens abundant later in the summer. The Savannah Sparrow is a common migrant; LeConte's and Nelson's Sharp-tailed Sparrows are occasionally seen. Before leaving the headquarters area, check the grassy creek crossing the road just south of the office, another spot where the King Rail is sometimes seen.

North about 1.3 miles, west of the road is a grassland (north) and farm field (south). This field is another traditional prairie-chicken booming ground. The grassland to the northwest is a good spot for Northern Harriers, Short-eared Owls, and Henslow's Sparrows.

Southwest of the crossroads (CR 1000E/600N) in 0.5 mile is a 40-acre prairie remnant (Walters Prairie) with a wetland in the center. If open for public access, check out the wetland for waterfowl and other birds such Black Terns and Least Bitterns. King Rails also frequent this area, but are difficult to detect. Depending upon recent fire history, willows growing around the wetland may hold Willow Flycatchers and Bell's Vireos.

Go east 1 mile and turn south at CR 1100E/600N and go 1.3 miles; another grassland will be to the east. Check overhead utility lines for Loggerhead Shrikes. You might also find Upland Sandpipers (spring/summer) and Rough-legged Hawks (fall/winter).

Head west at the next crossroads (CR 1100E/400N). Check the utility lines along the roadsides for Red-headed Woodpeckers, Northern Mockingbirds, and Loggerhead Shrikes. Continue a total of 2 miles to the crossroads of CR 900E/400N and turn north.

In about half a mile is a grassland, one of the better spots for locating migrating Bobolinks in late April and May. The crop fields to the north and west of this grassland are prime locations for finding Smith's Longspurs in April. Locating them on the ground requires patience, meticulous scanning, and luck. Listen for their dry clicking flight notes.

Turn west at the next crossroads (CR 900E/500N) and drive 0.3 mile. This is an extension of a much larger grassland to the north. Check for Upland Sandpipers and a prairie-chicken booming ground to the north.

Backtrack to CR 900E and go north for 0.8 mile to Pleasant Ridge Cemetery. Loggerhead Shrikes and Northern Mockingbirds are seen here in all seasons. The grassland west of the cemetery is a good area for Northern Harriers and Short-eared Owls.

Next head west 2 miles and north 1 mile to CR 700E/700N to part of Newton Lake State Fish and Wildlife Area. This area is open for public access year-round. Park and walk the gravel path heading west through the old fields, shrubby areas, and woodland edges. Yellow-billed Cuckoos and Baltimore and Orchard Orioles frequent this area. Also look for migrant thrushes, sparrows, and warblers. The path leads directly to Newton Lake, where you might find Ospreys, Bald Eagles, Double-crested Cormorants, and Wood Ducks. Walk south to a woodland where you might find Wild Turkeys, woodpeckers, Great Crested Flycatchers, and migrant warblers; the dense shrubs along the path usually hold Yellow-breasted Chats, Bell's Vireos, and sometimes Blue Grosbeaks.

To get to the dam of Newton Lake and scan the open water, go south 4 miles to CR 300N. Head west about 2.5 miles, and follow the bend of the road south before turning west onto CR 250N. A spur road heads northwest to the dam of Newton Lake. You'll find a parking lot on the north side. Birders often see Common, Forster's, Black, and Caspian Terns, and occasionally a Least Tern. Check the banks for herons and egrets and the spillway for Belted Kingfishers.

General information: This 1,700-acre site is actually 12 separate grasslands interspersed in the local landscape. The grassland property boundaries are clearly marked. Because of high densities of sensitive endangered species, access is restricted

The Short-eared Owl breeds at Prairie Ridge State Natural Area.
KANAE HIRABAYASHI PHOTO

on Prairie Ridge; check with the site staff for details. Also inquire about guided tours and field trips for groups. A second, smaller unit of Prairie Ridge is located near Kinmundy in Marion County, about 30 miles southwest. While there is no office, many of the same species, including Greater Prairie-Chickens, are present.

ADDITIONAL HELP

DeLorme IA&G grid:
Contact: Prairie Ridge and Newton Lake State Natural Areas.
Nearest gas, food, and lodging: Olney and Effingham; gas and food are available in Newton; camping at Sam Parr State Park northeast of Newton.

67 Rend Lake

Habitats: 18,900-acre manmade lake, mudflats, small sand ridges, and moist soil units.
Key birds: Migratory waterfowl, gulls, shorebirds, including Buff-breasted Sandpiper and songbirds; breeding songbirds, including American Redstart and Yellow-throated Warbler.
Best times to bird: Late July through October.

Directions: I highly recommend that before going, you obtain a free copy of the Watchable Wildlife guide to Rend Lake. The guide has detailed maps of all of the areas mentioned above. Call the U.S. Army Corps of Engineers Rend Lake contact listed in Appendix A.

You'll find three Rend Lake exits off Interstate 57 between the towns of Benton and Ina, Illinois. Here are directions to the Rend Lake Visitor Center. From I-57, take exit 71 (Illinois Highway 14) at Benton. Drive west on IL 14 for 2.5 miles. Turn right (north) on Rend City Road, drive north 3 miles to the main Dam Road. Turn right (east) and follow signs to the Rend Lake Visitor Center. To get to the Wayne Fitzgerrell State Park from I-57, take exit 77 (IL 154) off I-57. Travel west on IL 154 for 2.5 miles to the Rend Lake Resort Lodge entrance.

Birding: While walking the hot sandy, muddy flats adjacent to Rend Lake in extreme southern Illinois, we were immediately glad to have brought extra water, and to have worn hats. This is as close as I've ever come to desert in Illinois, but

67 Rend Lake

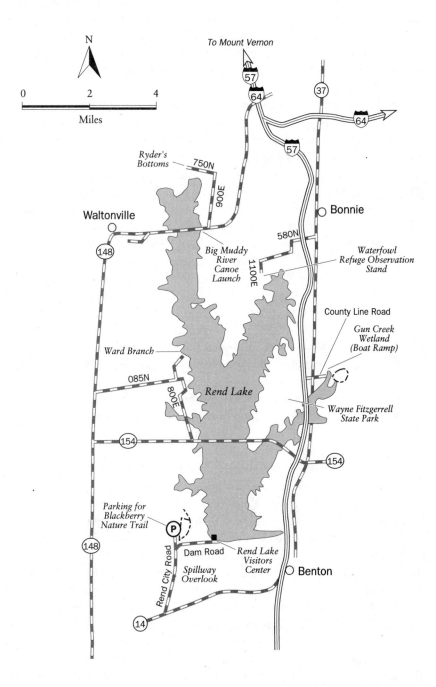

N

0   2   4

Miles

To Mount Vernon

57
64
37
64
57

Ryder's
Bottoms
750N
900E

Bonnie

Waltonville

148

Big Muddy
River
Canoe
Launch

580N

1100E

Waterfowl
Refuge Observation
Stand

County Line Road

Gun Creek
Wetland
(Boat Ramp)

Ward Branch

085N

800E

Rend Lake

Wayne Fitzgerrell
State Park

154

154

Parking for
Blackberry
Nature Trail

P

148

Rend City Road

Dam Road

Spillway
Overlook

Rend Lake
Visitors
Center

Benton

14

oases in the form of mudflats existed for the birds we had come to see: Buff-breasted Sandpiper, Western Sandpiper (very unusual in the East), and Pectoral Sandpiper. When conditions are right, you could count upwards of 23 species of shorebirds on a single day along the 162 miles of shoreline of this 18,900-acre lake surrounded by 21,000 acres of public land. A total of 272 bird species have been documented here and in the nearby Wayne Fitzgerell State Park, among them, 35 shorebird species.

Rend Lake, located on the flattest land in the state, can host wonderful mudflats when the lake drops just 1 inch, making this a shorebirder's mecca. Be aware that a sudden change in moisture, for example a 2-inch rainfall during the night, can affect the number of birds you'll see.

Start at the Rend Lake Visitor Center at the southeastern part of the lake, to get information on latest bird sightings and to secure maps. Then check the spill-way overlook. The spillway has held thousands of Common Goldeneyes and Ring-billed Gulls in winter, as well as occasional Canvasbacks. Rarities are possible; birders have recorded jaegers. Cliff and Barn Swallows nest beneath the bridge and can be seen feeding on the water, spring through fall.

Farther north is the Waterfowl Refuge Observation Stand where more than 150,000 Canada Geese winter. In winter, Bald Eagles loaf and feed nearby. Travel west out of Bonnie on County Road 550N, south on CR 1250E, then west on CR 500N, and south on CR 1100E 1.5 miles to the parking area.

The Gun Creek moist soil unit area (known as the Gun Creek Wetlands), features levee impoundments providing habitat for dabbling ducks, including shov-elers and teals, plus some of the longer-legged shorebirds, including dowitchers, yellowlegs, and occasionally godwits. An overlook is barrier-free. Go in spring and fall to observe duck and shorebird migration. To get there, take IL 37 to County Line Road. Turn east and drive 1 mile to Cypress View. You can also canoe here to bird the forested areas.

Ward Branch is one of the shorebirders' favorite spots at Rend Lake. Some-times you have to wade from Ward Branch in mucky mud to get to an island where shorebirds feed. You're almost guaranteed a good look at a Buff-breasted Sandpiper in fall, as well a Short-billed Dowitcher, Least Sandpiper, Lesser Yellow-legs, and sometimes Marbled Godwit. The area annually holds Baird's and West-ern Sandpipers, two of the more unusual shorebird species to be found in Illinois. Birders have recorded Whimbrels, Marbled and Hudsonian Godwits, Red Knots, American Avocets, and Red-necked Phalaropes. To get to Ward Branch, take IL 154 to CR 800E. Drive north to CR 085N. Go east to CR 725E, then north about a mile to the parking lot. Walk the farm road to the lake.

To enjoy woodland species in May and June, you can take several easy trails or some much-more-difficult-to-navigate ones. The 0.8-mile Blackberry Nature Trail goes through an oak hickory woodland, where songbirds, including nearly all of the warbler species known to occur in Illinois have been recorded. You'll find the parking lot on Rend City Road north of IL 14 at the south end of Rend Lake.

Green Tree Reservoir near the Gun Creek Wetlands (mentioned above) has an unmarked but easy to follow trail, where you can listen for singing warblers, including the Northern Parula and Black-throated Green beginning in April. Yellow-rumped Warblers sometimes winter.

To search for raptors as well as field and shrub birds, visit the Wayne Fitzgerrell State Park, where Ring-necked Pheasants abound. A mile-long trail leads through a woodland where you can watch and listen for migrating songbirds as well as breeding Cooper's Hawks, which are well into the nesting season by April.

For a challenging walk through hundreds of acres of mature old-growth hardwood forest, visit Ryder's Bottoms. Starting in early to mid-April, these woods come alive with bird song. Breeding are Scarlet Tanagers, Yellow-billed Cuckoos, Kentucky Warblers, woodpeckers, raptors, and many other upland woods species. You need to wear good hiking shoes here and bring a compass; there are no trails.

If you're adventurous and want to experience bird life in a unique way, try this part of the lake. But do be careful. Parking for Ryder's Bottoms is off CR 750N, west of CR 900E and IL 148. You can also canoe and bird at the Big Muddy River canoe launch, which is on IL 148 on the way to Ryder's Bottoms. You may find the Pileated Woodpecker, Cerulean Warbler, and other woodland species that breed in this 1,000-acre maple and sycamore forest.

General information: The U.S. Army Corps of Engineers created Rend Lake when it dammed the Big Muddy River in 1965 to control flooding, provide a water supply and recreational activities to local residents and visitors, and conserve wildlife. Sportsmen including hunters and fishermen, nature watchers, and boaters have access to a 40,000-acre area consisting of the lake, woods, and fields

You can spend several days exploring the rich bird life here.

Weather conditions change. Some days, walks are easy and comfortable. Other days, you might be walking ankle-deep in slippery mud. Bring plenty of water, wear a hat, and wear good boots. Summer can be quite hot. Side roads can be hazardous, especially during the wet season. Scopes are essential when looking for shorebirds.

ADDITIONAL HELP

DeLorme IA&G grid: 84 and 85.
Contact: U.S. Army Corps of Engineers, Rend Lake Management Office, Southern Illinois Tourism Council and the Wayne Fitzgerrell State Park Visitor Center.
Nearest gas, food, and lodging: Hotels and motels in the Mount Vernon area; camping at Wayne Fitzgerrell State Park; resort lodging at Rend Lake Resort Lodge 2.5 miles from the park.

68 Sauget Marsh

Habitats: Marsh and emergent wetlands, agricultural fields, including some grasslands and scrub/shrub wetland in a highly industrial area.
Key birds: American Bittern, Great Egret, Snowy Egret, Little Blue Heron, Cattle Egret, Black- and Yellow-crowned Night-Herons, King Rail, and Common Moorhen.
Best times to bird: Early spring for waders, early summer for breeding rails, moorhens, and grebes.

Directions: From the Mousette Lane exit off Interstate 255, go north 1.5 miles to a right curve in the road where you'll find the Wildlife Observation Parking Lot donated by St. Clair County and Sauget Industrial Park.

Birding: Birding Sauget can be difficult with the industrial park and nearby airport and interstate traffic creating much noise pollution. However, careful planning and visits at various times can be more rewarding than others. You'll enjoy the best birding in the early morning or as darkness approaches to maximize your chance of getting good views of both night-herons. Bitterns and rails are most active at these times, too.

Drive to the Wildlife Viewing Parking Lot just east of the main cattail-willow marsh on the curved road that traverses the park. At the time of this writing, local transportation officials were proposing building a three-lane road around an additional 15 to 20 acres of marsh at the site so birding may continue to thrive here.

American Bitterns migrate through Sauget Marsh. KANAE HIRABAYASHI PHOTO

At the main marsh, walk the road less than a block north until you reach the curve that goes east. You'll find the cattail areas that host foraging waders of all species, including the rare Glossy and White-faced Ibises that appeared in 1996. King Rails generally frequent this marsh as do Soras and Virginia Rails during migration.

East of the road, you might find Bell's Vireos and Willow Flycatchers in spring and summer. This area often attracts many displaying American Woodcocks in early spring. Check in early February in mild winters as these birds often begin their courtship long before other breeding bird species have even arrived.

To bird the rest of the marshy areas throughout the park, you need to drive the west road called Curtiss-Steinberg

68 Sauget Marsh

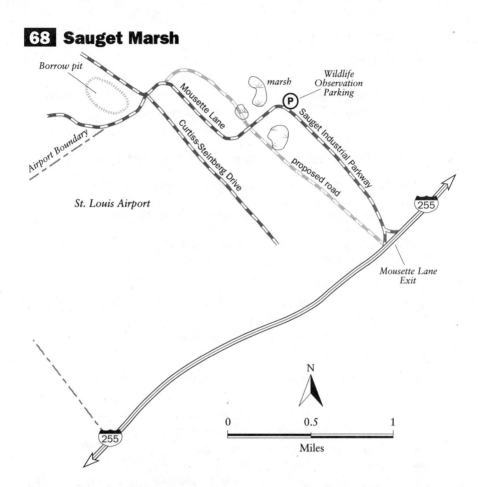

Road (which is off Mousette Lane) and park on the roadside for best viewing. Traffic is often heavy; be careful. Be sure to check the borrow pits just north of the airport for waders, including Yellow-crowned Night-Heron, most easily seen at dawn and dusk in late spring and summer.

All the small marshy spots are good for waders, sometimes waterfowl and even shorebirds, as evidenced by the Black-necked Stilt that frequented one area a few seasons ago. A large heron and egret roosting colony is on private property within 5 miles of the site, so you may see these birds visiting some of the wet areas in spring and fall.

General information: The approximate 15 acres of wetlands within the Sauget Marsh complex were created by St. Clair County in cooperation with the Sauget Industrial Park as compensatory wetland mitigation for the wetlands impacted as a result of the roads and adjoining development. The business park continues to grow, and plans for a new road are under way. The developers are required to create additional wetland habitats to compensate for taking of flood storage grounds within this flood-prone area. This should ensure additional foraging sites for the waders that utilize this area.

ADDITIONAL INFORMATION

DeLorme IA&G grid: 75.

Contact: Illinois Department of Natural Resources.

Nearest gas, food, and lodging: Cahokia on I-255 has food and gas. Lodging is recommended north and east in Caseyville or in downtown St. Louis, Missouri.

69 Crab Orchard National Wildlife Refuge

Habitats: Deciduous and coniferous forest, three lakes, wetlands, agricultural lands, and grasslands.
Key birds: Migratory loons, including Common and Red-throated; grebes, ducks, geese, gulls, and terns; many migratory rarities; wintering finches; Fish Crow, Black Vulture, and Bald Eagle.
Best times to bird: Fall through early spring; early summer.

Directions: From Interstate 57 at Marion, take Illinois Highway 13 west for 2 miles toward Carbondale. When you reach the intersection of IL 13/148, turn south on IL 148 to get to the viewing platforms and refuge headquarters, or continue west on IL 13 another 6 miles to Refuge Road, where you will drive south, following the birding tour outlined above.

Birding: This 43,600-acre refuge is managed for industrial and agricultural use as well as for migrating waterfowl. Many areas are closed to the public, and a user fee is required, but don't let that stop you from birding this major waterfowl migratory stopover. Several locations within the realm of public access provide good views of waterfowl as well as possibilities to see rarities including Iceland, Glaucous, Thayer's, Little, and Sabine's Gulls.

Some 100,000 waterfowl migrate through here annually; birders have documented 245 regularly occurring bird species, with an additional 29 accidentals. Of these, 20 duck, 9 hawk, 25 shorebird, 9 flycatcher, 7 vireo, and 30 warbler species have been reported. More than 100 birds breed on the site, including both nightherons, chats, Warbling and Bell's Vireos, and Scarlet and Summer Tanagers.

Twenty miles of roads bisect the refuge. A scope and warm clothing in winter are essential.

Starting at Refuge Road and IL 13, travel south on Refuge Road for about 2 miles to the top of a spillway where a small parking lot exists. You can view much of the lake from here. In spring, gull and waterfowl numbers can be incredible. Thousands of Bonaparte's Gulls visit annually. Search through these gulls to locate a possible Little Gull or Sabine's Gull. Most species of waterfowl recorded in Illinois have been observed from this spot at Crab Orchard Lake.

Many dabbling ducks gather in rafts, avoiding the fishermen as they pass. You'll likely find large flocks of Lesser Scaups, Canvasbacks, Ruddy Ducks, and Common and Red-breasted Mergansers in March and April as well as in fall and

69 Crab Orchard National Wildlife Refuge

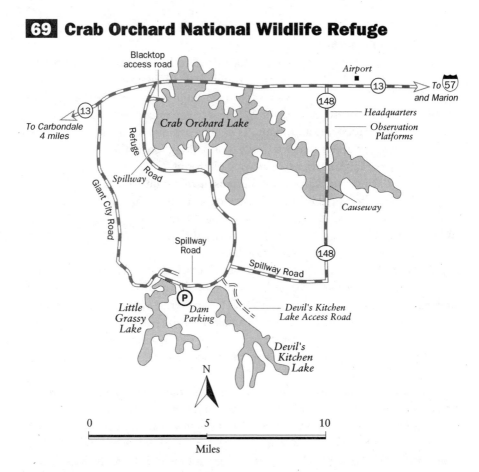

Blacktop access road

Airport

Crab Orchard Lake

Refuge Road

Spillway

Giant City Road

Spillway Road

Spillway Road

To Carbondale 4 miles

13

13 To 57 and Marion

148

Headquarters

Observation Platforms

Causeway

148

P Dam Parking

Little Grassy Lake

Devil's Kitchen Lake Access Road

Devil's Kitchen Lake

N

0   5   10

Miles

winter. Scoters occur every few years. In late fall, early winter, and again in February and March, large numbers of loons and grebes congregate on the lake. You should find Common Loons and Pied-billed Grebes easily. Look, too, for the less common Horned and Red-necked Grebes and Red-throated Loons, perhaps even a Pacific Loon on this large, deep lake.

Bald Eagles, Ospreys, and an occasional Black Vulture migrate over the lake, stopping at times to feed. You should have a good chance here to see Bald Eagles in various plumages, since they breed on the refuge. You'll probably see as many immature as adult Bald Eagles.

After scoping the waterfowl, return north on Refuge Road to IL 13. On your way, note a small blacktop access road with a gate and No Parking sign. Pull off to the side of the road and walk the road to search for wintering finches in the pines. You'll likely find Pine Siskins, Purple Finches, and Red-breasted Nuthatches. Pine and Yellow-throated Warblers breed here. Fish Crows sometimes outnumber American Crows. Listen for the American Crow's loud *"caw,"* and then the two-syllable nasal *"uh-uh"* call of the Fish Crow. The species look identical, and song is the only way to identify them. During spring migration, you should enjoy birding the trail to find warblers, vireos, thrushes, tanagers, and sparrows. Wild Turkeys may also be seen in this area.

When finished, return north on Refuge Road to IL 13 and drive east toward the town of Marion. In about 1.8 miles, you'll see the Williamson County Airport, a good spot to check for Upland Sandpipers in summer. Just before the airport is IL 148. Turn south here, driving for 1.8 miles to the refuge headquarters, where you can obtain brochures and maps, as well as ask about bird sightings. Then continue south for about a quarter mile to a parking lot on the west side of the road next to two large barrier-free viewing platforms.

In fall and winter you can view thousands of wintering geese and ducks foraging in the agricultural fields planted specifically for them. It can be quite windy and cold in winter. On the right day you should find Snow, Ross's, and Greater White-fronted Geese foraging with large flocks of Canada Geese. Sandhill Cranes and Tundra Swans also sometimes stop here.

You should find many teals and other dabblers, including Northern Shovelers and Redheads, as well as shorebirds in late spring if mudflats are available. This area has attracted the rare American Avocet, a western North American species.

Continue south on IL 148 for about a mile until you reach the causeway crossing Crab Orchard Lake. Stop at the parking lot on the north side of the lake to search for dozens to perhaps hundreds of Hooded Mergansers in fall, as well as other waterfowl.

If you want to search for more loons, grebes, and other waterfowl, you can continue farther south to visit Devil's Kitchen and Little Grassy Lakes, both popular camping and fishing spots. Drive south to Spillway Road, then southwest to the Devil's Kitchen Lake access road to check for waterfowl. A little farther along Spillway Road is the Little Grassy Lake Dam parking area. Here the lake reaches depths of 100 feet. You should find Common Loons, Forster's Terns, and Pied-billed Grebes during spring and fall migration.

General information: The area that is now the national wildlife refuge was once covered with corn and other crops. But in the 1930s, during the Depression, the government bought foreclosed farms and redesigned the site to become a major wildlife watching and recreation area. Workers planted millions of trees and created three lakes. The government also purchased more land here during World War II to build a munitions manufacturing plant. When the war ended, the U.S. Fish & Wildlife Service acquired the land and created the Crab Orchard National Wildlife refuge in 1947. Some munitions plants remain active. Also within the Refuge boundaries are 20 industrial plants and one of the nation's highest maximum security federal prisons. This is the most visited national wildlife refuge in the nation.

The Crab Orchard National Wildlife Refuge provides wildlife habitat management for one of the main waterfowl stops along the Mississippi Flyway, and serves as the U.S. Fish & Wildlife Service's contact station for wetlands restoration on private lands in the Missouri, Kentucky, Indiana, and the southern Illinois region. Stop at the refuge visitor center to obtain maps, and ask refuge personnel about user fees and areas you might be able to bird. Check for hunting season times and dates; many areas are closed to hikers during the hunting season. Office hours are 8 A.M. to 4:30 P.M. daily.

ADDITIONAL HELP

DeLorme IA&G grid: 89
Contact: Crab Orchard National Wildlife Refuge.
Nearest gas, food, and lodging: Marion and Carbondale; camping in the refuge.

70 Giant City State Park

> **Habitats:** Deciduous forests, agricultural lands, grasslands, streams, and creeks.
> **Key birds:** Migratory passerines; Fish Crow, Black Vulture; breeding Pileated Woodpecker, Whip-poor-will, Eastern Bluebird, Wood Thrush, 12 species of warblers, Summer and Scarlet Tanagers, and Orchard Oriole.
> **Best times to bird:** Spring and breeding season.

Directions: From the south, via Illinois Highway 51, take the Makanda exit eastbound through the small town of Makanda and across railroad tracks to the north road that leads in about a quarter mile to the Giant City State Park entrance. The entrance road turns right and curves several times. About 1.5 miles ahead, you'll see the large parking lot and picnic area where the Giant City Trail begins.

Birding: Some of southern Illinois' best birding is done at springtime in Giant City State Park, although breeding season has its own rewards. Within the park you should easily find both species of tanagers, Pileated Woodpeckers, Wood Thrushes, several vireos, and at least 12 breeding warbler species, including Louisiana Waterthrush, Worm-eating, Prairie, Pine, and Cerulean.

Black Vultures and Fish Crows fly over the park, sometimes stopping on a tree to give birders a good view. In fall and winter, Pine Warblers, Indigo Buntings, and Common Yellowthroats sometimes linger in the park.

Depending on where you access the park, usually from the southwest from Makanda or from the north out of Carbondale, one of the local birders' favorite trails in spring or summer is just past the lodge and Picnic Area 3. This loop trail called Giant City Nature Trail goes uphill into the large stands of forest, which contain many tall trees. The hike is fairly difficult at times, so be prepared. Wear comfortable hiking boots due to the rocks and potential for snakes.

70 Giant City State Park

To Carbondale

grasslands

Site Superintendent ■ Residence

Makanda

To 51

Main Entrance Road

Giant City Road

Fern Rock Nature Preserve

Picnic Shelter #2

Post Oak Trail

Little Grassy Lake

P

■ Giant City Lodge

Giant City Nature Trail

Picnic Shelter #3

N

To Cobden, 51 6 miles

0   0.5   1

Miles

As you ascend the trail, you'll near the tops of trees, where you can get eye-level views of migrating or breeding warblers, vireos, and tanagers. You may see both Scarlet and Summer Tanagers in the same tree, giving you the chance to compare the two. Northern Parulas and Yellow-throated Warblers frequent the tops of large sycamore trees, and can be easily seen from this vantage point. As you walk, look to the forest floor for migrating thrushes. In early spring, look for Hermit Thrushes, with their rufous tails that they often pump. A little later in spring, you'll find Gray-cheeked, Swainson's, and Wood Thrushes common, and Veeries occasionally.

Listen for the loud flicker-like call of the Pileated Woodpecker—though this species prefer the bottomlands. Red-shouldered and Broad-winged Hawks also frequent this area.

In spring and summer you should find breeding Eastern Phoebes, Eastern Wood-Pewees, and Acadian Flycatchers.

Once you complete this trail, you can drive the winding roads throughout the park and stop at any of the parking areas, which are near picnic shelters and trailheads. Any of these trails is worth a try. A drive on the main road at dusk in May and June, with windows rolled down, offers you the opportunity to hear

Whip-poor-wills calling. Sometimes this bird sits along the road, and when headlights shine, its eyes glare red. Drive carefully to avoid disturbing these birds.

Also walk the grounds near the lodge where you might find Orchard Orioles feeding young or hear Scarlet Tanagers singing its hoarse robin-like song.

One other trail in the park is worth mentioning: The Post Oak Trail has been specially designed for disabled visitors.

For another type of habitat, check the grasslands as you exit the park near the superintendent's house. You'll find Eastern Bluebirds, Yellow-breasted Chats, and White-eyed Vireos to be quite common in summer. This area has also attracted Bell's Vireos and Prairie Warblers to breed, and you may also find Blue Grosbeaks.

Finally, Little Grassy Lake on the park's east end attracts dabbling ducks during spring and fall migration.

General information: Owned and managed by the Illinois Department of Natural Resources, Giant City State Park's roads and trails reveal evidence of geologic forces from eons ago. Faulting and folding of the large sandstone bluffs have created a scenic vista for birders (and incidentally a place to hide for members of both the Union and Confederate Armies during the Civil War). Lush ferns, mosses, 75 species of trees, and more than that of wildflowers, grace this state park.

Hunting is allowed in some areas of the park; check at the lodge or call the park headquarters for more information. Many of the trails are rocky with excellent hiding places for reptiles, especially snakes. A little reminder: Never place your hand or foot where you can't see what lies on the other side.

ADDITIONAL HELP

DeLorme IA&G grid: 89.
Contact: Giant City State Park.
Nearest gas, food and, lodging: Carbondale; food and lodging are available at Giant City Lodge—reservations are necessary. Campgrounds exist in the park and nearby.

71 Union County Conservation Area and Associated Levees

Habitats: Deciduous and floodplain forest; flooded fields and mudflats, shallow open-water ponds, lakes, sloughs, grasslands, and agricultural fields.

Key birds: Migratory and wintering waterfowl and shorebirds, including American White Pelican, Snow, Canada, and Greater White-fronted Geese, migratory raptors, including Bald and Golden Eagles; foraging Least Tern and breeding Mississippi Kite, Black Vulture, Fish Crow, Blue Grosbeak, and many vireo and warbler species, including Prothonotary and Yellow-throated Warblers.

Best times to bird: Year-round, but especially in spring and fall for migrating waterfowl, shorebirds, raptors, warblers and sparrows; winter for waterfowl, raptors, and Bald Eagle; early in breeding season for nesting warblers, vireos, grosbeaks, and woodpeckers.

Directions: From Interstate 57, exit westbound at Anna/Vienna. Drive west on Illinois Highway 146 through the towns of Anna and Jonesboro 14 miles to the Union County Conservation Area main entrance, which is marked Refuge Drive. Turn south into the refuge. Birders advise you to bring a *DeLorme Illinois Atlas and Gazetteer* on your trip here.

Birding: Birders participating in the annual Union County Spring and Christmas Bird Counts often record one of the state's highest total species. Many noted amateur and professional ornithologists have spent considerable time conducting research or birding the area for at least 150 years. This rich history has produced a long list of rarities, including the White Ibis, Wood Stork, Least Tern, Western Kingbird, Clay-colored Sparrow, Prairie Falcon, Ruffed Grouse, Thayer's Gull, Common Ground Dove, Scissor-tailed Flycatcher, and Green-tailed Towhee, along with winter rarities such as Great Egret, Blue-winged Teal, Turkey and Black Vultures, American Woodcock, House and Marsh Wrens, American Pipit, White-eyed Vireo, Pine, Wilson's, and Nashville Warblers, Brewer's Blackbird, Western Meadowlark, Indigo Bunting, Vesper, and LeConte's, Lincoln's, and Harris's Sparrows. The state-owned refuge encompasses more than 6,200 acres and includes more than 850 acres of shallow sloughs and other open-water areas, including Lyerla (275 acres) and Grassey (350 acres) Lakes and is bordered on the east by Clear Creek Ditch, the south by Reynoldsville Road, the north by IL146, and the west by IL 3.

Although no real hiking trails exist on this refuge, which was designed for hunters, birders have access to the best sites via refuge roads, especially near the Clear Creek Levee Road, which runs the length of the refuge's east side. Keeping in mind that access is sometimes limited in some areas, especially during waterfowl hunting season, here's how you might best enjoy birding this large site.

Start by turning south onto Union County Refuge Road, a widened blacktop road bordered by bottomland hardwood forest. After the road enters the floodplain swamp forest habitat, drive slowly and be alert in spring and summer for

71 Union County Conservation Area and Associated Levees

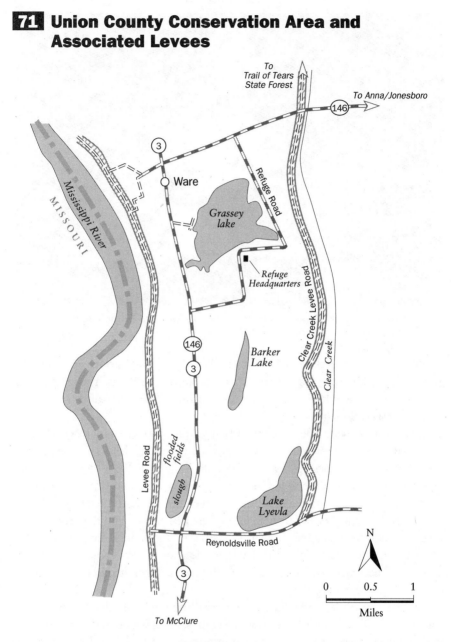

To Trail of Tears State Forest

To Anna/Jonesboro

146

MISSOURI

Mississippi River

3

Ware

Refuge Road

Grassey lake

Refuge Headquarters

Clear Creek Levee Road

Clear Creek

146

3

Barker Lake

Levee Road

flooded fields

slough

Lake Lyevla

Reynoldsville Road

N

0   0.5   1

Miles

3

To McClure

Yellow-crowned Night-Herons, Red-shouldered Hawks, and Barred Owls, which sometimes perch low just inside the forest. You're also likely to hear or see Pileated and Red-headed Woodpeckers, American Redstarts, Northern Parulas, and Yellow-throated and Prothonotary Warblers in spring and summer along this stretch of road.

After the road turns sharply to the right, you'll enter an area of large open fields planted with corn, milo, clover, and other crops for wintering waterfowl. In

The American White Pelican regularly migrates through the Union County Conservation Area. PETER WEBER PHOTO

spring, you may find Upland Sandpipers, Bobolinks, and various sparrows migrating, as well as Dickcissels that remain to breed. You'll pass the refuge headquarters near here, where you can obtain brochures and maps of this and other nearby conservation areas.

If you visit between late October and early April, you will find the next 2 miles of the Refuge Drive rewarding. In winter the refuge often harbors a large percentage of what has at times approached 200,000 Canada Geese. Often you can see several different sizes of Canada Geese in the same field. You might also find up to 20,000 Snow Geese, and usually at least a few Greater White-fronted Geese. Birders counted 350 Greater White-fronted Geese here one winter, and the area has also yielded several Ross's Geese. Numerous species of ducks, including thousands of Mallards, are usually sprinkled throughout the goose flocks. You may often see dozens of Bald Eagles and an occasional Golden Eagle perched in trees or patrolling the flocks of waterfowl.

As you scope the fields, be alert for small numbers of Killdeers, Common Snipes, Lapland Longspurs, and American Pipits, all of which have been found in this area on Christmas Bird Counts. Continue west out to IL 3, looking for the occasional Loggerhead Shrike perched on utility lines at any season.

At IL 3, turn north, driving toward the town of Ware. In about 2 miles, just before you reach town, you'll notice a small gravel access road on your right. If the gate is open, you can drive to Grassey Lake. If not, you'll have to walk. The gate is usually closed between October and March. The road leads to Grassey Lake, where you may find up to 1,000 migrating American White Pelicans in spring, as well as migrating loons and grebes. Swallows sometimes number in the thousands, and you may find Ospreys fishing as well as terns, including—very rarely—a Least Tern. You may also find some lingering diving ducks in late spring.

From late spring to late summer, the sloughs, swamps, and flooded fields just west of the intersection of IL 3/146 can be productive for migrating and summering herons and shorebirds. Begin in the town of Ware and head west from the Running Lake Ditch to the Mississippi River levee roads. Along with the abundant Great Blue Herons, you should find Great Egrets, sometimes numbering in the hundreds, and fewer numbers of Little Blue Herons, Black-crowned and Yellow-crowned Night-Herons, and Snowy and Cattle Egrets. Birders have recorded rarities at this spot, including Wood Storks, White Ibises, and Tri-colored Herons. Also look for American and Least Bitterns during migration.

Proceed east along IL 146 past Refuge Drive, about 2.3 miles to the Clear Creek levee. Drive south along the levee. This dirt road can sometimes be difficult to navigate, especially around the large potholes that usually develop in spring. Birders recommend you drive this road with a four-wheel-drive vehicle after heavy rains.

Most of the time any vehicle is fine on this road, which is one of the showcase areas for several of the refuge's birding specialties. Feel free to park off the edge of the road anywhere along the way and get out to explore the numerous bottomland fields, forests, and wetlands on foot. If you begin a walk down this levee road at daybreak on a winter's day, you will see and hear hundreds if not thousands of birds flying onto the refuge to feed from night-time roosting areas in the nearby Shawnee Hills just east of the refuge. You should also find small to large flocks of robins, waxwings, bluebirds, Yellow-rumped Warblers, various blackbirds (sometimes numbering in the tens or even hundreds of thousands), and winter finches. Also search the levee in winter for rarities, including Eastern Phoebes, House Wrens, Common Yellowthroats, Indigo Buntings, and LeConte's Sparrows, which have not only been found here but are also being recorded with increasing frequency on the Union County Christmas Bird Count. In winter this area can also be especially rewarding for large concentrations of waterfowl in the numerous small to large bottomland sloughs and lakes along the road. The swampy bottomland forest all along the road harbors numbers of woodpeckers, including sapsuckers as well as numerous Winter and Carolina Wrens, both kinglets, Brown Creepers, Hermit Thrushes, and Fox and White-throated Sparrows.

As the forest closes in on both sides of the road, you should begin to hear and see many migrant passerines, and if you're here in the breeding season, you should find Pileated Woodpeckers, White-eyed Vireos, Northern Parulas, Yellow, Yellow-throated, Kentucky, and Prothonotary Warblers, Louisiana Waterthrushes, Yellow-breasted Chats, and the especially numerous American Redstarts.

Also look for the most frequently sought after species, the Mississippi Kite. On sunny days, look for it perched on one of the numerous large dead cottonwoods, or soaring high in the sky, or performing graceful, midair acrobatics while pursuing flying insects low over the fields and levee road. You should find these species here any day between early May and late August, although on overcast or rainy days the kites perch next to the trunk of a large cottonwood, remaining well camouflaged.

Blue Grosbeaks often sit on the levee collecting grit or small insects. You should also find Baltimore and Orchard Orioles in spring and summer along with White-eyed Vireos and many Blue-gray Gnatcatchers. Other birds of interest along this road during the breeding season include most of the herons mentioned earlier, Red-shouldered Hawks, and Fish Crows, both of which nest in the bottomland woods just back from the levee.

After driving this road for about 5 miles, you'll reach Lake Lyerla, where you can search for Double-crested Cormorants, American White Pelicans, Fish Crows, and many tern and swallow species. A pair of Bald Eagles breeds near here. Lyerla Lake sometimes hosts good concentrations of waterfowl and other water-loving species, including Ospreys, Common Loons, gulls, terns, swallows, and the occasional rarity such as Tundra or Mute Swans and Surf Scoters.

Just past Lyerla Lake you'll reach a gate near the refuge portion of the levee road, which continues south. Turn west onto Reynoldsville Road. In spring and early summer you should hear singing Prothonotary Warbler and Orchard Orioles along the first mile of this road. When Reynoldsville Road crosses IL 3, continue driving west over the road and begin checking the often flooded field to the north just after crossing over a small slough for shorebirds and more herons and waterfowl in season. You'll be driving a gravel road west to the north/south levee, which overlooks the Mississippi River and its associated floodplain fields, forests, and sloughs.

The flooded fields just to the north, along the levee road on the east side, sometimes offer some of the best shorebirding in the area. In addition to more waterfowl, the areas adjacent to the levee can be good for such diverse species as American White Pelicans, Northern Harriers, Rough-legged Hawks, Short-eared Owls, gulls, cormorants, flickers, Red-headed Woodpeckers, Belted Kingfishers, all swallows, Fish Crows, Sedge and Marsh Wrens, American Pipits, Loggerhead Shrikes, Prothonotary Warblers, and flocks of Lapland Longspurs, blackbirds and sparrows, including Savannah, Vesper, Grasshopper, and the occasional Lark Sparrow. Also look for the rare Black-necked Stilt or Least Tern foraging in the flooded agricultural fields.

On a late-afternoon drive on this road during the breeding season, you can sometimes see many flocks of herons, including Great, Cattle, and fewer numbers of Snowy Egrets, and fair numbers of Little Blue Herons, returning to their nesting rookeries (mainly along the Missouri side) adjacent to the Mississippi River, from their daytime feeding areas in and around the Union County Conservation Area.

General information: The Illinois Department of Conservation, now the Illinois Department of Natural Resources, purchased this area to help the declining state goose population recover. Intensive management procedures accomplished the goal quickly, and since the late 1960s, the total population of wintering geese in the southern Illinois goose-hunting quota zone has steadily grown to sometimes well over half a million birds. About half of the acreage is planted to various crops to feed the thousands of wintering waterfowl using the area each fall and winter. The waterfowl attract hunters, so it's best to check in at the refuge headquarters to learn which areas are open to hiking during the hunting season.

The levee roads are generally very bumpy and after heavy rains can be slick and extremely muddy, even dangerous. Use extreme caution. Be aware some levees may have No Trespassing signs.

ADDITIONAL HELP

DeLorme IA&G grid: 92 and 93.
Contact: Illinois Department of Natural Resources or Union County Conservation Area refuge manager.
Nearest gas, food, and lodging: Fast food and gas in Anna and Jonesboro but limited lodging; more lodging and other facilities available in the town of Carbondale about 30 miles north.

72 Cypress Creek National Wildlife Refuge

Habitats: Deciduous upland and bottomland forest, grasslands, agricultural land, flooded fields, emergent and scrub/shrub wetland.
Key birds: Migrants, including bitterns and other herons, waterfowl, rails, shorebirds, Golden Eagle, Peregrine Falcon, American Pipit and Le Conte's Sparrow; breeding or summering species, including Bald Eagle, Wild Turkey, Eurasion Collared-Dove, Barn Owl (very rare), Chuck-will's-widow, Fish Crow, Loggerhead Shrike, vireos, warblers, tanagers, Blue Grosbeak, Baltimore and Orchard Orioles, and Grasshopper and Henslow's Sparrows.
Best times to bird: Migration for waterfowl, shorebirds, and passerines; breeding season for nesting or otherwise summering, uncommon-to-rare breeding species; winter for large numbers of waterfowl, eagles, harriers, and owls.

Directions: From Interstate 57, take exit 18, the Ullin exit. Drive east 9 miles to Shawnee Community College, where you will find the refuge headquarters and the starting point for the trip outlined below.

Birding: Much of the refuge is closed to the public or not easily accessed; however, you'll find plenty of places to bird if you plan accordingly. Stop at the refuge headquarters during visitor hours to obtain up-to-date information on areas open to the public with access for birding, or call before you go.

After you've located the office at the Shawnee Community College, and retrieved maps, brochures, and other information, proceed west on Shawnee College Road

72 Cypress Creek National Wildlife Refuge

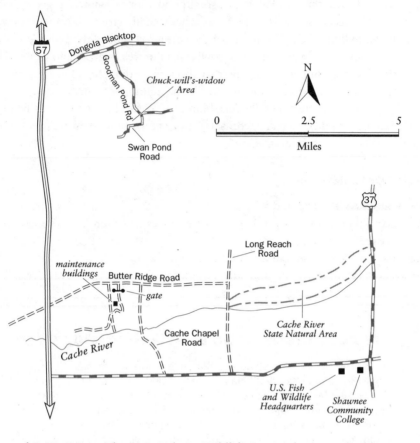

toward I-57. (Note: The U.S. Fish & Wildlife Service hopes to build a visitor center on Illinois Highway 37 just northeast of the college on the Cache River.) .

In about 2 miles, you'll see Long Reach Road, a gravel road that heads north past a large farm. The farmer often floods his fields, which attract ducks and shorebirds to pile onto his property. Use a scope to search for them in spring and fall.

The next crossroad west of Long Reach Road off of Shawnee College Road is Cache Chapel Road. You will want to turn north here shortly, but first continue west down Shawnee College Road a brief distance (about half a mile) and you will see standing water on both sides of the road. The area on the north side of the road is known as Easter Slough and holds water throughout the year. It almost always has at least a few herons and shorebirds in season. This is private property, but you can easily view birds from the road with a scope. The slough often holds one or a few Little Blue Herons or Snowy Egrets, and has hosted numerous shorebirds, including White-rumped Sandpipers, Black-necked Stilts, and Whimbrels to name a few of the rare species. The adjacent fields usually contain breeding Dickcissels and Grasshopper Sparrows.

Return to Cache Chapel Road and turn north, checking for Northern Mockingbirds, Loggerhead Shrikes, Blue Grosbeaks, and Orchard Orioles along the way. As you reach the fields north of the river on the east side of the road, look for shorebirds in spring and late summer, especially if there has been heavy rainfall or flooding conditions.

Farther north along the road to where it comes to a T intersection with Butter Ridge Road is another gravel road. Turn west and proceed less than half a mile to a sign announcing the Frank Bellrose unit of the Cypress Creek National Wildlife Refuge. A large gravel driveway leads south to several grain bins and buildings. Even though the entrance gate may be locked, you can still park here then hike in to enjoy birding.

The Frank Bellrose unit (commonly referred to as the DU unit for Ducks Unlimited's involvement in restoring the wetland complex) is probably the most birded area in the refuge. Walking, rather than driving through this area, makes the best sense for birders. The gravel lane leading to the maintenance building is an easy walk. You should find Dickcissels, Eastern Meadowlarks, and Horned Larks. American Golden-Plovers sometimes use the area during spring and fall migration, and sometimes flocks of blackbirds congregate, which may contain Rusty Blackbirds, and occasionally a few Brewer's Blackbirds.

In spring Savannah and Vesper Sparrows frequent the grassy areas along the entrance road. As you reach the maintenance compound you'll see the large, low-water marsh to the south. It has very little deepwater habitat but most ducks, including some diving ducks, utilize the area.

When Bald Eagles, which breed here, fly over, they force the ducks in the air every so often, giving you a good chance to see the variety of species. A Golden Eagle is a possibility in winter, and a Peregrine Falcon is possible during migration. As this spot dries in July and August, the herons and shorebirds pile into the shallow water areas at the marsh edges. Some rarities recorded include Black-necked Stilts, Marbled and Hudsonian Godwits, and Red-necked Phalaropes.

Follow the gravel access road around the maintenance buildings to the west and cross over the bridge for access to more herons, ducks, and shorebirds. The area beyond the bridge contains agricultural fields that are left in stubble for the waterfowl and in spring, when flooded, attract a large variety of water-loving species as well as American Pipits and LeConte's Sparrows during fall and spring migration.

You can walk roads along shallow levees in this area, but make sure you wear proper footgear because water sometimes can get quite deep. In March and April look for Least Bitterns, King Rails, Virginia Rails, Soras, and sometimes American Bitterns. At least seven pairs of Pied-billed Grebes nested in this area one spring and two Glossy Ibises once visited. Least Terns have foraged over the shallow-water wetlands, and probably breed nearby.

The levee makes a complete loop; however, you will have to wear at least knee boots to access the full circle to get to where you started. Follow the road back out to the maintenance compound and the entrance at Butter Ridge Road.

Drive east on Butter Ridge Road to Long Reach Road, then drive south for 3 miles to Shawnee College Road, where you can drive west back to I-57. If you want to search for Henslow's Sparrows and Chuck-will's-widows, go north on I-57 for 5.5 miles to the Dongola exit. Go east on the Dongola blacktop to Goodman Pond Road. Northeast of this intersection, you may find a large breeding population of Henslow's Sparrows. The property is private, but you can bird from the road. Listen for Chuck-will's-widows in spring and summer on Swan Pond Road, just west of Goodman Pond Road in the broken forested areas.

A special sidebar: As you traverse this area, listen for the nasal call of Fish Crows during breeding season and look for soaring Black Vultures year-round. Barn Owls have bred in the area; be alert for them while driving the roads at dusk.

General information: From the times of the earliest settlers in this former land of vast stretches of forested swamps and floodplain forest, humans have left their mark on the landscape by cutting and clearing the forests, draining the swamps, and channelizing and otherwise diverting the streams of the Cache River Basin. Historically, rains flooded several thousands acres of this region for six to eight months of the year.

Today's Cache River Natural Area (see Site 73), although impressive, represents a mere vestige of a vast swampland, which once included 11,000 acres of cypress-tupelo swamp, the largest of its kind north of the Ohio River. Much of Big Black Slough was densely forested with areas of deeper water sometimes described by early settlers as a lake. The water never completely disappeared, even during droughts.

Decades of draining and lumbering in the Cache Basin diverted water tables and reduced wetlands. The Nature Conservancy and U.S. Fish & Wildlife Service are restoring thousands of acres of bottomland areas to native floodplain forest. Someday this area may more resemble the once great forests of days gone by.

Be aware that biting insects and mosquitos as well as dense stands of poison ivy and stinging nettle can be fierce in summer.

ADDITIONAL HELP

DeLorme IA&G grid: 93.

Contact: U.S. Fish & Wildlife Service, Cypress Creek National Wildlife Refuge, The Nature Conservancy, and the Illinois Department of Natural Resources.

Nearest gas, food, and lodging: Camping at Dixon Springs State Park, about 14 miles east of Vienna along IL 146; at Ferne Clyffe State Park, about 20 miles north on IL 37; and at Horseshoe Lake (see separate account), about 30 miles southwest. Many of the small towns have a gas station and at least one restaurant; however, lodging is limited. Hotels and motels in Marion (30 miles north) or Vienna (15 miles northeast); one motel in Ullin.

73 Cache River and Heron Pond State Natural Areas

Habitats: Upland forest, bottomland forest, cypress-tupelo swamp, flooded fields, grassy upland fields, and floodplain forest along the Cache River.

Key birds: Migrating warblers and sparrows, including Le Conte's; breeding or otherwise summering Mississippi Kite, Bald Eagle, Red-shouldered and Broad-winged Hawks, Wild Turkey, Pileated Woodpecker, Acadian Flycatcher, Fish Crow, Brown Creeper, Loggerhead Shrike, Northern Mockingbird; Blue-winged, Northern Parula, Yellow-throated, Pine, Prairie, Cerulean, Black-and-white, Prothonotary, Worm-eating, Kentucky, and Hooded Warblers; American Redstart, Ovenbird, Louisiana Waterthrush, Yellow-breasted Chat, Blue Grosbeak, Dickcissel, Grasshopper and Henslow's Sparrows, and Orchard Oriole; wintering Northern Harrier, Short-eared Owl, and Red-headed Woodpecker; roosting Black Vulture at Heron Pond.

Best times to bird: Year-round but especially in spring for flycatchers, vireos, warblers, and sparrows, during the breeding season for southern specialties, and in winter for hawks, owls, and sparrows.

Directions: Exit Interstate 57 at Illinois Highway 146 (Anna/Vienna). Go east about 9.5 miles to Illinois Highway 37 and the town of West Vienna. Continue for another 0.5 mile on IL 146 until you see a sign for Wildcat Bluff Nature Preserve. Turn south and drive this unimproved gravel road to the entrance.

Birding: More than 8,200 acres of upland and bottomland fields, forests, swamps, and sloughs harbor a wide variety of not only birds, but also a large percentage of some of the state's rarest natural communities, including the bald cypress-tupelo swamp. The different units of this complex of state-owned lands are scattered along a large stretch of the Cache River. Many of the best areas for birding, especially the bottomland swamps and forests, contain many of the same breeding species.

The best times to bird this area are May for spring migrants, including most of the flycatchers, vireos, and warblers, as well as June for the breeders.

To begin your trip, follow the 5-mile-long twisting gravel road south off IL 146 east of IL 37 past grassy fields, successional areas, and upland forest until it dead-ends at the parking lot and the only access point into what is known as Wildcat Bluff. As you drive the road, check the utility lines for American Kestrels, Loggerhead Shrikes, Northern Mockingbirds, and occasionally Blue Grosbeaks. A few pairs of Blue-winged and Prairie Warblers breed in the old fields scattered with cedar trees along the way, but this is private property, so restrict your birding to the roadsides. After parking at the small lot, check the small grassy field on the east side of the road, north of the forest edge. Henslow's Sparrows have bred here, and you can usually find nesting Yellow-breasted Chats and Orchard Orioles. Arrive just before daybreak to listen for calling Whip-poor-wills or a Barred Owl.

You'll find trails leading southeast and southwest into the swamps and bottomland forest along the north side of the Cache River. The trail leaving east

73 Cache River and Heron Pond State Natural Areas

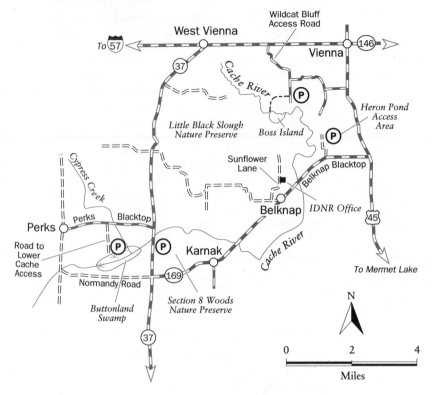

from the parking area leads you to an impressive view from the top of the bluffs overlooking a vast expanse of upland and bottomland forest. However, you can see the same birds, and pass through a more gradual (translation: "less steep") transition from the oak-hickory uplands into the silver maple–sycamore associated bottomlands, by taking the trail going west from the parking area.

Along the way during the breeding season, you should listen and look for Blue-gray Gnatcatchers, Carolina Wrens, Wood Thrushes, Red-eyed and Yellow-throated Vireos, Kentucky Warblers, and Scarlet and Summer Tanagers. As the trail starts downhill more steeply you may see or hear one of the few Worm-eating and Hooded Warblers in the area. Once the trail reaches the river, you have two choices, depending on conditions. If the river is low enough, you can wade across the Cache River where the trail/access road fords the river over to Boss Island. You can wander the trails on the "island" for quite a while, but bring a compass. Black Vultures have nested in the abandoned building just south of the river along the trail and elsewhere on exposed rocky bluffs on the island. In winter you may find Long-eared and Northern Saw-whet Owls in the pine plantations and overgrown fields. A few Blue-winged, Prairie, and Pine Warblers have bred here, and breeding Brown Creepers, rare nesters in Illinois, have been seen along the edge of the cypress-tupelo swamps alongside the trail.

If the river is too high, which is usually the case in spring and early summer, bring your compass and walk the edge of the river in either direction, for miles if you want. Especially from the river ford east, you should find numerous breeding birds such as Acadian Flycatchers, White-eyed Vireos, and warblers, including Northern Parula, Yellow-throated, Cerulean, American Redstart, Prothonotary, and Louisiana Waterthrushes. Be alert too for the more uncommon breeding species such as Yellow-crowned Night-Herons, Red-shouldered Hawks, Pileated Woodpeckers, and Fish Crows.

To see one of the finest and most accessible examples of bald cypress–tupelo swamp in Illinois, visit the Heron Pond State Natural Area. Although Heron Pond lies just across the river from Wildcat Bluff, you will have to return to your vehicle and proceed back to IL 146 to get there. Once at IL 146, go east to Vienna. Turn south onto U.S. Highway 45 at Vienna and go 5 miles to where a main blacktop road, known as the Belknap blacktop, meets US 45 from the west at a T intersection. Turn west on the blacktop road and watch for the sign for the Heron Pond Access Area and entrance road about 1.5 miles west of US 45. Follow the gravel access road north 1 mile to the parking lot. Walk the trail across the bridge over the Cache River and out to the boardwalk that brings you into Heron Pond. Here you will stand beneath towering bald cypress and tupelo trees.

As you walk the boardwalk, you should hear and see many of the same bottomland species you recorded in the Wildcat Bluff area. However, Yellow-throated Warblers are especially noticeable, and if you listen closely you might hear the faint, high-pitched, two-syllable, wheezy "song" of the breeding Brown Creeper. In the early evening, the amphibian chorus can be almost deafening as the gray tree frogs, green tree frogs, and rare bird-voiced tree frogs declare their intentions to potential mates. A group of bird-voiced tree frogs sounds like a "flock" of miniature Pileated Woodpeckers calling at once.

At dusk, Black and Turkey Vultures gather in the large cypress trees, offering close views for the patient birder. As you return to the parking area and go back out onto the Belknap blacktop, you may want to look south across Belknap toward a set of large powerline towers where vultures may also be roosting.

To continue to the next destination, drive south on the Belknap blacktop about 2 miles through the town of Belknap to the Illinois Department of Natural Resources office for maps and other information.

Check the Section 8 Woods Nature Preserve, which is on IL 37 north of IL 169. A small parking area is easy to miss, but it may soon be enlarged, and a short boardwalk may be constructed to aid in maneuvering this deepwater swamp. As of this writing, a new visitor center is scheduled to be built along IL 37. Look for the usual complement of swamp-loving birds, including Prothonotary and Yellow-throated Warblers, and

Cypress swamp along the Cache River. SHERYL DEVORE PHOTO

possibly Red-shouldered Hawks and Yellow-crowned Night-Herons. Chimney Swifts use their historical type of breeding habitat here, the inside of a large, mostly dead, hollow bald cypress tree along the west side of the highway.

If the tour above isn't adventurous enough for you, the next stop may be just the place. Just north of the Section 8 parking area and over the Cache River, a paved road intersects with IL 37 from the west. This is the Perks blacktop. Turn west here to reach the next site. After about 1.5 miles and shortly after crossing a channelized portion of Cypress Creek, you will see a sign for the Lower Cache River Canoe Access area. Watch for the gravel access road just beyond and off the south side of the Perks blacktop. Follow the gravel road to the dead end at the parking lot. This is one of very few public access points on the Lower Cache. (If you didn't bring a canoe, you can rent one at Cache Core Canoes on Long Reach Road near the town of Perks.)

This public access area on the Lower Cache is known as Buttonland Swamp, (for the dense growth of buttonbush shrubs that grow profusely out in the swamp). It has several miles of marked canoe trails, one of which takes you past the state champion bald cypress tree, which is more than 1,000 years old. In addition, you'll see a short boardwalk and raised viewing platform just west of the parking area that looks out over this remnant cypress-tupelo swamp. Look for Prothonotary Warblers and other river backwater birds.

Also check the fields adjacent to Normandy Road (a gravel road off a T intersection with Long Reach Road less than half a mile after crossing the Cache River). The U.S. Fish & Wildlife Service has purchased many large fields along both sides of this road, from Long Reach Road east to IL 169. Drive this road slowly to search for breeding Dickcissels, Henslow's Sparrows, and Eastern Meadowlarks as well as Loggerhead Shrikes, Northern Mockingbirds, Orchard Orioles, Eastern Bluebirds, Yellow-breasted Chats, Grasshopper Sparrows, and sometimes Sedge Wrens. If you're here in winter, these fields and others nearby often contain sizable roosts of Northern Harriers and Short-eared Owls.

General information: The Cache River runs for 110 miles in six Illinois counties. Its basin drains the entire southern tip of the state. The Lower Cache River basin, which includes all of the areas described in this site guide, once contained more than 250, 000 acres of swampy bald cypress-tupelo forest before humans settled here. In 1996, the United Nations Educational, Scientific, and Cultural Organization, added the Cache River and Cypress Creek wetlands to its list of 15 Wetlands of International Importance because of their critical role in providing resting and feeding areas for waterfowl and shorebirds.

Although only about 5,300 acres of swamp forest remain, much of these have been preserved in the three National Natural Landmarks and eight designated Illinois Nature Preserves of the Cache basin. In addition, surveys of the Illinois Natural Areas Inventory found 60 sites that contained ecosystems of statewide significance, with representatives of as many as 20 natural community types, including several that are the best or only examples of their type left in the state.

The wetland areas that make up the Cache contain more than 11 percent of the state's remaining high-quality floodplain forest habitat as well as 91 percent of the state's high-quality swamp habitat. The area is also one of only six places in the country where four or more physiographic regions come together, creating an extremely high diversity of biota (including avian diversity), including 104 species that are endangered or threatened in the state, 7 of which are federally threatened or endangered. These include not only birds, but also several species of bats, snakes, the river otter, and the bobcat.

If you are here in summer, the heat, humidity, mosquitos, and biting flies can be annoying at best. Three species of poisonous snakes occur in the area; water moccasins are more common here than in any other area of the state.

ADDITIONAL HELP

DeLorme IA&G grid: 93.

Contact: Cache River State Natural Area or Illinois Department of Natural Resources.

Nearest gas, food, and lodging: Camping at Dixon Springs State Park, about 14 miles east of Vienna along IL 146 and at Ferne Clyffe State Park, about 20 miles north on IL 37. Many of the small towns have a gas station and at least one restaurant; however, lodging is limited. Hotels and motels in Marion (30 miles north) or Vienna (15 miles northeast); one motel off I-57 at the Ullin exit.

74 Horseshoe Lake Conservation Area

Habitats: Natural oxbow lake with cypress-tupelo swamp, Mississippi floodplain forest, flooded fields and mudflats, agricultural fields, upland forest, and Mississippi River.

Key birds: Large concentrations of migrating and wintering waterfowl, including Greater White-fronted, Snow, and Ross's Geese, Bald and Golden Eagles; breeding or otherwise summering Little Blue Heron, Yellow-crowned Night-Heron, Snowy Egret, Mississippi Kite, Wild Turkey, Black-necked Stilt, Least Tern, Chuck-will's-widow, Pileated Woodpecker, Acadian Flycatcher, Fish Crow, Brown Creeper, Loggerhead Shrike, White-eyed Vireo, breeding warblers, including Blue-winged, Northern Parula, Yellow-throated, Prairie, Cerulean, American Redstart, Prothonotary, Worm-eating, Kentucky, Hooded, Louisiana Waterthrush, and Yellow-breasted Chat; breeding Scarlet and Summer Tanagers, Blue Grosbeak, and Baltimore and Orchard Orioles.

Best times to bird: Year-round but especially in migration for passerines and shorebirds; summer for uncommon-to-rare breeding/summering species; winter for large concentrations of waterfowl, eagles, and passerines.

Directions: From Interstate 57, exit at Mounds. Go west to U.S. Highway 51 and turn south. As you come into the north side of town, watch for one of the first streets (Sycamore Street) going west out of town. Turn right on Sycamore Street and proceed west out of town for 5 miles to the intersection of Illinois Highways 3 and 127. Continue west from the stop sign on IL 3 for a little more than 5 miles to the small village of Olive Branch. Watch for a sign (just before town) for the park office and stop and obtain a refuge map.

Birding: This area serves as one of the most ornithologically significant links to the state's past. Birding pioneers observed breeding species here that have disappeared from Illinois, possibly forever. Species that historically bred within 15 miles of Horseshoe Lake include the Trumpeter Swan, American Swallow-tailed Kite, Swainson's Warbler, Bachman's Warbler (now probably extinct), and the extinct Ivory-billed Woodpecker, Passenger Pigeon, and Carolina Parakeet.

Rarities that birders recently discovered here include the Magnificent Frigatebird, Neotropic Cormorant, Anhinga, White Ibis, and Rock Wren. Put this list in front of birders who haven't been to southern Illinois and they'll most likely guess we are talking about a place much farther south. Logging and draining have occurred on all but 5,000 acres of the original 250, 000 acres of floodplain swamp forest that originally covered this part of southern Illinois.

This 9,550-acre region includes bald cypress and tupelo trees, the ancient oxbow (of the Mississippi River) lake, which instantly transports you to an area more like a Louisiana bayou than the corn and soybean desert that you passed to get here. With its 30 miles of shoreline and 2,400 acres of open water, the conservation area provides a haven for thousands of ducks and geese and the dozens of Bald (and a few Golden) Eagles that feed on them in migration and throughout winter.

74 Horseshoe Lake Conservation Area

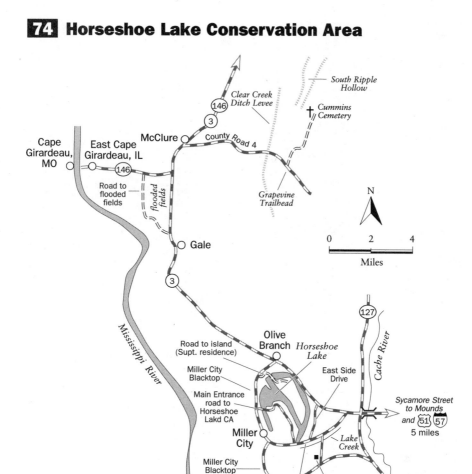

At the main entrance, follow West Side Drive along the lake. In the winter you should see waterfowl everywhere. Check the mowed grass areas for large flocks of geese, including mostly Canada Geese, but also fewer numbers of Snow and Greater White-fronted Geese, and occasional Ross's Geese. Check Horseshoe Lake for diving ducks, as well as the occasional Pied-billed Grebe and cormorant. Sometimes, several Bald Eagles sit in the large cypress trees along the edge of the lake.

In summer, listen for the songs of the common breeding warblers along the edges of the lake, including Northern Parula, Yellow-throated, and Prothonotary. Brown Creepers are also possible in summer.

Hooded Warblers breed at Horseshoe Lake Conservation Area. DENNIS OEHMKE PHOTO

Also search the north part of Horseshoe Lake just south of Olive Branch. Driving north on the Miller City blacktop, be alert for Red-shouldered Hawks and Barred Owls sitting in the cypress trees at any season. As an open stretch of the lake appears on the east, check the lake for more water birds. Watch for the gravel road leading to the "island" part of the refuge and the site superintendent's residence. This road, which is difficult to find, is 1 mile south of Olive Branch. Look for a small Wildlife Refuge sign near an abandoned motel. Turn east onto the gravel road and drive to the gate going out onto the island (gate may be locked). If you have time, you can walk onto the island. In winter, huge flocks of geese congregate. Search the wet fields during much of the year for Killdeer and Eastern Meadowlarks. In early winter and early spring, you might find Common Snipes, LeConte's Sparrows, and Lapland Longspurs, and occasionally American Pipits. A pair of Bald Eagles usually breeds nearby.

To visit another area of the refuge for migrant passerines, rails and shorebirds, and breeding or otherwise summering raptors, herons, and other nesting species, return to the Miller City blacktop and go south a little more than 3 miles to Promised Land Road and turn east. Drive for 3 miles to a T interesection with a gravel road to the right (which immediately crosses over Lake Creek). Turn south. You'll notice a few gravel roads leading west into a public hunting area along this short stretch of road. Unfortunately, many times the roads are closed, but you can park in the hunter parking area near the south end of this road, off the west side of the road near the hunter check-in station, and walk in. Various herons breed and/ or forage in the flooded fields and bottomland forest, including the Little Blue Heron, Yellow-crowned Night-Heron, and Great, Cattle, and Snowy Egrets.

Sometimes shorebirds and rails use the same flooded fields. Other breeding species include Red-shouldered Hawks, Mississippi Kites, Wood Ducks, Hooded Mergansers, Barred Owls, Pileated Woodpeckers, Acadian Flycatchers, Fish Crows, Carolina Wrens, Northern Parulas, Yellow-throated and Prothonotary Warblers, and Louisiana Waterthrushes.

Another productive spot, especially in migration and summer is south along the Miller City blacktop. During the 1993 Mississippi River floods, many sections of this road from here to where the road intersects IL 3 to the south, were flooded or destroyed by floodwaters, which actually broke through the protective dike. The river deposited millions of tons of sand over thousands of acres of agricultural fields. The area had already been a reliable and productive area for shorebirds, herons, and nesting Least Terns, but the floods provided much more breeding and foraging areas for these and several other species.

The large body of water on the west near the tiny town of Willard was formed during the 1993 flood when the Mississippi River breached the dike and gouged this large lake, and now provides a roosting and feeding area for various herons, shorebirds, gulls, terns, cormorants, and swallows. Drive the blacktop east from Willard toward IL 3, especially from June through late August, and scan the many pools and standing water areas for Little Blue Herons, Cattle and Snowy Egrets, Least Terns, Mississippi Kites, and Fish Crows. Look on the utility lines for Loggerhead Shrikes.

You can also drive the many dirt roads leading south from the blacktop (as they all eventually lead back to the blacktop in this extreme southern tip of Illinois). The 1993 flood created a rather eerie wasteland where virtually nobody lives or ventures into, except birders in search of some of the many rarities that have been found in this area over the years.

To search for upland forest birds, drive on IL 3 north to the town of McClure. Turn east at the grade school, which is County Road 4. Follow this road as it crosses over the Clear Creek ditch and levee and enters the rolling upland areas of the Shawnee National Forest, for about 4 miles. Just before a small parking area for the Grapevine Trail Trailhead and picnic area, a T intersection connects a gravel road. Drive north on this road for about a mile. The road will eventually lead down a steep hill and enter a large field. It then climbs again and levels at the small Cummins Cemetery on the west side of the road, and just before the road turns sharply east. Park along the road, bring a compass, and walk along the edge of the woods along the north side of the cemetery to where a short footpath leads northwest into the forest. Where the path comes to the edge of a tall, steep ravine, head west downhill to the stream-lined bottom of this large ravine system. This is known as South Ripple Hollow and serves as an outstanding example of what much of the Shawnee National Forest in the area used to be like. Although you'll find no well-maintained trails, you can walk parallel to the rock-bottom creek, cutting through a ravine, and heading north for more than 2 miles. Exploring this forest of huge trees (especially many immense American beeches) on a late spring or early summer morning can be rewarding. The forest attracts migrants as well as breeding Broad-winged and Cooper's Hawks, Whip-poor-wills, Pileated Wood-peckers, Acadian Flycatchers, Wood Thrushes, White-eyed, Yellow-throated, and Red-eyed Vireos, and warblers, including Northern Parula, Yellow-throated, Cer-ulean, Worm-eating, Ovenbird, Kentucky, Hooded, and Louisiana Waterthrushes and both tanagers. Driving Forest Service roads in the area can also produce an occasional Chuck-will's-widow, American Woodcock, and Blue Grosbeak, among other species.

Finally, check the flooded fields along IL 3 south of IL 146. A gravel road northeast of the town of Gale leads you past the flooded fields where you can stop along the road to search for shorebirds, herons, and possibly Least Terns and other rarities. American White Pelicans have summered and Black-necked Stilts bred here.

General information: John James Audubon traversed the Cape Girardeau region on the Mississippi River, birding close to this Illinois hotspot. Bird fossils remain from Native American campsites near the town of Thebes dating at least until as far back as A.D. 1000. Noted Illinois ornithologists spent thousands of hours exploring this region. The tradition continues today as contemporary ornithologists gather data. The Department of Conservation (as it was known then) purchased the first parcel of land here in 1927 to be used as a refuge for Canada Geese, and to provide water-fowl hunting. However, you can also picnic, camp, boat, fish, and bird here.

Two state-dedicated nature preserves exist on the site; these include a near-virgin forest of beeches, sugar maples, swamp chestnut oaks, and American elms. This forest was dedicated as a National Natural Historic Landmark in 1974.

The Horseshoe Lake ecosystem provides habitat for other state-threatened and endangered species besides birds. These include the bobcat, golden mouse, swamp rabbit, Rafinesque's big-eared bat, Illinois chorus frog, green and broad-banded water snakes, river cooter (a turtle), bantam sunfish, cypress minnow, and oxbow crayfish.

The massive flood of 1993 inundated the lake and much of the areas forests, with high-water marks stretching 12 to 15 feet or more up the trunks of the cy-press and tupelo trees. Although these water-loving trees were relatively unaf-fected by the flooding, it is yet to be seen how the floods have affected the local flora and fauna.

Hunting is allowed. Call before going in fall or early winter to learn which areas might be closed.

ADDITIONAL HELP

DeLorme IA&G grid: 92 and 93.
Contact: Horseshoe Lake Conservation Area.
Nearest gas, food, and lodging: Limited facilities in Olive Branch; more abundant facilities 20 miles away in Cape Girardeau, Missouri.

75 Pomona–Cave Creek

Habitats: Deciduous and coniferous forests, bottomland hardwood forests, scrub/shrub and agricultural lands.
Key birds: Spring migrants; breeding Black Vulture, Mississippi Kite, Cooper's and Broad-winged Hawks, Fish Crow, Pileated Woodpecker, Carolina Chickadee, Louisiana Waterthrush, Cerulean, Worm-eating, Prothonotary, and Yellow-throated Warblers (among others), and Blue Grosbeak.
Best times to bird: Spring and early summer.

Directions: Take Illinois Highway 127 south from Murphysboro or northbound from the Anna and Jonesboro area to Pomona Road. Drive west for 1.5 miles to the gravel road that leads north past the Pomona general store.

Birding: The Pomona–Cave Creek area, with its winding creeks amid woods, provides habitat for at least 12 breeding warbler species, including American Redstarts, Louisiana Waterthrushes, Yellow-breasted Chats, Hooded, Prairie, Pine, Yellow, Northern Parula, Kentucky, Worm-eating, and Blue-winged. In summer you should be able to find all these birds as well as both tanagers, both orioles, four species of vireos, Yellow-billed Cuckoos, and all the woodpeckers known to breed in Illinois. Pine Warblers, kinglets, and Hermit Thrushes often stay during mild winters. Spring arrives at Pomona two to three weeks earlier than it does in northern Illinois, and on a late April day, you should get a great dose of migrating songbirds, including copious warblers, thrushes, and tanagers.

You'll find no paved trails and no fancy nature centers, just lots of fairly easy walking and birding.

Begin your birding at the intersection of IL 127 and Pomona Road, 12 miles south of Murphysboro. Look for Blue Grosbeaks, a species that is nearly always encountered at this intersection in spring and summer. Drive west on Pomona Road for about a mile into town.

At the only stop sign in town, turn right (north) on an old Forest Service gravel road. Follow the road 1.5 miles past the bridge over Cave Creek and park just past the gravel road to your right. This is an old railroad bed that you can walk for miles. Begin here or go back across the bridge and take the trail to the east.

Walk the trail before the bridge, heading east to check for Broad-winged and Cooper's Hawks, which breed here. The pine trees along the trail attract Pine and Yellow-throated Warblers as well as Northern Parulas, especially in May and June. Just around the bend you may also hear the Louisiana Waterthrush singing, as well as Cerulean Warblers, Acadian Flycatchers, and Scarlet and Summer Tanagers.

Listen for the nasal call of the Fish Crow, which often flies over. This trail also offers you the chance to see a Pileated Woodpecker.

North of the bridge is a 3-mile gravel road trail that is easy to walk. You will find similar species as described above, but this route offers the best chances of

75 Pomona–Cave Creek

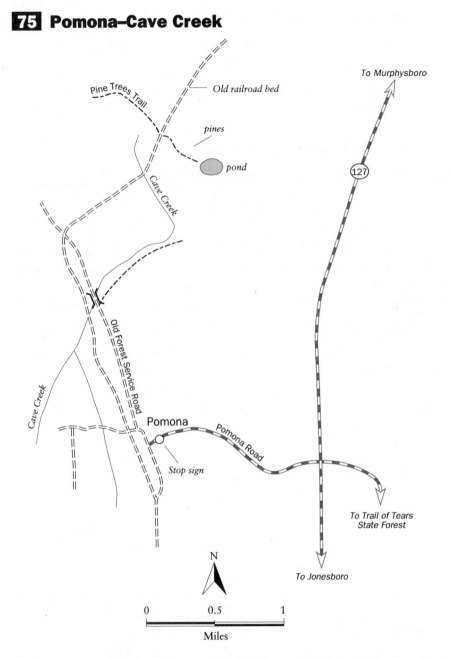

finding soaring Mississippi Kites and Black Vultures. Mississippi Kites have bred here, along with White-eyed Vireos, Blue-gray Gnatcatchers, Prairie Warblers, Indigo Buntings, and Common Yellowthroats. You'll need to search more carefully for the Kentucky and Worm-eating Warblers that breed here because they are skulkers. Your best chance to find them is to learn their songs, then listen for them in May and June when they are most vocal.

About a mile on the trail you'll see a hillside with pine trees. Follow the Forest Service trail sign to your right for 0.5 mile through pines and to a pond that hosts teals, Wood Ducks, and Mallards in spring. Herons and egrets frequent this spot, as well as all the swallow species known in Illinois. Look for Black Vultures, too. Cottonmouths also love this pond, so be careful.

Around the thickets bordering the trail west of the pond, you'll walk near where the Swainson's Warbler once bred. In the 1980s, birders could count on finding this species, but this bird may now be extirpated from Illinois. Also listen for the Cerulean Warbler; this is one of the most dependable spots in the state to find this bird, which is rapidly declining in numbers nationwide.

General information: Pomona is a favorite spot for turkey hunters. Early to mid-April is generally turkey season. Birders should wear blaze-orange vests to be visible. Consider calling first to check on hunting times. Much of southern Illinois is venomous snake country and Pomona is no exception. Cottonmouths, copperheads, and timber rattlesnakes have been encountered here. Cottonmouths are fairly numerous near the pond area and can be seen basking on the logs in the pond. Beware that they do move to the uplands, so they may cross your path. It's best to keep your eyes open and avoid disturbing them. Mosquitos, chiggers, and ticks can be bothersome, depending on the season. Bug spray may be necessary.

The Worm-eating Warbler breeds in southern Illinois. DENNIS OEHMKE PHOTO

ADDITIONAL HELP

DeLorme IA&G grid: 88.

Contact: Illinois Department of Natural Resources.

Nearest gas, food, and lodging: Gas and food are available in Murphysboro to the north and Anna/Jonesboro to the south. Lodging availability is best in Carbondale, about 7 miles east of Murphysboro on IL 13.

76 Atwood Ridge and Hamburg Hill

Habitats: Deciduous upland and bottomland swamp forest, pine and other plantations, old clearcuts, agricultural and pastured land (en route).

Key birds: Migrant passerines, especially warblers; wintering Golden and Bald Eagles; Black Vulture; breeding Broad-winged, Cooper's, and Red-shouldered Hawks, Wild Turkey, Pileated Woodpecker, Acadian Flycatcher, Fish Crow, Loggerhead Shrike, Northern Mockingbird, Wood Thrush, White-eyed Vireo, and warblers, including Yellow-throated, Northern Parula, Pine, Black-and-white, Kentucky, Worm-eating, Cerulean, Hooded, Prothonotary, Ovenbird, American Redstart, Louisiana Waterthrush, and Yellow-breasted Chat, Blue Grosbeak, Orchard Oriole, and Scarlet and Summer Tanagers.

Best times to bird: Spring for passerine migration, fall for raptor migration, early summer for breeders.

Directions: From Illinois Highway 146 in Anna/Jonesboro, traveling west, turn south on Berryville Road as you leave Jonesboro. Berryville Road goes past Lockard Chapel and winds for 3 miles to Water Plant Road. Turn south, going across Dutch Creek and past a water plant, where you will encounter a low-water crossing. This creek can be too deep if there's been heavy rains, so be aware of the weather. After crossing the creek, the road narrows and turns to gravel. After heavy rains this road is difficult to traverse without a four-wheel-drive vehicle. Continue up the hill 0.5 mile to the Y.

Birding: When it comes to birding, the Atwood Ridge area has its disadvantages; roads can be difficult to maneuver, turkey hunters can be everywhere in spring, and birding is sometimes hit or miss on the ridgetop sites. Even with these caveats, Atwood Ridge, Hamburg Hill, and Dutch Creek offer the birder a great chance to see some uncommon-to-rare Illinois birds, including Golden Eagles and Black Vultures. If you are there on the right day, the spring migration is superb, perhaps the best in the Midwest. Indeed, birders annually find 30 or more species of warblers during spring migration in one day, as well as large concentrations of flycatchers, vireos, thrushes, and other songbirds.

To search for migrating passerines at Atwood Ridge and Hamburg Hill, come in the morning. In the afternoon, the wind speed increases, sending birds to more sheltered areas; that's when you'll want to bird Dutch Creek.

76 Atwood Ridge and Hamburg Hill

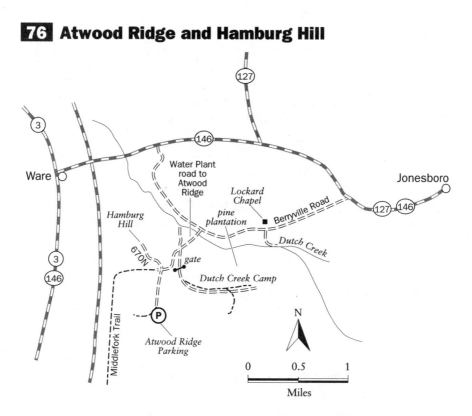

You'll find several areas accessible by motorized vehicle. After you park, be prepared to hike to find birds. Also note that after heavy rains some roads can be dangerous and should only be traveled with a four-wheel-drive vehicle.

The first access point is at a Y in the road. You have several options. You can park and walk the Middlefork Trail or walk south for about a quarter mile down a gravel road called Water Plant Road. For breeders, including Prothonotary, Hooded, and Worm-eating Warblers, and Louisiana Waterthrushes, take the Middlefork Trail, which you can walk for miles. Look for the locked gate with a Road Closed sign. That's where the trail begins. The Swainson's Warbler formerly bred in a huge stand of giant cane near this area, but no longer. This bird could be extirpated as a breeder in Illinois, but it doesn't hurt to check and report any sightings to the Illinois Natural History Survey.

For migrants, walk south down Water Plant Road (gravel). In late April, the Worm-eating Warbler returns to the deep ravines to breed, while Summer and Scarlet Tanagers sing from the treetops. When the road curves, you'll see an area of small trees and thickets, habitat for breeding White-eyed Vireos, Brown Thrashers, and Gray Catbirds. Ruby-throated Hummingbirds also frequent this spot. Also check this area for the late migrating warblers, including Connecticut and Mourning. The best time to find these two coveted warblers is from middle to late May. Also look overhead for Broad-winged, Sharp-shinned, Cooper's, and

Red-shouldered Hawks, as well as the occasional Black Vulture and Bald Eagle, which have all bred here or nearby. The Sharp-shinned Hawk is an uncommon breeder in Illinois, so you're more likely to see the similarly plumaged Cooper's Hawk. A section of large oak trees along this road attracts insects in May, which in turn, attract migrants, including Orange-crowned, Cape May, Blackburnian, Bay-breasted, Chestnut-sided, and Magnolia Warblers.

When you return to your car, drive 1 mile south on Water Plant Road until the road dead-ends, where you'll find a small place to park. One trailhead leads south and another goes west. Both offer excellent woodland birding especially in late April and early May. Hooded Warblers seem to favor the southwest trail. You should also find Worm-eating Warblers, Wood Thrushes, Acadian Flycatchers, Great Crested Flycatchers, Red-eyed and Yellow-throated Vireos, Scarlet and Summer Tanagers, Yellow-billed Cuckoos, and five woodpecker species. If you're on a quest for the Hooded Warblers, check the steep ravines near fallen trees.

Drive back to the Y in the road. Travel north on County Road 670N up a steep hill around the curves to Hamburg Hill. At this spot you can watch migrating raptors on a breezy fall day. Birders find this one of the best places in the area to see migrating Golden Eagles. More commonly you'll see Bald Eagles, Red-tailed Hawks, and other buteos and accipiters. The dead snags sticking out of the old clearcuts both here and along the road up to and at Atwood Ridge sometimes attract migrating Olive-sided Flycatchers from mid-May through the first few days of June. Also at the top of Hamburg Hill you'll find a dirt trail going south into forest habitat that attracts breeding Hooded and Cerulean Warblers.

To bird the more sheltered confines of the nearby Dutch Creek Camp and forested ravine, return to the road just west of the water treatment plant buildings and proceed south into the Dutch Creek Camp. If the gate is locked, park your car in a small pull-in, then bird by walking. The buildings in the clearing (surrounded by steep, rocky, forested hillsides) were built by the Youth Conservation Corps in the 1950s, and the area is now part of the Shawnee National Forest. Between 1989 and 1996, the Illinois Natural History Survey intensively studied Dutch Creek Camp for breeding birds.

Louisiana Waterthrushes, Yellow-throated Warblers, and Northern Parulas have bred along the creek and right around the buildings. Other breeding species include Cedar Waxwings, Ruby-throated Hummingbirds, Blue-gray Gnatcatchers, White-eyed Vireos, and Summer Tanagers. In the evening, Barred, Great Horned, and Eastern Screech-Owls call from the nearby woods, along with several Whip-poor-wills.

You'll note a steep hill north of the buildings. It's a tough climb, but you may find breeding Pine Warblers in an old pine plantation near the top of the hill. Look for the Black-and-white Warbler, a very rare Illinois breeder.

You'll find an old road/trail going east from the buildings into the surrounding forest. During breeding season search for Kentucky Warblers singing from the fern-covered areas along the creek running parallel to the trail as well as several pairs of Worm-eating Warblers on the steep ravines running up the hillside to the east. Other common or otherwise regular nesting species that you might see if you continue walking the trail include breeding Broad-winged and Cooper's Hawks, Pileated and Hairy Woodpeckers, Acadian Flycatchers, Carolina Wrens, Wood Thrushes, Red-eyed and Yellow-throated Vireos, Ovenbirds, Yellow-breasted Chats, and Scarlet Tanagers.

Eventually the trail veers away from the creek and past a fairly large clearing. You may want to explore this exceptional area even more, as the trails wind around through the forest for miles. Bring a compass, and be prepared for profuse mosquitos and poison ivy, as well as timber rattlesnakes and copperheads. When you reach open areas, look to the sky for raptors and other species, including Bald Eagles, Mississippi Kites, Black and Turkey Vultures, and Fish Crows. Also look for wintering Golden Eagles.

One more road worth exploring is Berryville Road, which meets with the west end of the town of Jonesboro on IL 146. Search this road for Belted Kingfishers, Northern Mockingbirds, Loggerhead Shrikes, Eastern Kingbirds, Orchard Orioles, and Eastern Bluebirds, which perch on the many utility lines and fences along the way, plus a possible Blue Grosbeak.

General information: Atwood Ridge attracts turkey hunters (as well as mushroom and ginseng hunters) in spring. The roads can be soft and full of ruts, and conditions continually worsen with rain, so be prepared.

ADDITIONAL HELP

DeLorme IA&G grid: 93.
Contact: Illinois Department of Natural Resources, Springfield, for information on hunting seasons and Shawnee National Forest, Jonesboro Ranger District for information on other hiking trails within the Shawnee National Forest.
Nearest gas, food, and lodging: Anna and Marion.

77 Trail of Tears State Forest

Habitats: Upland forested ravines, pine plantations, old field and successional areas, agricultural fields, and open park-like areas.
Key birds: Migrating passerines and breeding birds, including Mississippi Kite, Broad-winged, Cooper's, and Sharp-shinned Hawks, Wild Turkey, three owl species, Whip-poor-will, Chuck-will's widow, Pileated Woodpecker, Carolina and Sedge Wrens, Acadian Flycatcher, Fish Crow, 15 species of breeding warblers, including Blue-winged, Northern Parula, Yellow-throated, Pine, Prairie, Cerulean, Black-and-white, Worm-eating, Kentucky, Hooded, Louisiana Waterthrushes and Yellow-breasted Chat, Scarlet and Summer Tanager, Baltimore and Orchard Orioles, Blue Grosbeak, and Dickcissel.
Best times to bird: Year-round but especially in spring for migrant passerines and summer for uncommon-to-rare breeding species.

77 Trail of Tears State Forest

Directions: From Interstate 57, exit westbound at Anna/Vienna (Exit 30) and proceed west on Illinois Highway 146 through the towns of Anna and Jonesboro about 10 miles to the intersection of IL 146/127. Drive north for 1 mile on IL 127 to a blacktop road leading west. Drive west 3 miles to the main entrance, which leads you to the forest headquarters.

Birding: The 5,000-acre state-owned Trail of Tears State Forest (as well as the adjoining Bald Knob Wilderness Area) form one of the state's larger forested regions, and because of this, many uncommon-to-rare forest-interior breeding species reside here, including 15 species of warblers.

You'll encounter winding roads, some of them are not well kept. For easier maneuvering, bring a *DeLorme Illinois Atlas & Gazetteer* and a compass. The Trail of Tears State Forest has only one major blacktop road, which is called State Forest Road. A few side trips are mentioned, depending on your time or what you want to see. The important thing is to keep your bearings on how to return to the major blacktop road.

Begin birding by proceeding west from the towns of Anna and Jonesboro along IL 146/127. Where IL 127 splits north, continue west along IL 146 for a little over a mile where you will see a small roadside rest area and historic marker. Less than half a mile farther, you will see a dirt road angling north. Drive this road north for 3 miles, birding along the way. Be careful to remain off private property. The varied habitat along this rural road affords you the chance to see migrant flycatchers, wrens, warblers, and vireos in spring, plus possible Orchard Orioles and Blue Grosbeaks during the breeding season. At dusk in spring listen for Great Horned and Barred Owls and Eastern Screech-Owls as well as numerous Whip-poor-wills and occasionally, American Woodcocks (March and April).

The road ends at a T intersection with Clear Creek Ditch Levee Road. Turn north, being alert for birds in the open fields west of the levee. Some years Sedge Wrens and Dickcissels breed in the alfalfa and wheat fields. Check the wet areas in spring, fall, and winter for flocks of Horned Larks, which may contain some Lapland Longspurs and occasionally a Snow Bunting or two.

Proceed 1 mile to where the public portion of this levee road ends at a T intersection at the blacktop road. Turn east at the T intersection and drive 1.5 miles to the main entrance. Turn south onto Fire Tower Road, crossing over a rock-bottom stream and drive into the campground. Park and search this area for migrants as well as breeding Acadian Flycatchers, Wood Thrushes, Ruby-throated Hummingbirds, Carolina Wrens, Blue-gray Gnatcatchers, and White-eyed Vireos and sometimes a Hooded Warbler on the west hillside. Northern Parulas and Yellow-throated Warblers and Louisiana Waterthrushes should be easy to find along the creeks cutting through the campground and at the forest entrance.

Continue driving on Fire Tower Road, as it becomes a one-way dirt road that goes east through the forest. You'll drive up a steep ridge as you begin the loop. Park at any of the pull-outs where old logging access roads form trails into the forest. Most of the forested sections on the north side of the road are part of a state nature preserve, while the forested areas on the south contain a mixture of old second-growth and varying age selectively logged areas, providing a variety of forest types. If you spend much time hiking down into the forested slopes and stream-lined ravine bottoms you should encounter such relatively common nesting species as Cooper's and Broad-winged Hawks, Barred Owls, Whip-poor-wills, Wild Turkeys, Pileated Woodpeckers, and Hooded Warblers as well as Acadian Flycatchers, Wood Thrushes, Red-eyed and Yellow-throated Vireos, Carolina Wrens, Blue-gray Gnatcatchers, Worm-eating and Kentucky Warblers, and Scarlet and Summer Tanagers.

Trails 8 and 10, which join each other, are especially good for Hooded Warblers, which prefer the open areas in the forest created by the selective logging practiced here a few years ago. WARNING! Because of this logging and the abundance of deadfall and associated dense groundcover in these areas, this forest has a healthy population of poison ivy as well as equally healthy populations of copperheads and timber rattlesnakes.

You might also find a few breeding Pine and Yellow-throated Warblers in the scattered pines planted along the road and along a couple of the trails.

After exploring this part of the forest, it still may be worth your time to continue on the main blacktop loop and cross over to the north part of Trail of Tears State Forest. Here some of the ridgetops contain broad, flattened areas that provide nesting areas for Ovenbirds. In addition, you may find Cerulean Warblers, and possibly a breeding Black-and-white Warbler, an extremely rare occurrence in Illinois.

As this road comes downhill into a fairly large pine plantation with a dense understory of honeysuckle, you should encounter White-eyed Vireos, Northern Parulas, Yellow-throated and Pine Warblers, as well as Eastern Towhees. As the road circles back out to the main blacktop, look to the sky for soaring vultures, Cooper's and Broad-winged Hawks, and the Mississippi Kite, which has bred in the area for several years. Fish Crows also fly over daily as they traverse between breeding and foraging sites nearby. In winter the large pines around the forest headquarters buildings and all along the north side of the main blacktop attract roosting accipiters, sapsuckers, Red-breasted Nuthatches, and the occasional winter finch or Pine Warbler.

For a quick side trip, take the main blacktop east to IL 127 and turn north. Although this highway can sometimes be fairly busy, check the old fields with scattered small cedar trees for small numbers of breeding Prairie and Blue-winged Warblers and Yellow-breasted Chats. After dark in spring or summer, this stretch might produce numerous Whip-poor-wills as well as smaller numbers of Chuck-will's-widows and American Woodcocks. Listen, too, for Barred and Great Horned Owls and Eastern Screech-Owls.

General information: Trail of Tears State Forest includes a large upland forest containing oaks, hickories, beech, and tulip trees, as well as more than 620 species of other trees, flowering plants, and ferns.

This area, an east extension of the Ozark Hills region, is known not only for a wealth of avian diversity but also a large and interesting array of other wildlife, including skinks, salamanders, eastern pipistrelles, red bats, gray foxes, and bobcats.

This region has a rich historical background. One of the famous Lincoln-Douglas presidential debates occurred here. The forest's name was derived from the infamous march of the members of the Cherokee, Creek, and Chickasaw nations through this area during a bitter winter when thousands lost their lives.

Within this area is a state-dedicated nature preserve, the 222-acre Ozark Hills Nature Preserve. Trail of Tears State Forest also contains one of Illinois' two plant propagation centers, the Union State Nursery, occupying 120 acres within the forest.

Birders highly recommend you stop at the forest headquarters first to obtain maps. A compass is mandatory if you plan to go off the beaten path. The forest, which is selectively logged, attracts rattlesnakes and copperheads. Be extremely careful.

ADDITIONAL HELP

DeLorme IA&G grid: 92 and 93.
Contact: Trail of Tears State Forest.
Nearest gas, food, and lodging: Fast food and gas in Anna and Jonesboro but limited lodging; limited camping in nearby Pine Hills; campground and more lodging and other facilities available in the town of Carbondale about 30 miles north.

78 Pine Hills–LaRue Ecological Area

Habitats: Upland forested ravines, planted and native remnant pine stands, bottomland fields and sloughs, open swamp, agricultural fields, and levee roads associated with the Big Muddy and Mississippi Rivers.
Key birds: Migrating herons, egrets, shorebirds, and passerines; breeding birds, including Mississippi Kite, Red-shouldered, Broad-winged, and Cooper's Hawks, Black Vulture, Wild Turkey, Least Bittern, Barred Owl, Whip-poor-will, Chuck-will's widow, Pileated Woodpecker, Carolina Wren, Acadian Flycatcher, Fish Crow, 15 species of warblers, including Blue-winged, Northern Parula, Prothonotary, Yellow-throated, Pine, Cerulean, Worm-eating, Kentucky, Hooded, Louisiana Waterthrush, and Yellow-breasted Chat, Scarlet and Summer Tanagers, Orchard and Baltimore Orioles, and Blue Grosbeak.
Best times to bird: Year-round but especially in spring for migrant passerines and shorebirds, summer for uncommon-to-rare breeding species and late summer and fall for wandering herons and shorebirds.

Directions: From Interstate 57, exit westbound at Anna/Vienna and proceed west on Illinois Highway 146 through the towns of Anna and Jonesboro about 15 miles to the town of Ware at the intersections of IL 146/3. Travel north on IL 3 for about 4 miles to the south edge of the town of Wolf Lake. Watch for the sign for Pine Hills–LaRue Ecological Area and turn east onto the blacktop road about a mile to the entrance. To reach the nearby Trail of Tears State Forest (Site 77), continue east on the same blacktop another 4 miles to the main headquarters and entrance area.

Pine Hills. STEVEN D. BAILEY PHOTO

78 Pine Hills–LaRue Ecological Area
79 Oakwood Bottoms and the Big Muddy River Levee

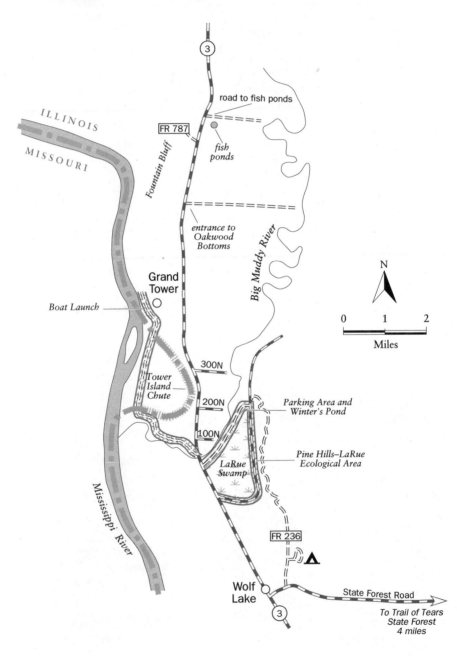

ILLINOIS

MISSOURI

road to fish ponds

FR 787

Fountain Bluff

fish
ponds

Big Muddy River

entrance to
Oakwood
Bottoms

N

0   1   2

Miles

Grand
Tower

Boat Launch

300N

Tower
Island
Chute

200N

100N

Parking Area and
Winter's Pond

Pine Hills–LaRue
Ecological Area

LaRue
Swamp

Mississippi River

FR 236

Wolf
Lake

3

State Forest Road

To Trail of Tears
State Forest
4 miles

Birding: The Pine Hills–La Rue Ecological Area contains some of the state's most pristine forest regions, including the few remaining native stands of shortleaf pines. In the upland forested ravines of this 4,200-acres site, you can easily add Kentucky and Worm-eating Warblers and Louisiana Waterthrushes without even venturing off the main park road. The same can be said for Northern Parula, Yellow-throated, and Prothonotary Warblers in the swamp forest. Including the nearby flooded fields, the number of bird species recorded at these areas approaches 260.

To begin your tour, start at the main entrance to the ecological area. Check the campgrounds for breeding (as well as numerous migrant) species, including Acadian Flycatchers, Wood Thrushes, Carolina Wrens, and Blue-gray Gnatcatchers as well as Northern Parulas, Yellow-throated Warblers, and Louisiana Waterthrushes. Ruby-throated Hummingbirds and Eastern Wood-Pewees place their nests right over the road through the campground. Look for small lichen-covered "knots" on horizontal branches for the nests. Hummingbird nests are the size of a half dollar; pewee nests are larger.

Continue north through large trees and lush vegetation. Acadian Flycatchers build their pendulous nests in trees right over the road. Summer and Scarlet Tanagers breed higher in the trees, where they are more difficult to find. Because of this high-quality habitat, many uncommon-to-rare species of forest interior nesting species can be found here. The breeding species list for Pine Hills includes Cooper's and Broad-winged Hawks, Barred Owls, Whip-poor-wills, Wild Turkeys, Pileated Woodpeckers, Acadian Flycatchers, Wood Thrushes, Red-eyed and Yellow-throated Vireos, Carolina Wrens, Blue-gray Gnatcatchers, Worm-eating and Kentucky Warblers, and Scarlet and Summer Tanagers.

As the road winds upward, you should hear the flat, Chipping Sparrow–like trills of the Worm-eating Warbler, which nests on steep-sided ravines. Also, as the road plateaus along the ridgetop bluffs, you'll enjoy spectacular views of the LaRue wetlands emanating into the Mississippi River floodplain from the base of the bluffs. Watch for soaring Turkey and Black Vultures.

The pull-outs and associated open shrubby areas near the parking areas along this section of the road can be quite good for migrant warblers and other passerines, especially in spring. You may notice a few scraggly stunted pines in some of the scenic overlook areas; these are some of the remnant pockets of native short-leaf pines.

For a different set of species, continue along the main road through Pine Hills as it winds its way back downhill to the base of the bluffs. Where the road comes to a T intersection, turn south and go a short distance to a small parking and picnic area off the west side of the road and just south of the Big Muddy levee road. The small pond and open swamp habitat attract migrant and breeding water birds, including several herons, Pied-billed Grebes, Wood Ducks, Hooded Mergansers, Belted Kingfishers, American Coots, Tree Swallows, Common Moorhens, and Red-headed Woodpeckers. You could spend most of the morning walking the road south along the base of the bluffs, or if you are rushed for time, simply drive slowly with your windows down, stopping and investigating promising areas as you go.

CAUTION! This stretch of road attracts large numbers of venomous snakes, including copperheads, timber rattlesnakes, and water moccasins that migrate twice annually out of the protective bluffs rising abruptly from the road. This road is closed for several weeks in early spring, typically sometime between March and early April, to protect the snakes as well as visitors.

The bottomland swamp forest on your right (west) and forested uplands going up the bluff on your left (east) can be swarming with migrants in spring and alive with nesting Northern Parula, Yellow-throated, and Prothonotary Warblers in summer.

General information: The Pine Hills–LaRue Ecological Area, an east extension of the Ozark Hills region of southern Illinois, contains large stands of immense oaks, hickories, beeches and tulip trees, with a dense understory of dogwoods, paw paws, spicebushes and such rare botanical treasures as azaleas, red buckeyes, and numerous ferns and wildflowers, growing in areas of great topographic relief. The region is equally well known by herpetologists for its amazing array of snakes (including the rare mud snake), lizards, salamanders (including the rare cave salamander), and other reptiles and amphibians. Some rare fish, including the pirate perch and the spring cave fish swim in the LaRue Swamp. The steep bluffs, with their majestic vistas of the LaRue Swamp and Mississippi and Big Muddy River floodplains stretching off toward Missouri, harbor one of the few populations of the state-listed endangered eastern wood rat. You may even see a bobcat within the forest. The state has dedicated 140 acres of LaRue Swamp as an Illinois State Nature Preserve.

ADDITIONAL HELP

DeLorme IA&G grid: 93.
Contact: Shawnee National Forest.
Nearest gas, food, and lodging: Fast food and gas in Anna and Jonesboro but limited lodging; a limited number of campsites are available at the Pine Hills campground but more lodging and other facilities are available in the town of Carbondale about 30 miles north.

79 Oakwood Bottoms and the Big Muddy River Levee

See map on page 298

Habitats: Forested wetlands, deciduous forests, grasslands, emergent and scrub/shrub wetlands.
Key birds: American Bittern, Yellow-crowned Night-Heron, Least Tern, Black-necked Stilt, King Rail, Fish Crow, Mississippi Kite, Louisiana Waterthrush, and Prairie Warbler.
Best times to bird: Year-round.

Directions: Oakwood Bottoms entrance is off Illinois Highway 3, about 15 miles southwest of Murphysboro in Jackson County and 3.4 miles north of Grand Tower. Turn east on the gravel entrance road to get to the birding sites. The entrance to the fish farms is east of IL 3; a gravel road travels immediately north of the ponds for easy viewing.

Birding: In southwest Jackson County, the Big Muddy River and Mississippi River floodplains meet, offering habitat for some of the state's rarest birds, including Least Terns and breeding Yellow-crowned Night-Herons near the Oakwood Bottoms.

You can bird the area by walking the Big Muddy River levee or driving a gravel road. Along the way you will see some of the more than 200 birds that have visited this region.

Birders who want to walk often park just east of the old silo, which is near a locked gate on the south side of the entrance road to Oakwood Bottoms, east of the railroad tracks. Park off the road to allow U.S. Forest Service employees access. Wear boots because the levee roads can be muddy. Walk the levee south for about a mile past the first set of levees going east and west to the second set that do the same. The levees all loop and head north toward where you parked, so it is difficult to get lost here. For those who wish to bird the area via automobile, go past the gate and drive east on the gravel access road, stopping along the way to look for birds.

As you walk or drive, search the emergent wetland areas for Yellow-crowned Night-Herons, Great Egrets, Green Herons, Little Blue Herons, and possibly Snowy Egrets in spring, summer, and during the postbreeding season. American Bitterns frequent the road ditches, remaining frozen even if you stop the car to look. Birders begin searching for the American Bittern and Yellow-crowned Night-Heron in April. The wetlands also attract King Rails, Soras, and Virginia Rails, especially at dawn in spring.

Some shorebirds as well as American Coots, Pied-billed Grebes, and an occasional diving duck utilize the emergent wetlands during migration. If water levels are deep, more divers are possible. During migration large numbers of dabbling ducks thrive in the flooded timber, including Wood Ducks, Hooded Mergansers, Mallards, and American Black Ducks.

Migrating songbirds also frequent the flooded timber area, and dozens of neotropical migrant species remain to breed including Bell's, White-eyed, Yellow-throated, and Red-eyed Vireos; Prairie, Yellow, Prothonotary, and Yellow-throated Warblers; Northern Parulas, American Redstarts, Louisiana Waterthrushes, and Common Yellowthroats.

While birding, look to the sky for Mississippi Kites and listen for the loud *"klee-yur"* shriek of the Red-shouldered Hawk. The hawks breed in the bottomland forests, and Mississippi Kites have possibly established some nests as well. This species spends a great deal of time foraging high in the sky for dragonflies and other insects.

Also inspect the fish ponds, 1 mile north of the bottoms on IL 3. Least Terns, which breed nearby, have foraged here occasionally, and Buff-breasted Sandpipers and other shorebirds forage along the pond levees in August and September.

You can search for Least Terns during late spring and summer along the Big Muddy River levee south of Oakwood Bottoms. Drive south on IL 3 for 5 miles, then drive east along the gravel levee road. Search the agricultural fields interspersed with emergent wetlands and small sloughs that usually contain standing water year-round. Shorebirds and ducks congregate in these wet fields, and loafing Least and Black Terns have been seen here as well. In addition, Black-necked Stilts, a very rare Illinois breeder, have been confirmed nesting in flooded agricultural fields.

Also check the levee road along the Mississippi River south of Grand Tower for Least Terns, shorebirds, and herons. The levee road between the north and south ends of Tower Island Chute is in Missouri, so any birds seen there can't be counted for Illinois. Be alert for Black-necked Stilts in the flooded agricultural fields along the gravel levee road south of the Tower Island Chute, a slough west of IL 3.

Another good birding spot near Oakwood Bottoms is Fountain Bluff, a large scenic upland forest that attracts migrating woodland species as well as breeding Pileated Woodpeckers and Worm-eating Warblers. Take Forest Road 787 west into the bluffs.

General information: The U.S. Forest Service owns and operates Oakwood Bottoms as a "greentree reservoir" for pin and other oaks and hickory trees. The service floods areas in fall to attract waterfowl, then drains some of the really wet areas the following spring. The bottoms attract turkey hunters in spring and waterfowl hunters in fall and winter, so call ahead to check times and dates if you plan to bird during these times. Summer can be hot and buggy, plus you might encounter a cottonmouth, so be careful and dress appropriately.

ADDITIONAL HELP

DeLorme IA&G grid: 88.
Contact: U.S. Forest Service in Murphysboro.
Nearest gas, food, and lodging: Murphysboro or Carbondale.

80 Mermet Lake

Habitats: Agricultural fields, grasslands, marshes and seasonal wetlands, bottomland hardwood forests and upland forests, and lake.
Key birds: Migrating waterfowl; breeding Double-crested Cormorant, Least Bittern, American Bittern, King Rail, Common Moorhen, Purple Gallinule, Black Vulture, Fish Crow, Wild Turkey, Yellow-throated and Prothonotary Warblers, and Blue Grosbeak.
Best times to bird: Spring migration for passerines; mid- to late summer for breeding Purple Gallinule; migrating waterfowl in fall.

80 Mermet Lake

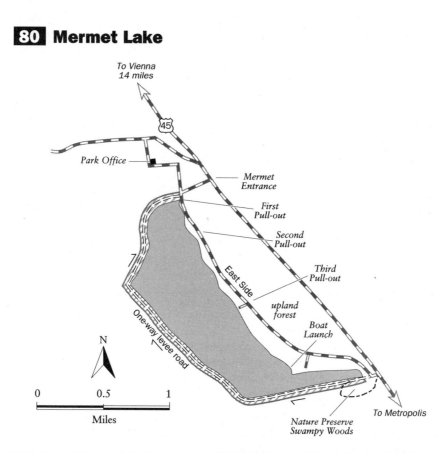

Directions: Mermet Lake is just west of U.S. Highway 45, 10 miles south of Vienna and 15 miles north of Metropolis. Interstate 24 gets you quickly to both towns from other locations in Illinois. Follow the sign off US 45, cross the railroad tracks, and go left at the first gravel road, which begins the one-way tour around Mermet Lake.

Birding: Birders have recorded 200 species at Mermet Lake in extreme southern Illinois. These include breeding Least Bitterns and Common Moorhens, both difficult to detect during any season in Illinois. Neotropical migrants arrive here sooner than most places in southern Illinois, and you may encounter Yellow-throated and Prothonotary Warblers the first week of April in most years.

A one-way 7-mile gravel road loop traverses the lake where birders can park cars along the road. Follow the gravel road south and park at the first gravel pull-out on your right. This is the spot, in spring, for Least Bitterns, American Bitterns, King Rails, and often times Soras, Virginia Rails, and Common Moorhens. Your best chance to find these species is right here. Arrive at dawn or dusk to hear them call.

At the next gravel pull-out on the right is where two pairs of Purple Gallinules were discovered with young in 1998. This is the northernmost breeding site for this bird in the United States, so if you want to add Purple Gallinule to your Illinois list, this is the place to come.

As you continue down the gravel drive 1 mile past the second pull-out, you'll enter an area with upland forest on both sides of the road. This spot, populated with oaks and hickories, attracts spring and fall warblers and vireos that enjoy the confines of the treetops, searching for insects. Some of the later spring warblers can be found, including Bay-breasted, Blackburnian, Magnolia, and Chestnut-sided. As you continue keep your eyes open for Wild Turkeys foraging in the agricultural fields on the east side of the road.

Red-shouldered Hawks are common in the woods around Mermet, often heard before seen. Blue Grosbeaks, Indigo Buntings, and American Goldfinches often forage in the dandelions along the road edges during cool periods of spring when other available food sources seem to be scarce.

As you reach the southernmost point of the lake, about 2.5 miles away from where you started, you may see hundreds of turtles basking in the sun on the logs. At the southwest corner of the drive is a small parking area with a trail that leads into the swampy woods.

If the spring weather cooperates and the trail is not flooded, you can enjoy a productive jaunt through the bottomland hardwood forest searching for species such as Prothonotary Warblers in spring and summer. Be alert for cottonmouth snakes, which frequent this area and can be alarmed into striking if you're not careful.

The west side of the lake has more pull-outs; most are utilized by fishermen but birders can use them, too. Many walk-in hunting areas exist to the west of the main road; however, wet spring weather generally makes these areas impossible without hip boots. Some lingering waterfowl and possibly some shorebirds may be encountered in these areas, but other birding areas are more accessible.

You should also look for Ospreys, which are usually seen perched atop a dead tree with a recently snagged prize out of the lake below. Ospreys have bred along the Ohio River, less than 60 miles away, and sometimes stop at Mermet in late summer and early fall after breeding. Spotted Sandpipers frequent this area in late spring and some breed here.

Also, look for Black Vultures and Mississippi Kites soaring on summer days. The largest colony of breeding Black Vultures in Illinois is just north of Mermet in Johnson County. The birds disperse daily, riding the thermals. The kites breed along the Mississippi River in southern Illinois, and are fairly easy to find at Mermet Lake in early to midsummer.

General information: Mermet Lake features excellent fishing; several large tournaments are hosted. You'll find the area heavily populated with boats during these times. Also, waterfowl hunting is allowed from early October through January and turkey hunting begins in early April, lasting for several weeks. Call first if you're planning to bird during these times to get information on closed areas and hunting dates.

The first of the spring season's migrating warblers, including the Magnolia pass through the Lake Mermet area. STEVEN D. BAILEY PHOTO

ADDITIONAL HELP

DeLorme IA&G grid: 94.

Contact: The Illinois Department of Natural Resources in Springfield for more information on hunting seasons and access at Mermet Lake.

Nearest gas, food, and lodging: Metropolis and Vienna.

7. *Illinois' Specialty Birds*

Following are 54 specialty birds in Illinois; many rare or that particularly interest birders both in and out of the state. Included is the best season in which to search for these birds plus some of the key sites mentioned in this book where they can be found. "Chances" refers to your ability to find the bird in proper habitat during the appropriate season.

Common Loon
Comments: Once bred in Illinois, now migrates through in spring and more commonly in fall, where dozens to hundreds may be seen on one lake.
Chances: Good to very good.
Key sites: 15, Gillson Park and Evanston Landfill. 54, Lake Springfield and Washington Park. 64, Carlyle Lake and Eldon Hazlet State Park. 69, Crab Orchard National Wildlife Refuge.

Red-throated Loon
Comments: A rare migrant seen more often in fall than in spring on lakes and large rivers.
Chances: Good.
Key sites: 15, Gillson Park and Evanston Landfill. 53, Clinton Lake. 54, Lake Springfield and Washington Park.

American White Pelican
Comments: Migrant whose numbers have increased in the past decade in Illinois. Much more common in western part of the state and along the Illinois and Mississippi Rivers. Migrating flocks have numbered in the 100s to the 1,000s in the past eight years.
Chances: Good to very good.
Key sites: 39, Mississippi River Corridor or 58, Lake Chautauqua National Wildlife Refuge. 59, Meredosia National Wildlife Refuge. 63, Pere Marquette State Park and Mark Twain National Wildlife Refuge–Brussels District. 64, Carlyle Lake and Eldon Hazlet State Park.

American Bittern
Comments: Common migrant, endangered as a breeder in the state. Not easily observed. Best chances at dawn or dusk in high-quality marshes during breeding season or spring migration.
Chances: Fair to good.
Key sites: 30, Goose Lake Prairie and Heidecke Lake. 56, Lake Shelbyville and Arcola Marsh. 50, Kennekuk County Park. 60, Beardstown Marsh and the Sanganois Conservation Area. 68, Sauget Marsh.

Least Bittern
Comments: Uncommon migrant, threatened as breeder in the state. Not easily observed. Best chances at dawn or dusk in high-quality marshes during breeding season or spring migration.
Chances: Fair to good.
Key sites: 50, Kennekuk County Park. 56, Lake Shelbyville and Arcola Marsh. 60, Beardstown Marsh and the Sanganois Conservation Area. 80, Mermet Lake.

Black-crowned Night-Heron
Comments: Fairly common migrant. Colonial breeder with other herons and egrets, endangered in the state.
Chances: Very good.
Key sites: 11, Baker's Lake and Ron Beese Park. 28, Lake Calumet and Vicinity. 29, Lake Renwick Heron Rookery Nature Preserve and Copley Nature Park.

Yellow-crowned Night-Heron
Comments: Uncommon migrant, endangered breeder. Numbers declining especially in north. Usually breeds in solitude in trees near good feeding habitats where crayfish thrive.
Chances: Good.
Key sites: 73, Cache River and Heron Pond State Natural Areas. 74, Horseshoe Lake Conservation Area. 79, Oakwood Bottoms and the Big Muddy River Levee.

Snowy Egret

Comments: Rare migrant, postbreeding wanderer, state-endangered, colonial breeder with other herons and egrets in southwestern part of state. Very rare elsewhere. Runs through water to catch prey.
Chances: Good.
Key sites: 68, Sauget Marsh. 71, Union County Conservation Area and Associated Levees. 74, Horseshoe Lake Conservation Area.

Black Vulture

Comments: Uncommon permanent resident in extreme southern Illinois. Found in swampy woodlands and soaring over bluffs.
Chances: Good to very good.
Key sites: 72, Cypress Creek National Wildlife Refuge. 73, Cache River and Heron Pond State Natural Areas.

Snow Goose

Comments: Hundreds to thousands stop at national wildlife refuge lakes or cornfields during migration. Flocks contain white-phase, blue-phase, and some mixed white and blue birds. Largest numbers found in many of the southern Illinois waterfowl refuges. In late November 1981, birders reported 10,000 Snow Geese at Mark Twain National Wildlife Refuge.
Chances: Excellent in November through early winter.
Key sites: 58, Lake Chautauqua National Wildlife Refuge. 63, Pere Marquette State Park and Mark Twain National Wildlife Refuge–Brussels District. 71, Union County Conservation Area and Associated Levees. 74, Horseshoe Lake Conservation Area.

Ross's Goose

Comments: Rare migrant and winter resident, numbers increasing, mostly seen in central and southern Illinois. Singles or small numbers found among flocks of Snow Geese.
Chances: Good.
Key sites: 19, Fermilab National Accelerator Laboratory. 71, Union County Conservation Area and Associated Levees. 74, Horseshoe Lake Conservation Area.

Mississippi Kite

Comments: Southern Illinois breeding specialty; very rare elsewhere in state. Population declined in the 1900s, now endangered in the state. Breeds in woods near water and open areas for foraging.
Chances: Good.
Key sites: 71, Union County Conservation Area and Associated Levees. 80, Mermet Lake.

Bald Eagle

Comments: Fairly common migrant and winter resident, rare breeder, state-threatened. Migrating and breeding populations have increased since the 1980s. Illinois harbors the second largest population of wintering Bald Eagles in the nation. Winters near locks and dams along Illinois and Mississippi Rivers.
Chances: Very good.
Key sites: 37, Mississippi Palisades State Park. 39, Mississippi River Corridor. 40, Starved Rock and Matthiessen State Parks. 58, Lake Chautauqua National Wildlife Refuge. 63, Pere Marquette State Park and Mark Twain National Wildlife Refuge–Brussels District. 71, Union County Conservation Area and Associated Levees. 74, Horseshoe Lake Conservation Area.

Red-shouldered Hawk

Comments: Fairly common migrant and winter resident; southern Illinois breeder. State threatened. Calls "klee-yur" from bottomland woods breeding grounds.
Chances: Good.
Key sites: 71, Union County Conservation Area and Associated Levees. 72, Cypress Creek National Wildlife Refuge. 74, Horseshoe Lake County Conservation Area. 79, Oakwood Bottoms and the Big Muddy River Levee.

Swainson's Hawk

Comments: Extremely rare migrant, state-endangered. A small population breeds in northern Illinois only. Documented in summer in Winnebago, Boone, Kane, and McHenry Counties. Found in savanna-like areas, with large open, grassy fields, interspersed with patches of woods.
Chances: Fair.
Key sites: 10, Crabtree Nature Center, Palatine Marsh, and Vicinity.

Gray Partridge

Comments: Introduced, uncommon permanent resident in northern Illinois, though numbers may be declining. Prefers cultivated fields and hedgerows in Lee, Ogle, and DeKalb Counties.
Chances: Poor.
Key sites: 33, Shabbona Lake State Recreation Area and Forest Preserve. 43, Nachusa Grasslands and Franklin Creek State Natural Area.

Greater Prairie-Chicken

Comments: Endangered. Rare and local permanent resident in southern Illinois grasslands. Only a few populations remain; habitat protected, but still may not be enough to maintain this bird in the state. Birds introduced from other parts of the country to sustain gene pool.
Chances: Very good in late April and May during courtship.
Key sites: 66, Prairie Ridge State Natural Area and Newton Lake State Fish and Wildlife Area.

Wild Turkey

Comments: Extirpated from state, then reintroduced; now permanent resident. Populations increasing statewide, though somewhat more common in south and northwest.
Chances: Fair to good in south. Very good in northwest.
Key sites: 37, Mississippi Palisades State Park. 41, Castle Rock State Park and the George B. Fell Nature Preserve. 57, Sand Ridge State Forest. 63, Pere Marquette State Park and Mark Twain National Wildlife Refuge—Brussels District. 76, Atwood Ridge and Hamburg Hill.

Yellow Rail

Comments: One of the most sought-after species in the nation. Rare migrant in Illinois. Finding one requires combing many wet fields in spring and hayfields in fall. More common in spring. Early to mid-April is best time to look.
Chances: Fair to poor.
Key sites: 53, Clinton Lake.

Sandhill Crane

Comments: Uncommon migrant and rare summer resident in northern Illinois; rare migrant in rest of state. Bred fairly commonly statewide until end of 19th century. Last nest found in 1972, until 1979 when one was discovered in Lake County. Now approximately 20 pairs breed in northern part of state. Hundreds to thousands fly over northeastern Illinois and along lakefront from late February through end of March and again from September through October. State-threatened.
Chances: Very good during migration and breeding season.
Key sites: 7, Chain O' Lakes State Park.

American Golden-Plover

Comments: Common migrant. Flocks seen in agricultural fields (especially when wet), mudflats, and along Lake Michigan shoreline on way to tundra breeding grounds. Most numerous in spring on east side of state. Numbers peak in mid-April, sometimes in the thousands. Much less numerous in fall, when they prefer short grassy areas, including sod farms.
Chances: Very good.
Key sites: 32, Kankakee River State Park, Momence Wetlands and Sod Farms in fall. 50, Kennekuk County Park. 52, Moraine View State Park in spring.

Upland Sandpiper

Comments: State-endangered. Few remaining breeding populations left. Requires large grasslands in which to nest.
Chances: Fairly good.
Key sites: 31, Midewin National Tallgrass Prairie. 43, Nachusa Grasslands and Franklin Creek State Nature Area.

Buff-breasted Sandpiper

Comments: Uncommon fall migrant; very rarely found in spring. Feeds in short grassy areas and sod fields, sometimes golf courses. Usually wearing immature plumage when seen.
Chances: Good in fall only.
Key sites: 32, Kankakee River State Park, Momence Wetlands, and Sod Farms. 58, Lake Chautauqua National Wildlife Refuge. 67, Rend Lake.

Black-necked Stilt

Comments: Several pairs have bred in southern Illinois since the 1993 floods.
Chances: Good during breeding season in specific locations.
Key sites: 71, Union County Conservation Area and Associated Levees. 74, Horseshoe Lake Conservation Area. 79, Oakwood Bottoms and the Big Muddy River Levee.

Thayer's Gull

Comments: Occasional migrant and winter resident along the Mississippi River and Lake Michigan shoreline. Sometimes seen with huge flocks of common gulls at landfill sites. Most arrive in November. Separation among Thayer's, Iceland, and Glaucous Gulls can be difficult; study identification clues before going on a winter gull trip.
Chances: Good.
Key sites: 1, Montrose Harbor, the Magic Hedge, the Lincoln Park Bird Sanctuary, and Belmont Harbor. 5, Waukegan Beach and Bowen Park. 28, Lake Calumet and Vicinity. 39, Mississippi River Corridor.

Iceland Gull

Comments: Rare migrant and winter resident along the Mississippi River and Lake Michigan shoreline. Separation among Thayer's, Iceland, and Glaucous Gulls can be difficult; study identification clues before going on a winter gull trip.
Chances: Fair.
Key sites: 1, Montrose Harbor, the Magic Hedge, the Lincoln Park Bird Sanctuary, and Belmont Harbor. 5, Waukegan Beach and Bowen Park. 28, Lake Calumet and Vicinity. 39, Mississippi River Corridor.

Lesser Black-backed Gull

Comments: Rare migrant and winter resident along the Mississippi River and Lake Michigan shoreline. A European species that began being recorded in Illinois in the 1980s. Most commonly seen in Illinois from November through February; its numbers are increasing in North America.
Chances: Fair to good.
Key sites: 1, Montrose Harbor, the Magic Hedge, the Lincoln Park Bird Sanctuary, and Belmont Harbor. 5, Waukegan Beach and Bowen Park. 28, Lake Calumet and Vicinity. 39, Mississippi River Corridor. 53, Clinton Lake.

Glaucous Gull

Comments: Occasional migrant and winter resident along the Illinois and Mississippi Rivers and Lake Michigan shoreline, as well as large lakes. Separation among Thayer's, Iceland, and Glaucous Gulls can be difficult; study identification clues before going on a winter gull trip.
Chances: Good.
Key sites: 1, Montrose Harbor, the Magic Hedge, the Lincoln Park Bird Sanctuary, and Belmont Harbor. 5, Waukegan Beach and Bowen Park. 28, Lake Calumet and Vicinity. 39, Mississippi River Corridor.

Least Tern

Comments: State-endangered. Occasional migrant and local summer resident in southern Illinois, rare migrant and postbreeding wanderer elsewhere. Rests on sandbars and mudflats.
Chances: Fair during breeding season.
Key sites: 71, Union County Conservation Area and Associated Levees. 74, Horseshoe Lake Conservation Area. 79, Oakwood Bottoms and the Big Muddy River Levee.

Monk Parakeet

Comments: Local year-round resident in Chicagoland. Accepted on state checklist in 1999. Lives in large stick nests atop light poles.

Chances: Very good, especially during breeding season.

Key sites: 2, Jackson Park and the Paul O. Douglas Nature Sanctuary (Wooded Island).

Snowy Owl

Comments: Occasional winter resident, more common in north. Chooses open areas, including fields, lake edges, and airfields for hunting. Generally irrupts once every four or more years, but can usually be found every winter along the Chicago lakefront.

Chances: Good.

Key sites: 3, Downtown Chicago Birding/Walking Tour. 5, Waukegan Beach and Bowen Park.

Northern Saw-whet Owl

Comments: Uncommon migrant and winter resident. More common in the north. Difficult to find; requires quiet, thorough searching of favored habitats of pines, cedars, and vine tangles and by locating whitewash on tree trunks and for small pellets on the ground.

Chances: Fair.

Key sites: 17, Morton Arboretum. 50, Kennekuk County Park. 51, Forest Glen Preserve and the Harry "Babe" Woodyard State Natural Area.

Short-eared Owl

Comments: Uncommon migrant and winter resident; rare breeder. Quickly losing large field habitat. Often shares feeding areas with Northern Harriers, which hunt by day. Found by visiting wintering grounds near dusk.

Chances: Good.

Key sites: 8, Glacial Park and Vincinity. 31, Midewin National Tallgrass Prairie. 46, Banner Marsh and Rice Lake State Fish and Wildlife Areas. 66, Prairie Ridge State Natural Area and Newton Lake State Fish and Wildlife Area. 73, Cache River and Heron Pond State Natural Areas.

Long-eared Owl

Comments: Uncommon migrant and winter resident. Most numerous in northern Illinois. Difficult to find; requires quiet, thorough searching groves of conifers and by locating whitewash on tree trunks and for medium-sized pellets on the ground. Sizable breeding population once existed in Illinois, but probably no longer breeds here.

Chances: Fair.

Key sites: 27, the Bartel and Orland Grasslands. 50, Kennekuk County Park. 51, Forest Glen Preserve and the Harry "Babe" Woodyard State Natural Area.

Chuck-will's-widow

Comments: Uncommon migrant and breeder in southern Illinois, rare in the north. Arrives in southern Illinois sometime in April. Best found by sound rather than sight as it calls its name at dusk.

Chances: Good.

Key sites: 57, Sand Ridge State Forest. 72, Cypress Creek National Wildlife Refuge. 74, Horseshoe Lake Conservation Area.

Pileated Woodpecker

Comments: Uncommon permanent resident in large wooded areas. Often heard by loud flicker-like call before seen.

Chances: Good.

Key sites: 48, Middle Fork State Fish and Wildlife Area. 70, Giant City State Park. 73, Cache River and Heron Pond State Natural Areas. 75, Pomona–Cave Creek. 77, Trail of Tears State Forest.

Loggerhead Shrike

Comments: State-threatened. Common permanent resident in southern Illinois, breeds as far north as Will County, but more common in south. Numbers declining. Inhabits open country, perching on wires, fenceposts, and tops of small trees. Feeds by impaling prey on thorns.
Chances: Good.
Key sites: 31, Midewin National Tallgrass Prairie. 60, Beardstown Marsh and the Sanganois Conservation Area. 61, Siloam Springs State Park. 66, Prairie Ridge State Natural Area and Newton Lake State Fish and Wildlife Area. 71, Union County Conservation Area and Associated Levees. 73, Cache River and Heron Pond State Natural Areas.

Northern Shrike

Comments: Uncommon winter resident in northern Illinois and very rare elsewhere in winter. Numbers change yearly; sometimes seen hardly at all in winter; most often seen December through February. Occurs singly, using large territory for feeding. Perches on tops of small trees in open woodlands.
Chances: Fair.
Key sites: 4, Illinois Beach State Park. 19, Fermilab National Accelerator Laboratory.

Bell's Vireo

Comments: Uncommon migrant and breeder; more common in south and the west than the north and east. More often heard than seen. Difficult to detect since it remains in thick vegetation. Numbers declining. Populations fluctuate as habitat changes; breeds near open willow-lined streams and shrubby areas. Typically arrives in Illinois in May.
Chances: Good.
Key sites: 47, Iroquois County Conservation Area. 43, Nachusa Grasslands and Franklin Creek State Natural Area. 44, Green River Conservation Area. 65, Horseshoe Lake State Park.

Fish Crow

Comments: Uncommon migrant and summer resident along the Mississippi and Ohio Rivers in southern Illinois. Distinguished from American Crow in the field by its nasal *"uh-uh"* call. Typically arrives in late March, departing sometime in October.
Chances: Good.
Key sites: 71, Union County Conservation Area and Associated Levees. 74, Horseshoe Lake Conservation Area. 76, Atwood Ridge and Hamburg Hill. 79, Oakwood Bottoms and the Big Muddy River Levee. 80, Mermet Lake.

Yellow-throated Warbler

Comments: Common migrant and summer resident in southern Illinois, decreasing northward; local population in northwestern Illinois. Arrives in April; heard and seen throughout summer.
Chances: Very good.
Key sites: 34, Sugar River Forest Preserve and Alder Tract. 42, Lowden–Miller State Forest. 49, Kickapoo State Park. 51, Forest Glen Preserve and the Harry "Babe" Woodyard State Natural Area. 74, Horseshoe Lake Conservation Area. 75, Pomona–Cave Creek.

Cerulean Warbler

Comments: Fairly common migrant and summer resident, fewer numbers and more localized in north; numbers declining nationwide. Often found by its fast buzzy song atop trees, May through summer.
Chances: Good.
Key sites: 7, Chain O' Lakes State Park. 35, Pecatonica River Forest Preserve. 36, Rock Cut State Park and Keiselburg Forest Preserve. 37, Mississippi Palisades State Park. 61, Siloam Springs State Park. 75, Pomona–Cave Creek.

Prothonotary Warbler

Comments: Common migrant and summer resident in southern Illinois, decreasing northward; small local breeding population in McHenry County. One of the most numerous breeding warblers in southern Illinois. Nests in tree cavities and manmade boxes along swamp and riverine backwaters. Rather abundant April through summer.

Chances: Very good.

Key sites: 9, Moraine Hills State Park. 63, Pere Marquette State Park and Mark Twain National Wildlife Refuge—Brussels District. 72, Cypress Creek National Wildlife Refuge. 74, Horseshoe Lake Conservation Area. 78, Pine Hills–LaRue Ecological Area. 79, Oakwood Bottoms and the Big Muddy River Levee. 80, Mermet Lake.

Worm-eating Warbler

Comments: Common breeder in southern Illinois; migrant and breeder elsewhere. Often found by song April through summer. Prefers nesting on wooded slopes.

Chances: Good.

Key sites: 61, Siloam Springs State Park. 76, Atwood Ridge and Hamburg Hill. 77, Trail of Tears State Forest. 78, Pine Hills–LaRue Ecological Area.

Louisiana Waterthrush

Comments: Common migrant and breeder in southern Illinois, rare in northern Illinois.

Chances: Very good.

Key sites: 40, Starved Rock and Matthiessen State Parks. 51, Forest Glen Preserve and the Harry "Babe" Woodyard State Natural Area. 61, Siloam Springs State Park. 75, Pomona–Cave Creek. 78, Pine Hills–LaRue Ecological Area.

Kentucky Warbler

Comments: Common breeder in southern Illinois; migrant and breeder elsewhere. Often found by song April through summer.

Chances: Good.

Key sites: 76, Atwood Ridge and Hamburg Hill. 77, Trail of Tears State Forest. 78, Pine Hills–LaRue Ecological Area.

Connecticut Warbler

Comments: Uncommon spring migrant; very rare fall migrant; most easily found along Chicago lakefront on way to northern United States breeding grounds. One of the most coveted migrating warblers in Illinois. Most often found singing in middle May through early June in wet, shrubby habitats where it skulks and is easy to miss. Requires some time in the field.

Chances: Good, especially along lakefront at appropriate time.

Key sites: 1, Montrose Harbor, the Magic Hedge, the Lincoln Park Bird Sanctuary, and Belmont Harbor. 2, Jackson Park and the Paul O. Douglas Nature Sanctuary (Wooded Island). 12, Ryerson Conservation Area and the Des Plaines River Corridor. 37, Mississippi Palisades State Park.

Hooded Warbler

Comments: Uncommon migrant and summer resident in southern Illinois; decreasing northward. Often found by song beginning in April through summer.

Chances: Good.

Key sites: 76, Atwood Ridge and Hamburg Hill. 77, Trail of Tears State Forest. 78, Pine Hills–LaRue Ecological Area.

Lark Sparrow

Comments: Locally common summer resident in sandy or poor soil locations. Arrives in late April.

Chances: Good.

Key sites: 47, Iroquois County Conservation Area. 48, Middle Fork State Fish and Wildlife Area. 57, Sand Ridge State Forest.

Henslow's Sparrow

Comments: Local summer resident. State-endangered. Nests in medium-grass prairies.
Chances: Fairly good.
Key sites: 27, The Bartel and Orland Grasslands. 30, Goose Lake Prairie and Heidecke Lake. 31, Midewin National Tallgrass Prairie. 51, Forest Glen Preserve and the Harry "Babe" Woodyard State Natural Area. 72, Cypress Creek National Wildlife Refuge.

Smith's Longspur

Comments: Common spring migrant; very rare fall migrant. Prefers agricultural fields with abundant foxtail; also inhabits clover and alfalfa fields, airport fields, golf courses, and sod farms. Observers need to walk farm fields to find them. April best time to search.
Chances: Very good.
Key sites: 50, Kennekuk County Park. 52, Moraine View State Park. 53, Clinton Lake. 54, Lake Springfield and Washington Park. 56, Lake Shelbyville. 66, Prairie Ridge State Natural Area and Newton Lake State Fish and Wildlife Area.

Blue Grosbeak

Comments: Uncommon migrant and local breeder, decreasing northward; most numerous in sandy and poor soil areas in central Illinois. Average arrival date mid-May. Builds nests in shrubs and short trees.
Chances: Good.
Key sites: 57, Sand Ridge State Forest. 65, Horseshoe Lake State Park. 72, Cypress Creek National Wildlife Refuge. 77, Trail of Tears State Forest. 80, Mermet Lake.

Bobolink

Comments: Fairly common migrant; somewhat common summer resident in the north, decreasing southward. Arrives on breeding grounds in May.
Chances: Very good.
Key sites: 27, the Bartel and Orland Grasslands. 30, Goose Lake Prairie and Heidecke Lake. 31, Midewin National Tallgrass Prairie. 43, Nachusa Grasslands and Franklin Creek State Natural Area.

Yellow-headed Blackbird

Comments: Locally uncommon migrant and summer resident in northern Illinois; rare migrant elsewhere in state; very rare winter resident. Arrives in northern Illinois sometime in April. State-endangered.
Chances: Very good.
Key sites: 6, Wadsworth Savanna and Wetlands Demonstration Project. 8, Moraine Hills State Park. 28, Lake Calumet and Vicinity.

Eurasian Tree Sparrow

Comments: Introduced, common permanent resident in west-central Illinois. Common in Mississippi River bottoms and levees. Expanding range into Minnesota.
Chances: Good.
Key sites: 58, Lake Chautauqua National Wildlife Refuge. 59, Meredosia National Wildlife Refuge. 60, Beardstown Marsh and the Sanganois Conservation Area. 63, Pere Marquette State Park and Mark Twain National Wildlife Refuge—Brussels District. 65, Horseshoe Lake State Park.

8. Illinois' State Checklist and Seasonal Distribution Charts

Pigeonholing every species of bird that passes through or breeds in Illinois as being either a north or south species is difficult. Indeed, the state of Illinois stretches 378 miles from the northern tip to the southern border. However, although a north/south separation is somewhat arbitrary, it does have merit, especially regarding breeding and wintering ranges of many of the bird species seen. For the purposes of this distribution chart, the state is divided into a northern half and a southern half, except for just a few species. The dividing line runs at a southeastern angle from the northern edge of Hancock County to the southern third of Vermilion County.

The top distributional line, marked N, is for the northern part of Illinois; the bottom distributional line, marked S, is for the southern part of Illinois. Some species' distribution is similar statewide; you'll find only one distributional line for these.

Consider this distribution chart as a guideline, noting that abundance and time of occurrence vary within these divisions. Populations often increase or decrease from north to south or south to north depending upon the season. Also, some pockets of habitat exist north and south of the distributional lines for some of these species. Good habitat may attract or hold isolated populations of birds not normally seen within these distribution lines. For example, Starved Rock State Park, which is included in the north section, holds good breeding populations of typical southern species such as Acadian Flycatchers and several warbler species.

Note, too, that climate, including seasonal rainfall, wind direction, and temperatures, can affect the distribution, as well as habitat alteration here and throughout the world, wherever these birds migrate.

Most species in Illinois enter and traverse the state on a broad front from south to north in spring and vice versa in fall. But some spring migrants enter the state from the southwest or west only, and spread east or northeast, usually in decreasing numbers. Some examples include American White Pelicans, Western Meadowlarks, and Lark Sparrows. For a few of these species, distribution charts are included for the eastern and western half of the state, rather than north and south.

Sometimes the opposite is true. Species such as Sandhill Cranes, Gray-cheeked Thrushes, and Black-throated Blue Warblers enter the state from the southeast or east and so are much less common, if seen at all, in the western half of Illinois. Part of this is due to the prevailing winds at the season in which these birds migrate, but it is also due to long-established migratory paths of these species.

For other species such as several shorebirds, Smith's Longspurs, and Connecticut Warblers, the migration charts here show that some are more common in spring or fall. It's important to know these particular patterns if looking for a Baird's Sandpiper, for example, in Illinois. This species is more commonly seen and in much higher numbers during fall migration in Illinois than it is in spring.

Two distributional charts for Illinois formed a strong basis for the charts you see here. These charts are found in *Birds of the St. Louis Area: Where and When to Find Them* (1998, Webster Groves Nature Study Society) and *Chicago Area Birds* (1984, Chicago Review Press) by Steven Mlodinow. However, these charts reflect only small portions of the state within a time frame before 1997.

To create an up-to-date, one-of-a-kind bird distributional chart for the entire state, we also incorporated information from *Meadowlark* Volumes 1-8, *Illinois Birds & Birding*, Vols. 5-7, *The Birds of Illinois*, by H. David Bohlen (1989, Indiana University

Press), *Southern Illinois Birds*, by W. Douglas Robinson (1996. Southern Illinois University Press), the author's experience, and the experience of Steven D. Bailey, an Illinois Natural History Survey ornithologist. Bailey conducts statewide bird surveys, gathering distributional data used for the Illinois Critical Trends Assessment Project.

The checklist itself is published here with kind permission from the Illinois Ornithological Society and its standing committee, the Illinois Ornithological Records Committee. This checklist, published in 1999, reflects the American Ornithologists Union's Seventh edition to the Check-list of North American Birds.

KEY

Common to abundant ▰▰▰
Difficult to miss in proper habitat and season, usually in good numbers.

Fairly common ▬▬▬
Can usually be found most days in some numbers by most observers.

Uncommon ▨▨▨
Difficult to find or can be missed in proper habitat in a day by an experienced observer.

Rare to casual _____
Not seen more than a few times in any one season and sometimes may not be seen every season by an experienced observer.

Accidental—listed only
Species for which accepted records exist in no more than two of the past ten years.

Extirpated—listed only
Species formerly casual or regular in Illinois, but that have not been recorded in the wild in the state for at least 50 years.

Extinct—listed only
Species that have occurred in the state but no longer occur anywhere in the world.

ABBREVIATIONS

B	Species that currently breed in the state. Breeding evidence is greater than or equal to eight times in the past 10 years or 40 or more times in the past 50 years.
b	Species that have bred at least once in the past 50 years but no longer breed regularly.
(B)	Species that have formerly bred more or less regularly in the state, but have not been confirmed as breeding in the past 50 years.
(b)	Species that have been confirmed as breeding in the state but never regularly, and with no confirmed records of breeding in the past 50 years.
B(L)	Breeding populations are local, not widespread in region.
L	Migratory populations are local, not widespread in region
W or E	Species distribution tied to eastern half or western half of state.
I	Irruptive species; populations vary extremely from year to year depending on food supply.
*	The Black-capped Chickadee is a common permanent resident in northern and most of central Illinois; the Carolina Chickadee is a common permanent resident in southern Illinois and the eastern edge of central Illinois. The boundary counties between these two species are Madison, Bond, Fayette, Shelby, Moultrie, Champaign, Ford, and Kankakee.

315

Status and distribution

Bird Species		Region	Month of Occurrence J F M A M J J A S O N D
LOONS			
☐ Red-throated Loon *(Gavia stellata)*		Statewide	
☐ Pacific Loon *(Gavia pacifica)*			
☐ Common Loon *(Gavia immer)*	(b)	N	
		S	
☐ Yellow-billed Loon *(Gavia adamsii)* Accidental			
GREBES			
☐ Pied-billed Grebe *(Podilymbus podiceps)*(threatened)	B	N	
		S	
☐ Horned Grebe *(Podiceps auritus)*	(b)	N	
		S	
☐ Red-necked Grebe *(Podiceps grisegena)*		Statewide	
☐ Eared Grebe *(Podiceps nigricollis)*		Statewide	
☐ Western Grebe *(Aechmophorus occidentalis)*		Statewide	
☐ Clark's Grebe *(Aechmophorus clarkii)* Accidental			
BOOBIES			
☐ Northern Gannet *(Morus bassanus)* Accidental			
PELICANS			
☐ American White Pelican *(Pelecanus erythrorhynchos)*		W	
		E	
☐ Brown Pelican *(Pelecanus occidentalis)* Accidental			
CORMORANTS			
☐ Neotropic Cormorant *(Phalacrocorax brasilianus)*		Statewide	
☐ Double-crested Cormorant *(Phalacrocorax auritus)*	B	N	
		S	
DARTERS			
☐ Anhinga *(Anhinga anhinga)*		S	
FRIGATEBIRDS			
☐ Magnificent Frigatebird *(Fregata magnificens)* Accidental			
BITTERNS, HERONS *and* EGRETS			
☐ American Bittern *(Botaurus lentiginosus)* (endangered)	B	Statewide	
☐ Least Bittern *(Ixobrychus exilis)* (threatened)	B	Statewide	
☐ Great Blue Heron *(Ardea herodias)*	B	N	
		S	
☐ Great Egret *(Ardea alba)*	B	N	
		S	

See abbreviations on page 315

Bird Species	Region	Month of Occurrence J F M A M J J A S O N D
Snowy Egret *(Egretta thula)* (endangered)	B(L),L	N
		S
Little Blue Heron *(Egretta caerulea)* (endangered)	B(L),L	N
		S
Tricolored Heron *(Egretta tricolor)*	Statewide	
Reddish Egret *(Egretta rufescens)* Accidental		
Cattle Egret *(Bubulcus ibis)*	B(L)	N
		S
Green Heron *(Butorides virescens)*	B	N
		S
Black-crowned Night-Heron *(Nycticorax nycticorax)* B(L) (endangered)		N
		S
Yellow-crowned Night-Heron *(Nyctanassa violacea)* B(L) (endangered)		N
		S

IBISES *and* SPOONBILLS

White Ibis *(Eudocimus albus)*	S	
Glossy Ibis *(Plegadis falcinellus)*	Statewide	
White-faced Ibis *(Plegadis chihi)*	Statewide	

STORKS

Wood Stork *(Mycteria americana)* Accidental		

AMERICAN VULTURES

Black Vulture *(Coragyps atratus)*	B(L)	S
Turkey Vulture *(Cathartes aura)*	B	N
		S

WHISTLING-DUCKS, GEESE, SWANS, *and* DUCKS

Fulvous Whistling-Duck *(Dendrocygna bicolor)* Accidental		
Greater White-fronted Goose *(Anser albifrons)*	Statewide	
Snow Goose *(Chen caerulescens)*	b	N
		S
Ross's Goose *(Chen rossii)*		N
		S
Canada Goose *(Branta canadensis)*	B	N
		S
Brant *(Branta bernicla)*	Statewide	
Mute Swan *(Cygnus olor)* (introduced)	B(L)	Statewide
Trumpeter Swan *(Cygnus buccinator)* (reintroduced) (unestablished)	B	
Tundra Swan *(Cygnus columbianus)*	Statewide	

Common to abundant   Uncommon
Fairly common   Rare to casual

317

Bird Species	Region	Month of Occurrence J F M A M J J A S O N D
☐ Wood Duck *(Aix sponsa)*	B N	
	S	
☐ Gadwall *(Anas strepera)*	b N	
	S	
☐ Eurasian Wigeon *(Anas penelope)*	Statewide	
☐ American Wigeon *(Anas americana)*	(b) N	
	S	
☐ American Black Duck *(Anas rubripes)*	b N	
	S	
☐ Mallard *(Anas platyrhynchos)*	B	
☐ Blue-winged Teal *(Anas discors)*	B N	
	S	
☐ Cinnamon Teal *(Anas cyanoptera)*	S	
☐ Northern Shoveler *(Anas clypeata)*	B N	
	S	
☐ Northern Pintail *(Anas acuta)*	b N	
	S	
☐ Garganey *(Anas querquedula)* Accidental		
☐ Green-winged Teal *(Anas crecca)*	b N	
	S	
☐ Canvasback *(Aythya valisineria)*	b N	
	S	
☐ Redhead *(Aythya americana)*	b N	
	S	
☐ Ring-necked Duck *(Aythya collaris)*	N	
	S	
☐ Tufted Duck *(Aythya fuligula)* Accidental		
☐ Greater Scaup *(Aythya marila)*	L N	
	S	
☐ Lesser Scaup *(Aythya affinis)*	b N	
	S	
☐ King Eider *(Somateria spectabilis)*	Statewide	
☐ Common Eider *(Somateria mollissima)* Accidental		
☐ Harlequin Duck *(Histrionicus histrionicus)*	Statewide	
☐ Surf Scoter *(Melanitta perspicillata)*	Statewide	
☐ White-winged Scoter *(Melanitta fusca)*	L N	
	S	
☐ Black Scoter *(Melanitta nigra)*	L N	
	S	
☐ Oldsquaw *(Clangula hyemalis)*	N	
	S	

See abbreviations on page 315

Month of Occurrence

Bird Species	Region	J F M A M J J A S O N D
Bufflehead *(Bucephala albeola)*	N	
	S	
Common Goldeneye *(Bucephala clangula)*	N	
	S	
Barrow's Goldeneye *(Bucephala islandica)*	Statewide	
Hooded Merganser *(Lophodytes cucullatus)* B	N	
	S	
Common Merganser *(Mergus merganser)*	N	
	S	
Red-breasted Merganser *(Mergus serrator)* b	N	
	S	
Ruddy Duck *(Oxyura jamaicensis)* B	Statewide	

OSPREYS, KITES, HARRIERS, HAWKS, *and* EAGLES

Bird Species	Region	J F M A M J J A S O N D
Osprey *(Pandion haliaetus)* (endangered)		
Swallow-tailed Kite *(Elanoides forficatus)* Accidental (b)		
White-tailed Kite *(Elanus leucurus)* Accidental		
Mississippi Kite *(Ictinia mississippiensis)* (endangered) B(L)	S	
Bald Eagle *(Haliaeetus leucocephalus)* (threatened) B	Statewide	
Northern Harrier *(Circus cyaneus)* (endangered) B	Statewide	
Sharp-shinned Hawk *(Accipiter striatus)* B	Statewide	
Cooper's Hawk *(Accipiter cooperii)* B	Statewide	
Northern Goshawk *(Accipiter gentilis)* I	Statewide	
Red-shouldered Hawk *(Buteo lineatus)* (threatened) B	N	
	S	
Broad-winged Hawk *(Buteo platypterus)* B	Statewide	
Swainson's Hawk *(Buteo swainsoni)* (endangered) B(L)	N	
	S	
Red-tailed Hawk *(Buteo jamaicensis)* B	Statewide	
Ferruginous Hawk *(Buteo regalis)* Accidental		
Rough-legged Hawk *(Buteo lagopus)* I	Statewide	
Golden Eagle *(Aquila chrysaetos)*	N	
	S	

FALCONS

Bird Species	Region	J F M A M J J A S O N D
American Kestrel *(Falco sparverius)* B	Statewide	
Merlin *(Falco columbarius)*	Statewide	
Gyrfalcon *(Falco rusticolus)* I	Statewide	
Peregrine Falcon *(Falco peregrinus)* (endangered) B(L)	N	
	S	
Prairie Falcon *(Falco mexicanus)*	Statewide	

■ Common to abundant   ■ Uncommon
■ Fairly common   ── Rare to casual

PARTRIDGES, PHEASANTS, GROUSE, *and* TURKEYS

☐ Gray Partridge *(Perdix perdix)* (introduced) — B N

☐ Ringed-necked Pheasant *(Phasianus colchicus)* (introduced) — B Statewide

☐ Ruffed Grouse *(Bonasa umbellus)* — (B) N

☐ Sharp-tailed Grouse *(Tympanuchus phasianellus)* Extirpated — (b)

☐ Greater Prairie-Chicken *(Tympanuchus cupido)* (endangered) — B S

☐ Wild Turkey *(Meleagris gallopavo)* — B Statewide

NEW WORLD QUAILS

☐ Northern Bobwhite *(Colinus virginianus)* — B Statewide

RAILS, GALLINULES, *and* COOTS

☐ Yellow Rail *(Coturnicops noveboracensis)* — (b) Statewide

☐ Black Rail *(Laterallus jamaicensis)* (endangered) — (b) Statewide

☐ King Rail *(Rallus elegans)* (endangered) — B(L) Statewide

☐ Virginia Rail *(Rallus limicola)* — B N / S

☐ Sora *(Porzana carolina)* — B N / S

☐ Purple Gallinule *(Porphyrula martinica)* Accidental — b

☐ Common Moorhen *(Gallinula chloropus)* (threatened) B(L) Statewide

☐ American Coot *(Fulica americana)* — B Statewide

CRANES

☐ Sandhill Crane *(Grus canadensis)* (threatened) — B(L) E / W

☐ Whooping Crane *(Grus americana)* Accidental

PLOVERS

☐ Black-bellied Plover *(Pluvialis squatarola)* — Statewide

☐ American Golden-Plover *(Pluvialis dominica)* — Statewide

☐ Snowy Plover *(Charadrius alexandrinus)* Accidental

☐ Semipalmated Plover *(Charadrius semipalmatus)* — Statewide

☐ Piping Plover *(Charadrius melodus)* (endangered) — b Statewide

☐ Killdeer *(Charadrius vociferus)* — B Statewide

STILTS *and* AVOCETS

☐ Black-necked Stilt *(Himantopus mexicanus)* — b Statewide

☐ American Avocet *(Recurvirostra americana)* — Statewide

See abbreviations on page 315

Bird Species	Region	Month of Occurrence J F M A M J J A S O N D

SANDPIPERS, CURLEWS, GODWITS, TURNSTONES, DOWITCHERS, SNIPES, *and* WOODCOCKS

Bird Species	Region	Month of Occurrence
☐ Greater Yellowlegs *(Tringa melanoleuca)*	N / S	
☐ Lesser Yellowlegs *(Tringa flavipes)*	N / S	
☐ Solitary Sandpiper *(Tringa solitaria)*	Statewide	
☐ Willet *(Catoptrophorus semipalmatus)*	Statewide	
☐ Spotted Sandpiper *(Actitis macularia)* B	Statewide	
☐ Upland Sandpiper *(Bartramia longicauda)* (endangered) B	N / S	
☐ Eskimo Curlew *(Numenius borealis)* Extirpated		
☐ Whimbrel *(Numenius phaeopus)* L	Statewide	
☐ Long-billed Curlew *(Numenius americanus)* Accidental		
☐ Hudsonian Godwit *(Limosa haemastica)*	Statewide	
☐ Marbled Godwit *(Limosa fedoa)*	Statewide	
☐ Ruddy Turnstone *(Arenaria interpres)* L	N / S	
☐ Red Knot *(Calidris canutus)* L	Statewide	
☐ Sanderling *(Calidris alba)* L	Statewide	
☐ Semipalmated Sandpiper *(Calidris pusilla)*	Statewide	
☐ Western Sandpiper *(Calidris mauri)*	Statewide	
☐ Least Sandpiper *(Calidris minutilla)*	Statewide	
☐ White-rumped Sandpiper *(Calidris fuscicollis)*	Statewide	
☐ Baird's Sandpiper *(Calidris bairdii)*	Statewide	
☐ Pectoral Sandpiper *(Calidris melanotos)*	Statewide	
☐ Sharp-tailed Sandpiper *(Calidris acuminata)* Accidental		
☐ Purple Sandpiper *(Calidris maritima)* L	N	
☐ Dunlin *(Calidris alpina)*	Statewide	
☐ Curlew Sandpiper *(Calidris ferruginea)* Accidental		
☐ Stilt Sandpiper *(Calidris himantopus)*	Statewide	
☐ Buff-breasted Sandpiper *(Tryngites subruficollis)*	Statewide	
☐ Ruff *(Philomachus pugnax)*	Statewide	
☐ Short-billed Dowitcher *(Limnodromus griseus)*	Statewide	
☐ Long-billed Dowitcher *(Limnodromus scolopaceus)*	Statewide	
☐ Common Snipe *(Gallinago gallinago)* B(L)	N / S	

Legend:
- ■ Common to abundant
- ■ Fairly common
- ▨ Uncommon
- — Rare to casual

Bird Species		Region	Month of Occurrence
			J F M A M J J A S O N D
☐ American Woodcock *(Scolopax minor)*	B	N	
		S	

PHALAROPES

Bird Species		Region	
☐ Wilson's Phalarope *(Phalaropus tricolor)* (endangered)	b	Statewide	
☐ Red-necked Phalarope *(Phalaropus lobatus)*		Statewide	
☐ Red Phalarope *(Phalaropus fulicaria)*		Statewide	

JAEGERS, GULLS, TERNS, *and* SKIMMERS

Bird Species		Region	
☐ Pomarine Jaeger *(Stercorarius pomarinus)*	L	Statewide	
☐ Parasitic Jaeger *(Stercorarius parasiticus)*	L	N	
		S	
☐ Laughing Gull *(Larus artricilla)*		Statewide	
☐ Franklin's Gull *(Larus pipixcan)*		Statewide	
☐ Little Gull *(Larus minutus)*		Statewide	
☐ Black-headed Gull *(Larus ridibundus)*		Statewide	
☐ Bonaparte's Gull *(Larus philadelphia)*		Statewide	
☐ Mew Gull *(Larus canus)*		Statewide	
☐ Ring-billed Gull *(Larus delawarensis)*	B	N	
		S	
☐ California Gull *(Larus californicus)*		Statewide	
☐ Herring Gull *(Larus argentatus)*	B	N	
		S	
☐ Thayer's Gull *(Larus thayeri)*		Statewide	
☐ Iceland Gull *(Larus glaucoides)*		Statewide	
☐ Lesser Black-backed Gull *(Larus fuscus)*		Statewide	
☐ Slaty-backed Gull *(Larus schistisagus)* Accidental			
☐ Western Gull *(Larus occidentalis)* Accidental			
☐ Glaucous-winged Gull *(Larus glaucescens)*		Statewide	
☐ Glaucous Gull *(Larus hyperboreus)*		N	
		S	
☐ Great Black-backed Gull *(Larus marinus)*		Statewide	
☐ Sabine's Gull *(Xema sabini)*		Statewide	
☐ Black-legged Kittiwake *(Rissa tridactyla)*		Statewide	
☐ Ross's Gull *(Rhodostethia rosea)* Accidental			
☐ Ivory Gull *(Pagophila eburnea)* Accidental			
☐ Gull-billed Tern *(Sterna nilotica)* Accidental			
☐ Caspian Tern *(Sterna caspia)*		N	
		S	

See abbreviations on page 315

Bird Species	Region	Month of Occurrence J F M A M J J A S O N D
☐ Royal Tern *(Sterna maxima)*	N	—
☐ Sandwich Tern *(Sterna sandvicensis)* Accidental		
☐ Common Tern *(Sterna hirundo)* (endangered)	B N / S	■ / ■
☐ Arctic Tern *(Sterna paradisaea)*	Statewide	—
☐ Forster's Tern *(Sterna forsteri)* (endangered)	B N / S	■ / ■
☐ Least Tern *(Sterna antillarum)* (endangered)	B(L) S	—
☐ Large-billed Tern *(Phaetusa simplex)* Accidental		
☐ Black Tern *(Chlidonias niger)* (endangered)	B(L) N / S	■ / ■
☐ Black Skimmer *(Rynchops niger)* Accidental		

AUKS, MURRES, *and* ALLIES

Bird Species	Region	Month of Occurrence
☐ Dovekie *(Alle alle)* Accidental		
☐ Ancient Murrelet *(Synthliboramphus antiquus)* Accidental		

PIGEONS *and* DOVES

Bird Species	Region	Month of Occurrence
☐ Rock Dove *(Columba livia)* (spec.) (introduced)	Statewide	■■■■■■■■■■■■
☐ Band-tailed Pigeon *(Columba fasciata)* Accidental		
☐ Eurasian Collared-Dove *(Streptopelia decaocto)* (introduced) Accidental	b	
☐ White-winged Dove *(Zenaida asiatica)* Accidental		
☐ Mourning Dove *(Zenaida macroura)*	B Statewide	■■■■■■■■■■■■
☐ Passenger Pigeon *(Ectopistes migratorius)* Extinct		
☐ Common Ground-Dove *(Columbina passerina)* Accidental		
☐ Monk Parakeet *(Myiopsitta monachus)* (introduced)	B(L) N	■■■■■■■■■■■■

PARAKEETS *and* PARROTS

Bird Species	Region	Month of Occurrence
☐ Carolina Parakeet *(Conuropsis carolinensis)* Extinct		

CUCKOOS *and* ANIS

Bird Species	Region	Month of Occurrence
☐ Black-billed Cuckoo *(Coccyzus erythropthalmus)*	B,I N / S	■ / ■
☐ Yellow-billed Cuckoo *(Coccyzus americanus)*	B,I N / S	■ / ■
☐ Groove-billed Ani *(Crotophaga sulcirostris)* Accidental		

BARN OWLS

Bird Species	Region	Month of Occurrence
☐ Barn Owl *(Tyto alba)* (endangered)	B N / S	—

■■■ Common to abundant   ▬▬ Uncommon
▬▬ Fairly common   —— Rare to casual

TYPICAL OWLS

Bird Species		Region
☐ Eastern Screech-Owl *(Otus asio)*	B	Statewide
☐ Great Horned Owl *(Bubo virginianus)*	B	Statewide
☐ Snowy Owl *(Nyctea scandiaca)*	I	Statewide
☐ Northern Hawk Owl *(Surnia ulula)* Accidental	I	
☐ Burrowing Owl *(Athene cunicularia)*		Statewide
☐ Barred Owl *(Strix varia)*	B	N
		S
☐ Long-eared Owl *(Asio otus)*	b	Statewide
☐ Short-eared Owl *(Asio flammeus)* (endangered)	B	Statewide
☐ Boreal Owl *(Aegolius funereus)* Accidental	I	
☐ Northern Saw-whet Owl *(Aegolius acadicus)*	b	Statewide

NIGHTHAWKS *and* NIGHTJARS

Bird Species		Region
☐ Common Nighthawk *(Chordeiles minor)*	B	Statewide
☐ Chuck-will's-widow *(Caprimulgus carolinensis)*	B	N
		S
☐ Whip-poor-will *(Caprimulgus vociferus)*	B	N
		S

SWIFTS

Bird Species		Region
☐ Chimney Swift *(Chaetura pelagica)*	B	Statewide

HUMMINGBIRDS

Bird Species		Region
☐ Broad-billed Hummingbird *(Cynanthus latirostris)* Accidental		
☐ Ruby-throated Hummingbird *(Archilochus colubris)*	B	N
		S
☐ Rufous Hummingbird *(Selasphorus rufus)*		Statewide
☐ Allen's Hummingbird *(Selasphorus sasin)* Accidental		

KINGFISHERS

Bird Species		Region
☐ Belted Kingfisher *(Ceryle alcyon)*	B	Statewide

WOODPECKERS

Bird Species		Region
☐ Red-headed Woodpecker *(Melanerpes erythrocephalus)*	B	Statewide
☐ Red-bellied Woodpecker *(Melanerpes carolinus)*	B	Statewide
☐ Williamson's Sapsucker *(Sphyrapicus thryroideus)* Accidental		
☐ Yellow-bellied Sapsucker *(Sphyrapicus varius)*	B	N
		S
☐ Downy Woodpecker *(Picoides pubescens)*	B	Statewide

See abbreviations on page 315

Bird Species		Region	Month of Occurrence J F M A M J J A S O N D
☐ Hairy Woodpecker *(Picoides villosus)*	B	Statewide	
☐ Black-backed Woodpecker *(Picoides arcticus)* Accidental			
☐ Northern Flicker *(Colaptes auratus)*	B	N	
		S	
☐ Pileated Woodpecker *(Dryocopus pileatus)*	B	Statewide	

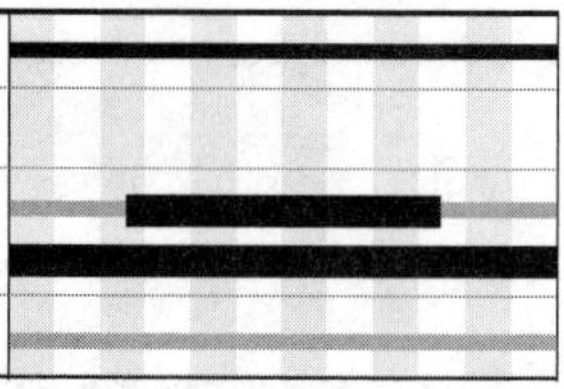

TYRANT FLYCATCHERS

Bird Species		Region	Month of Occurrence J F M A M J J A S O N D
☐ Olive-sided Flycatcher *(Contopus cooperi)*		N	
		S	
☐ Eastern Wood-Pewee *(Contopus virens)*	B	N	
		S	
☐ Yellow-bellied Flycatcher *(Empidonax flaviventris)*		N	
		S	
☐ Acadian Flycatcher *(Empidonax virscens)*	B	N	
		S	
☐ Alder Flycatcher *(Empidonax alnorum)*		N	
		S	
☐ Willow Flycatcher *(Empidonax traillii)*	B	N	
		S	
☐ Least Flycatcher *(Empidonax minimus)*	B	N	
		S	
☐ Eastern Phoebe *(Sayornis phoebe)*	· B	N	
		S	
☐ Say's Phoebe *(Sayornis saya)* Accidental			
☐ Vermilion Flycatcher *(Pyrocephalus rubinus)*		Statewide	
☐ Ash-throated Flycatcher *(Myiarchus cinerascens)* Accidental			
☐ Great Crested Flycatcher *(Myiarchus crinitus)*	B	Statewide	
☐ Western Kingbird *(Tyrannus verticalis)*	B(L)	Statewide	
☐ Eastern Kingbird *(Tyrannus tyrannus)*	B	Statewide	
☐ Scissor-tailed Flycatcher *(Tyrannus forficatus)*		Statewide	

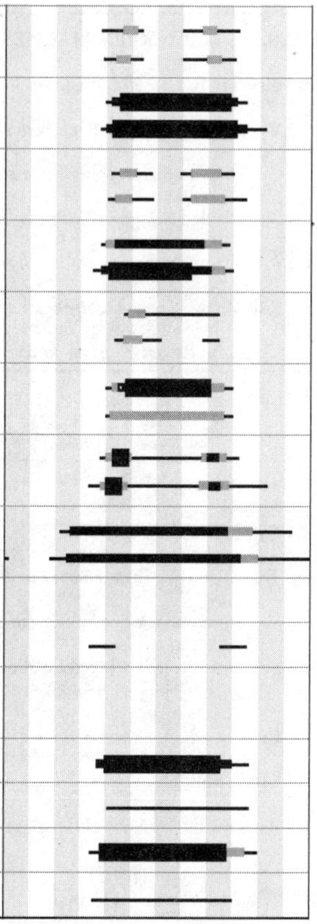

SHRIKES

Bird Species		Region	Month of Occurrence J F M A M J J A S O N D
☐ Loggerhead Shrike *(Lanius ludovicianus)* (threatened)	B(L)	N	
		S	
☐ Northern Shrike *(Lanius excubitor)*	I	N	

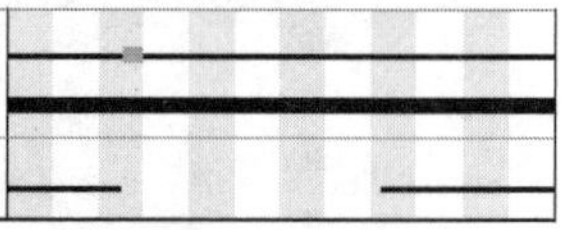

VIREOS

Bird Species		Region	Month of Occurrence J F M A M J J A S O N D
☐ White-eyed Vireo *(Vireo griseus)*	B	N	
		S	
☐ Bell's Vireo *(Vireo bellii)*	B	Statewide	
☐ Yellow-throated Vireo *(Vireo flavifrons)*	B	Statewide	

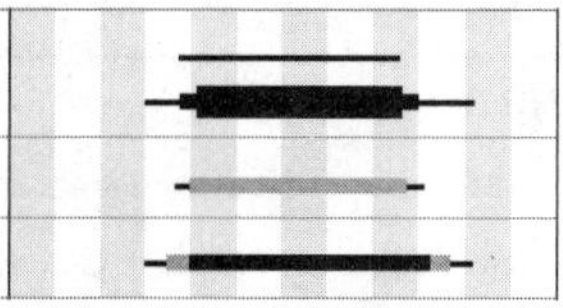

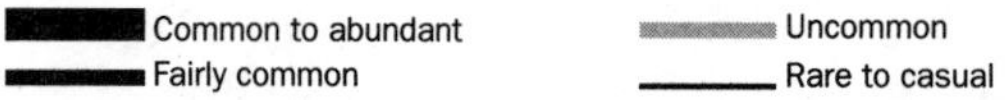

Legend:
- ▇▇▇ Common to abundant
- ▆▆▆ Fairly common
- ░░░ Uncommon
- ─── Rare to casual

Bird Species	Region		Month of Occurrence J F M A M J J A S O N D
☐ Blue-headed Vireo *(Vireo solitarius)*	b	N	
		S	
☐ Warbling Vireo *(Vireo gilvus)*	B	Statewide	
☐ Philadelphia Vireo *(Vireo philadelphicus)*		N	
		S	
☐ Red-eyed Vireo *(Vireo olivaceus)*	B	N	
		S	

JAYS, NUTCRACKERS, MAGPIES, *and* CROWS

☐ Blue Jay *(Cyanocitta cristata)*	B	Statewide	
☐ Western Scrub-Jay *(Aphelocoma californica)* Accidental			
☐ Clark's Nutcracker *(Nucifraga columbiana)* Accidental	I		
☐ Black-billed Magpie *(Pica pica)* Accidental			
☐ American Crow *(Corvus brachyrhynchos)*	B	Statewide	
☐ Fish Crow *(Corvus ossifragus)*	B	S	
☐ Common Raven *(Corvus corax)* Extirpated	(B)		

LARKS

☐ Horned Lark *(Eremophila alpestris)*	B	Statewide	

SWALLOWS

☐ Purple Martin *(Progne subis)*	B	Statewide	
☐ Tree Swallow *(Tachycineta bicolor)*	B	Statewide	
☐ Violet-green Swallow *(Tachycineta thalassina)* Accidental			
☐ Northern Rough-winged Swallow *(Stelgidopteryx serripennis)*	B	N	
		S	
☐ Bank Swallow *(Riparia riparia)*	B	Statewide	
☐ Cliff Swallow *(Petrochelidon pyrrhonota)*	B	Statewide	
☐ Barn Swallow *(Hirundo rustica)*	B	N	
		S	

CHICKADEES *and* TITMICE

☐ Carolina Chickadee *(Poecile carolinensis)*	* B	N	
		S	
☐ Black-capped Chickadee *(Poecile atricapillus)*	* B	Statewide	
☐ Boreal Chickadee *(Poecile hudsonicus)* Accidental			
☐ Tufted Titmouse *(Baeolophus bicolor)*	B	N	
		S	

NUTHATCHES

☐ Red-breasted Nuthatch *(Sitta canadensis)*	B,I	Statewide	
☐ White-breasted Nuthatch *(Sitta carolinensis)*	B	Statewide	

See abbreviations on page 315

Bird Species	Region	Month of Occurrence J F M A M J J A S O N D

CREEPERS

Bird Species	Region	
☐ Brown Creeper *(Certhia americana)* (threatened)	B	Statewide

WRENS

Bird Species	Region	
☐ Rock Wren *(Salpinctes obsoletus)*		Statewide
☐ Carolina Wren *(Thryothorus ludovicianus)*	B	N S
☐ Bewick's Wren *(Thryomanes bewickii)* (endangered)	B	Statewide
☐ House Wren *(Troglodytes aedon)*	B	N S
☐ Winter Wren *(Troglodytes troglodytes)*		N S
☐ Sedge Wren *(Cistothorus platensis)*	B	Statewide
☐ Marsh Wren *(Cistothorus palustris)*	B	N S

KINGLETS

Bird Species	Region	
☐ Golden-crowned Kinglet *(Regulus satrapa)*	b	N S
☐ Ruby-crowned Kinglet *(Regulus calendula)*		N S

GNATCATCHERS

Bird Species	Region	
☐ Blue-gray Gnatcatcher *(Polioptila caerulea)*	B	N S

WHEATEARS, BLUEBIRDS, SOLITAIRES, *and* THRUSHES

Bird Species	Region	
☐ Northern Wheatear *(Oenanthe oenanthe)* Accidental		
☐ Eastern Bluebird *(Sialia sialis)*	B	N S
☐ Mountain Bluebird *(Sialia currucoides)* Accidental		
☐ Townsend's Solitaire *(Myadestes townsendi)*	I	Statewide
☐ Veery *(Catharus fuscescens)*	B	N S
☐ Gray-checked Thrush *(Catharus minimus)*		N S
☐ Swainson's Thrush *(Catharus ustulatus)*		N S
☐ Hermit Thrush *(Catharus guttatus)*		N S
☐ Wood Thrush *(Hylocichla mustelina)*		N S
☐ American Robin *(Turdus migratorius)*		N S

Common to abundant Uncommon
Fairly common Rare to casual

Bird Species	Region	Month of Occurrence J F M A M J J A S O N D
☐ Varied Thrush *(Ixoreus naevius)*	I Statewide	

CATBIRDS, MOCKINGBIRDS, *and* THRASHERS

Bird Species	Region	Month of Occurrence
☐ Gray Catbird *(Dumetella carolinensis)*	N S	
☐ Northern Mockingbird *(Mimus polyglottos)*	N S	
☐ Sage Thrasher *(Oreoscoptes montanus)* Accidental		
☐ Brown Thrasher *(Toxostoma rufum)*	B N S	
☐ Curve-billed Thrasher *(Toxostoma curvirostre)* Accidental		

STARLINGS

Bird Species	Region	Month of Occurrence
☐ European Starling *(Sturnus vulgaris)* (introduced)	B Statewide	

PIPITS

Bird Species	Region	Month of Occurrence
☐ American Pipit *(Anthus rubescens)*	N S	
☐ Sprague's Pipit *(Anthus spragueii)* Accidental		

WAXWINGS

Bird Species	Region	Month of Occurrence
☐ Bohemian Waxwing *(Bombycilla garrulus)*	I	
☐ Cedar Waxwing *(Bombycilla cedrorum)*	B Statewide	

AMERICAN WOOD WARBLERS

Bird Species	Region	Month of Occurrence
☐ Blue-winged Warbler *(Vermivora pinus)*	B N S	
☐ Golden-winged Warbler *(Vermivora chrysoptera)*	b N S	
☐ Tennessee Warbler *(Vermivora peregrina)*	N S	
☐ Orange-crowned Warbler *(Vermivora celata)*	N S	
☐ Nashville Warbler *(Vermivora ruficapilla)*	b N S	
☐ Northern Parula *(Parula americana)*	B N S	
☐ Yellow Warbler *(Dendroica petechia)*	B N S	
☐ Chestnut-sided Warbler *(Dendroica pensylvanica)*	B N S	
☐ Magnolia Warbler *(Dendroica magnolia)*	Statewide	
☐ Cape May Warbler *(Dendroica tigrina)*	Statewide	
☐ Black-throated Blue Warbler *(Dendroica caerulescens)*	N S	

See abbreviations on page 315

Month of Occurrence

Bird Species		Region	J F M A M J J A S O N D
☐ Yellow-rumped Warbler *(Dendroica coronata)*		N	
		S	
☐ Black-throated Gray Warbler *(Dendroica nigrecens)* Accidental			
☐ Black-throated Green Warbler *(Dendroica virens)*	b	N	
		S	
☐ Townsend's Warbler *(Dendroica townsendi)* Accidental			
☐ Blackburnian Warbler *(Dendroica fusca)*		N	
		S	
☐ Yellow-throated Warbler *(Dendroica dominica)*	B	N	
		S	
☐ Pine Warbler *(Dendroica pinus)*	B	N	
		S	
☐ Kirtland's Warbler *(Dendroica kirtlandii)* Accidental			
☐ Prairie Warbler *(Dendroica discolor)*	B	N	
		S	
☐ Palm Warbler *(Dendroica palmarum)*		N	
		S	
☐ Bay-breasted Warbler *(Dendroica castanea)*		N	
		S	
☐ Blackpoll Warbler *(Dendroica striata)*		N	
		S	
☐ Cerulean Warbler *(Dendroica cerulea)*	B	N	
		S	
☐ Black-and-white Warbler *(Mniotilta varia)*	B	N	
		S	
☐ American Redstart *(Setophaga ruticilla)*	B(L)	N	
		S	
☐ Prothonotary Warbler *(Protonotaria citrea)*	B	N	
		S	
☐ Worm-eating Warbler *(Helmitheros vermivorus)*	B	N	
		S	
☐ Swainson's Warbler *(Limnothlypis swainsonii)* (endangered)	b	N	
		S	
☐ Ovenbird *(Seiurus aurocapillus)*	B	N	
		S	
☐ Northern Waterthrush *(Seiurus noveboracensis)*		N	
		S	
☐ Louisiana Waterthrush *(Seiurus motacilla)*	B(L)	N	
		S	
☐ Kentucky Warbler *(Oporornis formosus)*	B	N	
		S	

▬▬▬ Common to abundant ▦▦▦ Uncommon

▬▬▬ Fairly common ———— Rare to casual

Bird Species		Region	Month of Occurrence J F M A M J J A S O N D
☐ Connecticut Warbler (Oporornis agilis)		N	
		S	
☐ Mourning Warbler (Oporornis philadelphia)	b	N	
		S	
☐ MacGillivray's Warbler (Oporornis tolmiei) Accidental			
☐ Common Yellowthroat (Geothlypis trichas)	B	Statewide	
☐ Hooded Warbler (Wilsonia citrina)	B	N	
		S	
☐ Wilson's Warbler (Wilsonia pusilla)		Statewide	
☐ Canada Warbler (Wilsonia canadensis)	b	N	
		S	
☐ Yellow-breasted Chat (Icteria virens)	B	N	
		S	

TANAGERS

Bird Species		Region	Month of Occurrence
☐ Hepatic Tanager (Piranga flava) Accidental			
☐ Summer Tanager (Piranga rubra)	B	N	
		S	
☐ Scarlet Tanager (Piranga olivacea)	B	N	
		S	
☐ Western Tanager (Pirange ludoviciana)		Statewide	

TOWHEES, SPARROWS, JUNCOS, LONGSPURS, *and* OLD WORLD BUNTINGS

Bird Species		Region	Month of Occurrence
☐ Green-tailed Towhee (Pipilo chlorurus) Accidental			
☐ Spotted Towhee (Pipilo maculatus)		Statewide	
☐ Eastern Towhee (Pipilo erythrophthalmus)	B	N	
		S	
☐ Cassin's Sparrow (Aimophila cassinii) Accidental			
☐ Bachman's Sparrow (Aimophila aestivalis) Accidental			
☐ American Tree Sparrow (Spizella arborea)		N	
		S	
☐ Chipping Sparrow (Spizella passerina)	B	N	
		S	
☐ Clay-colored Sparrow (Spizella pallida)	B(L)	Statewide	
☐ Brewer's Sparrow (Spizella breweri)		N	
☐ Field Sparrow (Spizella pusilla)	B	N	
		S	
☐ Vesper Sparrow (Pooecetes gramineus)	B	Statewide	
☐ Lark Sparrow (Chondestes grammacus)	B(L)	Statewide	
☐ Black-throated Sparrow (Amphispiza bilineata) Accidental			

Bird Species		Region	Month of Occurrence J F M A M J J A S O N D
☐ Lark Bunting (*Calamospiza melanocorys*)		Statewide	
☐ Savannah Sparrow (*Passerculus sandwichensis*)	B	N	
		S	
☐ Grasshopper Sparrow (*Ammodramus savannarum*)	B	N	
		S	
☐ Henslow's Sparrow (*Ammodramus henslowii*) (endangered)	B	Statewide	
☐ Le Conte's Sparrow (*Ammodramus leconteii*)	b	N	
		S	
☐ Nelson's Sharp-tailed Sparrow (*Ammodramus nelsoni*)	b	Statewide	
☐ Fox Sparrow (*Passerella iliaca*)		N	
		S	
☐ Song Sparrow (*Melospiza melodia*)	B	N	
		S	
☐ Lincoln's Sparrow (*Melospiza lincolnii*)		N	
		S	
☐ Swamp Sparrow (*Melospiza georgiana*)	B	N	
		S	
☐ White-throated Sparrow (*Zonotrichia albicollis*)		N	
		S	
☐ Harris's Sparrow (*Zonotrichia querula*)		Statewide	
☐ White-crowned Sparrow (*Zonotrichia leucophrys*)		N	
		S	
☐ Golden-crowned Sparrow (*Zonotrichia atricapilla*)			
☐ Dark-eyed Junco (*Junco hyemalis*)		N	
		S	
☐ Lapland Longspur (*Calcarius lapponicus*)		Statewide	
☐ Smith's Longspur (*Calcarius pictus*)		Statewide	
☐ Chestnut-collared Longspur (*Calcarius ornatus*) Accidental			
☐ Snow Bunting (*Plectrophenax nivalis*)		N	
		S	

NEOTROPICAL GROSBEAKS and BUNTINGS

Bird Species		Region	Month of Occurrence J F M A M J J A S O N D
☐ Northern Cardinal (*Cardinalis cardinalis*)	B	Statewide	
☐ Rose-breasted Grosbeak (*Pheucticus ludovicianus*)	B	N	
		S	
☐ Black headed Grosbeak (*Pheucticus melanocephalus*)		Statewide	
☐ Blue Grosbeak (*Guiraca caerulea*)	B(L)	N	
		S	
☐ Lazuli Bunting (*Passerina amoena*) Accidental			

■■■ Common to abundant   ▨▨▨ Uncommon
▬▬ Fairly common   ── Rare to casual

331

Bird Species		Region	Month of Occurrence J F M A M J J A S O N D
☐ Indigo Bunting *(Passerina cyanea)*	B	N	
		S	
☐ Painted Bunting *(Passerina ciris)* Accidental			
☐ Dickcissel *(Spiza americana)*	B	Statewide	

BOBOLINKS, BLACKBIRDS, MEADOWLARKS, GRACKLES, COWBIRDS, *and* ORIOLES

Bird Species		Region	Month of Occurrence
☐ Bobolink *(Dolichonyx oryzivorus)*	B	N	
		S	
☐ Red-winged Blackbird *(Agelaius phoeniceus)*	B	N	
		S	
☐ Eastern Meadowlark *(Sturnella magna)*	B	N	
		S	
☐ Western Meadowlark *(Sturnella neglecta)*	B(L)	E	
		W	
☐ Yellow-headed Blackbird *(Xanthocephalus xanthocephalus)* (endangered)	B(L)	N	
		S	
☐ Rusty Blackbird *(Euphagus carolinus)*		N	
		S	
☐ Brewer's Blackbird *(Euphagus cyanocephalus)*	B(L)	N	
		S	
☐ Common Grackle *(Quiscalus quiscula)*	B	N	
		S	
☐ Great-tailed Grackle *(Quiscalus mexicanus)* Accidental			
☐ Brown-headed Cowbird *(Molothrus ateri)*	B	N	
		S	
☐ Orchard Oriole *(Icterus spurius)*	B	N	
		S	
☐ Baltimore Oriole *(Icterus galbula)*	B	N	
		S	

HOLARCTIC FINCHES

Bird Species		Region	Month of Occurrence
☐ Gray-crowned Rosy-Finch *(Leucosticte tephrocostis)* Accidental			
☐ Pine Grosbeak *(Pinicola enucleator)*	I	Statewide	
☐ Purple Finch *(Carpodacus purpureus)*	(b)	Statewide	
☐ House Finch *(Carpodacus mexicanus)* (introduced)	B	Statewide	
☐ Red Crossbill *(Loxia curvirostra)*	b,I	Statewide	
☐ White-winged Crossbill *(Loxia leucoptera)*	I	Statewide	
☐ Common Redpoll *(Carduelis flammea)*	I	N	
		S	
☐ Hoary Redpoll *(Carduelis hornemanni)* Accidental	I		
☐ Pine Siskin *(Carduelis pinus)*	b, I	Statewide	

See abbreviations on page 315

Bird Species		Region	Month of Occurrence J F M A M J J A S O N D
☐ American Goldfinch *(Carduelis tristis)*	B	Statewide	
☐ Evening Grosbeak *(Coccothraustes vespertinus)*	I	Statewide	

WEAVER FINCHES

☐ House Sparrow *(Passer domesticus)*	B	Statewide	
☐ Eurasian Tree Sparrow *(Passer montanus)* (introduced)	B	S	

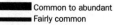
■■■■ Common to abundant   ▨▨▨ Uncommon
■■■■ Fairly common   —— Rare to casual

333

Appendix A: Contact information for Birding Illinois

INTRODUCTION

Illinois Department of Natural Resources Hunting and trapping regulations; phone: 217-785-8610; Illinois Camping Guide; phone: 217-782-7454.

Illinois Bed & Breakfast Association, P.O. Box 82, Port Byron, IL 61275; phone: 309-523-2406.

Illinois Visitors Guide; phone: 1-800-2CONNECT or on the Internet: http://www.enjoyillinois.com.

Rare Bird Alerts

DuPage County, Illinois Rare Bird Alert; phone: 630-406-8111. To report rare birds, call 630-406-1535.

Chicago, Illinois Rare Bird Alert; phone: 847-671-1522. To report rare birds in the Chicago region, call 847-671-1534.

Illinois State Museum Central Illinois—Rare Bird Alert; phone: 217-785-1083. To report rare birds in the central Illinois region, call 217-782-6697.

Northwest Illinois Rare Bird Alert; phone: 815-965-3095.

NATIONAL BIRDING ORGANIZATION: American Birding Association ABA, P.O. Box 6599, Colorado Springs, CO 80934; phone: 1-800-850-2473.

ILLINOIS-BASED BIRDING ORGANIZATIONS: A PARTIAL LIST

Bird Conservation Network, c/o Chicago Audubon Society. See below.

Chicago Audubon Society, a chapter of the National Audubon Society, 5801-C North Pulaski Road, Chicago, IL 60646-6057; phone: 773-539-6793. Information line: 847-299-3505. Email address: chicago_audubon@juno.com

Chicago Ornithological Society, c/o Michael Kutska, 599 Clinton Place, River Forest, IL 60305; phone or fax: 708-366-2409.

DuPage Birding Club, 4308 Nutmeg Lane #244, Lisle, IL 60532.

Evanston North Shore Bird Club. P.O. Box 1313, Evanston, IL 60204-1313.

Illinois Audubon Society, P.O. Box 2418, Danville, IL 60834-2418, USA; phone: 217-446-5085. Fax: 217-446-6375. Contact the society for a list of statewide chapters.

Illinois Ornithological Society, P.O. Box 931, Lake Forest, IL 60045. Website address: http://www.chias.org/ios/

North Central Illinois Ornithological Society, a chapter of the National Audubon Society, 737 N. Main Street, Rockford, IL 61103; phone: 815-965-3095.

Prairie Woods Audubon Society, a chapter of the National Audubon Society, P.O. Box 1065, Arlington Heights, IL 60006; phone: 847-818-4041.

Sinnissippi Audubon Society, a chapter of the National Audubon Society, 737 N. Main Street., Rockford, IL 61103-6971; phone: 815-965-3433.

Southern Illinois Ornithology Society, a chapter of the National Audubon Society, P.O. Box 222, Carbondale, IL 62903-0222.

Thorn Creek Audubon Society, a chapter of the National Audubon Society, P.O. Box 895, Park Forest, IL 60466.

Vermilion County Audubon Society, a chapter of the National Audubon Society; phone: 217-427-5563.

ILLINOIS BIRDERS EXCHANGING THOUGHTS—Email ListServ

Illinois Birders Exchanging Thoughts, IBET, is an Email list for the discussion of wild birds and birding issues relating to Illinois. IBET's mission is to promote the joy of birding by keeping the membership updated on rare and interesting birds and birding opportunities. The list is administered by Sue Friscia at Q4BIRDS@aol.com.

To subscribe, send Email to majordomo@lists.enteract.com. In the body of the text type the words "subscribe ibet," then follow directions from Emails sent to you.

The last 50 (about a week's worth) IBET postings are available on the World Wide Web at: http://www-stat.whsrton.upenn.edu/~siler/IBET.html.

BIRDING SITES 1-80

1. Montrose Harbor, the Magic Hedge, the Lincoln Park Bird Sanctuary, and Belmont Harbor. Chicago Park District Administration Building, 425 East McFetridge Drive, Chicago, IL 60605; phone: 312-747-1457 or 1560. The Chicago Audubon Society, 5801-C North Pulaski Road Chicago, IL 60646-6057; phone: 773-539-6793. Website: http://www.audubon.org/chapter/il/chicago/. Regional Transportation Associaton (RTA); phone: 312-836-7000.

2. Jackson Park and the Paul O. Douglas Nature Sanctuary (Wooded Island). Chicago Park District Administration Building, 425 East McFetridge Drive, Chicago, IL 60605; phone: 312-747-1457 or 1560. The Chicago Audubon Society, 5801-C North Pulaski Road Chicago, IL 60646-6057; phone: 773-539-6793. Website http://www.audubon.org/chapter/il/chicago/. The

Museum of Science and Industry, 57th Street and Lake Shore Drive, Chicago, IL 60637; phone: 773-684.1414 or 1-800-468-6674; TDD, 773-684-3323. Chicago Transportation Association (CTA):

3. Downtown Chicago Birding/Walking Tour, the Chicago Audubon Society, 5801-C North Pulaski Road Chicago, IL 60646-6057; phone: 773-539-6793. Website: http://www.audubon.org/chapter/il/chicago. The Field Museum of Natural History, Roosevelt Road at Lake Shore Drive, Chicago, IL 60605-2496; phone: 312-922-9410. The Chicago Academy of Sciences 2060 North Clark Street, Chicago, IL 60614; phone: 773-549-0606 or Email cascol@chias.org.

4. Illinois Beach State Park, Lake Front Drive, Zion, IL 60099; phone: 847-662-4828. Illinois Beach Resort and Conference Center Reservations; phone: 847-625-7300.

5. Waukegan Beach and Bowen Park, Waukegan Park District, 2000 Belvidere Street, Waukegan, IL 60085; phone: 847-360-4700.

6. Wadsworth Savanna and Wetlands Demonstration Project. Lake County Forest Preserves, 2000 North Milwaukee Avenue, Libertyville, IL 60048; phone: 847-367-6640; TT/TDD, 847-367-6649.

7. Chain O' Lakes State Park. Chain O' Lakes State Park, 8916 Wilmot Road, Spring Grove, IL 60080; phone: 847-587-5512.

8. Glacial Park and Vicinity. McHenry County Conservation District, 6512 Harts Road, Ringwood IL, 60072; phone: 815-678-4431.

9. Moraine Hills State Park. Moraine Hills State Park, 914 S. River Road, McHenry, IL 60050; phone: 815-385-1624.

10. Crabtree Nature Center, Palatine Marsh, and Vicinity. Crabtree Nature Center, 3 Stover Road, Barrington, IL 60010-5342; phone: 847-381-6592.

11. Baker's Lake and Ron Beese Park. Baker's Lake, 3 Stover Road, Barrington, IL 60010-5342; phone: 847-381-6592. Ron Beese Park, Barrington Park District, 235 Lions Drive, Barrington, IL 60010; phone: 847-381-0687.

12. Ryerson Conservation Area and the Des Plaines River Corridor. Ryerson Conservation Area, 21950 Riverwoods Road, Deerfield, IL 60015; phone: 847-948-7750. Lake County Forest Preserves, 2000 North Milwaukee Avenue, Libertyville, IL 60048; phone: 847-367-6640; TT/TDD, 847-367-6649.

13. Chicago Botanic Garden. Chicago Botanic Garden, 1000 Lake Cook Road, Glencoe, IL 60022; phone: 847-835-5440; TDD, 847-835-0790.

14. Skokie Lagoons. The Chicago Audubon Society, 5801-C North Pulaski Road, Chicago, IL 60646-6057; phone: 773-539-6793. Website: http://www.audubon.org/chapter/il/chicago. Forest Preserve District of Cook County,

General Headquarters; phone: 312-261-8400; city, 847-366-9420; suburban, 847-771-1190 for hearing impaired.

15. Gillson Park and Evanston Landfill. Wilmette Park District, 1200 Wilmette Avenue, Wilmette, IL 60091; phone: 847-256-6100.

16. O'Hare Post Office Ponds. The Chicago Audubon Society, 5801-C North Pulaski Road Chicago, IL 60646-6057; phone: 773-539-6793. Website http://www.audubon.org/chapter/il/chicago/.

17. Morton Arboretum, 4100 Illinois Route 53, Lisle, IL 60532; phone: 630-719-2400.

18. Blackwell Forest Preserve. Forest Preserve District of DuPage County, 185 Spring Avenue, P.O. Box 2339, Glen Ellyn, IL 60138; phone: 630-790-4900.

19. Fermilab National Accelerator Laboratory, P.O. Box 500, Batavia, IL 60510; phone: 630-840-5588. If you see any unusual birds here, Peter Kasper, who works at the lab and keeps a bird list, would appreciate a phone call.

20. Conkey Woods. Forest Preserve District of Cook County, 637 North Harlem Avenue, River Forest, IL 60305; toll-free phone: 1-800-870-3666.

21. McClaughry Springs Woods. Forest Preserve District of Cook County, 637 North Harlem Avenue, River Forest, IL 60305; toll-free phone: 1-800-870-3666.

22. Little Red Schoolhouse Nature Center and Nearby Sloughs, 9800 S. Willow Springs Road, Willow Springs, IL 60480; phone: 708-839-6897.

23. Swallow Cliff Woods. Forest Preserve District of Cook County, 637 North Harlem Avenue, River Forest, IL 60305; toll-free phone: 1-800-870-3666.

24. Camp Sagawau, 12545 W. 111th Street, Lemont, IL 60439; phone: 630-257-2045.

25. Saganashkee Slough. Forest Preserve District of Cook County, 637 North Harlem Avenue, River Forest, IL 60305; toll-free phone: 1-800-870-3666.

26. McGinnis Slough, Forest Preserve District of Cook County, 637 North Harlem Avenue, River Forest, IL 60305; toll-free phone: 1-800-870-3666.

27. The Bartel and Orland Grasslands. Forest Preserve District of Cook County, 637 North Harlem Avenue, River Forest, IL 60305; toll-free phone: 1-800-870-3666.

28. Lake Calumet and Vicinity. The Chicago Audubon Society, 5801-C North Pulaski Road, Chicago, IL 60646-6057; phone: 773-539-6793. Web-site: http://www.audubon.org/chapter/il/chicago/.

29. Lake Renwick Heron Rookery Nature Preserve and Copley Nature Park. Forest Preserve District of Will County, 22606 S. Cherry Hill Road. P.O. Box 1069, Joliet, IL 60434; phone: 815-727-8700.

30. Goose Lake Prairie and Heidecke Lake. State Natural Area Park Office, 5010 N. Jugtown Road, Morris, IL 60450; phone: 815-942-2899.

31. Midewin National Tallgrass Prairie, 30071 South State Route 53, Wilmington, IL 60481; phone: 815-423-6370. http://www.fs.fed.us/outernet/mntp/index.htm. For tour reservations, ask for extension 14.

32. Kankakee River State Park, Momence Wetlands, and Sod Farms. Kankakee River State Park, P.O. Box 37, Bourbonnais, IL 60914; phone: 815-933-1383.

33. Shabbona Lake State Recreation Area and Forest Preserve, 4201 Shabbona Grove Road, Shabbona IL 60550; phone: 815-824-2106. Afton County Forest Preserve, 1350 Crego Road, DeKalb, IL; phone: 815-756-6633.

34. Sugar River Forest Preserve and Alder Tract. Winnebago County Forest Preserve District, 5500 Northrock Drive, Rockford, IL 61103; phone: 815-877-6100; North Central Illinois Ornithological Society, Burpee Museum of Natural History, 813 N. Main Street, Rockford, IL 61103; phone: 815-965-3433. Birding Hotline: 815-965-3095.

35. Pecatonica River Forest Preserve. Winnebago County Forest Preserve District, 5500 Northrock Drive, Rockford, IL 6110; phone: 815-877-6100; North Central Illinois Ornithological Society, Burpee Museum of Natural History, 813 N. Main Street, Rockford, IL 61103; phone: 815-965-3433. Birding Hotline: 815-965-3095.

36. Rock Cut State Park and Keiselburg Forest Preserve, 7318 Harlem Road, Loves Park, IL 61111; phone: 815-885-3311.

37. Mississippi Palisades State Park, 16327A Illinois Route 84, Savanna, IL, 61074; phone: 815-273-2731.

38. Savanna Army Depot, 2612 Locust Street, Sterling, IL 61801; phone: 815-625-2968.

39. Mississippi River Corridor. Phone Kelly McKay at 309-755-6731 or Tom Stalf at 309-799-7017.

40. Starved Rock and Matthiessen State Parks. Starved Rock State Park, Box 509, Utica, IL 61373; phone: 815-667-4906.

41. Castle Rock State Park and the George B. Fell Nature Preserve, 1365 W. Castle Road, Oregon, IL 61061; phone: 815-732-7329.

42. Lowden-Miller State Forest. Castle Rock State Park, 1365 W. Castle Road, Oregon, IL 61061; phone: 815-732-7329.

43. Nachusa Grasslands and Franklin Creek State Natural Area. The Nature Conservancy, 2055 Lowden Road, Franklin Grove, IL 61031; phone: 815-456-2340.

44. Green River Conservation Area. Illinois Department of Natural Resources, 524 S. Second Street, Springfield, IL 62701-1787; phone: 217-782-7454.

45. Woodford State Fish and Wildlife Area, R.R.1, Lowpoint, IL 61545; phone: 309-822-8861. Illinois Department of Natural Resources, 524 S. Second Street, Springfield, IL 62701-1787; phone: 217-782-7454.

46. Banner Marsh and Rice Lake State Wildlife Areas, R.R.3, Box 91, Canton, IL 61520; phone: 309-647-9184. Illinois Department of Natural Resources, 524 S. Second Street, Springfield, IL 62701-1787; phone: 217-782-7454.

47. Iroquois County Conservation Area, R.R.1, Beaverville, IL 60912; phone: 815-435-2218. Illinois Department of Natural Resources, 524 S. Second Street, Springfield, IL 62701-1787; phone: 217-782-7454.

48. Middle Fork State Fish and Wildlife Area. Middle Fork State Fish and Wildlife Area, R.R.1, Box 374, Oakwood, IL 61858; phone: 217-442-4915. Illinois Department of Natural Resources, 524 S. Second Street, Springfield, IL 62701-1787; phone: 217-782-7454.

49. Kickapoo State Park, 10906 Kickapoo Park Road, Oakwood, IL 61858; phone: 217-442-4915. Illinois Department of Natural Resources, 524 S. Second Street, Springfield, IL 62701-1787; phone: 217-782-7454.

50. Kennekuk County Park, Box 215, Danville, IL 61832; phone: 217-442-1691. Recreation Ventures, Danville; phone: 217-443-4939.

51. Forest Glen Preserve and the Harry "Babe" Woodyard State Natural Area, 20301 E. 900 North Road, Westville, IL 61883; phone: 217-662-2142. Harry "Babe" Woodyard State Natural Area, Illinois Department of Natural Resources, 524 S. Second Street, Springfield, IL 62701-1787; phone: 217-782-7454.

52. Moraine View State Park, R.R.2, LeRoy, IL 61752; phone: 309-724-8032. Illinois Department of Natural Resources, 524 S. Second Street, Springfield, IL 62701-1787; phone: 217-782-7454.

53. Clinton Lake, R.R.1, Box 4, DeWitt, IL 61735; phone: 217-935-8722. Illinois Department of Natural Resources, 524 S. Second Street, Springfield, IL 62701-1787; phone: 217-782-7454. Champaign County Audubon Society; phone: 217-367-6766.

54. Lake Springfield and Washington Park. Springfield Park District, P.O. Box 5052, Springfield, IL; phone: 217-522-8434.

55. Carpenter and Riverside Parks. Springfield Park District, P.O. Box 5052; Springfield, IL; phone: 217-522-8434. Riverside Park, 4105 Sandhill Road, Springfield, IL 62702; phone: 217-789-2353.

56. Lake Shelbyville, R.R.1, Box 42A, Bethany, IL 61914; phone: 217-346-3336.

57. Sand Ridge State Forest, Site Superintendent, Box 111, Forest City, IL 61532; phone: 309-597-2212.

58. Lake Chautauqua National Wildlife Refuge, 19031 E. County Road 2105N, Havana, IL 62644; phone: 309-535-2290.

59. Meredosia National Wildlife Refuge Lake Chautauqua National Wildlife Refuge Manager, U.S. Fish & Wildlife Service, R.R.2, Box 61-B, Havana, IL 62644; phone: 309-535-2290.

60. Beardstown Marsh and Sanganois Conservation Area, R.R.2, Box 80, Chandlerville, IL 62627; phone: 309-546-2628. Illinois Department of Natural Resources, 524 S. Second Street, Springfield, IL 62701-1787; phone: 217-782-7454.

61. Siloam Springs State Park, R.R.1, Box 204, Clayton, IL 62324; phone: 217-782-7454. Illinois Department of Natural Resources, 524 S. Second Street, Springfield, IL 62701-1787; phone: 217-782-7454.

62. Mark Twain National Wildlife Refuge—Keithsburg Division, 10728 County Road X61, Wapello, IA 52653; phone: 319-523-6982.

63. Pere Marquette State Park and Mark Twain National Wildlife Refuge—Brussels District, HCR Box 107, Brussels, IL 62013; phone: 618-883-2524; Pere Marquette State Park, P.O. Box 158, Grafton, IL 62037; phone: 618-786-2204.

64. Carlyle Lake and Eldon Hazlet State Park. State Fish and Wildlife Area, R.R.1, Box 233, Vandalia, IL 62471; phone: 618-425-3533. Eldon Hazlet State Park, 20100 Hazlet Park Road, Carlyle, IL 62331; phone: 619-594-3015.

65. Horseshoe Lake State Park, 3321 Highway 111, Granite City, 60240; phone: 618-931-0270. Illinois Department of Natural Resources, 524 S. Second Street, Springfield, IL 62701-1787; phone: 217-782-7454.

66. Prairie Ridge State Natural Area and Newton Lake State Fish and Wildlife Area. Prairie Ridge State Natural Area, 4295 N. 1000th Street, Newton, IL 62448; phone: 618-783-2685. Newton Lake State Fish and Wildlife Area, 3490 E. 550th Avenue, Newton, IL 62448; phone: 618-783-3478.

67. Rend Lake, Rt. 1, Box 338, Bonnie, IL 62816; phone: 618-29-3110. Wayne Fitzgerrell State Park, 11094 Ranger Road, Whittington, IL 62897; phone: 618-629-2320.

68. Sauget Marsh. Illinois Department of Natural Resources, 524 S. Second Street, Springfield, IL 62701-1787; phone: 217-782-7454.

69. Crab Orchard National Wildlife Refuge, U.S. Fish & Wildlife Service, 8588 Route 148, Marion, IL 62959; phone: 618-997-3344 or P.O. Box J, Carterville, IL 62918; phone: 618-997-3344.

70. Giant City State Park, P.O. Box 70, Makanda, IL 62958; phone: 618-457-4836.

71. Union County Conservation Area, Refuge Manager, R.R.#2, Jonesboro, IL 62952; phone: 618-833-5175.

72. Cypress Creek National Wildlife Refuge, U.S. Fish & Wildlife Service, Route 1, Box 53D, Ullin, IL 62992; phone: 618-634-2231. The Nature Conservancy, Route 1, Box 53E, Ullin, IL 62992; phone: 618-634-2231.

73. Cache River and Heron Pond State Natural Areas. State Natural Area, 930 Sunflower Lane, Belknap, IL 62908; phone: 618-634-9678. Illinois Department of Natural Resources, 524 S. Second Street, Springfield, IL 62701-1787; phone: 217-782-7454. Cache Core Canoes, phone: 618-845-3817.

74. Horseshoe Lake Conservation Area, P.O. Box 85, Miller City, IL 62962; phone: 618-776-5689 or 776-5215. Illinois Department of Natural Resources, 524 S. Second Street, Springfield, IL 62701-1787; phone: 217-782-7454.

75. Pomona–Cave Creek. Illinois Department of Natural Resources, 524 S. Second Street, Springfield, IL 62701-1787; phone: 217-782-7454.

76. Atwood Ridge and Hamburg Hill. Illinois Department of Natural Resources, 524 S. Second Street, Springfield, IL 62701-1787; phone: 217-782-7454.

77. Trail of Tears State Forest, Route 1, Box 1331, Jonesboro, IL 62952; phone: 618-833-4910.

78. Pine Hills–LaRue Ecological Area, Shawnee National Forest at Route 45 South, Harrisburg, IL 62946; phone: 618-253-7114

79. Oakwood Bottoms and the Big Muddy River Levee. Illinois Department of Natural Resources, 524 S. Second Street, Springfield, IL 62701-1787; phone: 217-782-7454.

80. Mermet Lake, R.R.1, Box 118, Belknap, IL 62908; phone: 618-524-5577. Illinois Department of Natural Resources, 524 S. Second Street, Springfield, IL 62701-1787; phone: 217-782-7454.

Appendix B: Documentation form for rare birds in Illinois

The Illinois Ornithological Record Committee (IORC), founded in 1985, evaluates the evidence for records of birds that are rare or unusual in Illinois. As a standing committee of the Illinois Ornithological Society, IORC strives to improve the quality of submitted ornithological field data both through example and dissemination of pertinent information and techniques.

The committee is responsible for publishing and maintaining the official checklist of Illinois birds. It also publishes in the journal, the reports on rare birds, indicating whether the sighting has been accepted. The committee houses all bird records and evaluations of evidence thereof (including the evidence itself) at the Department of Natural Resources archives at the Avian Ecology Program, 600 North Grand Avenue West, Suite 4, Springfield, Illinois 62702. Students and professional ornithologists are welcome to inquire or review any bird records housed there.

Observers are encouraged to submit documentation of rare and unusual birds to IORC. The committee maintains a review list of birds that require documentation in the state. To receive more information about IORC, a copy of the committee's by-laws, report forms, or the review list, contact the IORC secretary, David B. Johnson at 504 Crown Point Drive, Buffalo Grove, Illinois 60089.

ILLINOIS DOCUMENTATION
FOR UNUSUAL BIRD SIGHTINGS

Submitted to Illinois Ornithological Records Committee (IORC) IORC RECORD NUMBER: _____

This form submitted as supporting documentation of (check all that apply):
___Unusual species ___Unusual date ___Unusual number ___Unusual plumage
___Unusual breeding record ___Christmas Bird Count record ___Spring Bird Count record
___Breeding Census record ___Other _____

1. Species _____
2. Number of birds _____
3. Date(s)_____
4. Location (include county)_____
5. Observers: _____
    5b. Documentor: Your name _____
        Mailing Address _____
        Others agreeing with identification _____
        Observers NOT agreeing with identification _____
6. Description of bird (size, shape, proportions, details of both color and patterns on head, back chin, throat, breast, flanks, undertail, wings, and tail, etc.; coloration of soft parts: bill, eye, legs, and feet) include only details actually seen in the field _____
    _____
    _____
7. Description of behavior _____
    _____
    _____
8. Description of vocalizations _____
    _____
    _____
9. Description of immediate and surrounding habitat(s) _____
    _____
    _____
10. Viewing conditions _____
    _____
    Optical equipment used for observation (type, power)_____
    _____
    Distance/how measured? _____
    Time(s) of observation _____
    Total time of observation _____
11. Previous experience with this species and similar species _____
    _____
    _____
12. Please eliminate other similar species and/or hybrids (use additional paper, if necessary)
    _____
13. Were photos obtained? _____
    If so, by whom?_____ Attached? _____
14. Books and illustrations consulted, and advice received. How did these influence this description?
    _____
15. How long after the observation were field notes recorded? _____
16. How long after observation was this form completed? _____
17. Additional remarks _____

Signed _____ Dated _____

Mail directly to: IORC Secretary, David B. Johnson, 504 Crown Point Drive, Buffalo Grove, IL 60089 or to IORC Secretary c/o Avian Ecology Program, Natural Heritage Division/Dept. of Natural Resources, Springfield, IL 62701

FORM REVISED AUGUST 1998

Appendix C: Sensitive bird species of Illinois

Status	Species
Extinct	Passenger Pigeon *(Ectopistes migratorious)*
	Carolina Parakeet *(Conuropsis carolinensis)*
Extirpated	Sharp-tailed Grouse *(Tympanuchus phasianellus)*
	Trumpeter Swan *(Cygnus buccinator)* reintroduced/unestablished
	Common Raven *(Corvus corax)*
State-listed Endangered	American Bittern *(Botaurus lentiginosus)*
	Snowy Egret *(Egretta thula)*
	Little Blue Heron *(Egretta caerulea)*
	Black-crowned Night-Heron *(Nycticorax nycticorax)*
	Yellow-crowned Night-Heron *(Nyctanassa violacea)*
	Osprey *(Pandion haliaetus)*
	Mississippi Kite *(Ictinia mississippiensis)*
	Northern Harrier *(Circus cyaneus)*
	Swainson's Hawk *(Buteo swainsoni)*
	Peregrine Falcon *(Falco peregrinus)*
	Greater Prairie-Chicken *(Tympanuchus phasianellus)*
	Black Rail *(Laterallus jamaicensis)*
	King Rail *(Rallus elegans)*
	Piping Plover *(Charadrius melodus)*
	Upland Sandpiper *(Bartramia longicauda)*
	Wilson's Phalarope *(Phalaropus tricolor)*
	Common Tern *(Sterna hirundo)*
	Forster's Tern *(Sterna forsteri)*
	Least Tern *(Sterna antillarium)*
	Black Tern *(Chlidonius niger)*
	Barn Owl *(Tyto alba)*
	Short-eared Owl *(Asio flammeus)*
	Bewick's Wren *(Thryomanes bewickii)*
	Swainson's Warbler *(Limnothlypis swainsonii)*
	Henslow's Sparrow *(Ammodramus henslowii)*
	Yellow-headed Blackbird *(Xanthocephalus xanthocephalus)*
State-listed Threatened	Pied-billed Grebe *(Podilymbus podiceps)*
	Least Bittern *(Ixobrychus exilis)*
	Bald Eagle *(Haliaeettus Leucocephalus)*
	Red-shouldered Hawk *(Buteo lineatus)*
	Common Moorhen *(Gallinula chloropus)*
	Sandhill Crane *(Grus canadensis)*
	Loggerhead Shrike *(Lanius ludovicianus)*

KEY

Extinct   Species that have occurred in the state but no longer occur anywhere in the world.
Extirpated   Species that were formerly casual or regular in Illinois but have not been recorded in the wild in the state for at least 50 years.
Endangered   Species whose breeding populations are in danger of extirpation within Illinois; listed as endangered by the Illinois Department of Natural Resources.
Threatened   Species whose breeding populations are at risk of becoming endangered within Illinois; listed as threatened by the Illinois Department of Natural Resources

Bibliography

Bohlen, H. David. 1989. *The Birds of Illinois*. Indiana University Press, Bloomington, Indiana.

Bohlen, H. D. 1978. *An Annotated Check-List of the birds Of Illinois*. Illinois State Museum Popular Science Series, location?

Fawks, Elton (compiler) and Paul Lobik (editor). 1975. *Birding in Illinois*. The Illinois Audubon Society (formerly in Downers Grove, Il., today in Danville, Il.).

Graber, Richard R. and Jean Graber. 1963. *A Comparative Study of Bird Population in Illinois:* 1906–1909 and 1956–1958. Illinois Natural History Survey Bulletin 28(3):383–528.

Kaufman, Kenn. 1990. *Advanced Birding: Peterson Field Guides*. Houghton Mifflin, Boston, Mass.

Mlodinow, Steven. 1984. *Chicago Area Birds*. Sponsored by the Chicago Audubon Society. Chicago Review Press. Chicago, Ill.

Nelson, E. W. 1876. *Birds of Northeast Illinois*. Essex Institute Bulletin 8(9–12).

Pettingill, Olin Sewall. 1977. *A Guide to Bird Finding East of the Mississippi*. Oxford University Press, New York.

Ridgeway, Robert. 1889 and 1895. *The Ornithology of Illinois*. The State Laboratory of Natural History, Springfield, Ill.

Robinson, W. Douglas. 1996. *Southern Illinois Birds: An Annotated List and Site Guide*. Southern Illinois University Press, Carbondale, Ill.

Webster Grove Nature Study Society. 1998 (Rev.) *Birds of the St. Louis Area: Where and When to Find Them*. Webster Groves, Miss.

Index

Bold page numbers indicate photographs.

Mockingbird, Northern 115, 146, 155, 164, 176, 177, 198, 255, 277, 281, 293
Momence Sod Farms 121–23, **122**
Momence Wetlands 121–23, **122**
Montrose Harbor 30–33, **31**
Moorhen, Common 53, 66, 101, 106, 107, 173, 210, 228, 299, 303
Moraine Hills State Park 61–63, **62**
Moraine View State Park 192–94, **193**
Morton Arboretum 83–85, **84**

N

Nachusa Grasslands 162–65, **163**
Newton Lake State Fish and Wildlife Area 253–56, **254**
Nighthawk, Common 146
Night-Heron
  Black-crowned 33, 65, 67, 69, 106, 107, 108, 111, 146, 187, 190, 193, 210, 222, 229, 238, 250, 253, 271, 306
  Yellow-crowned 78, 109, 155, 181, 190, 229, 236, 238, 261, 269, 271, 279, 280, 284, 301, 306
Nuthatch
  Long-eared 131
  Red-breasted 90, 98, 131, 143, 263, 296
  White-breasted 155, 168

O

Oakwood Bottoms **298**, 300–302
O'Hare Post Office Ponds 81–83, **82**
Oldsquaw 43, 46, 50, 79, 101, 115, 150, 197, 199, 202, 245
Oriole
  Baltimore 60, 95, 103, 119, 136, 146, 157, 173, 234, 255, 272
  Orchard 60, 76, 95, 100, 103, 105, 115, 119, 129, 138, 143, 146, 164, 166, 173, 177, 190, 198, 207, 251, 255, 267, 272, 275, 277, 281, 293, 295
Orland Grassland 103–5, **104**
Osprey 46, 76, 87, 140, 154, 187, 210, 233, 238, 255, 263, 271, 272, 304
Ovenbird 72, 131, 138, 142, 143, 148, 159, 161, 183, 188, 189, 231, 237, 286, 293
Owl
  Barn 276
  Barred 94, 121, 131, 132, 132, 134, 155, 159, 169, 178, 179, 181, 183, 191, 204, 227, 239, 269, 277, 284, 285, 292, 295, 296, 299

Great Horned 57, 74, 84, 164, 191, 204, 292, 295, 296
Long-eared 57, 90, 119, 139, 167, 176, 181, 182, 186, 189, 191, 200, 245, 247, 278, 310
Northern Saw-whet 84, 132, 181, 184, 189, 190, 199, 200, 245, 278, 310
Short-eared 60, 81, 90, 116, 119, 174, 177, 181, 186, 191, 194, 226, 245, 252, 253, 254, 255, 256, 272, 281, 310
Snowy 33, 38, 43, 43, 50, 245, 310

P

Palatine Marsh 63–67, **64**
Parakeet
  Carolina 282
  Monk 32, 36, 36, 310
Partridge, Gray 127, 129, 165, 308
Parula, Northern 75, 131, 142, 146, 164, 183, 186, 188, 191, 204, 231, 237, 259, 266, 269, 271, 279, 283, 285, 286, 287, 292, 295, 296, 299, 300, 301
Paul O. Douglas Nature Sanctuary 34–37, **35**
Pecatonica River Forest Preserve **131**, 133–35
Pelican, American White 101, 112, 140, 154, 169, 173, 207, 208, 210, 220, 222, 225, 226, 233, 237, 239, 245, 247, 250, 270, 270, 272, 286, 306
Pere Marquette State Park 234–40, **235**
Phalarope 275
  Red 198, 210, 249
  Red-necked 82, 102, 187, 192, 220, 258
  Wilson's 82, 90, 108, 187, 225, 228, 238
Pheasant, Ring-necked 103–4, 129, 189, 229, 233, 259
Phoebe, Eastern 119, 142, 204, 237, 266, 271
Pigeon, Passenger 282
Pine Hills-LaRue Ecological Area 297–300, **298**
Pintail, Northern 65, 100, 140, 151, 202, 233, 239
Pipit, American 32, 187, 225, 239, 268, 270, 272, 275, 284
Plover
  Black-bellied 33, 42, 50, 82, 90, 109, 122, 138, 187
  Piping 50, 175, 225, 252
  Semipalmated 32, 42, 50, 60, 82, 108, 138, 227, 233
Pomona-Cave Creek 287–90, **288**
Prairie-Chicken, Greater 253, 256, 308
Prairie Ridge State Natural Area 253–56, **254**

About the illustrator

Denis Kania is a freelance wildlife artist living in Naperville, Illinois. He has done commissioned works for The Nature Conservancy, the Land Conservancy of Lake County, and other organizations. He also served as art editor for the Illinois Ornithological Society for seven years.

About the author

Sheryl DeVore at Ryerson Woods.

Born in Chicago in 1956 and a lifelong Illinoisan, Sheryl DeVore has spent the past 17 years involved in writing, editing, education, and research projects related to birds, people, and nature.

She serves as the Chief Editor for *Meadowlark*, the quarterly journal of the Illinois Ornithological Society, a position she has held since the Society's founding in 1992. Sheryl is also the Assistant Editor for *Chicago Wilderness Magazine* and the Assistant Managing Editor for Pioneer Press Newspapers, where she was named Journalist of the Year in 1997.

During her 17 years with Pioneer Press, Sheryl has won many national and regional awards for her environmental writing. These include the Harry E. Schlenz Medal, awarded annually to one environmental journalist nationwide; several First Place awards for environmental reporting by the Suburban Newspapers of America; and the Chicago Audubon Society's Excellence in Environmental Reporting Award. For seven consecutive years, Sheryl has won First Place for Best Locally Developed Science and Technology writing from the Northern Illinois Newspaper Association. She has also won numerous First and Second Place Awards for investigative articles.

For 12 years, Sheryl has also done volunteer and commissioned work for the Lake County Forest Preserves and Friends of Ryerson Woods, including conducting breeding bird surveys, presenting bird song and warbler identification workshops, and editing and designing nature publications.

Sheryl serves on the Chicago Audubon Society Board as the Chair of the Conservation Committee, and on the Advisory Board of the Friends of Ryerson Woods. She possesses a particular penchant for bird song, no doubt related to her college training as a musician. A professional flutist, she continues to perform in the Chicagoland region.

This is Sheryl's second book. Her first book, *Northern Flights: Tracking the Birds and Birders of Michigan's Upper Peninsula* was published by Mountain Press in June 1999.